PRAISE FOR SONG OF ARIRANG

"Fighting against the mighty Japanese empire was a hopeless cause. But some Koreans dedicated themselves to that cause even in the 1920 and 1930s when Japan appeared invincible. Kim San, né Jang Ji-rak, was one of those who joined a few dozen other Korean young men who had gathered around the Chinese communist army in northwestern China. The perceptive young man met Nym Wales (Helen Foster Snow), the American journalist then in Yan'an, the capital of Chinese communist movement, to whom he poured out his heart. Little did he know then that their book, first published in 1941, would become a classic memoir of Korean and Chinese revolutionary movements and immortalize Kim San himself."

— Chong-Sik Lee, author of *Revolutionary Struggle in Manchuria: Chinese Communism and Soviet Interest, 1922-1945*

"Beginning with the portentous event of Kim San's own birth on the very battlefield of the Russo-Japanese War, this book offers us a micro-level perspective on global intellectual history that is captivating and compelling. Belonging nowhere and an enemy of the state everywhere, Kim offers us an insider's behind-the-scenes perspective on major world events. What did it mean to conduct a moral life in the colonial context? How could transnational 'peace,' 'freedom,' 'liberation' and 'equality' be imagined, defined, and practiced in the world of empires? Autobiographically narrated by Kim, *Song of Arirang* asks us all to reconceive our shared global imagination of the future. This is a must-read in modern East Asian history."

—Sho Konishi, author of *Anarchist Modernity: Cooperatism and Japanese-Russian Intellectual Relations in Modern Japan*

"A moving portrait of a Korean revolutionary active in the Chinese Communist Party (CCP), *Song of Arirang* is a story that could have disappeared along with those of countless other forgotten revolutionaries in East Asia. This new edition of *Song of Arirang*, with its extensive and meticulous historical notes for the reader, is a rousing tribute to those who have dedicated themselves to emancipatory struggles."

— Namhee Lee, author of *The Making of Minjung: Democracy and the Politics of Representation in South Korea*

SONG

OF

ARIRANG

Song of Arirang
Copyright © 2022 by Brigham Young University
(on behalf of the Helen Foster Snow Literary Trust)
All rights reserved. Printed in the United States
25 24 23 22 4 3 2 1
Published by Kaya Press // kaya.com
Distributed by D.A.P./Distributed Art Publishers // artbook.com (800) 388-BOOK
ISBN: 9781885030566
Library of Congress Control Number: 2018967240
Cover and Text Design by Chris Ro (adearfriend.com)
Magpie Series Editors: Sunyoung Lee & Sunyoung Park
Magpie Series Design Editor: Chris Ro
Illustration of Kim San: Eugene Park

This book was made possible by support from the USC Dana and David Dornsife College of Arts, Letters, and Sciences; the USC Department of American Studies and Ethnicity; Stephen CuUnjieng; and the Choi Chang Soo Foundation.

Additional funding was provided by generous contributions from: Fuad Ahmad, Tanzila Ahmed, Kamil Ahsan, Jasmine Ako, Christine Alberto, Hari Alluri, Stine An, Akhila Ananth, Tiffany Babb, Manibha Banerjee, Tom and Lily So Beischer, Terry Bequette, Piyali Bhattacharya, Roddy Bogawa, Paul Bonnell, Thi Bui, Hung Bui, Cari Campbell, Nate Cavalieri, Susan Chan, Sonali Chanchani, Jade Chang, Wah-Ming Chang, Alexander Chee, Anelise Chen, Anita Chen, Jean Chen, Lisa Chen, Leland Cheuk, Floyd Cheung, Amy Chin, Elaine Cho, Jayne Choi, Judy Choi, Jennifer Chou, Seo-Young Chu, Elizabeth Clements, Tuyet Cong Ton Nu, Timothy Daley, Matthew Dalto, Kavita Das, Lawrence-Minh Bùi Davis, Steven Doi, Susannah Donahue, Daniel Dyer, Irving Eng, Jessica Eng, Fan Fan, Matthew Fargo, Peter Feng, Sia Figiel, Sesshu Foster, Christopher Fox, Sylvana Freyberg, Naomi Fukuchi, Kelsey Grashoff, Anthony Hale, KA Hashimoto, Jean Ho, Skye Hodges, Ann Holler, Heidi Hong, Huy Hong, Abeer Hoque, Jonathan Hugo, Jimmy Hwang, Ashaki Jackson, Jayson Joseph, Theresa Kang, Mia Kang, Lisa Kang, Andrew Kebo, Vandana Khanna, Bizhan Khodabandeh, Swati Khurana, Ian Kim, Helen Kim Lee, Gwendolyn Knight, Sabrina Ko, Robin Koda, Karen Koh, Juliana Koo, Sun Hee Koo, Eileen Kurahashi, Paul Lai, Jenny Lam, Iris Law, Samantha Le, Catherine Lee, Hyunjung Lee, Whakyung Lee in memory of Sonya Choi Lee, Winona Leon, Andrew Leong, Edan Lepucki, Claire Light, Janine Lim, Edward Lin, Jennifer Liou, Carleen Liu, Mimi Lok, Leza Lowitz, Pauline Lu, Abir Majumdar, Jason McCall, Sally McWilliams, Rajiv Mohabir, Faisal Mohyuddin, Russell Morse, Samhita Mukhopadhyay, Nayomi Munaweera, Adam Muto, Wendy Lou Nakao, Jean Young Naylor, Dominique Nguyen, Kathy Nguyen, Kim Nguyen, Vinh Nguyen, Viet Thanh Nguyen, Sandra Noel, Yun and Minkyung Oh, Gene & Sabine Oishi, Chez Bryan Ong, Eric Ong, Tiffany Ong, Camille Patrao, Perlita Payne, Leena Pendharker, Thuy Phan, Eming Piansay, Cheryline Prestolino, James Pumarada, Zhiyao Qiu, Jhani Randhawa, Amarnath Ravva, Sam Robertson, Brendan Ryan, Jonathan Sands, Chaitali Sen, Prageeta Sharma, Andrew Shih, Paul H. Smith, Roch Smith, Luisa Smith, Nancy Starbuck, Rachana Sukhadia, Robin Suhkhadia, Rajen Sukhadia, Kelly Sutherland, Willie Tan, Zhen Teng, Isabella Tilley, Wendy Tokuda, Frederick Tran, Monique Truong, Kosiso Ugwueze, Patricia Wakida, Monona Wali, Kelli Washington, Aviva Weiner, Heather Werber, Rachel Will, Duncan Williams, William Wong, Koon Woon, Amelia Wu & Sachin Adarkar, Andrea Wu, Anita Wu & James Spicer, Ann Yamamoto, Jihfang Yang, Nancy Yap, Max Yeh, Stan Yogi, Shinae Yoon, Mikoto Yoshida, and many others.

Additional support for Kaya Press is provided by the National Endowment for the Arts; the Los Angeles County Board of Supervisors through the Los Angeles County Arts Commission; the Community of Literary Magazines and Presses and the Literary Arts Emergency Fund; and the City of Los Angeles Department of Cultural Affairs.

SONG

OF

ARIRANG

BY KIM SAN

&

NYM WALES (HELEN FOSTER SNOW)

The Story of a Korean Revolutionary in China

Edited by George O. Totten III & Dongyoun Hwang
Foreword by Arif Dirlik

TABLE OF CONTENTS

XI **FOREWORD** | by Arif Dirlik

XIII **INTRODUCTION** | by George O. Totten III

SONG OF ARIRANG

1 **PRELUDE** | by Nym Wales

PART 1

DECLARATION OF INDEPENDENCE

27	CHAPTER 1	Recuerdo (Memories)
39	CHAPTER 2	Korean Childhood
50	CHAPTER 3	Declaration of Independence
67	CHAPTER 4	Tokyo School Days
77	CHAPTER 5	Crossing the Yalu River

PART II

THOSE WHO LIE IN WAIT

91	CHAPTER 6	Shanghai, Mother of Exile
106	CHAPTER 7	They Who Lie in Wait
118	CHAPTER 8	Reflections on Women and Revolution
126	CHAPTER 9	From Tolstoy to Marx

PART III

IN THE RANKS OF CHINA'S GREAT REVOLUTION

139	CHAPTER 10	In the Ranks of China's "Great Revolution"
158	CHAPTER 11	The Guangzhou Commune
182	CHAPTER 12	Life and Death in Hailufeng
214	CHAPTER 13	Reunion in Shanghai

PART IV

CLIMBING THE HILLS OF ARIRANG

229	CHAPTER 14	A Revolutionary is Also a Man
236	CHAPTER 15	Return to Manchuria
245	CHAPTER 16	A Revolutionary Marriage
251	CHAPTER 17	Climbing the Hills of Arirang
270	CHAPTER 18	Party and Personal Wars
278	CHAPTER 19	Fate and Fortune

PART V

THE KOREAN NATIONAL FRONT

293	CHAPTER 20	Back to the Mass Movement
302	CHAPTER 21	Japanese Prisoner Again and Exile
317	CHAPTER 22	Two Women and Marriage
327	CHAPTER 23	The Korean National Front Against Japan
335	EPILOGUE	"Only the Undefeated in Defeat ..."

343 **POSTLUDE** | by Nym Wales

351 ENDNOTES

373 BIOGRAPHICAL NOTES

385 **AFTERWORD: KIM SAN AFTER 1937** | by Dongyoun Hwang

APPENDIX I

398 Kim San's Aliases and Pennames

400 A Chronological Account of the Life of Kim San

APPENDIX II: WRITINGS BY KIM SAN

415 The Basis for the Korean National Front

417 Program for Action of the Union for the Korean National Front

421 A Strange Weapon (Short Story)

443 Mourning Comrade Han Hae (Poem)

APPENDIX III

449 Foreword to the Second Edition by Nym Wales (Ramparts Press)

462 Bibliographical Abbreviations Used in Notes

463 Bibliography

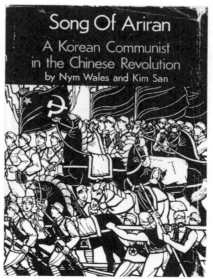

Top: *Song of Ariran* (John Day edition, 1941)
Bottom: *Song of Ariran* (Ramparts Press edition, 1974)

Foreword

ARIF DIRLIK

Students of socialism and revolution will be in debt to George O. Totten III and Dongyoun Hwang for this updated and expanded republication of Korean revolutionary Kim San's classic autobiography, as told to and by Nym Wales (the pseudonym of Helen Foster Snow) in Yan'an in the late 1930s. *Song of Arirang* was not as momentous in its revelations as Edgar Snow's *Red Star Over China*, published at about the same time, which told the world of the unfolding of the Communist movement in China under Mao Zedong's leadership. But despite its more modest autobiographical scope, it is a rich source of information and insight about both the Korean and the Chinese revolutions.

Kim San's account of his revolutionary itinerary during the previous two decades is enriched by his reflections on the revolutions in which he was a participant, offering a rare glimpse into the psyche of a dedicated and thoughtful revolutionary.

The account draws our attention to the importance of a regional (in contrast to a national) perspective in grasping the dynamics of radicalism in eastern Asia, stretching from Japan in the northeast across China and southeast Asia. In the earlier part of the 20th century, radicals from across the region inspired one another, learned from one another, and participated in one another's movements. The new national consciousness that provided the impulse for their radicalization was tempered by an internationalism and utopianism that found expression in an attraction to anarchist and Marxist communisms. Kim San's account offers cogent testimonial to this eastern Asian internationalism: he remains focused on the Korean revolution as his ultimate goal, but he also claims the Chinese Revolution as his own. He was not the only Korean or foreigner to participate in the revolutionary events he describes. A sizable contingent of Koreans was trained by the Comintern and sent to China to provide guidance in the revolution. Radicals from Japan and Vietnam also participated in some of the events he describes. Kim himself counted on Japanese communists to help out in the Korean struggle against Japanese colonialism.

Kim San's choice of a beloved Korean folk song for the title of his memoir underlines his desire to impart to the reader a quintessentially

"Korean" sensibility. The associations of the song also suggest a tragic sense of revolution, which must be pursued even with foreknowledge of its ultimate failure. As he puts it:

> *The "Song of Arirang" has come to symbolize the tragedy of Korea. Its meaning is symbolic of constantly climbing over obstacles only to find death at the end.*
>
> *It is a song of death and not of life. But death is not defeat. Out of many deaths, victory may be born. There are those of us who would write another verse for this ancient "Song of Arirang." That last verse is not yet written.*

Our times are far removed from Kim San's revolutionary milieu in China of the 1930s. And he speaks in a Korean voice. Yet the voice reaches us across these historical and cultural divides.

—EUGENE, OREGON
AUGUST 13, 2017

"[O]f all my experiences in China, none was more productive of knowledge and understanding than my talks with Kim San in Yan'an during those rainy days in 1937... Such a life story will never be told again." —NYM WALES

Introduction*

GEORGE O. TOTTEN III

Raw human drama—that is what this book is. Vividly it describes the Chinese Revolution and the Korean Independence Movement from the inside, as seen, felt, and experienced by a revolutionary who wonders about the meaning of life and shares mankind's urge to set things right in societies where the moral order has been smashed. As such, it speaks to men and women, young and old, of all ages.

In a compound in Yan'an, soon after the Japanese onslaught of July 7, 1937, "Nym Wales"—Helen Foster Snow—took down the words of "Kim San," the former a young American journalist who knew she was in on one of the scoops of the century, the latter a Korean who had decided to struggle against the Japanese occupiers of his homeland by joining the Chinese Communists. He was old beyond his thirty-two years due to sickness, imprisonment, torture, and privation brought on by voluntary participation in the struggles against the decaying social system and the rising new order of foreign imperialism. In a moment of truth, this revolutionary revealed his innermost thoughts in a way few human beings do.

As a Korean member of the Chinese Communist Party, Kim San was in a unique position to observe and report on the Chinese Revolution and its relation to movements in neighboring Korea and Japan. But as important as this book is to those interested in the history of revolution in Asia, it directly alerts modern radicals to some of the questions any movement on the left must face: the relation between study and practice, love and revolution, ends vs. means. Beyond that, as a gripping tale of adventure, it can enthrall even the most politically disinterested.

---

* Originally published in the 1972 Ramparts Press edition of *Song of Ariran*. Portions of the essay that are outdated or have been superseded by current research have been placed into endnotes.

We shall never come so close to Mao Zedong or Kim Il Sung as we do here to Kim San. While volumes have been, and will be, written on those leaders, they can never escape the teleology of chairman-to-be and predestined premier. But here is a man of leadership potential who has not yet stepped onto a pedestal. Here is a hardened revolutionary, still horrified at the necessity to kill, who does not hide the romanticism that originally motivated him. Most revolutionary autobiographies and histories are written either by outsiders or by people who have left or been expelled from the party. Only from the outside do such authors have the time and (for former members) the pressing need for self-justification. One thinks of the bulk of Leon Trotsky's work (not including his powerful early account, entitled simply 1905) or the autobiography of Zhang Guotao,* who unsuccessfully vied with Mao Zedong for leadership in the Chinese Communist Party. Humility, security considerations, and party discipline are no doubt involved in this silence of active revolutionaries, but more important probably are limitations of time and duty that tend to restrict their writings to matters of theory, strategy, and tactics.

For Kim San in 1937 the atmosphere of waiting in Yan'an afforded him the opportunity to tell his story to Helen Snow and the leisure to collaborate with her on this book. Though not yet such a "successful" revolutionary, he nevertheless was still very much committed to, and actively engaged in, his life's work. It is thus an authentic historical document, unique of its kind. True, some of the scenes have been reconstructed and at times given different dates and places; but it must be remembered that at the time Kim San told his story, the fight was not yet won, and it was necessary for him to protect himself and his comrades. True, he did apparently at times incorporate the experiences of others into his own narrative—the better to tell the Korean story in the context of the larger revolutionary upheaval in China. And although in 1937 in Yan'an Kim San did not have the luxury of access to documentation—if indeed any records would have been available—he had for many years kept a diary, in code. Part of the enormous and rare value of this work lies in its firsthand personality descriptions of im-

---

* *autobiography of Zhang Guotao:* Chang Kuo-t'ao [Zhang Guotao], *The Rise of The Chinese Communist Party 1921-1927: The Autobiography of Chang Kuo-tao,* 2 Vols. (Lawrence, Kansas: The University Press of Kansas, 1971-72).

portant historical figures* and its on-the-spot accounts of such usually glossed-over battles as the abortive Guangzhou Commune of 1927 and the fall of China's first soviet at Hailufeng shortly thereafter.

But it is Kim San himself who springs forth from these pages as a many-faceted individual in his own right, bringing understanding and respect for the thousands of others like him who fought for their ideals and did not break under pressure. Perhaps without realizing it, Helen Snow produced a classic in its genre with a power she scarcely expected.[1]

This book moved me deeply when I first read it in the spring of 1944 when I was studying Japanese and undergoing officer training in the U.S. Military Intelligence Service at Camp Savage, Minnesota. When I was shipped overseas, I brought the book along and kept it with me throughout the battle in Southeast Asia. It helped me feel that I was part of the same struggle for the liberation of the Korean, Chinese, and other peoples overrun by Japanese imperialism, as well as for the emancipation of the Japanese people themselves from the clutches of a government that had led them into a disastrous war. So I never shared any of the racial hatred that was promoted by much of the anti-Japanese war propaganda of the time against the "yellow Jap rats." I was able easily to establish rapport with the Japanese prisoners of war I dealt with. This book was an eye-opener to surrendered Japanese when I passed it around. Those with sufficient English to read it told others about it. It helped them realize what Japan had done in China and Korea. It helped raise in their minds all kinds of questions, from that of war guilt to the position of women in society.

The events Kim San relates cover the years 1905 to 1937. He was born during the Russo-Japanese War of 1904–05 when the Japanese decisively routed Russian influence on the Korean peninsula, having first defeated the Chinese there in the Sino-Japanese War of 1894–95.

---

* *important historical figures*: These include the Chinese Communists Peng Pai and Ye Ting; the Korean Nationalists Ahn Chang-ho and Yi Gwang-su; the terrorists Kim Won-bong and Oh Seong-ryun; and the Korean Communists Yi Dong-hwi and Kim Chung-chang. Two other notable historical biographies emerged from the same period: Edgar Snow's collaboration with Mao Zedong that appears as part of *Red Star Over China* (New York: Random House, 1938) and Agnes Smedley's collaboration with Zhu De published under the title *The Great Road: The Life and Times of Chu Teh* (New York: Monthly Review Press, 1956).

INTRODUCTION

Thereafter the Japanese consolidated their position, formally annexing Korea in 1910 in the face of the helpless rage of the Korean people.

Kim's story begins, really, with the euphoric demonstrations of 1919, when oppressed peoples throughout the world rally to the hopes raised by President Woodrow Wilson, demonstrating peacefully against their oppressors not only in Korea but in China, Indonesia, Turkey, and elsewhere. The Japanese drown the Korean demonstrations in a river of blood. Over the next few years, hundreds of thousands of Koreans flee their homeland, some going to work or study in Japan, where conditions are slightly less harsh for them than at home. Kim San himself goes to Tokyo, but soon leaves to join other Korean refugees in Manchuria, where Koreans are settling on the land and beginning to train fighters for the long war of liberation.

In hopes of getting an education in a big city in China, Kim is drawn to Shanghai, where the Korean Provisional Government has been set up by Korean exiles in reaction to the suppression of the March First (Samil) Movement of 1919. He sides with the anarchist faction, which advocates direct action against Japanese authority, in opposition to the moderate faction, which proposes diplomatic pleading with the putatively democratic powers to pressure Japan to give up Korea. (Syngman Rhee, destined to become the American strongman in South Korea after Japan's defeat, is among the latter group.) Soon Kim is attracted to the communist alternative, which repudiates individual anarchist terrorism and advocates a whole panoply of means—mass movements within Korea, guerrilla tactics across the border in Manchuria, collaboration with the Russian and Chinese Communists. By 1924 Kim becomes a communist.

The second stage of Kim's life, between 1925 and 1928, is one of open revolutionary activity and fighting in the Chinese Revolution. This is the era of collaboration between the Chinese Nationalists (Guomindang or GMD) and the Chinese Communists (Gongchandang or CCP), the period of the "First United Front." For more than a decade the country has suffered internal strife among the Chinese warlords and has succumbed to the political demands and economic inducements of the imperial powers; now the two parties agree that China must be reunited. But their longer-range visions of China's future differ. The Communists call for a bourgeois democratic government under which the workers and peasants will have the freedom to organize and win mass support. The right wing of the Nationalist party, led by Chiang Kai-shek, favors an economy led by financiers and capitalists in collaboration with landlords in which workers' and peasants' organizations would be carefully controlled so as not to hinder production (roughly along the model of contemporary Fascist Italy). At first the differences are veiled. Chiang Kai-shek visits the Soviet Union for training and the Soviets help set up the Huangpu Military Academy in Guangzhou. The Guomindang-Communist collaboration is symbolized by Chiang serving as head of the Huangpu Academy, while Zhou Enlai serves as its political commissar. In 1926 a joint army, whose officers are a product of the Academy, sets out from Guangzhou, in South China, on a Northern Expedition to defeat the warlords. Winning battle after battle, it is awaited in Shanghai by a victorious workers' movement which has rebelled and ousted Shanghai's warlord just before the coastal wing of the Northern Expedition arrives.

It is at this point that Chiang Kai-shek makes his main bid for supreme power. With the assurance of support from foreign business interests and reactionary elements in the city, he crushes the workers' movement and their Communist leaders with a wanton massacre beginning April 12, 1927.

With the United Front in shambles, Communists and other leftists regroup and begin to fight back, though they have few weapons. Some gather in Guangzhou and plan an uprising to create a revolutionary base there. Kim San participates in this brief Guangzhou Commune (December 11–14, 1927) and in the desperate retreat to the first Chinese soviet, at Hailufeng. But the effort to save Hailufeng—the last physical vestige of the revolution up to that point—is doomed by the Nationalists' control of the army. Kim San and the other survivors emerge from the counterrevolutionary bloodbath, defeated in battle but strengthened by the experience and with a new determination.

For the next ten years Kim works underground in North China. He is twice imprisoned and severely tortured. As a leading member of the Chinese Communist Party branch in Beijing, he tries to develop new strategies and tactics but is frustrated both by imprisonment and by the dogmatism and inflexibility of some of his Chinese comrades. During this period, too, Kim's emotional life rises to his first serious love affair and falls to the contemplation of suicide.

By 1935 Kim San solves his identity crisis. Earlier he had taken out

Chinese citizenship papers; now he devotes himself anew to the role of representing the Korean liberation struggle in the Chinese Revolution. In this capacity he travels to the North China areas held by the Chinese Communists. Here in Yan'an, in the summer of 1937, just after the Second United Front with the Nationalists, Helen Snow finds him, a stable and mature individual, showing the effects of torture and privation but strong and confident in his leadership ability. He has come to Yan'an to represent the Korean United Front of Communists and Nationalists as a Korean delegate to the Chinese soviets. This new role is his more natural one for through his many years of exile, the beautiful Geumgang mountains of his native land beckon in his mind's eye, and the poignant refrain of Arirang, Korea's most beloved song, rings always in his ears.[2]

—TOKYO, JAPAN
JULY 1972[3]

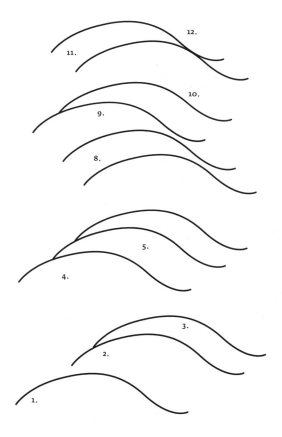

SONG

OF

ARIRANG

The Story of a Korean Revolutionary in China

EDITOR'S NOTES

Title and Subtitle
For this edition, we have decided to change the spelling of the title from *Song of Ariran* to *Song of Arirang*. "Arirang" is close to the actual pronunciation of the word by Koreans, and is also the correct spelling of the word according to the new romanization system recognized by the South Korean government and used throughout this edition. At the time Nym Wales first published this book in 1941, there was no romanization system in place for Korean, so it is possible that she chose to romanize "Arirang" as "Ariran" in accordance with the Japanese pronunciation: unlike in Korean, there is no "ng" ending consonant in Japanese.

We have chosen to adopt a new subtitle for the current edition as well, combining elements from the ones used for the 1941 edition published by John Day (also referred to throughout as the first edition) and the 1974 edition published by Ramparts Press (also referred to throughout as the second edition).

Romanization
In romanizing Korean throughout this volume, we have chosen to use the revised system adopted by the South Korean Ministry of Culture and Tourism in 2000, albeit with several exceptions for Korean names and places such as Syngman Rhee (not Yi Seungman) and Pyongyang (not Pyeongyang). In romanizing Chinese, we have followed the pinyin system, with exceptions again for names of significant historical figures such as Chiang Kai-shek and Sun Yat-sen or official names of institutions. Romanization of Japanese terms follows the Hepburn system, with exceptions for commonly used words that have entered the English lexicon, including place names such as Tokyo and Osaka.

Throughout both the text and notes, Korean, Chinese, and Japanese names are rendered with the family name first and the personal name last, as is typical throughout East Asia. The only exception to this is for Syngman Rhee. While Chinese and Japanese personal names appear as one word without a hyphen, Korean personal names appear mostly as one word with a hyphen, though there are a few exceptions to this as well.

Places (or events and institutions associated with them) that are better known today by another name, we have chosen to use the more contemporary names with a few exceptions (i.e. for Mukden).

Historical Notes
Throughout this edition, we have endeavored to be as complete as possible in our annotation of the work. so have In order to provide as comprehensive a reading experience as possible, we have divided up these annotations into three categories: in-text footnotes, which include all of Kim San's and Nym Wales' original footnotes, along with any additional notes we felt were necessary to understanding the text; historical notes that clarify and give further contextualization of what is being described; and biographical notes on the numerous people referenced in the text.

Most of these notes have been provided by George O. Totten III and Dongyoun Hwang, and are labeled GT and DH respectively. References for these notes, where available and appropriate, have also been included.

Throughout the multiple other editions of this book that have been published in multiple languages, different editors have felt it necessary to append notes of their own that give additional historical, political, or other contextual information. We have drawn on a number of these sources, in addition to providing our own. Notes that were provided in the first and second editions of the book by Kim San and Nym Wales have been mostly kept in this new edition and are labeled KS and NW. respectively. Any further clarification or information we have added to their notes or to the main text are placed in brackets.

In addition, certain passages attributed to Kim San that had originally been placed in the appendices of the first English-language edition of the book have been interpolated back into the main narrative text or as notes.

Finally, we have retained additional notes from the second edition that had themselves been taken in whole or in part from different Japanese editions of *Song of Arirang*: if by Andō Jirō (from the Misuzu shobō edition published in 1965), they are taken from the Ramparts edition and labeled AJ; and if by Matsudaira Ioko (from the Iwanami edition published in 1987), they are labeled MI. Notes provided in the Japanese editions by Professor Kang Tok-sang are labeled KTS and those by Professor Mizuno Naoki are labelled MN. Notes by Mizuno Naoki (MN) have also been taken from *"Ariran no uta" oboe gaki: Kimu San to Nimu Wēruzu* (Notes on *Song of Arirang*: Kim San and Nym Wales), edited by Yi Hoe-seong and Mizuno Naoki and published by Iwanami Shoten in 1991.

All notes have, when necessary, been modified and/or updated by Dongyoun Hwang in this edition. When a note has been added to or adjusted by multiple editors, multiple initials are indicated. For information on bibliographical abbreviations used in the notes, please refer to Appendix III at the end of this book.

Abbreviations

Throughout the notes and essays accompanying this text, the Chinese Nationalist Party, known more commonly these days as the Guomingdang, is referred to as the GMD. Similarly, the Chinese Communist Party (Zhongguo Gongchangdong) is referred to as the CCP.

Acknowledgments

The editors are grateful to Iwanami Shoten and to Professor Mizuno Naoki and Mr. Yi Hoe-seong for their permission to use these modified and/or updated footnoted materials. The editors would also like to thank Brigham Young University, Arif Dirlik, Moonji Publishing, Co. Ltd., the *Sisa Journal*, Iwanami Shoten, and the Unam Kim Seong Suk Memorial Foundation for granting permission to reproduce several of the images used in this edition. The photos used for the section on the Canton Commune and the anti-communist purge were originally owned by Professor Dirlik, who later gave them to me.

TO THE RETURN OF THE EXILES ACROSS THE YALU RIVER

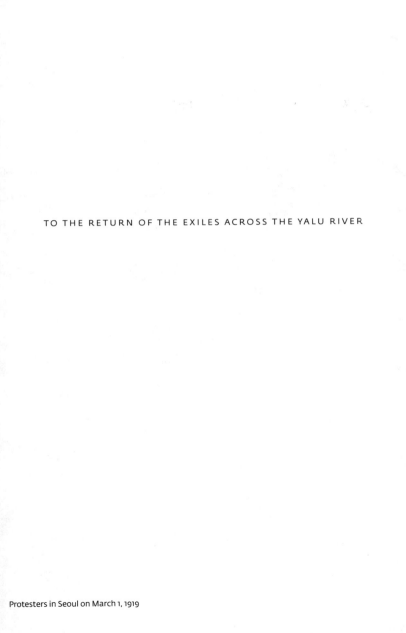

Protesters in Seoul on March 1, 1919

Prelude

NYM WALES

I MET HIM IN YAN'AN.[4] One day during my stay there in the early summer of 1937, I was casually looking over the

Yan'an in 1937

list of borrowers of English books from the Lu Xun Library. Only a few books seemed to be in demand, including V. I. Lenin's *Left-Wing Communism: An Infantile Disorder* and O. Tanin and E. Yohan's *When Japan Goes to War*. One borrower's name led all the rest; he had taken out dozens of books and magazines on all subjects during the summer.

"Who is this omnivorous reader?" I asked, immediately interested, for I was always in sad need of someone who could talk with me in English.

"He is a Korean delegate to the Chinese soviets.[5] He teaches Japanese economics and physics and chemistry at the Military and Political Academy."[6]

"Where can I find him?"

"At the Foreign Office."

I sent a messenger with a letter asking when I might talk with him about Korea. No reply. I dispatched another. Still no reply.

"He is a very secret delegate," someone informed me. "Perhaps he doesn't want to meet you."

"Oh," I nodded, and decided that I should not be able to learn anything about Korea that summer.

About a week later, my bodyguard, Demmy-erh,* came in and announced that a stranger wanted to see me.

"Bring him in."

A thin scholar's hand held back the blue padded curtain that served as a makeshift door to my room in the walled hostel compound, and a tall, arresting figure stood poised in the shaft of light. He bowed in a proud and dignified manner and looked at me with steady composure as we shook hands. It was raining heavily, and the paper windowpanes did not provide much light, but I saw that his strongly profiled face was curiously un-Chinese and quite handsome in a semi-Spanish sort of way. For a moment I thought he looked European.

"Did you send me this note?" he asked in English.

"Oh, yes," I said. "You're the Korean delegate I've been wanting to see."

"I've brought some information on Korea for you," he stated in an impersonal, businesslike way, putting a pile of notebooks on the table.

He had a forbidding personality and obviously did not want to be asked any embarrassing personal questions.

I pulled out my fountain pen, Demmy-erh lighted a candle, and we sat down to work. After an hour or so my hand cramped from writing statistics. It was cold, too, for this mountain capital of the Chinese soviets is only fifty miles from the far northwest bastion of the Great Wall where it forms the border between China and Inner Mongolia and Manchuria. Demmy-erh brought in two bowls and a steaming pot of tea.

---

* *Demmy-erh*: My bodyguard was a Red soldier, armed at all times. He was assigned to me for my own protection, and also to serve as a kind of orderly. All the top communists, as well as the three other foreigners in Yan'an—Otto Braun [1900-1974], Dr. George Hatem [1910-1988] and Agnes Smedley [1892-1950]—had bodyguards. When Demmy-erh was found to have tuberculosis and sent to the hospital, he was replaced by Guo Sunhe, a hero of the Long March [see note 165] who later escorted me on the trek from Yan'an to Xi'an. –NW [The bodyguard's actual name was Dai Ming'er. –DH]

This Korean was definitely the conspirator type, I decided. An exile who had lived his life doing dangerous underground revolutionary work, he was somber, quiet, and self-disciplined, but sensitive and nervous. Was that prison pallor on the thin, expressive face? The intelligent bright eyes encouraged me, however, for they seemed frank and understanding.

"I spent most of last summer in Korea and Manchuria," I ventured. "I went to Korea to climb the Diamond Mountains and to learn something about Korea. I didn't learn much, but I had plenty of mountain climbing. I was caught on the top of the highest peak in the Geumgang-san* in the worst typhoon in years. Nearly all the bridges and paths and chains were destroyed, but a Korean guide brought me down safely in spite of the torrents we had to cross everywhere."

"Yes, there was a big flood in Korea at that time."

"I saw it later from the bridge at Seoul. Chickens and pigs and cows and houses tumbling down the muddy river."

"But did you notice how clear and beautiful the streams are in Korea on ordinary days?" The question was not a little nostalgic. "I have never seen any clean rivers and creeks in China. We Koreans say it is a pleasure to commit suicide in a Korean river. Chinese rivers are too dirty for this purpose."

"Are you Koreans as fond of suicide as the Japanese?"

"That is one of the few dignities a colonial people should be able to claim, but we are not even free to choose this way out. On the bridge you speak of in Seoul, the Japanese put up a sign long ago. It reads, 'Please wait five

---

* *Geumgang-san*: The Korean name for the previously referenced Diamond Mountains. "Geumgang" literally means "diamond" and "san" means mountain. Located in what is now North Korea, it is one of the most famous mountains in Korea, and beloved for its beautiful scenery as well as the many historical stories about it that have been handed down from the past. –DH

PRELUDE

minutes.' Hungry mothers often throw their babies into the river and then themselves. Special police are detailed to watch anyone who comes there alone and stares at the water with a certain expression. This is considered a fine courtesy to us Koreans. The Yalu River near Andong* is also a favorite place for suicide. The alternative is to become an exile on the other side."

"I have no patience with people who prefer suicide to fighting for their rights," I remarked unkindly. "Koreans are too gentle and resigned and tolerant. They seemed to me as pastoral as the landscape."

"You are wrong about that. Never a day has passed since 1910[**] that Koreans somewhere have not struck a blow against the Japanese. This is a long story. It has been impossible to overthrow the regime in the peninsula so far, and the armed struggle has been carried out from Manchuria.[7] But thousands have been imprisoned and executed. The prisons are always full. Koreans are not resigned. They are merely preparing for the right moment. They are by nature gentle and tolerant, yes. But there is no anger like the anger of a patient man who has suffered a little too long. Beware the gentle water buffalo."

"That may be true," I said. "Beware the fury of a patient man, we say."

"In the Orient, Koreans are considered a high-tempered race. They quarrel and fight easily, and they are proud and sensitive. They are quick to avenge, and they do not easily forgive. They nurse their wrongs and never forget. Every Korean has bitter enemies and dear friends. The Japanese

---

* *Yalu River near Andong:* Because the Yalu ("Amnok" in Korean) forms a large section of Korea's natural border with China, it is indelibly linked in the Korean imagination to the idea of exile. Andong, known now as Dandong, is the largest Chinese city across the Yalu River from the Korean city of Sinuiju. –GT, DH

[7] *since 1910:* Korea was annexed by Japan in 1910 and remained as its colony until 1945. –DH

are individually much afraid of Koreans because we are too much like themselves. We are medium between the Japanese and Chinese. Koreans are a peninsular people—half island and half continental. And a mountain people, too."

"Do you think Japan is worried now* about Korea?"

"Japan is always worried about Korea. The place is swarming with spies. They watch every minor symptom of dissatisfaction and revolt. Sometimes I almost think they read every letter that was ever mailed there. Japan has trained a whole army of secret service men in Korea. No Japanese will ever rest easy until Korea is surrounded on every side by an army of occupation. They dare not press the military boot too heavily on internal Korea nor continue the past tempo of exploitation. That's one reason for wanting the military occupation of Manchuria and north China. Japan must seek new colonies to ease the pressure on Korea. Korea is thus a great storehouse of retribution for Japan. It does not require a Buddhist to see this. And today Japan's ruling class has another worry. It is afraid of cooperation between the people of Japan itself and the people of Korea. Their common interests and geography are much too close for comfort. The Koreans are a vital ally of those Japanese who want revolution and the victory of the Japanese proletariat. Japan will spread her army in military adventures all over China and Mongolia before she will permit the bottled-up internal pressure at home to rise to meet that in Korea."

"But nothing is happening in Korea now."

"Nothing needs to happen there right now. History awaits its due moment. When the time comes, enough will happen. And it will not be long in coming, I think.

---

* *now*: All references to "now" and "today" that are in the main text are meant to refer to the year 1937, when Kim San was speaking to Nym Wales. –DH

PRELUDE

Little things are going on in Korea that the world never hears about. When there is no censorship on news from Korea, then I'll begin to lose hope. Japan never lets any news come out of Korea—have you noticed that?"

"I have noticed!" I exclaimed. "It's a closed country. While I was there, I felt as if I were living in a hermetically sealed tube in which no sound could travel. The atmosphere was deadly. The missionaries would not talk about anything. They said every letter was read and that spies came to every gathering where Koreans were present. I could not even get any books on Korea. Before I went on my trip, I wanted to read everything I could find on the subject, and three books were all Beijing[8] could produce. I got no information out of any of them. I looked up the publishers' lists, and there was not a single volume on present-day political and economic conditions. I was very annoyed about it."

"Yes, I have read all the books on Korea too. None of them really touches on any of the vital problems. There are only half a dozen worth reading at all."

"Then you must tell me all about the Korean-Japanese situation, or how else will I ever know anything about it?"

"I'll be very glad to do this—to the extent of my abilities. It is important to us Koreans that the world should know about Korea's problems. Whenever you are free, send me a note, and I'll come at that time."

I thanked him and made an appointment for the next afternoon.

❖

Korea is in many ways the most beautiful country in the Far East, so rainy-fresh and green with beautiful sharp-profiled mountains and swift-moving rivers. It reminds one a little of Japan, but on a full scale instead of miniature. The landscape has a rustic quality dramatically relieved by hills and valleys. The little grass-roofed houses snuggle together among crooked lanes in the quaint Arcadia village style. Along the bright-pebbled brooks, women and girls are constantly washing their linen clothes to snowy whiteness. Only a nation of idealists and martyrs would suffer so much backbreaking labor in the name of white, white cleanliness.

Japan is gay and a little artificial with a postcard sort of design. Korea is pure and natural. Japan is a country of sounds—geta,* staccato voices, traffic noises, shōji windows and doors** being always opened and closed, and tiny bits of furniture being moved back and forth. Korea is quiet and smooth-moving. No bobbing up and down in eternal bowing. Human relations seem unstrained and casual. Korean women are sweet and modest and shy in their white and pale blue flowing dresses fitted high at the waist, their hair dress simple and smooth in the Madonna style.

I had decided immediately that the Koreans are far and away the best-looking people in the Far East. Tall and strong and muscular and always well proportioned, they make excellent athletes. While I was in Korea the news came that a young Korean named Son Gi-jeong had won a contest in the Olympics.[9] The Koreans were highly excited and published the news everywhere. The Japanese suppressed all the papers and put out a statement that the man was actually a Japanese with a Korean name! In Japan they heralded the feat widely as a Japanese triumph.

"Well, is he a Korean or is he a Japanese?" I had asked

---

* *geta*: Wooden Japanese clogs used for protection against mud. —NW

** *shōji windows and doors*: Japanese sliding panels of wooden lattice covered by opaque paper that makes a swishing sound when opened or closed. —GT

the clerk at the hotel desk.

"Maybe he is a Korean." The Japanese clerk smiled and drew in his breath. "But it would make them too conceited to publish this. It might cause trouble. They might try to start celebrations here."

Son Gi-jeong at the 1936 Berlin Olympics

Many Koreans have very handsome faces, with well-chiseled profiles. Their features are often a mixture of Japanese and Chinese. Koreans are much in demand in both Japan and China as movie stars. Some have curly hair and remind you of Sessue Hayakawa of the silent film days, the only Oriental man ever to become a film idol for American audiences. Philip Ahn, the Korean actor now in Hollywood, has a more typical face, however. The No. 1 film idol of China, King Shan,[10] is a Korean—he was the hero in the movie *The Sable Cicada*, which was shown in New York. Korean women are often extremely beautiful, with a delicate, ethereal quality.

It is somehow biologically incongruous to see such a comparatively beautiful, intelligent, and superior-looking race under the subjugation of the little Japanese, who are certainly not noted for their appearance. As I watched a squat bandy-legged Japanese officer arrogantly ordering some of these people around in Korea, almost tripping over his sword, I asked a missionary who was with me how such a phenomenon was possible.

"Maybe that's why," she answered. "An inferiority complex can be the cause of great accomplishments."

"But the Koreans must be stupid," I said.

"No, they are far more intelligent than the Japanese. I think the Japanese just happened to get a head start with modern armaments."

The missionaries in Korea really loved and admired the Koreans. They seemed to have none of the racial troubles that have marked their work in Japan and China.

❖

Kim San—that is only one of his five or six noms de guerre[*]—came the next afternoon at the appointed hour. And the next. And the next. I asked him many questions about Korea, and also about Japan, that led to long discussions. I had thought to finish up within a few days, but found myself getting in deeper and deeper.

"You know," I commented to reassure myself, "I am not at all personally interested in Korea. Of course, I am anxious to learn about it for general background on the Far East. But my time and energies are limited. I don't see how I can possibly use all this material. I am really only interested in vital, immediate things, in movements that are making history. Affairs are moving so fast in the world today that one has no time for anything else. That's why I took the trouble to come here to learn something about the Chinese soviet movement, and I intend to write a book on this[**] as soon as possible. I must concentrate on collecting and organizing material for this. I think we must finish up tomorrow, or I'll get lost in a thousand notebooks."

He looked a little hurt. "That is true, of course. I have

---

[*] *five or six noms de guerre*: Kim San used at least nineteen pseudonyms and three pen-names in China. See Appendix I for a more detailed discussion of the question of Kim San's true name. –DH

[**] *I intend to write a book on this*: This book was later published under the title *Inside Red China* (New York: Doubleday-Doran and Co., 1939). –NW

always thought China more important than Korea, and the Koreans often call me a traitor for this reason. In fact, I have been either actively fighting or doing underground work for the Chinese Revolution* since 1925. As soon as war breaks out here in the Far East,** however, Korea will be in a strategic position, and before long, things will begin to happen. Because of the close relation between the Japanese and Korean working classes, as well as between Korea and the Manchurian partisan movement, the Korean Revolution will soon become a vital factor in the Far East. We even have over 300,000 Korean workers in Japan itself now. I myself intend to go to Manchuria to lead the Korean partisans there against Japan as soon as the war situation comes about. My best friend is in

---

° *Chinese Revolution*: Here and throughout the book, whenever Kim San or Nym Wales refer to the "Chinese Revolution," they mean the Chinese Communist Revolution. The GMD also uses the term "Chinese Revolution" but with a different periodization and meaning.

Chinese communist scholars usually explain the Chinese Revolution as consisting of four historical periods: the Great Revolution (1923/1925-1927), the Land Revolution (1927/1928-1936), the Anti-Japanese War (1937-1945), and the Liberation War (1946-1949), which led to the birth of the People's Republic of China. Kim San's activities in China corresponded to the former three periods: the Great Revolution, in which the CCP pursued a "bourgeois democratic revolution" (as opposed to a proletarian revolution) under the GMD's leadership by forming a United Front with the GMD to wipe out warlords (i.e. "feudal forces") and imperialism; the Land Revolution, in which, after its break up with the GMD and internal disputes over revolutionary strategy, the CCP adopted Mao Zedong's peasantry-focused strategy of "surrounding the cities from rural areas"; and the Anti-Japanese War for which the CCP prioritized "national struggle" over "class struggle" and formed a second United Front with GMD.

GMD scholars use the term "Chinese Revolution" to refer to the period starting with the revolutionary activities of Sun Yat-sen that began in the late 19th century and succeeded in 1912 with the establishment of the Republic of China. However, China remained divided by warlords. The Nationalist Revolution thus began when Sun reorganized the party in 1923 with the Soviet Union's support and then in 1924 formed the United Front with the CCP so as to unify China under the banner of the GMD. After Sun's demise in 1925, the GMD established its National Government, which launched a military campaign (the Northern Expedition, see note 96) against warlords in 1926. The Nationalist Revolution ended in 1928 when the National Revolutionary Army (NRA) under Chiang Kai-shek's leadership occupied Beijing after the break-up with both the Soviet Union and the CCP in 1927. Unlike the Chinese Communist Revolution, the GMD's "Chinese Revolution" gradually moved away from anti-imperialism, "anti-warlordism," and "anti-feudalism," and instead primarily served Chiang's military dictatorship. –DH

°° *war breaks out in the Far East*: i.e. the Sino-Japanese War of 1937–1945. –DH

Manchuria leading a division of the First Front Army right now, and he has written several times for me to join him. This division is made up of seven thousand Koreans."

"We must discuss all these things," I groaned; "I am really afraid I'll take too much interest in Korea. I am always getting involved in lost causes and oppressed minorities. I can find an oppressed minority by the scent. I suppose that's how I happened to find you here. I can't seem to miss. It's a very unscientific if not morbid type of interest, and I have made a firm resolution never to pay any attention to such things again. It simply distracts one's energies on relatively unimportant subjects. The world is full of them now."

"Majorities don't need help. And anyway Korea is not a lost cause—"

"Yes, I know. But I've got a big 'oppressed majority' on my mind right now. China's a large subject. I grant, however, that oppressed majorities command less sympathy than oppressed minorities. They ought to be able to hold their own. Anyway, I'll see you tomorrow."

The next day, July 7, 1937, brought sudden news of the incident at the Marco Polo Bridge.* Yan'an was astir with excitement and speculation. Had the war with Japan come at last? Or would there be more compromise and peace?

When Kim San arrived, I asked his opinion.

"War is inevitable, and I think it has come," he said. "If it is not started by this incident, it will be started by the next or the next. Because Japan has no surplus capital to

---

* *incident at the Marco Polo Bridge*: The "Marco Polo Bridge Incident," also called the "Lugouqiao Incident" or the "July 7th Incident" in China, marked the beginning of the full-scale war between China and Japan between 1937 and 1945 (the Sino-Japanese War). Japanese military units stationed near Beijing and the Tianjin area were holding military exercises southwest of Beijing near the city of Wanping. On the night of July 7th, the Japanese, after briefly exchanging shots with the Chinese, demanded to enter the city of Wanping to conduct a search for a missing soldier. The Chinese refused, and the Japanese then attacked the Marco Polo Bridge (Luqouqiao) and bombarded the wall of the city. –GT, DH

carry out a program of slow economic imperialism, she must depend on the army for robber tactics and outright military and political seizure. She is too weak financially to make economic 'cooperation' with China possible. She must destroy China's power before she can begin to exploit the country safely."

"What do you think will be the outcome of the war between China and Japan?"

"There are only two alternatives: either the Japanese will occupy the whole of China and have a great victory, or they will lose everything and be destroyed. A small military adventure in north China will only rouse China, and if the mass movement gets started quickly, it will engulf Japan. Therefore, the Japanese army is prepared for a big gamble before China can mobilize. If Japan is defeated, a revolution at home is sure. Then Japan will join with China and Korea in a strong democratic revolutionary union, and the center of world political forces will shift to the East, with Soviet Russia strategically in the middle. The British know this."

We talked for a long time that afternoon about the war possibilities.

"It looks as though you will be starting for Manchuria right away," I remarked as he left.

❖

I was very busy the next few days, but my mind kept reverting to all this Korean had told me, and, although I had a long list of unanswered questions on China, and Yan'an was full of valuable information, I could not avoid the conclusion that this new subject was a highly important one. It was also apparent that Kim San himself was a unique personality and that I might never again have the rare opportunity of talking with such a person.

He was one of the most fascinating characters that I had met in seven years in the Orient. He had certain qualities that seemed unusual among the revolutionaries I had met—and I had, with some pains and a good deal of writer's cramp, written down the autobiographies of about twenty-five of them during the summer. I could not quite analyze these qualities at first. Then I recognized what they were: He had an independent, fearless mind and perfect poise. His opinions were decisive and showed that they had all been carefully reasoned out, both from theory and from experience. He thought as a leader, not as a follower. I realized that, since he was one of the most important leaders of the Korean revolutionary movement, this was natural enough. And under the surface, though he was gentle-mannered and reclusive, there was POWER. Here was by no means a harmless person. I would not care to be his enemy, though he might make a loyal, devoted friend. I felt that he had not only no fear of death or of killing but was morally and intellectually incorruptible and without evasion. Here was a man who had been hammered and shaped in the white heat of the great tragedies that have molded recent history in China and Korea and who had emerged from the ordeal, not only as a steel instrument of tempered will and determination, but as a sentient being of feeling and consciousness.

I determined that I must not fail to learn more about him. The problem was how to win the confidence of this aloof, reserved personality. He was not likely to volunteer any personal information about himself. Such active revolutionaries are seldom free to tell their stories, and I was not a little afraid to ask, for life and death must hang on the careless handling of the secrets of men whose lives are spent in underground activities. The offensive is sometimes the best tactic.

"It seems to me that you must be a very interesting

person. Are you?" I came to the point directly.

He laughed, showing a set of strong white teeth in a stubborn jaw; I think it was the first time I saw him laugh. "I am not so simple as some and less complex than others."

"I think I'd like to write a book about you. You know, I must finish up here as quickly as possible and I have been a little sick and I am very tired, as well as being still busy with other things here, but if you are willing to tell me the story of your life, I am prepared to write it. I have always wanted to write a novel about someone like you, and I think you would make a good subject."

"It is dangerous for me to let my activities be known publicly. I have already been in a Chinese prison, and twice in a Japanese prison. The next time will be serious for me. I could perhaps tell you some of it, but not all."

"You can think it over and let me know when you have decided. I don't see why you don't write a book about Korea yourself, there are so few."

"As a matter of fact, I have already started a book in Korean about a Korean exile in Manchuria. I call it *Shadows of the White-Clothed People*.[11] I don't know when I'll ever have time to finish it. When I go back to Manchuria to join the partisans, I'll get the material for the last part."

"Why do you call your book by that title?"

"Because all Koreans like to wear white. We are always called 'the white-clothed people.'"

The next afternoon, Kim San returned, happier than I had ever seen him. This made me realize that he had another characteristic rare in Yan'an, where everyone was cheerful and gay: he was serious-minded and unhappy, though not without optimism.

"I have decided that we should do the book," he announced. "In fact, I am grateful that you want to write about Korea. I only hope it is read by Chinese and

Japanese and by Koreans abroad, as well as by Americans and British, to remind them that Korea is not a lost cause. For this reason I am prepared to tell you the whole story. It will be worthwhile, even though I may have to suffer for it. No Korean plans his grave, anyway. It may be anywhere, anytime. But if you will wait two years from now before publishing it, it will be better for me. Then I hope to be safely in Manchuria among the Korean partisans there. By that time all these things can be told without harm to anyone because the war will change the entire situation. Such a book will be really valuable then, especially when the Korean movement rises again."

❖

So we started to work. The rain came down unceasingly every day for weeks. Nearly every afternoon I wrote down his story by candlelight until my fingers were too cramped to continue. At first his English was halting and slow, but soon it was surprisingly fluent and expressive. His vocabulary, gained entirely from reading books, was excellent—though many pronunciations were hardly orthodox. He was also a teacher of Japanese, knew Chinese perfectly, as well as a little Mongolian, and had studied German and Latin as a medical student.

"Your English is remarkable," I said. "Especially when you say that you have never before attempted to carry on a long conversation in it."

"All Koreans learn foreign languages easily for some reason," he replied dryly. "The Japanese say that it is proof that we are a natural colony. And they say that the reason they cannot learn foreign languages is because they are a dominant race."

After I had got into the heart of the story, I saw that it was going to be dramatic and interesting. The breadth of his experiences amazed me. The book was going to cover, not only Korea, Japan, and Manchuria, but the exciting course of the Chinese Revolution as well. Only a wandering Korean revolutionary could have had such broad and differentiated experiences, and only an outsider could have such a clear perspective on all these movements and peoples of the three countries. The story of his life gave a kaleidoscopic picture of the whole Far East. It was a new and fresh interpretation. Moreover, it did not take me long to realize I had been right in supposing that Kim San had an extraordinarily interesting and complex mind and personality. His intellectual life had not been simple and easy but full of every conceivable problem of political and revolutionary struggle. How he resolved these problems was of philosophical as well as practical interest. Rarest of all was the fact that he had not only gone through all these varied experiences but was able to tell about them in the spirit and style of good narrative.

Everywhere the intellectual is being put to the test today, and he is crumpling up between the lists of struggle like a piece of his own waste paper. These are the times that try men's minds. We must grasp a hundred years in a day. History moves faster than the vibrations of the brain cell. Nations collapse and empires shift before we comprehend. The meteoric rush of new worlds in creation leaves us dizzy in a paralysis of confusion and fear as we feel the old world cut from under our feet. Sandbags cannot defend the ivory tower, and the tears of self-pity merely add dampness to the dugout of despair and disillusionment. I often think of Kim San telling me his story simply and quietly in that miserable room in Yan'an, and wonder how many American and British intellectuals could have survived his ordeal with philosophical objectivity. Kim San was a sensitive intellectual,

at heart an idealist poet and writer, hurled into one of
the bloodiest, ugliest, and most confusing cataclysms
of our time. He had no illusions left but was not a cynic.
He acknowledged things as they are but affirmed change
and progress. Suffering and defeat had not destroyed his
vision but fired his thinking with deeper meaning and
significance. He was master of objective fact and not a
slave of the subjective word. The body feeds on bread but
the spirit on hunger and pain. The intellectual is capable
of action and decision only when he ceases to think in
symbols instead of concrete realities. Kim San overcame
this weakness and did not fall victim to the pathology of
intellectual defeatism. Actually, the intellectual cannot be
betrayed. He can only betray himself and his profession.
His job is not only to paint pictures of the future but to
recognize and analyze the materials of historical change
as they exist. What utter vanity to expect the multiform
world to mold itself to his single limited design! History
is not so dull in action and so narrow in plan as those who
criticize it. From their Olympic seats of petty judgment,
they hurl not thunderbolts but firecrackers.

❖

I have organized, rewritten, and cut down the mass of
material in my seven notebooks on Kim San, but it is as
nearly like the original story told to me as possible. It is
strictly authentic in all details, including the conversa-
tions. I insisted on getting these from Kim San, while
writing down the narrative, with much labor and prodding. He had a phenomenal memory and a good narrative
sense, which simplified this task very much indeed. He
had kept a diary for many years, written in code, and
though he had periodically destroyed these notes, it served
to fix incidents in his mind so well that he had no diffi-

culty remembering minor details. I dared not spoil the authenticity of a valuable piece of research on a practically unknown subject, but have let the subject speak for himself without interpretation, aside from the necessity of converting it into readable English. The virtue of this book lies, therefore, in its historical and autobiographical value. It seems to me that it is a new contribution to our very limited knowledge of the mind, psychology, and experience of revolutionary leaders in the Orient, as well as a first-hand description of some of the most dramatic events of the period. It tires me even to remember the amount of clinical cross-examination through which I put this man so mercilessly during those two months in Yan'an.

Very little of the detailed historical information contained in these pages has ever before been written in any language. Even Kim San's account of the Guangzhou Commune* is unusual personal experience. The story of Hailufeng** has never before been written, and only three or four persons are now alive to recount the tragic tale. (André Malraux has written the only two novels about the 1925–1927 revolution in China: *The Conquerors*, dealing with the Hong Kong Strike in 1924–1925, and *Man's Fate*, describing the April events in Shanghai in 1927.) The files of the Comintern*** may contain the records, but it has

---

* *Guangzhou Commune*: An armed uprising by the CCP against GMD military forces that took place from December 11–13, 1927 in Guangzhou (known also in the West by its older Romanization, "Canton"), the capital of Guangdong Province and today China's third largest city. This led to the establishment of the short-lived "Workers and Peasants Democratic Government" aka the Guangzhou Commune. (See Chapter 11). Also referred to throughout the book as the Guangzhou Uprising. –DH

** *the story of Hailufeng*: Hailufeng, an area in Guangdong Province southeast of Guangzhou that encompasses Haifeng and Lufeng, was the site of the first Chinese soviet, established by the CCP in November 1927. In 1928 it fell to the GMD, as Kim San explains at length in Chapter 12. See note on p. 182. –DH

*** *Comintern*: An international communist organization, also known as the Communist International or the Third International, established in 1919 under the leadership of the Soviet Union that set the strategies and policies for the international communist movement as well as for national communist parties. –DH

been impossible for Chinese or Koreans to publish such stories even illegally since the Civil War in 1927.[12] Most of the original leading participants are dead.

There are several things about which it has been literally impossible to obtain inside information: the Manchurian guerrillas, particularly Koreans; illegal Korean activities and prison records; and underground communist activities in China or Korea. Kim San's story throws much new light on these subjects.

This is the record of the experiences of a typical leader in the vast interrelated social upheaval now spreading throughout the nations of the Far East, where history is moving a thousand years in a generation. It is primarily, however, the story of the Korean revolutionary movement from its early beginnings in Korea and Manchuria to its coordination with the Chinese struggle after 1925. Kim San's career followed closely the general trend of the movement. It is also the story of three companions: of Kim San and his two best friends, Oh Seong-ryun (also called "Ham-seong" in Manchuria) and Kim Chung-chang, a trio in the vanguard of Korean leadership—one the famous terrorist and man of action now leading a partisan army in Manchuria; one the ex-monk and theoretical intellectual; the other, Kim San, their one-time disciple in action and theory, ten years younger.

As our conflict with Japan approaches, we in the United States and Britain shall soon be as eager to inform ourselves about the potentialities of the underground opposition to Japanese fascism and conquest as we are today about a possible internal revolt against Hitler. Kim San and his Korean friends have spent twenty years in this opposition. The Japanese have always called Korea "the dagger pointing at the heart of Nippon."

As we started work, I said to Kim San: "First you must tell me the general development of your career and next about your early youth."

"My youth?" he answered quizzically. "It's true that I am now only thirty-two, but I have lost my youth somewhere, where I do not know. . ."

—BAGUIO, PHILIPPINES
1939

"Arirang" is pronounced with broad a's and accented on the last syllable: "Ah-ree-rahng." The Hills of Arirang refers to a section of hills in the center of the Korean peninsula. They bring up feelings of a kind of sad nostalgia. This refrain is probably the most well-known and beloved folk song in Korean history and continues to be sung with many word variations up until today. –NW, GT

The "Song of Arirang" has many different versions and lyrics corresponding to different places in Korea. Accordingly, it used to be called with the name of a place attached to it, such as "Jindo Arirang" and "Miryang Arirang." The lyrics above are a more common version (i.e. "Gyeonggi Arirang") that is now widely known to most Koreans. The lyrics presented on the facing page are a version of the song that is particularly relevant to the story of Korean exiles in China who engaged in independence struggle against Japanese colonialism. –DH

Song of Arirang

(OLD KOREAN FOLKSONG OF EXILE,
PRISON, AND NATIONAL HUMILIATION)

Arirang, Arirang, A-ra-ri-yo!
Crossing the hills of Arirang.
There are twelve hills of Arirang
And now I am crossing the last hill.

Many stars in the deep sky—
Many crimes in the life of man.
Arirang, Arirang, A-ra-ri-yo!
Crossing the hills of Arirang.

Arirang is the mountain of sorrow
And the path to Arirang has no returning.
Arirang, Arirang, A-ra-ri-yo!
Crossing the hills of Arirang.

Oh, twenty million countrymen—where are you now?
Alive are only three thousand mountains and rivers.
Arirang, Arirang, A-ra-ri-yo!
Crossing the hills of Arirang.

Now I am an exile crossing the Yalu River
And the mountains and rivers of three thousand li*
    are also lost.
Arirang, Arirang, A-ra-ri-yo!
Crossing the hills of Arirang.

* A "li" is a traditional measure of length in China, Japan, and Korea. It is equivalent to 0.5 kilometers or 0.31 miles. Its pronunciation in Chinese is "li"; in Japanese and Korean it is "ri." It is used without an "s," even when plural. —GT, DH

Women protesting on March 1, 1919

PART 1

DECLARATION

OF

INDEPENDENCE

Koreans migrating to Jiandao ("Gando" in Korean), a border region along the north bank of the Tumen ("Duman" in Korean) River circa 1936

CHAPTER 1

Recuerdo (Memories)

I SUPPOSE THAT I must have been very young at one time or another. There was a small boy of eleven who ran away from home and lived his own life afterward, but I cannot remember that he was very young. There was a shabby eager student who carried a three-language dictionary next to a hungry belly on his travels to Japan and Manchuria and China. But I only remember that he was not young. There was a revolutionary romantic of sixteen and twenty-two who burned with a pure devotional flame. I know now that he was very young, but he did not know it then. He must have been very young before he went to prison, for he felt so very old afterward. I remember that he was young on the day he met his first great love. I know that he was old before he had finished with this subject.

Perhaps the reason he was never young is that Korea had no youth to suffer what she felt. She was a nation weeping in ancient bondage long before Japan made orphans of her sons. The widow of nations, still she stands, holding out

sorrowful arms to her exiled children across the Yalu River.*
We shall return one day but not to weep.

I hated Korea when I ran away that autumn day in 1919,[13] vowing never to return until the weeping was changed to fighting slogans. She wanted peace, and peace she got—after the "peaceful demonstrations" had been dispersed in helpless blood. She was a foolish old woman naively mouthing feminine pleas to the great powers for "international justice" and a promise of "self-determination." We were betrayed by her foolishness. I resented the accident of birth that made me the child of such shameful helplessness. In Russia and Siberia, men and women were fighting and winning. They did not beg for freedom. They earned it by right of hard struggle. I wanted to go there to learn the secret of human emancipation; then I would return and lead two million exiles in Manchuria and Siberia to recapture their homeland.

I stole money for my trip but could not pass the lines of the foreign intervention in Siberia.[14] So I studied military science in Manchuria, then I went on to Shanghai to join the little knot of Korean revolutionaries there. I became an anarchist, placing futile hope in terrorist reprisals against both the conquerors and traitors of Korea. At least we would die heroically, flaunting our individual courage to a world in denial of the helpless impotence of the country of our birth. In that period, I wanted to fight for ideas and principles with a nihilist disregard for those geographical expressions called countries. When these beautiful gestures in the name of justice failed, I saw the meaning of organized internationalism. We would emancipate all oppressed nations. China and Korea and later Japan together would bear the bright torch of liberty over the Far East. I became a Chinese citizen and a member of the

---

* *to her exiled children across the Yalu River*: A poetic way of saying "in China." —GT, DH

Chinese Communist Party. Gladly we went to Guangzhou in the hundreds to die for China in the name of internationalism.* The flower of the Korean revolutionary leadership was annihilated there—and we failed. Some of my comrades committed suicide when they learned of this great sacrifice. In Hailufeng, I suffered more than those who died, but this only kindled my faith. For the Korean nationalist movement, the great tragedy of the reaction in China in 1927** was a blow from which it never recovered. With no ally, Korea went back to helplessness under the Japanese.

After 1928, my romantic days of action were over. Ahead lay only a hard, slow struggle full of ideological and tactical problems. I had to prepare myself for leadership and responsibility in a secret underground movement where the slightest mistake meant death, not only for myself but for others.

My life's purpose then became the strengthening and rebuilding of the defeated Chinese Revolution, and the coordination of the Chinese and Korean revolutionary movements in a common struggle. In 1929 and 1930 I took leadership in organizing the revolutionary work in north China and Manchuria.

---

* *we went to Guangzhou...to die for internationalism*: Guangzhou emerged as the revolutionary center in China from 1924 when the United Front between the GMD and the CCP was established there with the support and sponsorship of the Soviet Union. Many radicals and revolutionaries from China and abroad, including Korea, streamed into the city for the Nationalist Revolution of China, which was launched under the banner of the GMD. —DH

** *the reaction in China in 1927*: Reference to the anti-communist campaigns initiated on April 12, 1927 in Shanghai by the GMD under Chiang Kai-shek (also known as the April 12th Coup), which ultimately led to the break-up of the first United Front between the GMD and the CCP. Chinese communists describe these campaigns, which resulted in the execution or imprisonment of vast numbers of Chinese communists and anti-Japanese Korean fighters who were living in exile in China at the time, as a "betrayal" or "reaction" by the GMD and the beginning of civil war between the two parties. The GMD describe these same events as the beginning of the separation from the communists — i.e. the "purification of the party." —DH

RECUERDO (MEMORIES)

The year 1931 was a year of political crisis in China[15] like 1927. Japan had taken Manchuria. The crisis in my own life coincided with the general crisis—and these internal and external blows struck me with tremendous force. After my release in 1931 from torture and illness in a Japanese prison, I found that many old comrades did not trust me. This injustice angered and embittered me. I contemplated murdering a political enemy who had lied about me. Then I decided upon suicide. Next I thought of giving up revolutionary work and walking around the world for seven years. This brief period, however, was only a bookmark in my life where I found my way.

I went through a grueling self-examination and study of general revolutionary principles and came out victorious, with complete confidence in myself and with moral and physical courage that has never since failed. Until this time, I had never asked questions, never sincerely thought of theoretical problems. I had been too busy taking action and following orders. Now I searched for answers and fundamental principles, both in philosophy and action. I was reinstated into the Chinese Party* and went into underground work in the mass movement.

In 1933 I was again a prisoner. But freedom was of little use when I regained it. The mass movement in White areas** had failed, and the Chinese Party in north China was broken. I was unhappy but not in despair, for I now had a solid philosophy to tread on. One must await the next forward movement in the ebbing and surging of history.

But the struggle against Japan was fast approaching,

---

* *the Chinese Party*: Throughout the book, the Chinese Communist Party is often referred to as the "Chinese Party." –DH

** *White areas*: A reference to the anti-communist areas ruled by the GMD. "Red areas"—i.e. areas controlled by the communists—would have been referred to at the time by people in Kim San's political circles as "liberated areas." –DH

and a new day was near. In 1935, I went to Shanghai, where I helped reorganize the Korean revolutionaries into an internally united front and into a common front with China against Japan. In August 1936, these groups sent me as a delegate to Yan'an.

And now Korea... Will not this war in the Far East lead to the liberation of Korea at last? I think it will, and soon I must go back to the service of my own country and help to lead her forward, for now we are "crossing the last hill of Arirang."

In Korea we have a folk song, a beautiful, ancient song which was created out of the living heart of a suffering people. It is sad, as all deep-felt beauty is sad. It is tragic, as Korea has for so long been tragic. Because it is beautiful and tragic, it has been the favorite song of all Koreans for three hundred years.

Near Seoul there is a hill called the Hill of Arirang. During the oppressive Yi Dynasty[16] there was a giant solitary pine at the top of this hill, and this was the official place of execution for several hundred years. Tens of thousands of prisoners were hanged until dead on a gnarled branch of that ancient tree, their bodies suspended over a cliff at the side. Some were bandits. Some were common criminals. Some were dissident scholars. Some were political and family enemies of the Korean emperor. Many were poor farmers who had raised their hands against oppression. Many were rebel youths who had struggled against tyranny and injustice. The story is that one of those young men composed a song during his imprisonment, and as he trudged slowly up the Hill of Arirang, he sang this song. The people learned it, and after that whenever a man was condemned to die he sang this in farewell to his joys or sorrows. Every Korean prison echoes with these haunting notes, and no one dares deny a man's death-right to sing it at the end.

The "Song of Arirang" has come to symbolize the tragedy of Korea. Its meaning is symbolic of constantly climbing over obstacles only to find death at the end. It is a song of death and not of life. But death is not defeat. Out of many deaths, victory may be born. There are those of us who would write another verse for this ancient "Song of Arirang." That last verse is not yet written. We are many dead, and many more have "crossed the Yalu River" into exile. But our return will not be long in the future.

When the Japanese took Korea in 1910, a fifth verse was added to the original song. But since then and in the future, we will have hundreds more, including "love songs." Today we have a whole book of nearly a hundred different versions. We even have a popular "Love Song of Arirang." Already the "Song of Arirang" has been sung all over the plains of Manchuria, both by Korean volunteers and Chinese. In Japan also it is popular. Even now, three versions of the "Song of Arirang" are available on phonograph records. The word "Arirang" is such a favorite that inns and cafes use it as their name. Yi Gwang-su has written a play on the subject.

Many of these versions are banned in Korea. The Japanese are almost as afraid of "dangerous songs" as of "dangerous thoughts." In 1921, a communist intellectual wrote a "dangerous" version as he was about to die, and someone else wrote another secret revolutionary version called "Moving the Hills of Arirang." Middle-school students have been given six months in prison for singing certain versions of this song. I knew one who received this punishment in Seoul in 1925.

There are "twelve hills of Arirang," the song says. When I first read Dante, I was surprised to find that he used the same number—twelve heavens and twelve hells—and that his theme was also, "Abandon all hope, ye who enter here." I suppose it is a universal number for misfortune.

Korea has passed painfully over more than twelve hills of Arirang, however. Our little peninsula has always been a stepping stone from Japan to China and back again, and from Siberia to the south. She was for hundreds of years the center of culture in the north, and every barbarian invasion passed over on its way to China, devastating Korea's fair cities and fields of civilization. Yet in spite of conquest she retained her identity under temporary suzerainty and never submitted, but awaited the opportunity to rise again. Against the frail wall of our "twenty million countrymen,"[*] fifty to seventy million Japanese have been pressing since the nineteenth century on their inexorable drive to Manchuria and China. We could not hold them back, and the iron-nailed boot is pressing hard on Korea today, but when Japan loses her stride, the sunny green grass will grow again where darkness has been.

I have seen Korea climb several hills of Arirang already in my short life, only to find death at the summit. I was born at the time she was being trampled by foreign armies during the Russo-Japanese War.[**] I saw the Korean Army of seventy thousand men demobilized and forced to retreat across the borders after their country became a Japanese protectorate in 1905. I saw the country become a colony in 1910, and year after year I saw over a million exiles driven across the Yalu River into Manchuria and Siberia and China. There are now over two million Korean exiles, one million in Manchuria, 800,000 in Siberia, 300,000 in Japan, and the others in China, Mexico, Hawaii, America, and elsewhere.

---

[*] *"twenty million countrymen"*: According to a census of October 1, 1935, Korea had a population of 22,898,695, of whom 561,384 were Japanese and 50,639 were other foreigners, mostly Chinese. –NW

[**] *Russo-Japanese War*: The Russo-Japanese War was fought in Korea and Manchuria from 1904 to 1905 over, among other things, influence in Korea. Russia's loss and signing the Treaty of Portsmouth effectively recognized Japan's right to a sphere of influence over Korea and southern Manchuria –DH

RECUERDO (MEMORIES)

I saw the whole country turned into a prison after the Christian "peaceful demonstrations" during the March First National Movement in 1919*—fifty thousand prisoners and seven thousand killed. I was one of three thousand Korean students in Japan in 1919, four years before a thousand of them and five thousand other Koreans were massacred during the earthquake in 1923,[17] a pogrom to warn the Japanese population against a repetition of the great Rice Riots of 1918,[18] for they were murmuring that "the gods were punishing" the corrupt ruling class. I lived the life of the exiles in Manchuria in 1920, a few weeks before over six thousand of them (including all my friends but one) were killed by Japanese troops in revenge for the activities of the Korean Army of Independence.**

I met the young terrorists in Shanghai who tried to avenge these deaths by turning to desperate personal heroism and mourned the tragic result—300,000 in the Uiyeol-dan*** alone were executed by the Japanese from

---

* *March First National Movement in 1919*: A nationwide protest against Japan's colonial rule in Korea that took place on March 1st, 1919 and that called for the return of Korea's independence. The reaction by the Japanese colonial authorities was extremely fierce, with the number of dead amounting to over seven thousand, and more than fifteen thousand wounded, according to some accounts; the military police burned down 715 homes, forty-seven Christian churches, and two schools. The Declaration of Independence issued in Seoul on that day can be easily found in the many historical accounts of this memorable episode. Although the protests failed at the time, they led to the establishment of the Korean Government-in-Exile in Shanghai (the Korean Provisional Government) the following month, and inspired the whole subsequent independence movement. Also referred to throughout the book as the "March First Movement." –AJ, GT, DH

** *the Korean Army of Independence*: What Kim San refers to again and again throughout the book as the Korean Army of Independence was not a regular armed force under the command of the Korean Provisional Government but a series of irregular guerrilla fighters or various groups of armed force scattered throughout Manchuria and later in China proper. –DH

*** *Uiyeol-dan*: Often translated as "the Righteous Group," this anti-Japanese terrorist group was organized by Kim Won-bong (aka Kim Yak-san) and others in December 1919 in Jilin Province in Manchuria. Targeting important Japanese and pro-Japanese Koreans for assassination, they carried out numerous bombings in Korea, China, and Japan until the middle of the 1920s, when the Uiyeol-dan changed its emphasis from terrorism to more organized political struggle. –DH (*HSIS*, 103)

1919 to 1927. I was one of three thousand Koreans who gathered in the French Concession in Shanghai to support the Korean Provisional Government,* which was organized there in 1919 in opposition to the Japanese set-up in Seoul, and which collapsed in 1924, leaving only a coterie of old men with broken hearts and broken hopes.

Ahn Chang Ho (seated in center of the front row) and other members of the Provisional Government of the Republic of Korea in Shanghai. Photo taken on October 11, 1919.

With eight hundred other Koreans, I joined the Chinese Revolution in Guangzhou and saw the flower of Korean revolutionary leadership sacrificed during the two years from 1925 to 1927—two hundred communist leaders participated in the "Guangzhou Commune" alone, and most were killed. I fought in China's annihilated first soviet, at Hailufeng, with fifteen other Korean comrades—and only

---

* *Korean Provisional Government*: The Korean Provisional Government was formally inaugurated as a government-in-exile in Shanghai in April of 1919 with Syngman Rhee as its head of state. As Kim San notes here, internal power struggles and divisions gradually weakened this government and its activities throughout the 1920s, though it was revived in the 1930s and 1940s. –GT, DH

two of us are alive to tell the story. Japan took the occasion to arrest one thousand others in Korea as "communists"[19] at the same time, on March 15, 1928, though we had only four hundred communists in all Korea then. When our allies in the Chinese Great Revolution failed, we said, "The world is broken for Korea."

I returned to Jilin in Manchuria in 1929 to coordinate revolutionary activities between Chinese and Koreans against Japan. And what happened to this? There I found the Chinese nationalists under Zhang Xueliang vying with the Japanese in their efforts to split up Korean-Chinese unity at a time when most Koreans wanted to become Chinese citizens! Two years later these efforts came to a crisis. Through the stupidity of the Chinese in taking out petty reprisals against Japan by attacking the anti-Japanese Koreans, the Korean nationalists broke with the Chinese. At the same time, Zhang Xueliang's government was executing as many Korean revolutionaries as could be found. The Chinese executed forty of my Korean communist comrades at one time in Jilin. In 1932, eight hundred young Korean farmers were arrested from Jilin City to Panzu in an attempt to destroy the Korean communist movement. How bitterly the inexperienced "Young Marshal" learned to regret this! Long before the Xi'an Incident in 1936,[20] he was begging Korean revolutionaries of all kinds to work with him, preferably communists.

The Korean and Chinese volunteers now work together again, and every year hundreds of Koreans in Manchuria give up their lives fighting the Japanese.

I have seen scores of my countrymen in prison cells next to mine—many of them later executed or mentally deranged from torture. There are now some six thousand political prisoners in Korea.

Every year since 1905,* the story has been the same—hundreds imprisoned or executed in Siberia under the Czars, in Manchuria, in China, in Japan, as well as in Korea. For a revolutionary to be a man with four countries is worse than to be a man without a country. All are only a passport to death. We Koreans are "legally" arrested by the Japanese, the Chinese, the British and French in Shanghai, and the Korean police. We have no protection anywhere. So Korea is the most religious and Christian nation in the Orient—hoping for surcease from sorrow in the Kingdom of Heaven, where presumably there are no prisons for people with "dangerous thoughts" of freedom.

Korea is a small country to lose so many men and to bear so much oppression and suffering. But the end is not yet. We can still hope that the last sacrifice will finish in victory. Korea still has strength to climb the last of the hills of Arirang and tear down her old gallows of death. I believe that the next "October Revolution"** will be in Japan—and the Korean Revolution will either precede or follow in November.

As I survey the rugged contours of my life's experience, I see only a succession of hard-won defeats, and the highest mountain lies wearily ahead. My life has not been a happy one. It has been lived close to history, and history does not dance to the piping of shepherds. It is moved only by the groans of the wounded and the sounds of battle. To struggle is to live. All else is without meaning in my world. Within the oppositions of that struggle lies my identity with the life of man, my unity with his history.

---

* *since 1905*: 1905 was the year in which Russia was defeated in the Russo-Japanese War of 1904-1905, clearing the way for Japan's annexation of Korea in 1910. (See note on p. 33). –DH

** *the "October Revolution"*: Reference to the Russian Revolution of 1917, the success of which resulted in the establishment of the first communist government. This came to represent the possibility of emancipation from their oppressors and colonizers for many oppressed/colonized peoples. –DH

RECUERDO (MEMORIES)

But let us get on with the story. We can philosophize as we proceed....

CHAPTER 2

Korean Childhood

I WAS BORN on a mountain in the middle of a battlefield. The Korean villagers had all fled to the mountains for safety during the constant fighting, and my mother had escaped to the site of our ancestral graves. That was on March 10, 1905, and the Russo-Japanese War did not end until August.

My home in the little village of Chasan-ri* on the outskirts of Pyongyang** was under Japanese occupation, while the Russian base was farther north. The mountain that was the scene of my arrival into the world was near

---

* *little village of Chasan-ri*: Recent evidence indicates that Kim San's home was not Chasan-ri near Pyongyang. A newly discovered photo of Kim San taken during his 1931 detention at the Japanese Consulate in Tianjin, China, shows his permanent home address as 299 Hajang-Dong, Bukjung-Myeon, Yongcheon-Gun, Pyong-an Bukdo, close to the Yalu River. (This photo can be seen on page 384.) Kim San obviously must have wanted to hide his actual identity and home address. —DH (Baek and Hong 1998, 1515-1529)

** *Pyongyang*: It [Pyongyang] is now [in 1937] called Heijō by the Japanese, just as Seoul, the capital [of the Japanese colony of Korea], has been renamed Keijō, but the Koreans still use the old names. Pyongyang is the third largest city in Korea and was for some years the most important munitions depot and airplane base which Japan had on the mainland." —NW [In 1948, Pyongyang became the capital of the Democratic People's Republic of Korea (DPRK or North Korea). —GT]

the sea. Russian ships could be seen in the harbor below, my mother told me. At the beginning of the war, the Koreans hoped for a Russian victory, she said, but their sympathies turned toward Japan during the struggle. For the conduct of the Russian troops angered the villagers. They oppressed the people, mistreated their daughters, and took their oxen. The Japanese at that time wisely avoided antagonizing the population and always paid for anything they wanted.

My home life was not a happy one. My father was an independent farmer but very poor and always in debt. He owned only one chō* of farm land, though we also raised 60 or 80 yen worth of silk cocoons a year. I lived in a typical rustic Korean house with a grass roof. It had only one large room and three small storerooms at the side. The raised floor was made of stone covered with oiled paper and heated by a flue underneath for warmth in winter. We took off our shoes, leaving them outside, and sat on the floor on cushions. It was shining, clean, and comfortable. My pleasantest childhood memory is of snuggling close to that warm floor while the bitter winds howled through the thick grass roof. But it was not always warm. Fire was an expensive luxury, and the flue was hot only while food was being prepared on the kitchen stove. Even then coal was cheaper than wood; what forests remained were soon despoiled by the Japanese for their own use.

Those were stormy years for Korea. My first permanent impression of the outside world was of seeing people crying everywhere. Men gathered in groups and talked excitedly. Women stood in knots over the smoky kitchen fires and wiped their eyes endlessly as they fed the flames with bunches of dry grass. On the nearby hills you could

---

* *chō*: A Japanese term for a measurement equal to 2.45 acres of land. Sometimes called "chōbu" ("jeongbo" in Korean). –NW, GT, DH

hear war cries as swordplay and boxing were practiced.

"What is it?" I clung to my mother's skirts in terror.

"The Japanese are coming," she answered.

The word took on a sinister meaning for me. It was the bugbear of my childhood. That was a month or two before Japan officially occupied Korea on August 22, 1910.

I remember there were arguments among the men about whether or not to cut off the topknot,* and the question seemed to be the most important thing in the world. Those who had cut the topknot were beings apart from the rest, and we children pointed our fingers at them excitedly as they passed. It meant they were members of the Korean Independence Party.[21] New schools were opened to teach the people the meaning of what was about to happen, and the villagers marched to these classes like troops, shouting and making speeches as they went.

The first time I remember seeing one of the dreaded Japanese conquerors up close was when I was seven years old. Two policemen came to our house and slapped my mother's face until blood ran down where her teeth had bitten into her lips. I ran out screaming in tears and wanted to pound my fists against them, but my mother pulled me back.

"Hush, hush," she begged. "You must never strike back. Don't make any trouble."

"Why did they slap you?" I asked when the policemen had gone.

"The Japanese are forcing everyone to be vaccinated, and I did not go to have this done quickly enough to suit them. When I told them I had been too busy with my housework

---

* *whether or not to cut off the topknot*: Following a Confucian teaching, Koreans believed that their body, hair, and skin were all inherited directly from their parents and so, in order to demonstrate filial piety, should not be harmed. The long hair that resulted from this belief was worn by men in a topknot. However, the Japanese forced Koreans to cut their topknots into Western-style short hair, which came to symbolize the modern. –DH

and that I would surely do it tomorrow, they got angry," she explained sadly. "They have no respect for women. But you must never do anything to annoy them."

It was always the same. You must never strike back no matter what the Japanese might do. It would "cause trouble." That was the commonest phrase I heard on the subject. I thought there must be some good reason for this attitude, but I could not see it. There were so many of us Koreans and so few Japanese. How easy it looked to drive them into the sea!

That same week I learned that there were pro-Japanese traitors too, and I was angrier at them than at the Japanese. One of our village elders, who could speak a little Japanese, had a feud with another family. The old father of this family resisted vaccination and talked against it. The village elder reported this fact to the Japanese and asked them to punish him. I watched the Japanese police tie this old man to the wooden pestle of a rice mortar and beat him severely. After that the neighbors avoided the village elder and warned each other that they must not speak against the Japanese in his presence or he would report it.

Eleven of us lived in the same house. I was the third son. My eldest brother, whose wife and children lived with us, had gone to an old-fashioned school, but my second brother had finished at the new primary school. My father was an old-type Confucianist and could read a little Chinese as well as Korean. Mother had never attended school but could read a little Korean, [22] which is very easy to learn. Nobody else in the house could read. My mother and my elder brother's wife were devout Christians and never missed going to church. They prayed over every problem that came up, small or great.

Meals were prepared only twice a day because of lack of

fuel for cooking. At nine in the morning, our achimbap[*] consisted of dry white rice, soup, salted sardines, and a vegetable—usually dried chopped radish or salted cabbage, with soy sauce. Jeomsim[**] at midday was exactly the same, saved over from the morning, except that it was cold to avoid heating. In the evening, jeonyeokbap[***] was served at five or six in winter and at six or seven in summer. It was not much different from the other two meals, though two or three times a month we had a little chicken or beef. Our family was poor but not too uncomfortable. Poor peasants in Korea eat meat only at festival times—on the New Year, the Cheongmyeong Festival, the Old May First Athletic Meet, and the Autumn Festival. Many poor women and children never get enough to eat and are always half-hungry. They cannot afford white rice except on holidays, even though they raise it themselves, but must eat millet.[****] We have no sweet food in Korea, and ordinarily do not drink tea but only cold water.

Our eating customs are more like the Japanese than the Chinese. We always use a spoon and chopsticks made of metal or silver; if of wood, they are used only once and thrown away. This is a regulation in all Korean inns. No one ever uses the chopsticks belonging to someone else. Each has an individual little table and bowl and individual side dishes. Even a very poor man has his table, though his wife has none. We sit on the raised floor like the Japa-

---

[*] *achimbap*: Korean word for breakfast. –DH

[**] *jeomsim*: Korean word for lunch. –DH

[***] *jeonyeokbap*: Korean word for dinner. –DH

[****] *but must eat millet*: According to a story in the *Oriental Daily News* [Dong-a Ilbo; see note 33] in 1926, the average annual expenditure in a Korean family was 19.70 yen, while the income was only 16.30 yen. Always in debt, the farmer loses his land and goes hungry. Conditions are now [i.e. in 1937] worse. The farmer makes an average of about 6 sen [or 0.06 yen] for eight days of labor. The Korean [i.e. the Japanese colonial] government estimates this at 13 sen, but this is incorrect, because the average [farmer] works only half the year and the idle six months should be reckoned in. –KS

nese on tatami,* and the mother serves. We never eat from a single common dish as in China, and this is one reason why Koreans have so much less sickness. I have never learned to like the Chinese habit. We never wait if others are late, and it is the custom not to talk during meals. The men smoke a very long pipe and talk afterward. In China there is constant chatter during meals. The Koreans are much more individualistic than the Chinese. In a Korean inn, travelers never talk and get acquainted. All are served individually and privately.

I started primary school at seven and walked eight li** to classes every day in good weather. After school I helped on the farm. In the cold winter months, I lived in a boys' dormitory near the school.

In school I learned three languages. It was compulsory in every primary school to study Japanese seven hours a week, Korean five hours, and Chinese characters three hours. No Japanese attended these schools. They had their own institutions. The Korean government*** supported both the Korean and Japanese public schools out of tax money. Some were entirely free, but others required a monthly fee of one yen. Few poor children could go to school for more than a year or so, though it was easier in the cities than in the countryside. The children of poor farmers had to work in the fields as soon as they were strong enough. Yet all Koreans have a great zeal for education, and if one member of a family learns to read, he teaches all the others. The Christian churches, especially the Methodists and Presbyterians, also held classes on Sundays.

Often we children heard news of interesting happen-

---

* *tatami*: Japanese word for the reed mats used to cover the floors in traditional Japanese houses, temples, etc. –GT

** *eight li*: i.e. a little over two and a half miles. –GT

*** *the Korean government*: i.e. the Japanese colonial government in Korea. –DH

ings on the nearby Manchurian border.

"A ten-man group came two days ago and killed six Japanese near Sinuiju," one of the boys would say. "Only one of our soldiers was shot, and the rest got away across the border."

"My brother came home last week and stayed with us two days," another would relate after pledging us all to absolute secrecy. "He came with five other soldiers, and they fired on the Japanese sentries near Pyongyang. He had to hide in a paddy field for a whole day so they couldn't catch him."

Our eyes would grow big with hero worship, and we would decide anew to join the Korean Army of Independence in Manchuria when we were grown up and come back with the raiding bands into north Korea every month to ambush the Japanese invaders.

Korean "Righteous Army" (Uibyeong) soldiers circa 1908

"There will be millions of us young men then," we said. "The Japanese will all run away like chickens."

And we would retell the stories of our boyhood hero, General Yi Dong-hwi—of how many Japanese he had killed and how many tigers he had stalked while hiding with his troops in the mountains. And we wondered

KOREAN CHILDHOOD

how many new troops he was training in Siberia and
Manchuria to come back and save their fatherland.

In the school dormitory on the long cold winter
evenings, we would talk of how Ahn Jung-geun had shot
Prince Itō in Harbin as he stepped down from the train
with a large entourage, and of many, many other stories
of those who had done deeds, daring and bold, for Korean
independence.

Ahn Jung-geun in Japanese prison

I was fond of athletics and
always participated in sports,
especially wrestling. All Korean
boys wrestle and fight. Korea has
had a long tradition in athletics
and has produced some of the
best athletes in the Far East.
Every year there were national
"Olympic" games. This was called
the "Great Athletic Meet," on the
holiday "Old May Fifth." It was an
ancient planting-time festival.
On August 15, there was also a rice harvest festival,
with songs and symbolic dances. If the harvest was
good, everyone was gay and happy; if bad, there was no
dancing. The autumn festival is uncommon now; there is
little happiness to sing and dance about in Korea today.

I used to go to the games wearing an old-fashioned
flowing linen gown tied on the side, which flapped in
the wind like the wings of a bird. I never wore long hair,
though. The boy students now all wear foreign-style
uniforms, black in winter and blue or white in summer.
The girls wear white middies and black skirts.

The Old May Fifth holiday was always celebrated on
the mountains, and you could see a long vista from the
top. Everyone wore new clothes, and the father had to
give spending money to each member of the family. The

mountainside billowed with the men's wide pantaloons blowing in the wind and the women's three full skirts flying about in layers like the petals of a flower. The strong men of Korea gathered to show off their prowess, while the old gentry sat around as spectators with their topknots secure under their funny little black horsehair hats. Prizes were given. The farmers received farm implements and oxen. The first prize was the finest ox procurable, all covered with flowers like Europa's bull in Greek mythology. The first prize for little boys was a calf. I once threw six other boys at wrestling and proudly received as a prize a notebook and pencil. Wrestling was the chief sport—but Korean wrestling is not the same as Japanese sumo, though both try to force the opponent out of the ring. It has no religion mixed up in it but is a healthy, natural sport.

❖

I have always had a strong temper and a proud, stubborn disposition. It was not for many years that I learned to control these faults. As a child I could never submit to punishment. When my father struck me, I never cried but ran away to the hills, refusing to eat or speak with anyone except my mother, whom I loved dearly. I was always a leader and always inclined to dominate those around me. At the age of eleven, I got into a fight with one of my rivals at school and broke his nose. Father was furious. I defied him and decided to run away from home forever. I have never gone back except for brief visits.

My second brother then owned a small shoe shop in a nearby city, and I went to him.

"Why do you run away now? In another year you can finish primary school," he said when I told my story.

He gave me eight yen to go back. I took the money but refused to lose face by going home. Instead I called on a rich man who was one of my schoolmate's relatives. This man took a liking to me and helped me to prepare for the middle-school examination, but I failed. I worked in his house for four months, never letting my brother or parents know where I was.

Then one day my brother happened to see me on the street as I was carrying a market basket for the woman whose husband I lived with. I tried to hide, but he ran up and talked to me sympathetically.

"Your mother is very sad, but your father is still angry," he said. "You needn't go home. You can stay with me and study at a preparatory school."

I went back with him and worked in his shop to earn my way, while studying to pass the middle-school examination.

Both this brother and his young wife were very kind to me. He was a good man and later on often helped me during my troubles. The family always blamed him for encouraging my rebel tendencies. He was sympathetic with me because at nineteen he had also run away from home. He stole some money from Father and walked to Seoul, where he earned his way through commercial school as an apprentice in a shoe shop. After two years, he had learned machine work so well that he returned to Pyongyang and opened his own little shop, buying Japanese leather for shoes. This work prospered, as his was one of the first modern machine shops in the city, and when he died from illness fifteen years later, the shop had a capital of 30,000 yen. My family had no idea how much money he had. Father would never have anything to do with this truant son after he ran away. He was a stern master of his house, like others of the Confucian patriarchal tradition, and never forgave an offense against filial piety. But mother came to see my brother and me secretly, and he often gave money to help her and my sisters. Father was always heavily in debt, so life was constantly difficult for the family.

My eldest brother, like most privileged first sons in patriarchal families, seemed to bear no relation to his younger brothers. He was arrogant, selfish, and cruel. My second brother and I never had more than polite, formal relations with him. The whole family hated him, while they secretly loved the truant second son. This eldest brother was a farmer and rice merchant, hulling his rice by machine. When he took a second wife, he left his neglected first wife and her four children to live with the family, while the other went with him to a separate establishment.

When my second brother died later, he left 10,000 yen in trust at the bank for his two young sons and a total of 20,000 yen for his wife. My eldest brother was surprised to learn of this and set about greedily to take it away from her—trying to assert some medieval right of primogeniture. The gentle, helpless widow did not know the law, and before she was aware of what was happening, the rascal had stolen her 20,000 yen and was trying to get control of the trust fund, too. My mother tried to defend her, and the widow begged me by letter to return for a little while to help, but I was busy with revolutionary work in Guangzhou at that time. She and her son always liked and had confidence in me, and she wanted me to direct the education of the two boys. But I have never been free to help any of my family members at any time.

CHAPTER 3

Declaration of Independence

AFTER SEVERAL MONTHS of preparatory study while working in my brother's shoe shop, I was able to pass the middle-school examinations. I entered a Christian school of about three hundred students.[23] The teacher of history and geography happened to come from my home village and liked me, so I was invited to his house for a meal every week. He also taught me literature, and we often talked about China.

We also talked of religion and similar problems. "You and I are both good Christians," he would comment. "We must never forget that Christianity provides the only unity in Korea today and that it has been a great educational force. It is a movement for human emancipation, and that is why Korea is a Christian nation. We Koreans are all idealists, and idealism creates history. The Chinese are too mercenary to be a Christian nation, and they will be destroyed by their materialism. The Japanese are too far backward in the stage of samurai feudalism. Korea will lead them both."

Brave words! I thought of my mother and sisters and

sister-in-law—always praying in the church and receiving nothing but sorrow for their faith.

"But it is futile only to be a Christian and never to act. We have turned the other cheek long enough," I declared.

"You will see," he said mysteriously. "Christianity will be the mother of Korean independence. In Korea it is a symptom of revival, not a mere spiritual religious institution. In the name of religion, many great historical happenings have been brought to pass."

Soon afterward something historical did come to pass: March 1st, 1919.[24] On that morning the teacher stood solemnly and dramatically before my middle-school class and made a speech full of fine phrases that I have never forgotten—how ironic they sound today!

"Today marks the declaration of Korean independence. There will be peaceful demonstrations all over Korea. If our meetings are orderly and peaceful, we shall receive the help of President Wilson and the great powers at Versailles,[25] and Korea will be a free nation—"

The students shouted, and tears of jubilation streamed down our faces. We jumped up and danced with our arms around each other.

We gathered closely in a little knot to hear what more the teacher had to say.

"They cannot refuse to listen to the voice of a whole nation. President Wilson is fighting at the Peace Conference for the principle of the self-determination of nations and for the principle of democracy for all countries and all peoples. Behind him stands the mightiest nation in the world. America will not permit Japan to enslave Korea. We ask only for independence and democracy. That is the birthright of any nation. We do not oppose with arms or any kind of violence. Our just demand cannot be denied. Ten Thousand Years of Korean Independence!"

"Ten Thousand Years of Korean Independence!" We

shouted the slogan again and again. "Man-se! Man-se!"*

"How can we be sure the Peace Conference will help Korea?" we asked the teacher eagerly.

"Every newspaper in the world will carry the story of our great mass demonstrations," he declared fervently. "When they hear of this in Versailles, they will not forget Korea. Their consciences will be awakened. Japan has only a very small voice in the Peace Conference. The people will not permit their leaders to betray the weak nations. A new world is beginning. You do not know what great things are happening for mankind. Listen: Since 1914, millions of men have been killed in the Great War in Europe. The soldiers of the Allies died to make the world safe for democracy. After this great sacrifice of their sons, the people of every nation are rising to demand justice and freedom for every other nation. Korea today joins hands with all the peoples in the world for liberty! The brotherhood of man will soon be realized! Even Germany will be a democracy with the rest of us. We will join hands with Japan, too, if she abides by the decisions of the Peace Conference and agrees to the equality of nations. We ask only for friends. We wish to make no enemies.

"You have all been told many times about President Wilson's Fourteen Points. He will defend Korea at the Peace Conference, if we strengthen his hand by our peaceful demonstrations. The armistice was granted only on condition that the Fourteen Points be realized. The Fifth Point says clearly that, on questions of colonial sovereignty, the interests of the colonial population shall have equal weight with those of the governments concerned." The teacher pulled a sheaf of ragged propa-

---

* *Man-se*: Korean word that literally translates to "ten thousand years," though this exclamation is generally used to express something akin to "hurrah!" Pronounced "wansui" in Mandarin and "banzai" in Japanese. –GT, DH

ganda leaflets from his pocket and referred to them as he talked, though he knew by heart all the glorious phrases that had been spoken, as indeed who did not among the Korean intellectuals in those hopeful days. We students knew them too.

Description of the Korean Declaration of Independence from a Red Cross pamphlet

"President Wilson has declared that every arbitrary power everywhere must be destroyed to save the peace of the world and that the settlement of every question of sovereignty must be based only upon the free acceptance of that settlement by the people of the nation concerned and not upon the material advantage of the strong military powers which want mastery over such nations.

"Six weeks ago the Peace Conference held its first meeting at Versailles. A few days ago President Wilson made a great speech before the delegates, standing firm on everything he has always stood for. He has said that 'governments derive all their just powers from the consent of the governed and that no right anywhere exists to hand peoples about from sovereignty to sovereignty as if they were property.' That means he will insist that the will of the people of Korea be respected. Let us make that will heard from heaven to earth! As soon as our patriotic Korean leaders read this speech, they decided to organize a nationwide demonstration today. We must all join it—men, women, and children—and we Christians must lead. Come with me now."

He led us out into the street where we formed a line with thousands of other students and townspeople and paraded through the city, singing and shouting slogans. I was so happy I thought my heart would burst. Everyone was jubilant. I was so excited I forgot to eat all day. I think millions of Koreans forgot to eat on March First.

One old white-haired man came out on the steps as we passed and shouted with a cracked voice, "Now I can see the independence of Korea before I die!"

A mass meeting was called in the city during the demonstrations at which the new Declaration of Independence, patterned after the American document, was read. I edged my way to the front of the vast throng and listened to it as if it contained the words of eternal destiny. It made the blood pound in my ears, especially the sentence, "If every Korean were to die for this sentiment, the last man would still demand independence." As I look back on this now, it seems strange that there was so much idealistic hope in the world. This manifesto was strongly international in feeling and upheld the principle of peace and common international moral support against that of armed struggle. It called upon China and India to join, and China soon responded after it was discovered that secret treaties between Britain and Japan had already arranged to give part of Shandong to the Japanese.[26]

This was my first awakening to political consciousness, and the power of mass movement shook me to the very roots of my being. I ran through the streets all day and joined every passing demonstration, shouting until my voice was too hoarse to be heard. At night I helped edit a school paper, where we feverishly repeated again and again the grand phrases that were on everybody's lips and that burned into my very soul. I believed that I was an important part of a great world movement and that the millennium had come. The shock of the betrayal from Versailles[27] that came a few weeks later was so great that I felt as though the heart had been torn out of me. What pathetic, naive creatures we Koreans were then, believing in words!

I had many shocks during those few days. It was like living through an earthquake. I learned the meaning of force and the futility of nonviolence. At first the Christian spirit of martyrdom seemed very heroic to me; then it appeared stupid. Several times I saw Japanese soldiers fire on groups of Christian women gathered in the street singing hymns and songs of national independence. They also attacked them with swords, and many of the wounded later died in hospitals. The women did not run but stood quietly and raised their eyes to the sky as they redoubled their prayers. When I saw this, my first reaction was anger at the Japanese, but this was quickly followed by impatience and irritation at the Christians who would stand so passively waiting for death. My hands itched to take revenge.

One incident made a deep impression on me. I saw a Korean Christian leader crucified outside the west gate of the city. The Japanese nailed him to a cross "as a Christian so he can go to heaven," they said. Many women came to kneel and pray beside the cross, but they only wept and did nothing. It was my first experience of cold, studied cruelty without provocation.

The next day the Christian congregations all held meetings to pray for the success of the demonstrations. They prayed for President Wilson at the Peace Conference. And they prayed that Japan would listen reasonably to Korea's demands so there would be no bloodshed. Then they marched through the streets singing hymns and other songs. The women and girls all joined. I think every Christian in Korea participated—about three hundred thousand of them.

At that time in Korea there were only two organized groups which formed the mass basis of the movement on March First: the Christians and the old Cheondogyo.[28] The Cheondogyo is a Korean political-religious organization founded in Korea eighty years ago, just after the Taiping Rebellion in China.[29] Its peasant followers occupied southern Korea in opposition to the corrupt feudal dynasty. This religion teaches that "Man is God" and is humanistic in feeling.

In 1919, the Cheondogyo numbered about two million adherents, and had a Farmer's Union, a Women's Union, and a Young Men's Union. It was a nationalist movement against the Japanese. The Young Men's Union and the Farmer's Union are revolutionary forces in Korea, but the Women's Union is much less so.

The Cheondogyo called on all its followers to join the March First demonstrations, and village after village participated from one day to another. The members also marched in formation through the streets, singing the old national song of Korea with grim determination. Each time, the movement reached down deeper and deeper into the strata of society, beginning with the intellectuals and finally rousing even the remotest farm villagers and the lowest of the coolie class.

Even the Buddhist priests from Geumgang-san formed a "Priests' Independence Party" and went about among the people encouraging the nationalist movement. Their lands had become smaller and smaller every year,[30] and they were in a strongly anti-Japanese mood. Many of these priests did not believe in Buddhism except as a philosophy and said it was the same as Hegelian idealism.[*] Geumgang-san became a safe retreat for patriotic idealists, and after 1919 many young intellectuals went there to study and talk with the priests. Like all educated Koreans, I myself like Hegel and Feuerbach and have studied all the old religions and philosophies. I understood early in life that at a certain stage religion is social idealism in practice and not merely spiritual fancy.

Altogether, no fewer than two million people participated in the demonstrations throughout Korea. Property, farm work, and personal safety were all forgotten in the wave of patriotic feeling. I suppose it was one of the most peculiar movements the world has ever seen. It was a spontaneous uprising that was not an uprising but an idealistic "Christian" protest movement, ready for martyrdom but refusing any form of violence. The slogan of the whole movement was very simple: "Struggle Peaceably for Korean Independence." Peacefulness was insisted upon everywhere.

The movement was organized and led by a group called the "Thirty-Three Men," who formed the Korean national committee. Most of the leaders were Christians. The rest were members of the Cheondogyo. The head of the Cheondogyo, Son Byeong-hui, was the principal mass leader, while an intellectual named Choe Nam-seon, who

---

[*] *Hegelian idealism*: Some Geumgang-san priests later became Marxists, and many studied this philosophy. Others became nationalists. I know four who became Communist Party members. Two of these died in Guangzhou in 1927. One of these, when he died from a wound, said, "Now I am twenty-eight years old. I have acquired no merit. Nor have I ever once kissed a girl. Yet now I must die." A Korean friend sent for his wife to come kiss him before he died, but it was too late. The other, also not yet thirty, died in the Guangzhou Commune, when sixteen other Koreans were killed by a machine gun. Both had been active priests in the Geumgang-san. –KS

was believed in by all the Korean intelligentsia, was the ideological inspiration. Choe Nam-seon wrote the Korean Declaration of Independence, and it was signed by the "Thirty-Three."

Every year on the anniversary of March First, Koreans everywhere reread this Declaration of Independence and retell the story of the Independence movement and the tales of later patriotic terrorist acts. They make speeches and cry and pray for future success. The police surround all the towns in Korea and detain all the "dangerous thoughts" suspects for this one day. In all the prisons the inmates shout and demonstrate for independence.

What was the result of this experiment in peaceful demonstrations? It was as was to be expected.

The Japanese were very confused. They did not know what to do. Such a movement puzzled them by its intensity no less than by its peaceableness. But they quickly decided. On the second day they arrested the leaders and until up to May 21, when the movement stopped, arrested altogether three hundred thousand people. All the hospitals and schools were turned into prison camps. My middle school was one of these temporary prison camps. Two-thirds of those arrested were freed after a short detention, after having been beaten. The other hundred thousand were "legally" arrested and sent to court. About fifty thousand of these were sentenced to imprisonment. Not one was executed—there was no legal excuse for this. Korean civil law forbade this, as the demonstrators had openly and insistently announced, "We struggle only for Korean independence and not against Japan." Execution was legal only for murder, so the Japanese killed the people on the streets instead of arresting them—a nice Japanese technicality.

On March 7, I was arrested with some other students in a street demonstration and held for three days.

"Why do you demand Korean independence?" the police asked, striking me with a bamboo rod.

"I don't know why, but I do," I answered.

"Will you go out again in a demonstration? If you don't promise not to, you will never be free again."

The Japanese governor rushed through seven decrees, one after another, to suppress the movement. These provided punishment by imprisonment for up to ten years for writing, making speeches, participating in demonstrations, or propagandizing in any way for revolution. There was no Christianity in the methods the Japanese used.

Nearly seven thousand Koreans were killed during the period of suppression. Stories of new atrocities came in hourly. Many of them were doubtless exaggerated. Some of them were not.

Three villages near Suwon were burned. The Japanese burned the Christian church in one village and shot the people as they tried to run out. At Cheongju, the church was also a target of Japanese revenge. About a thousand people were wounded and killed in these two incidents.[31]

The American missionaries were very angry about this. One American was arrested for hiding a Korean student in his house. The Japanese demanded a fine of 10,000 yen or one year in prison. The American refused both. Finally he paid a small sum and was released.

Another incident occurred near the town of Daegu, where about two thousand farmers

Photo of burnt church taken at Jeam-ri in 1919

demonstrated before the police station. The police officer said to them:

"I have telephoned the government to ask for Korean independence as you wish, and they will soon reply. Please wait thirty minutes, as the officials are now in a meeting. After that you may go back to your homes."

The simple, honest farmers believed these words. While they waited, Japanese troops sped up in three motor cars and killed thirty men before they could run away.

The Christian churches were special objects of Japanese fury because they represented a cohesive spirit of cooperation as well as of religious independence and were the centers of American influence, which was then very strong in Korea. The Japanese occupied all the churches in our city and forbade religious gatherings.

Before March First, I had attended church regularly. I had never questioned the fact that the Christian church was the best institution in Korea, though I thought praying futile. After this debacle, my faith was broken. I thought there was certainly no God and that the teachings of Christ had little application for the world of struggle into which I had been born. One thing in particular made me angry. That was hearing an American missionary tell the people, "God is punishing Korea for the mistakes she has made. Now Korea is suffering to pay for these. Later God will let her recover after penance is done. When God wills, Korea will get her independence, not before."

Why should Korea be the only nation to practice Christian ethics? I asked myself. In Europe the Christian nations did not turn the other cheek. Millions of Christians killed each other in the Great War. To fight was to gain victory. Only to pray was to ensure failure.

I was dissatisfied with all the teachings of my youth. A torment entered my soul and mind. March First was the beginning of my political career. All over Korea, young men felt the same. The desperate terrorist movement followed logically from the tragedy.

"CUSHIONED-PAW IMPERIALISM"

Yet the movement did not fail completely. It came as a great shock to the Japanese and caused them to move more discreetly in Korea afterward. They had a new respect for our people and a new fear. Reprisals have never ended since—every occasion was made an excuse for new punishment.

Tokyo decided that the movement was not against the imperial government but against the local Japanese governor general and his policy of armed force. Hence they concluded that it was better to establish a new policy of political and cultural control instead of merely brandishing the sword. In September 1919 a new governor general was appointed—Admiral Saitō.

He changed the policy to one of peaceful control and tried to utilize the right wing against the mass movement. This method we called "cushioned-paw imperialism." Formerly no Korean could open a factory without the permission of the governor general. Saitō changed the industrial laws so that factories could be started freely. He granted civil liberties and freedom of speech and of the press in name, but in practice, of course, suppressed it as much as possible. This tactic served to do away with the explosion point. Until 1919 there was not a single Korean newspaper except the official organ of the government.* (In 1910, there had been the *Korean Daily News*,[32] but it was suppressed.) In 1919 the new *Oriental Daily News*[33] was started, representing the

---

* of the government: i.e. of the Japanese colonial government. –DH

bourgeoisie. Since then it has been the most influential organ of opinion in Korea, and useful to the Japanese as a barometer of public feeling.*

Before 1919 there was very little collaboration between the Japanese and the Korean bourgeoisie. From 1910 to 1929 Japan had controlled the country by using the feudal elements as a buffer and a puppet bureaucracy. After 1919 the power of the Korean bourgeoisie was recognized, and Saitō began to utilize the right wing of the bourgeoisie instead of the feudal elements. This policy cleverly broke the right wing away from the nationalist movement.

While the immediate cause of the March First demonstrations was the news of President Wilson's speech at the Versailles Conference promising self-determination to all nations, it was the expression of a long, slowly cumulative nationalist movement that had begun in 1907. The greatest driving factor was the Korean nationalist movement across the border in Manchuria, where the active center of anti-Japanese resistance existed. This movement was led by exiled Korean soldiers and officers. When Korea became a Japanese protectorate after the Russo-Japanese War, the Korean Army had been demobilized. This started one day when about three thousand Korean soldiers were drilling on the parade ground in Seoul. They were ordered to stack their guns, and each was given a letter from the Korean government and the Japanese saying that the army was to be

---

* *barometer of public feeling*: In 1920, the *Joseon Daily* [Joseon Ilbo] was also started more leftist in character [than the *Oriental Daily News* (i.e. Dong-a Ilbo, see note 33)]. It was impossible to edit a revolutionary paper in Korea, and the secret *Korean Independence Daily News* [Daehan dongnip sinmun] was started by Yi Gwang-su in Shanghai in 1920, with branches in Manchuria and elsewhere. Copies were smuggled into Korea from the outside. Later, [in 1926], the *Jung-oe Ilbo*, or *Inside-and-Outside News*, was established by a small middle group; it was a liberal paper between the right and left. Several other newspapers were later started. –KS

Koreans leaving for Manchuria in the 1930s

demobilized and each man must return home. In each letter was 10 yen. The soldiers were so surprised they could not speak. Tears rushed to the eyes of some of them, and every man tore up his letter. One officer committed suicide. The Japanese quickly gathered all the guns and put them in the ordnance room. Then some of the unarmed soldiers started to struggle against the armed Japanese, while others broke down the door of the ordnance room and grabbed guns. The Japanese killed three hundred within minutes, and the fighting continued for three days.

The Korean soldiers struggled against the Japanese for three years until 1910, when a Japanese expedition occupied Korea. During that time the whole country rose to support the soldiers. When the principal struggle had failed, some of the soldiers ran away to Manchuria.

The commander-in-chief, Yi Dong-hwi, led several thousand soldiers to the mountains, and the next year they were driven away to Manchuria.

DECLARATION OF INDEPENDENCE

About five thousand soldiers retreated to Jilin in eastern Manchuria. There they organized a military school with several hundred students. In the spring and summer and autumn these soldiers farmed the land to produce their food, and in the winter they studied and kept in training. Every year until 1924 small groups of five, ten, or twenty men came secretly to north Korea and fought guerrilla warfare against the Japanese.

The headquarters of this Korean Army of Independence was a mountain in Jilin Province, but they also had centers in Fengtian Province. They established many schools and training centers. During those years, about a million Korean farmers migrated to Manchuria, so the army had a strong base among these exiles. Every one of them dreamed of recapturing his homeland someday.

The idea of Korean independence and democracy came directly from America—just as the hope for its immediate realization in 1919 stemmed from President Woodrow Wilson. When Japan occupied Korea in 1910, all the nationalist intellectuals fled to America. There they studied political methods, and in 1919 they returned to Korea. These "returned students" were called the "American Democracy" group. Most of them were Christians. They represented a middle-class political group—nearly all were teachers, students, journalists, lawyers, or doctors.

A basic internal reason for the nationalist movement was that, during the Great War, Korean industry developed somewhat, stimulated by war demands, and the Korean bourgeoisie felt strong enough to demand independence. Still another reason for the nationalist movement was that Japan itself was affected by the postwar wave of liberalism that flooded over the whole world and was considered therefore to be likely not to oppose some form of change for Korea.

The Chinese students and teachers in Beijing were

considerably affected by the news of the demonstrations in Korea, and even before the movement stopped, they organized the May Fourth Movement in Beijing,[34] the first demonstration of its kind in China. The Koreans in the city participated in these enthusiastically. Korean students and exiles in Beijing did a good deal of propaganda work there. They organized plays and lectures and had small demonstrations and tried to rouse the Chinese to common action. They gave copies of the Korean Declaration of Independence to the Chinese to read, emphasizing the words it contained: *"Our struggle is breaking the sleep of four hundred million Chinese. China can join with Korea, and India will also rise. This is a world movement, and it will carry on."*

China was then having its own troubles with Japan and the Peace Conference. The powers seemed willing to give over Jiaozhou in Shandong Province to the Japanese, who had taken it away from the Germans during the war, and the Chinese students rose to demand "justice" from Versailles. The Korean movement served to waken the Chinese to the dangers of Japanese imperialism and also encouraged them to make similar demands and protests against the Peace Conference, which was betraying Korea and China equally. The movements were similar in nature. Both pledged themselves to democracy. Both were against Japanese imperialism. Both based their hopes on Wilson's promises to weak nations. Both were demonstrations organized to influence the great powers to render aid. In Korea, however, it was a mass movement throughout the peninsula, while in China it was merely a student uprising and cultural movement, only indirectly supported by the people in general, though its influence was widely felt after a time.

What a great disillusionment was to come for the eager peoples of the Far East—for Japan and China and India no less than for Korea! The solution of the colonial question was only a mockery. "Self-determination" was only a slogan under which the great powers consolidated their empires. America deserted the League of Nations, and Britain and France utilized it to maintain the status quo in their own interests. Youth in China and Korea soon turned to Soviet Russia for hope, and China redirected its wrath against the British.

The uncompromising Japanese response to a peaceful appeal for some basis of equality had the effect of rousing Korean youth to wild individual action and terrorism. Hundreds went to Shanghai, where terrorist societies were formed to harass the Japanese. The nationalists and the "American Democracy" group set up their own exiled independent Korean Provisional Government in Shanghai out of the fabric of a broken dream.

Since 1919, there has been no other important mass uprising in Korea. Activities were carried on from exile. The movement at home went into a preparatory period for the day of final struggle. My own life has followed closely this tortuous double path.

CHAPTER 4

Tokyo School Days

SHORTLY AFTER the March First Movement of 1919 had subsided, I decided to try to earn my way through college in Japan. Tokyo then was the Mecca for students all over the Far East and a refuge for revolutionaries of many kinds. Every Korean student wanted to go there for higher education, as no good colleges existed at home and Japanese schools were at that time liberal and full of postwar intellectual excitement.

Father had no money, however, and strongly opposed my desire. I decided that if no one should help me, I would run away secretly. In the end, my second brother came to the rescue, as always—and was blamed again for making a rebel of me. He wanted me to study medicine and gave me 100 yen, which was enough for about five months' schooling.

THE LUMPEN-INTELLIGENTSIA AND THE EGGSHELLS

I found a room with a friend named Bak Geun[35] and another student. We paid twelve yen a month for this.

I soon found a job delivering eighty newspapers before eight o'clock in the morning, for which I received ten yen a month. Another student tutored me in chemistry and algebra while I prepared to enter Tokyo Imperial University.

Over a third of the Korean students in Tokyo then earned their way through school by part-time jobs. Usually they pulled jinrikisha,* delivered newspapers or milk, or corrected proofs at printing houses. (So many hungry students stole the still-warm milk off the streets in the morning, however, that the Japanese installed little milk boxes with keys to prevent this.) Other students worked in the many little sweatshop factories. These Korean boys were a picturesque element in the life of Tokyo, though most of the Japanese thought them a very bad element. Six hundred of the students pulled rickshaws. Several times I myself pulled one to meet the trains, and the fare from a single ride was enough to live on for a whole day. It was good money, but no Chinese or Japanese students would stoop to do this work. We bought their cast-off clothes at secondhand shops. Since 1910 Korean students had migrated to Tokyo and struggled through school in this manner. They were menials for the Japanese, but these wages made Japan pay for their education.

We poor Korean students sometimes went out in small groups to ask for old books and magazines and clothing at people's houses. All the Japanese housewives and girls were kind. They liked the Korean students and often gave us new things. We did not beg but always paid a little for what was given us. If a pretty Japanese girl came to the door, the group usually tried to be invited in to sit down awhile—and got a very good bargain. If the owner of the house were rude and refused them, the students would

---

80 *jinrikisha*: A Japanese word for man-powered vehicles. More commonly known in English as "rickshaws." –DH

become impudent and demand to examine the house to see whether he was lying. We divided all the old books, magazines, and newspapers collected in this way and sold them to secondhand bookshops and stalls.

I delivered my eighty newspapers early in the morning, went to school, then every afternoon at four put on working clothes for whatever job I happened to have.

Once, when Bak Geun and I went to a house to "buy" old books, we got into a fight with the owner because he swore at us. This Japanese happened to be good at jiujitsu, and Bak Geun received a broken nose. After that we always tried to call when the husbands were not at home.

Bak Geun was put into prison in 1929. Even in 1919 his attitude—often expressed to the Japanese—was that "we should confiscate the property of the Japanese to pay for all they have looted from Korea."

There were two definite classes among the Korean students in Japan—those who worked and those who had money. The one-third of the students who were poor "work-and-study" students were called by the other the "lumpen-proletariat."* We, however, usually referred to ourselves as the "lumpen-intelligentsia" and called them "eggshells," meaning that they had pretty white skin and nothing but softness inside. Korean workers traditionally refer to the upper class as "eggshells," and we borrowed this from them.

"One blow of the fist is enough to smash their pretty faces in," we would say.

We also referred to them scornfully as the "hothouse class."

---

* *lumpen proletariat*: From the German, "lumpen" literally means "rags," so "lumpen proletariat" refers to the very poor who have dropped out of the proletariat or working classes. Although they have the physical ability to work, they have lost the will to do so and live on handouts or by thievery or selling rags. The Marxists considered this group as an inevitable result of the growth of capitalism. The Nazis used them to attack organized labor in the period of Hitler's rise to power. Here the term is used in a humorous sense. —GT

We eight hundred "lumpens" dominated the entire body of Korean students and called our rule the "dictatorship of the proletariat." We ran all student meetings and lectured the "eggshells" at will, with plentiful doses of proletarian philosophy. Our work-and-study section was far more advanced intellectually than the others. All studied Marxism. Poverty and struggle sharpen the brain and give reality to knowledge. The rich "eggshells" were terrified of us and privately referred to us as "bandits."

Once, at a big festival, many rich students spent a good deal of money for a feast. We "lumpens" went in a body to the restaurant, ordered chopsticks, and sat down to eat with them without being invited. Some rich students were smart enough to pay us tribute and often invited us, especially to birthday dinners and other such feasts—just as gangsters are paid off.

Sometimes we were more romantic. We would burst in on a feast and in high Tolstoyan phrases demand to know how the rich could eat while we hundreds were starving. Then we would overturn the tables and walk out in great disdain—nursing our hunger and pride.

The Japanese hated to rent rooms to the "lumpens" because we seldom paid our rent but moved out in high dudgeon whenever it was suggested by the landlord, caring nothing about being arrested. We called the police station "the only free hotel."

The heyday of the student "lumpen" period in Tokyo was during the days following the World War. After that the movement declined, and by 1927 it had practically disappeared. However, it revived in Japan later.

Many famous Korean leaders earned their way through college pulling rickshaws in Tokyo. Three of these founded the Korean Young Men's Independence Party[36] in Tokyo just before I arrived.

Before 1919 there were usually from one thousand to

two thousand Korean students in Japan, and in the years immediately following, the number increased to about three thousand or more. Since 1927 it has averaged from two thousand to three thousand. From a third to a half earn their way entirely or partly. When they have finished school, most Korean students can find no work. Under Japan, Korea has little use for an educated class—yet what a vast need would be created if she had a free and independent existence for natural development!

Korean intellectuals and students have to work so hard to keep alive that actually they are half-proletarian. Their status is not at all the same as in other countries where the economic system can take care of its educated youth. We estimate that today seventy percent of the Korean students are communist sympathizers. Most of those who return from Japan, Germany, and Russia would like to be Party members. Those who study in America and France are not in this class—they are "gentlemen" and only want good positions and the "Christian" type of activity. They could never have gone abroad without money originally, and their economic status is usually good. Before 1919, the nationalist leaders were mostly returned students from America, and most of the higher-educated intellectuals went to school either in America or Japan. After 1919, all the leadership came from Japan. The communists are nearly all Japan-returned students. They learn their theory in Tokyo and their tactics in organization and action from China.

I was surprised to find the Japanese in Japan so different from those in Korea. This was logical enough, as the clerks and agents of imperialism are naturally hired to suppress the colonials, and their attitude becomes entirely different from those at home. I liked many of the Japanese I became acquainted with in Tokyo. In 1919, a revolutionary class began to develop in Japan. At that time, the anarchists were the principal radical element, but soon the communist movement gained momentum. Japanese make very good comrades. Japanese communists are honest and strong and not afraid to sacrifice. They become passionately devoted to their cause. I like those I have known very much indeed. In China, the nationalist tendency, even in the communist movement, is very strong because of fighting against colonialism, but there is none of this tendency in the Japanese communist movement. They never distinguish between Korean and other foreign comrades, as the Chinese do, but are really international-minded.

Student life in Japan was very stimulating. Many excellent new magazines were being published there, dealing with all kinds of social science and any kind of orthodox or unorthodox economic theories. There was a big Korean Young Men's Christian Association (YMCA) in Tokyo, which was a center of Korean student life, and also a large Korean Association. Tokyo not only harbored the three thousand Korean students, but a thousand other Korean intellectuals, including revolutionary exiles of various kinds. About 200,000 Korean laborers lived in various parts of Japan. Relations between the liberal Japanese and the Koreans were good, and a spirit of Far Eastern internationalism was developing under the leadership of these Japanese. Both Japanese and Koreans watched eagerly for signs of new international democratic movements in the West. Japan relaxed its nationalistic vigilance for a while, feeling relieved of the danger of threats from rival imperialist aggression after Versailles. Yet only four years later, with the Japanese earthquake, came the great pogrom, breaking up this dream....

EARTHQUAKE AND POGROM

The earthquake of September 1923 was the greatest natural disaster in Japanese history. Nearly the whole of Tokyo and Yokohama were destroyed. Telephone and telegraph wires were broken, and the population was in a state of extreme tension.

After the earthquake, Japan went into a pathological state of fanatical terrorism, as sometimes happens there, and carried out a pogrom against the Koreans. Six thousand Koreans living in Japan were massacred, including a thousand students, while six hundred Chinese were also killed.

The reason is not difficult to explain. Japan was in the throes of a postwar economic crisis. When the earthquake came, the ruling class feared a new uprising comparable to the great Rice Riots of 1918 that would involve not only the peasantry but also the factory workers, whose livelihood had been destroyed by the disaster. Hence they quickly organized terrorist action against a minority in order to forestall such an uprising and frighten the Japanese people themselves. The government tried to divert the wrath of the people away from itself and to distract their attention.

On September 3, 1918, the government authorized a broadcast to the people by the chief of police in Tokyo, warning that Korean anarchists and nationalists, in cooperation with Japanese anarchists, were burning houses, killing people, and stealing money and property. The people were asked to "use all necessary measures" to protect themselves and their property. This announcement was posted in all public places. It was a lie, and the majority of the people did not know what to think. But the reactionaries were already secretly mobilized in squads of twenty to one hundred and lost no time in starting the massacre, using knives, bamboo poles, swords, hammers, and scythes.

Many Koreans were put to death by slow torture with bamboo stakes, while their torturers stood around and applauded. Young girl students and women were tortured with bamboo spikes, then tossed up and down on blankets by the men until they died. If a Korean were found on a train, he was thrown off when the engine was moving at high speed. In Tokyo, Koreans were asked to come to military headquarters for protection. Eight hundred went, and every one of them was killed inside the headquarters.

The some three thousand reported deaths occurred mostly in Tokyo, Osaka, and Nagoya—the industrial centers of unrest. On September 5, the Tokyo government ordered that the killing stop and that all Koreans must be protected by the police. They then deported about 100,000 to Korea.

During those days when our fellow countrymen were being massacred, *every Korean family had to contribute free rice to help the Japanese*. Two million dan* of rice we gave to save Japan from starvation! This is the pleasure derived from being a subject race. At the same time, the Japanese government in Korea robbed the people indirectly by keeping the local price of rice low and making a good profit thereby. Rice sold in Japan for thirty sen** was forcibly bought from our farmers for seven.

Since 1923 the Koreans have never trusted the Japanese, nor do the Japanese trust them. Some have had to work with their conquerors because they must either earn a living or die, and a certain element has been degraded to the status of rōnin*** mercenaries because of their economic helplessness. But in his heart every Korean is only waiting for "der Tag," "the Day," and the Japanese know it.

---

* *dan*: A Chinese measure (usually translated as "picul") that equals about 133 pounds. –GT

** *sen*: A Japanese unit of money equal to one-hundredth of a yen. The exchange rate at that time was about two or three yen to a US dollar. –GT

*** *rōnin*: A Japanese term for [masterless samurai that] was corrupted in China and Korea in the 1920s to mean irresponsible rascals who follow the Japanese army, usually to loot and kill or seize personal property. Many were opium traffickers. –NW

The events of 1923 had many repercussions. Several important Japanese politicians became frightened at what they had done, realizing that after that treacherous massacre no nation in the Far East would be deceived as to the true nature of Japanese "friendship." Korea stood out as an object lesson to all. For this reason, Japan began ardently promoting the "Pan-Asiatic brotherhood" idea and has been elaborating frantically upon this theme ever since. The reactionary movement that later became fascist in Japan also dates from the fears and uncertainties of that year. At the same time, this affair had a great political influence upon all Koreans and led to an important political realignment: the radicalization of the nationalist movement and the destruction of even passive friendliness for Japan. Everywhere in Korea you can find families whose relatives were killed in Japan in 1923. The nationalists are so bitter that when the communists talk of cooperating with the Japanese proletariat, they always point to 1923, and it is hard to convince them that any Japanese can be trusted.

I remember that when we read in the papers that America had rushed nurses, doctors, food, and clothes by the ship-load to Japan after the earthquake, we wondered how Americans could be so kind and friendly to a country which was reviling America with every kind of epithet and whose government was cruelly ordering the massacre of thousands of helpless Koreans who received no sympathy or aid from anywhere. That was the period of Japan's greatest antipathy toward America because of the Washington Conference a few months before.[37]

After 1923 many students and other Koreans went to China instead of Japan, and for two years I think none went to Japan. Koreans turned to China for cooperation against imperialism and reaction. Most of these students participated in revolutionary activities, either for the

Chinese Revolution or the Korean cause. Then, when the Guomindang turned reactionary in 1927, few Korean students went to China, and circumstances forced them again to turn to Japan for education. Since 1927 I think there has been an average of two or three thousand Korean students in Japan. Because the level of culture in China was low and no jobs for educated Koreans were available, student life there was extremely hard. Having no families, nor any source of support in China, it required the greatest sacrifice on the part of those Koreans engaged in revolutionary or anti-Japanese activities there. It was difficult even to keep alive.

The Guomindang reaction had a very bad effect upon the Korean movement. Had it not occurred, a good revolutionary alliance would have been formed between China and Korea. With the combined forces of the proletariat, peasantry, and national bourgeoisie of both countries, including Manchuria, our mutual success might easily have been assured. Thus the Guomindang reaction was of signal aid to the Japanese in destroying the spirit of Korea, a fact of which Japan was gratefully aware at the time. After the counterrevolution in China in 1927, Koreans of every political group said bitterly, "Our whole world has been broken."

I have seen much of class hatred, of racial hatred, of personal hatred, of hatred between nations—so much that cruelty no longer has any meaning for me as a moral value. I am stirred by victories and roused by defeats, but the cruelty by means of which these are achieved I take for granted. I would be greatly stirred by some historic change without cruelty, but this would be like the realization of a beautiful dream. Long ago I lost all the utopian fancies of my youth.

CHAPTER 5

Crossing the Yalu River

IN THAT SAME YEAR, 1919, I decided to leave Japan and try to make my way to Soviet Russia to attend school. I had discovered that Tokyo was merely a secondary intellectual center and that Moscow was the primary source of the "new thought." By this time I had studied a little social science, and Kropotkin,[38] in particular, had influenced me. I then thought communism and anarchism were the same thing.

I went back to Korea to try somehow to get money for my trip. I had to be very careful to let no one suspect my intention. Luck was with me: I was staying with my second brother, and he entrusted me with 200 yen to take to my family. I ran away with the whole sum and took a small boat to Andong where I slipped over the border into Manchuria and escaped the officials. Freedom and high adventure lay before me. I had "crossed the Yalu River."

At a small station, I took the train to Harbin. There I discovered that no trains were running because of the war conditions due to the Allied Intervention in Siberia. I decided to go instead to the Korean nationalist military school in south Manchuria. In an unhappy frame of mind because of my failure, I set out alone to walk the seven hundred li.[39]

It took me over a month....

A TREK OF SEVEN HUNDRED LI

I could have hired a Chinese cart the whole distance for only $30, but my confiscated treasure now amounted to only $130,[40] and I hoarded it like a miser. I was only fifteen years old, and life seemed very precarious.

There were no Korean inns on the way, and I stayed at Chinese inns in the villages. For fifteen cents you could have all you wanted of gaoliang,* tofu, and Baikal wine, and spend the night on a communal kang.** The inns were so dirty that I could hardly eat there and often went out to buy noodles and cakes at street stalls instead. There were as many men on a lice-ridden kang as it would hold, and I could not sleep. I was afraid of the rough men I consorted with—muleteers and farmers and, I imagined, some robbers among them. They got drunk and snored loudly. This did not keep anyone but myself awake, however. Though I had a Korean-Chinese dictionary with me, I could not speak Chinese, and they seemed suspicious of me.

I was in constant fear of bandits on the road and of robbers at night, though actually I had no trouble. Every night I went out and buried my money in the ground. Then at daybreak I dug it up and left the inn without breakfast.

Often I ran to hide myself at the side of the road from

---

* *gaoliang:* Mandarin word for a kind of sorghum prevalent in the northern half of China that functions as a basic food staple, much like rice does in the south. –GT, DH

** *kang:* Mandarin word for a brick bed warmed by fire or smoke that passes through a flue under it. –GT, DH

the curiosity of the farmers who came along. I could not answer their greetings, not daring to betray that I was a foreigner.

Day after day I stumbled through the deep cart ruts, stopping to rest in the bushes when I was too tired to keep on. The cold winter winds swept slowly over these broad plains, as slowly as the ancient peasant women, too poor to buy a new broom, sweeping the snow from their cottage doors inside the courtyard as I passed by.

Near the end of my trip I met a young Korean in one of the inns, and we traveled together. He took me with him to stay at the house of a Korean farmer the next night. This poor farmer had a big family with only two rooms to live in, but he would not take any money from us and let us sleep with his boys in one room. His house was made of rice stalks, and he owned only one ox.

At one village we went to a Korean school. The teacher welcomed us and said to me, "In a few days our school will have to close. The Chinese government has ordered that all Koreans must go to Chinese schools. If you will wait a few days, we will all go together."

I decided to wait, and my young companion went on without me.

Everyone in the village was unhappy about the oppression of Koreans by the local Chinese governor, and the fifty students sat discussing it uneasily. A mass meeting was called, and some Korean farmers came to have tea and listen to the speeches. I learned that the immediate reason given for closing the school was this: A few days previously a group of Chinese bandits had passed on their way to hide in the mountains. That afternoon the government troops arrived in pursuit and demanded to know where the bandits had gone. There were two roads, and the teacher directed the troops to the wrong road so they would be sure to take the right one. The troops always went in the opposite direction from what the people told them in order to *avoid* finding the bandits!

The troops took the road opposite from the one indicated by the teacher, as he knew they would, and to their surprise met the bandits and had a fight. The troops retreated with many wounded and dead, and when they returned to the village the commander accused the teacher of lying and was very angry because he had accidentally met the enemy he did not want to find and had suffered a big loss. The result of his displeasure was the closing of the school.

All the Koreans in Manchuria wanted to go back to Korea and dreamed of the day of independence for which they were waiting impatiently. Their houses all leaked, and they did not trouble to repair them, for, they said, "Why should we make repairs? Soon Korea will be independent, and we will go back home." That was nearly twenty years ago! In every Korean community along the way, the atmosphere was stiflingly religious, either Presbyterian or Methodist. The people were in an emotional state, and mass prayers for independence were held morning and night everywhere we went.

One of my experiences was very exciting. At Sanyu-anpu[41] I was sleeping in the dormitory of a primary school near the river. This was a democratic little town. Together with three thousand Chinese, there were about one thousand Koreans living in the town, and seven thousand nearby. The Koreans had their own "people's government" and court, and practiced real self-government. They were true nationalists and spoke only Korean. The schools taught English and a little Japanese but no Chinese.

After midnight on January 3, we heard firing and the hoofbeat of horses. Bandits surrounded the school and held prisoner all eighty schoolchildren and the teacher. They also brought thirty Korean men as prisoners and demanded a ransom of $200 each for every man and child or else the prisoners would be kidnapped. The Koreans immediately brought $200 for each of the thirty men and for twenty of the children. These were all released, as were those who looked ragged and poor, but there was no money to pay for the rest. But when they were convinced the village really had no more money, the bandits released everyone and decamped at seven o'clock in the morning.

Eight hundred "mounted bandits" had occupied the town, all romantically riding white horses, and twenty Koreans were killed in the fighting. The bandits had demanded money from every shop and ordered that pigs and chickens be killed and that the women prepare food for them instantly. Manchurian bandits have a very strict code. They never harm women but only demand money. They always send a letter in advance telling the exact time they will arrive and stating how much money to have ready for them. This they estimate carefully. They never demand anything from the No. 1 feudal landlords[42] because in Manchuria these pay a regular tribute to the bandits and sometimes give money and bullets to help the bandit raids, afterward sharing the profits. They do not rob the poor, but raid the middle class. When a person is kidnapped, they have a regular routine. First they send back the ears, then the fingers, and finally the head if no ransom is paid.

That afternoon, the Chinese troops arrived.

"We must stay to protect you," they said. "Perhaps the bandits will return."

Then they ordered food and drink, and the whole town had to pay for them, poor and rich alike. They stayed for a week, getting fat.

Of course, everyone knew the bandits would not return. No doubt the troops had an understanding with them all along.

These two raids "washed the town clean," as the saying was. Then it would be left in peace until enough money and pigs and chickens had been accumulated to make another raid worthwhile.

❖

I lived for three weeks in the home of the pastor in this town. He took a fancy to me and offered to adopt me as a son, and said that if I did not want this, he would like me to marry his daughter later anyway. But I refused, saying that I had parents enough already and that I had vowed never to marry. He was very unhappy about my refusal.

I liked his daughter well enough. I was then fifteen, and the interest she showed in me suddenly awakened my awareness of girls. Until that time I had had no consciousness of sex. Now I found myself shy and tongue-tied in her presence. I wanted to talk with her, but every time I came near I felt oppressed and unfree and wanted to run away. I thought she was the prettiest girl I had ever seen, and my heart used to beat fast whenever I looked at her. Though she was only fourteen, I felt that she was mysterious and beyond my understanding. I wanted to know more about her but dared not talk with her about anything personal at all. Instead, I threw myself with silent devotion into helping her with her lessons. I wrote many essays for her and toiled over her mathematics every day.

I began to lose my appetite and to stay awake nights wondering if marriage were so bad after all. I decided that I might come back someday and that if I still liked her I might consider it. But she would have to be worthy of being a hero's wife. By that time, I reasoned, I would no longer fall in love with a pretty face, and unless she measured up to all requirements in education and intelligence, I would naturally not like her at all, and my problem would solve itself.

The two sons taught in primary school and also in Sunday school. I became well acquainted with them and with other teachers. I liked them all very much, and they offered to give me a job as a primary-school teacher. However, I clung to my resolution to attend the military school, and at the end of three weeks one of the sons took me to Hanihe.

THE KOREAN

At last I had arrived at my destination—the military school of the Korean Army of Independence at Hanihe.[43] The "New Development School," it was called—a more discreet title. But when I tried to enter the school they would not even consider me, a small boy of fifteen. Eighteen was the minimum age. I was heartbroken and wept tragically. Finally, when the full story of my long pilgrimage was known, they decided I must be exceptional material and let me take the examinations. I passed in geography, mathematics, and the Korean language, but failed in Korean history and in the stiff physical examination. Nevertheless, I was permitted to enter the school for the term of three months, free of tuition.

The place was mountainous, and the school consisted of eighteen separate classrooms ranged along the mountainside for secrecy. Nearly one hundred students were enrolled, from eighteen to thirty years of age. I was the youngest ever to enter the school, they told me. Classes began at four o'clock in the morning, and lights were out at nine in the evening. We studied military tactics and drilled with firearms. But the strictest requirement was to be able to climb up the mountains quickly—guerrilla tactics. The other men were iron-muscled and long skilled in climbing. I was able to trundle along after them only by courtesy. We practiced carrying stones on our backs so that we could run very easily when without any burden. Careful study was given to Korean topography, especially that of northern Korea—in preparation for The Day. In my time off I dug into Korean history with a will.

I found that I could live the hard life after a little practice and enjoyed my training. The mountain was very beautiful in the spring. Hearts were buoyant with hope, and eyes were bright with expectancy. What could we not do for freedom?

Sinheung school students farming

Were there not nearly a million Korean exiles in Manchuria, all eager to recapture their homeland? And hundreds of thousands of others in Siberia?[44] Three hundred thousand of us were here together in the south, and there were other legions of hard-headed farmers in the north. Some had immigrated to Manchuria long before, during a great famine, pioneers in the wilderness where only tribes had roamed. Not until towards the end of their dynasty in China had the Manchus permitted the Chinese to enter[45]—then about thirty million strong flooded in. After 1907 a million

Koreans left their homeland for Manchuria. We have a saying that "for every Japanese who came to Korea, thirty Koreans left the country." One Korean in every twenty was exiled from the land of his twenty million countrymen, as the population of Korea is roughly estimated. Most of these went to Manchuria and Siberia. Some became fishermen in the North Pole areas. Some went to China, others to America or Mexico or Hawaii. Three hundred thousand workers were in Japan. Most of those who went abroad were Christians.

Every fighting Korean exile felt his power multiplied by a million. But it was not true. Space rendered us alien to each other. But it was a comfortable thought, and the tide of nationalism ran high.

On the first anniversary of March First, big memorial meetings were held. Our school had a holiday, and I went back to Sanyuanpu where a memorial meeting was held. In addition to the three hundred students at the middle school, other Koreans came from nearby, and the occasion was tense with patriotic feeling. There were then three Korean middle schools in Manchuria and 1,200 primary schools, as well as the two secret military schools started by the Army of Independence to keep young men in training. Every winter the Korean irregulars in Manchuria went back to Korea to struggle against the Japanese there and get money to buy guns. The people of Korea were eager to help them, but the army did not know how to organize such support effectively.

❖

When my three months' term was up in June, I stayed one week at the school just for the fun of it. Then I went back to Sanyuanpu to see the pastor again—and his pretty daughter. I spent nearly a month there, playing tennis, swimming in the lake, and fishing with a net. And I liked the daughter better and better.

In June the pastor secured a job for me as the teacher at a primary school eighty li away that was under his administration. I received no money but lived in the homes of the students one month at a time. I taught everything except drawing and singing, and on Sunday I had to lead prayers and teach Sunday school. Religion was very dear to these mountain farmers, and I could not criticize it but had to submit to the orthodoxy of the place. The church was not only a place of worship but the social center, and even I could see the value of this. I thought to leave the form and revolutionize the content. And here in Manchuria the content was already far more revolutionary than in Korea itself.

I did not intend to bury myself in any village, however idyllic in appearance, and after only three months of teaching determined to go to Shanghai to study politics and science and to join the revolutionary movement. Shanghai was then the new center of the nationalist movement where the Korean Provisional Government was functioning. I still had $80 of the $130 with which I had left Harbin the year before, and this was more than enough to pay my traveling expenses.

I went to tell the pastor of my plan and to say good-bye to his daughter. When I told him that I wanted to go away to study, he said, "That is good. If your father cannot help, I will send you money when you need it, because I believe you are a fine boy and that you have a splendid future." He said that he also wanted to send his daughter to a good school after two more years and asked me to help her and to take care of her in Beijing or elsewhere when the time came. I promised to do this faithfully.

There were tears in my eyes as I left the old pastor and his family, for I had learned to love all of them very much.

He was a very kind and generous man. I think of him even now when I need a memory of true goodness to sustain my faith in human nature. But I never saw Ahn Dong-hui or his daughter again...

❖

It was lucky for me that I did not decide to stay with Ahn Dong-hui. A great tragedy was to befall all these good people only a few weeks after I left.

At the end of 1920, the Korean Army of Independence occupied Hunchun,[46] killing nearly all the Japanese there. Tokyo sent two divisions of troops to destroy the army, which managed to escape to Siberia. In revenge, the Japanese massacred the civilian population, killing over six thousand Koreans.[47] Women and babies were bayoneted, and many of the leaders were buried alive.

And what happened to Ahn Dong-hui and his family? He and his wife and daughter were forced to look on while his two sons were cut alive into three parts. Then the old pastor was forced to dig his own grave with his bare fingers and to lie in it while the Japanese soldiers slowly buried him alive. After being forced to witness these deaths, the wife drowned herself in a river. What happened to the fourteen-year-old daughter, my first schoolboy love, I never could find out.[48] But I have always hated to think of it. The only person who survived among the many I had met in Sanyuanpu was Jo Un-san,[49] the school teacher, who told me about the incident when I met him in Beijing two years later.

The Korean Army did not stop fighting the Japanese for long, however. Four thousand partisans fought during the winter with little food and no warm clothing, until only one thousand were left. During the fighting they killed nearly two thousand Japanese troops.

Members of the Uiyeol-dan on a card taken from Japanese police files. From top left: Yi Seong-u, Kim Gi-deuk, Gang Se-u, and Gwak Jae-gi. Kim Won-bong stands on the far right. Seated: Jeong I-so. On the bottom right is a photo of Kim Ik-sang that has been attached separately by Japanese police.

PART 2

THEY WHO LIE IN WAIT

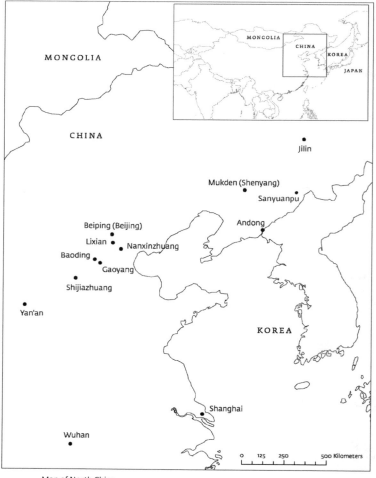

Map of North China

CHAPTER 6

Shanghai, Mother of Exiles

AS THE S.S. Fengtian moved slowly up the yellow Huangpu River on that winter's day in 1920, the great city of Shanghai reared its skyline challengingly at me from

View of the Shanghai Bund

the bund.* But I was nearly sixteen and unafraid.
  I bargained with the driver of a horse carriage to take

---

* *bund*: A word meaning "embankment" or "waterfront" that was used in Shanghai to refer to part of the International Settlement, a territory initially ceded by the Qing Dynasty to the British. Also referred to in China as "waitan." –DH

me to the office of the Korean Provisional Government for eighty cents. He had asked for $1. When I arrived he demanded $3 and would not let me get out of the carriage. There was nobody on the street to help me, so I firmly demanded to drive on to the Korean People's Association,[50] where I nonchalantly handed him $1.50 and hoped I had removed his impression of me as a country yokel. I had expected him at any moment to drive me to some side street and rob me of my money.

At the Association I introduced myself to one of the officers. He took me to a Korean hostel where I could get room and board for $15 a month. There I ate at the same table with him, and we became well acquainted. Later this man figured in a terrorist bombing escapade with a beautiful actress, and after imprisonment for this in Korea, he joined the Manchukuo army and secretly released thirty Korean prisoners of war.

I easily secured a job as proofreader and typesetter at the *Korean Independence News*[51] for $20 a month. This was the secret radical nationalist paper edited by Yi Gwang-su that was first established in Shanghai and afterward published elsewhere. Copies were smuggled into Korea.

In the evenings I went to the Korean Inseong School[52] where I studied English. I also studied Esperanto and the theory of anarchism and in my free time explored every phase of Korean life and activity in Shanghai, becoming acquainted with all of the Korean revolutionary exiles there. I rode all over the city on tram cars just to look around.

Shanghai was a new world to me, my first glimpse of Western material culture and of Western imperialism at work. I was fascinated by this vast, polyglot city with all its opulence and all its misery.

After the March First movement in 1919 was suppressed by the Japanese, the French Concession in Shanghai* became the principal directing point for Korean revolutionary activity. Three thousand Korean political exiles gathered there, where they formed the Korean Provisional Government in opposition to the Japanese setup in Seoul and to Governor General Saitō's spurious plans for Korean "self-government." The preliminary meetings for the formation of this government[53] began in August 1919, and in the winter of that year it opened its office in the French Concession, with the Korean flag flying proudly over the building. The principal organizers were General Yi Dong-hwi and some returned students from abroad, and the government received secret financial support from sympathizers in Korea and Manchuria. Syngman Rhee was elected president** and General Yi Dong-hwi chairman or premier. The government had its

Korean Provisional Government building in Shanghai in the 1920s

---

* *French Concession*: An area of Shanghai that was under the legislation of the French. At the time, various foreign powers had been granted control over sections of the city of Shanghai. The French maintained theirs independently, while the other imperial powers consolidated theirs together into the International Settlement. Residents of the French Concession enjoyed extraterritorial rights untouched by Chinese law, as French law was enforced there. The International Settlement was ruled by a Council of Ratepayers, which made their own laws. At the time, the French Concession was thought to be the safest area for a foreign government-in-exile to operate. –GT

** *elected president*: Syngman Rhee was still technically the elected president of Korea [in 1937]. He went on to Geneva after Japan took Manchuria on September 18, 1931 [see note on p. 328], to demand more "diplomatic" solutions to the Korean problem. –KS

own parliament and press, and established branch offices everywhere Korean centers existed abroad. It had a military school in Shanghai, which graduated two hundred students the first term and eighty the second.

Photo of Korean Provisional Government in Shanghai taken in December 1928. Standing behind the white table from left to right: Yi Dong-hwi; Syngman Rhee (wearing flowers); and Ahn Chang-ho.

The French refused to suppress Korean activities, for the provisional government paid squeeze (bribes) to the French authorities for protection and sent delegates to Paris to explain its reason for existence. At that time France was anxious to extend "French culture" and influence in the Orient.*

The first parliament was held on March 1, 1920, when a

---

* *influence in the Orient*: After 1925 the French Concession was not so safe any more, as the French were not sympathetic with the new Korean communist movement. The French now [i.e. in 1937] no longer protect the Koreans, but do refuse to permit the Japanese to come in and arrest them secretly as is the case in other places. The French began to extradite Koreans in 1926 because of their participation in the Chinese Revolution. This frightened the French imperialists. The British have never protected the Koreans in Shanghai, and many were arrested on the streets of the International Settlement. During 1926 and 1927 and up to the present [1937], the French and Japanese have cooperated in arresting Korean revolutionaries. After the Hongkou Park bombing by a Korean in 1932 [see note on p. 103], the French arrested twenty, including old revolutionaries who had been living there over ten years, such as Ahn Chang-ho, Yi Won-hun [dates unknown], Jo Bong-am [1899-1959], and Hong Nam-pyo [1888-1950]. –KS

democratic constitution was adopted. Two slogans were for democracy and independence. I often went as a spectator to the meetings of this parliament.

From 1919 to 1924 there were two nationalist groups in opposition to each other: the "American" group versus the "Siberian-Manchurian" group.

The "American" group gained its name from the fact that it had depended upon America and President Woodrow Wilson to aid Korean independence. Its leader, Syngman Rhee, the Ph.D. from America, had been at Princeton when Wilson was its President. Wilson had complete confidence in him. We must use the diplomatic method and put pressure on the great democratic powers to secure international justice for Korea, they said devoutly. Practically, they based their hopes upon the contradictions between Japan and America in the Pacific.

Most of the Koreans from Korea followed the "American" group, especially the Christians, as well as returned students from abroad and intellectuals generally. These were all "gentlemen." Most of them spoke good English. They actually expected to get Korean independence by being able to speak persuasive English! They would not even help the terrorists in their program for demoralizing the Japanese. The "American" group had a majority in the parliament, with one hundred members.

The "Siberian-Manchurian" group had only eighty representatives. It was led by General Yi Dong-hwi, the earliest nationalist leader, who had fought the Japanese for years. This group wanted to organize open warfare with the Japanese. They said ten thousand Korean troops could cross the Yalu River in a month and annihilate all the Japanese in Korea. Most of its members came from exile in Manchuria and Siberia, where they had constantly waged partisan warfare along the Korean border.

When parliament rejected his program, General Yi

was so disgusted at their "gentlemanly" naiveté that he resigned and said he would never cooperate with the government again but would only do work for the Communist Party.

GENERAL YI DONG-HWI: AN OFFICER, NOT A "GENTLEMAN"

The most picturesque figure I met in Shanghai was this old General Yi Dong-hwi, my childhood hero. He had been a folk hero of Korea before 1900 and was at this time over fifty years of age. General Yi was tall and strong and full-chested, with a big bushy military mustache that made him look like the pictures of the marshals of France.

Yi Dong-hwi

I often went with him and other friends to the French Park near Avenue Joffre in Shanghai, where he told us stories of his life and numerous adventures and made us pledge to keep up the good fight for freedom and independence that he had started so long ago. His life represents the period of the nationalist and revolutionary movement from 1907 to the formation of the first Korean Communist Party.[54]

General Yi told us that his father was a Confucian scholar and his family a feudal landlord house. He was born in Hamgyeong Province in northern Korea, and I thought him typical of the best kind of Han River people,* who are brave and eager for struggle, while the South-

---

* *Han River people*: Poetic way of referring to Koreans. The Han River, one of the largest rivers in Korea, flows from the mountains in eastern Korea through Seoul to the Yellow Sea. –DH

erners are more cultured and passive. He was a very fine officer, but he despised the gold-braided "gentlemen" of the cadet school as much as he deplored the golden-tongued "gentlemen" of the diplomatic school, though he himself was a graduate of Tokyo Imperial Military Academy.[55] He admired the hard-handed Korean pioneers in Siberia and Manchuria* and had great faith in the people's volunteers and in any kind of armed struggle, though he had fought and failed many times in his life.

Upon his return from Tokyo, Yi Dong-hwi helped organize the new army school in Seoul. He was one of the most promising young officers and even before the Russo-Japanese War was given command of one division in the Korean Army. By 1910 he was commander-in-chief.[56]

When the Japanese troops drove Yi and his soldiers out of Korea in 1911, they fled to Manchuria. Yi immediately started new resistance movements and schools among the Koreans in Manchuria and Siberia, doing educational work and organizing Korean cooperatives among the farmers.

Yi Dong-hwi was one of the first Koreans to become a communist, influenced by the Russian example. Korea is very close to Soviet Russia, you know. Thousands of Koreans fought in the October Revolution. The Korean communist movement is the oldest such movement in the Far East. In 1918 Yi organized the first Korean Communist Party, called the "Irkutsk Party"[57] and went to Moscow, though he kept his membership secret. That was four years before a Communist Party was set up in China.[58]

After the Great War and the Versailles Treaty, when Korea hoped to receive some justice from the victorious nations and the Nationalist Revolution broke out, the

---

* *Korean pioneers in Siberia and Manchuria*: By the end of WWI, there were significant Korean populations in cities such as Vladivostok, Irkutsk, Chita, and Khabarovsk, and Korean farms existed throughout Siberia. –DH

Koreans in Siberia organized a "Siberian Korean People's Association" of some tens of thousands of members and sent General Yi to Shanghai as its delegate in 1919.

As leader of the "Siberian-Manchurian" group in the Korean nationalist movement, Yi was anxious to organize an army and start a war against the Japanese. He established the military school under the Provisional Government in preparation for this, and planned to develop a big Korean army in Manchuria and Siberia. At that time there were six thousand troops in the Korean Army of Independence in Manchuria, and I do not know how many partisans in Siberia.

In 1922 a special parliament was called in Shanghai, and Yi fought against the "American" group of the nationalists and lost. He then cut relations with the Provisional Government, as he thought it useless, and went to Moscow to discuss Korean problems. His idea was that we must first organize a strong revolutionary mass party.

At the time Yi first went to Moscow from Siberia in 1918, he had no theory at all but only believed in the mass movement and the soviets. When Lenin asked him how many workers there were in Korea—in the factories, in the railways, on the farms—he could not answer. He had no idea. Lenin smiled and called in Zinoviev,* saying, "We must help Comrade Yi here. He has hot blood for Korean independence but no method. This is a natural Oriental condition. They have no revolutionary base but only a background of terrorism and military action."

When Yi returned to Moscow in 1922, he talked against the Korean Provisional Government and also said it was too early to form a Communist Party; that it was necessary for revolutionary elements to join a broad nationalist

---

* *Zinoviev:* i.e. Grigory Zinoviev, Bolshevik and close associate of Vladmir Lenin. (See Biographical Notes.)

party for independence and strengthen it. Lenin said this was correct. Yi then asked for help, and Lenin promised him 500,000 rubles.[59] A Korean lawyer named Ahn Byeong-chan carried 300,000 rubles of this money from Russia to Mongolia, but on the way he was killed by robbers, and the money was stolen. In the winter of 1923 a Korean communist named Kim Rip brought the other 200,000 rubles to Shanghai.

Kim Rip was a democratic leader from Korea who had studied in Moscow before the October Revolution. In 1919 the Comintern sent him to Shanghai. He aided General Yi Dong-hwi in organizing the Korean Communist Party there and accompanied Yi to Moscow on the 1922 journey. He and Lenin agreed on the party line of building up a big nationalist party as opposed to a provisional government.

When Kim Rip returned to Shanghai, he asked the Provisional Government to call a "Korean People's Delegates Congress."[60] For this, six hundred delegates came from Korea, Russia, America, and Manchuria. Kim Rip refused to give the 200,000 rubles to the Provisional

Korean socialists in the 1920s. Yi Dong-hwi is seated in the front row with his arms crossed. Kim Rip sits on the far right of the front row.

Government, turning it over instead to the Preparatory Committee for the People's Congress. For a month during 1924 this meeting struggled to reach a basis for work, but in the end no unity was achieved, and it broke into two parts. The meeting had two antagonistic lines: (1) to reorganize the Provisional Government and strengthen it to lead the Korean revolution, or (2) to organize one big national revolutionary party for independence, because the government had demonstrated itself to be useless.

One June evening in 1924, as he was riding in a rickshaw, Kim Rip was shot[61] from behind by political enemies in the Provisional Government. After this, the Provisional Government drew the 200,000 rubles from the bank and used it.

When Yi Dong-hwi heard of the death of Kim Rip, he was furious. Yi himself died in 1928 at his home near Vladivostok.[62] He was over sixty years old then. After 1924,[63] Yi was very unhappy.

After this affair the Provisional Government lost all power and influence.

AHN CHANG-HO AND YI GWANG-SU

When I arrived in Shanghai in 1920 I was a nationalist, with only a slight tendency toward anarchism. I met all kinds of people and was thrown into a maelstrom of conflicting political ideas and discussions. At first I fell naturally into the nationalist cultural group, then, after a little study and observation, gravitated to the terrorists and anarchists, for I sensed the importance of the nationalist program. The communist movement was in its infancy, and I knew little of Marxism and nothing of Leninism.

The first influence I felt in Shanghai was that of the famous nationalist pair, Ahn Chang-ho and Yi Gwang-su, who had been close comrades ever since they had been teacher and pupil together in Korea. Yi was editor of the *Korean Independence News*, on which I worked, and also of the magazine *Young Korea*. He was also chairman of the committee formed to rewrite Korean history and destroy the myths the Japanese textbooks were trying to build up. Ahn Chang-ho was Minister of Labor in the Korean Provisional Government and leader of the Heungsa-dan,* which he had founded in 1916. I joined the Heungsa-dan, which had eighty members in Shanghai and branches wherever there were Koreans.

The influence of Yi Gwang-su on me was not lasting, but Ahn Chang-ho had the second greatest total personal influence on my life. The most important personal influence was to be that of Kim Chung-chang, a communist ex-monk from the Geumgang-san, whom I did not meet until later in Beijing in 1922, while the third personality to influence me was Peng Pai, a Chinese leader of the Hailufeng Soviet, whom I met in 1928. Ahn Chang-ho taught me practical politics. Kim Chung-chang taught me Marxist theory. Peng Pai taught me revolutionary tactics in the field. No other individuals have influenced my life more deeply, and after 1922 my theoretical background was determined, though I had yet to receive any training in action and tactics.

Ahn Chang-ho and Yi Gwang-su liked to influence

---

* *Heungsa-dan*: "Heungsa-dan" may be translated as the "Society for the Development of Scientists," though "sa" was the old term designating a scholar of the highest rank. - KS [Ahn Chang-ho actually founded this organization on May 13, 1913. Organized in San Francisco as a "national campaign organization…for the independence and prosperity of the nation," its goals were "to develop the self-reliant independence movement based on the development of power and skill to regain the lost country" and ultimately "to build a true democratic republic where every citizen can live a free and even life." The formal English-language translation of "Heungsa-dan" today is the "Young Korean Academy." According to its homepage, the Heungsa-dan is still active in South Korea and working towards the goals of national unification as well as increasing transparency in society and supporting education. (The Young Korean Academy) –DH]

Korean youth, and I went to their house nearly every day with a few older boys. Occasionally Korean girls joined us. These meetings were like a forum or discussion class. We talked over political and historical problems at great length. Yi and Ahn said to us, "The revolution is very far away. You must study now in preparation for the future, and your families must help to pay your way."

❖

Ahn Chang-ho was born in the Gangseo district near Pyongyang to a middle-class landlord family. He received no formal education but studied by himself. Ahn joined the Korean reform movement at sixteen, making fiery speeches to the public that would be long remembered, and became its political leader, while Yi Dong-hwi became its military leader. Ahn was a persuasive and powerful speaker, though habitually silent and noncommittal on small things in daily life. When determined on a line of action, however, he spoke out decisively and firmly, and usually carried his point. [64]

Ahn Chang-ho

In 1907 Ahn Chang-ho was very active, organizing demonstrations and lecturing to the public. From 1907 to 1910 he was the leader of all the Korean nationalists; then, when Japan annexed Korea, he escaped to Qingdao and from there to California in 1910. [65] In California he organized a nationalist Korean People's Association, and also a newspaper. This was his second visit to California.

Ahn learned many songs and stories in America. He

loved Negro songs especially and taught me several. We used to gather with him in Shanghai and sing "Old Black Joe," "My Old Kentucky Home," and "Massa's in the Cold, Cold Ground." His schools in Korea also taught these, and they became very popular there on moonlit nights. Koreans all love sad music dedicated to thoughts of bereavement, homesickness, and misery, so Negro melodies have a great appeal. I also loved these old songs. Another American song which I like is "My Blue Heaven," which I heard first in a café in Korea just a few days after my release from prison in 1931. In Korea it is called "River at Evening," and we sing it very slowly in a melancholy tone....

When the nationalist movement rose in 1919, Ahn Chang-ho returned to Shanghai to join the Korean Provisional Government, but five years later he split with the government and went back to California. He was arrested in San Francisco in 1924 for having communist books in his house, but he was not a communist and was released the next day. The next year again he returned to Shanghai and organized many groups there. In the spring of 1932, after the Shanghai War,[66] he was arrested in the French Concession and turned over to the Japanese because of a bombing incident* in which several Japanese

---

* *a bombing incident*: This bombing incident, in which several Japanese officials lost their lives, is often referred to as the Hongkou Park Incident. Nym Wales considered this to be one of the most effective pieces of terrorism ever accomplished. On April 29, 1932, Japanese army and civil officials gathered in Hongkou Park, which was located in the Japanese sector of the city, to celebrate the Japanese victory in the Shanghai War as well as the Japanese Emperor's birthday. A Korean named Yun Bong-gil threw a bomb and hit and killed Shirakawa Yoshinori, the Japanese Army's Commanding Officer in Shanghai, and also seriously wounded Shigemitsu Mamoru, the Japanese Minister stationed in Shanghai, and others. Yun was arrested and executed. As a result of this incident, the pressure on Koreans living in Shanghai became extremely severe. Ahn Chang-ho and other activists were arrested. On the other hand, due to this incident, Chinese who were resisting Japanese aggression became more interested in the Korean independence movement. It was said that after this incident even Chiang Kai-shek began to aid the Korean Provisional Government. –MI, GT.

Yi Gwang-su

officials were either killed or wounded, though he had no connection with this. He was sent to Seoul, where the court released him. The police arrested him again, however, and he was sent to prison for a year because of his connection with the independence movement. Yi Gwang-su mobilized all his newspapers and influence and secured Ahn's freedom. The *Oriental Daily News* in Korea wanted Ahn to become its editor, but he refused. Now he is inactive and silent although he is in Seoul; he is still the most important political leader of the bourgeoisie.

Ahn Chang-ho represents a democratic mass movement following bourgeois principles, while Yi Gwang-su represents a parallel liberal cultural movement of the upper bourgeoisie and bourgeois intellectuals. Yi opposes the rise of the proletariat, but Ahn Chang-ho concedes its revolutionary role. Yi tends toward paternal aristocracy, while Ahn is a true liberal democratic leader. Ahn became interested in communist theory and tactics at the same time as Sun Yat-sen and the Chinese nationalists turned to Marxism for solutions to their complex problems. He never became a communist, but he never opposed the young Korean Communist Party.

I have already told how Yi Gwang-su, in his early days in Tokyo, pulled a rickshaw to earn his way through college. About 1924, Governor Saitō invited Yi to return to Korea, and he became editor of the *Oriental Daily News* and of a liberal forum for youth called *The Light of the Orient*.

Yi was the first modern Korean writer and is still the best. He has written nearly twenty books—novels, short stories, essays, poetry, and history. He is a Tolstoyan, full of the tragic spirit of sacrifice and paternalism.

CHAPTER 7

They Who Lie in Wait

IN THE MIDDLE of all the political argument in Shanghai was a little knot of youthful terrorists who shrugged their shoulders at talk and went in for direct action against the Japanese.[67] Their activities fascinated me, as they did all young Koreans, and I myself became an anarchist. I met nearly all the terrorist leaders and learned the whole history and background of this movement, so curiously Korean in character.

Terrorism has been an integral phase of the Korean struggle against the Japanese. Like anarchism, it develops in a society of isolated peasant units where mass action is difficult. It is a reaction against constant suppression and revulsion against a sense of frustration and futility. It expresses the yearning for freedom that only those who are slaves can really feel.

Koreans are a gentle folk, peaceful and quiet and religious. Out of the exasperation caused by this general passivity and toleration of unrelieved suffering, young people turned to direct action and seized the only weapons available to them for redress of suffering and injustice—

the bomb, the gun, or the knife. Out of its gentlest people, society often produces its most fiery individual heroes, seeking immolation in sacrifice. That is a dialectical process. Because of this spirit of daring and sacrifice, Koreans are renowned throughout the Far East as its most redoubtable terrorists. Whenever the Chinese want an act of terrorism done against the Japanese, they usually turn to the Koreans for volunteers.

THE UIYEOL-DAN AND THE ANARCHISTS

In the winter of 1919 two terrorist groups were created secretly. One was the Uiyeol-dan[68] or "Practice Justice Bravely Society." This group existed in Korea proper and in Shanghai, Beijing, Tianjin, and south Manchuria. The other was the Jeokki-dan, the "Red Flag Society,"[69] centered in Manchuria and Siberia.

Of these two the Uiyeol-dan was the more active and carried out three hundred acts of terrorism against the Japanese in Korea from 1919 to 1924. Their big plans failed, but the little ones often succeeded. From 1919 to 1927 the Japanese executed three hundred members of the Uiyeol-dan alone. Only a handful are now alive. This group was dominated by anarchist ideology, and the Korean anarchist heyday was during 1921 and 1922.

The Uiyeol-dan had only a few members. It did not want many. The nucleus was a unit of fifty men, all strictly secret. Each of these was connected with some other group. Altogether the Uiyeol-dan had several hundred members at different times.

The Uiyeol-dan members lived like a special cult, keeping themselves in perfect physical condition with swimming, tennis, and other exercises. They practiced sharp-shooting every day. These young men also studied books and took recreation to keep themselves cheerful and psychologically fit for their particular duties. Their life was a strange combination of gaiety and seriousness. Death was always before them, so they lived life to the full while it lasted. They were a strikingly handsome lot. Uiyeol-dan members always wore good-looking foreign-style sports clothes, took good care of their hair, and were at all times shiningly clean and fastidious in appearance. They were very fond of taking photographs—thinking them always to be their last—and of walking in the French Park. All the Korean girls admired the Uiyeol-dan, and they had many love affairs. The girls from Vladivostok were part Russian and part Korean, very beautiful and quite intelligent. Affairs of the heart with these girls were short-lived but intense.

All the money to support the Uiyeol-dan came from rich men in Korea through the Provisional Government. The government floated bonds of $30,000,000 to be paid in thirty years—after Korean independence was achieved. We were very optimistic in those days! Some Americans and missionaries joined the "Friends of Korean Independence" movement[70] at that time also.

The Uiyeol-dan had twelve secret arsenals in Shanghai for making bombs, which were directed by Martin, a German,[71] who was a member of the secret nucleus.

The Koreans gave Martin a motorcycle, which he dearly loved. He used to ride around on it nearly every day from 1921 to 1924. His salary was $200 a month, of which he spent only $70, so he saved money. Sometimes he took messages to Korea and returned with replies.

I met Martin in Shanghai in 1923. He was about forty years old, with very deep-set eyes and black brows, tall and strong and very proud in bearing. He made good friends with the Koreans. He had no political ideas but greatly admired the terrorists. He was a little sympathetic with the Italian movement, but hated Germany and the Japanese. He used to say they were exactly alike.

Martin smoked all the time and loved to play cards. He also liked to drink, and spent most of his $70 on brandy or beer. He ate with us Koreans usually or bought Russian food at cheap émigré restaurants.

When the Uiyeol-dan split in 1924, the Party gave Martin $10,000 as a gift of gratitude, and he left Shanghai. I never heard anything about him afterward.

In 1921 an anarchist party was first started in Korea proper.[72] It was called the "Black Youth League."[73] It was small and made up entirely of intellectuals. That same year a Beijing branch was organized that had both Taiwanese and Japanese in it, as well as a few Chinese. The Black Youth League was dissolved after 1924, though there is still an "Anarchist Federation"[74] with a few members. As soon as the Communist Party rose, the anarchists lost all influence. The founder,* Shin Chae-ho, is now in prison in Korea.

While I was in Shanghai about twenty leaders of the Uiyeol-dan were gathered in the French Concession. I was not permitted to become a regular member, but after I joined the anarchist group,[75] I was accepted among them as a promising disciple and thereby entered into the life of their little circle.

In 1924, at a time of general reorientation in Korean politics when Korean class relations were plainly changing, the Uiyeol-dan split into three parts: nationalists, anarchists, and communists. These three elements, dominated by anarchist philosophy, had existed within its ranks before, but the organization had been a cohesive unit. The reason for this split was that the mass movement in Korea itself was rising to a high point and tended toward communist ideology

---

* *the founder*: i.e. of the Black Youth League. –DH

by 1924. This rise of the masses had a great influence upon the minds of the Uiyeol-dan members and gave a new validity to Marxism. It was no longer necessary to practice individual terrorism—a mass movement existed in which one could do political work. By that time the workers' and farmers' unions and the youth associations had large memberships. The Japanese did not suppress them because these unions opposed terrorism and the Uiyeol-dan. Instead, from 1919 to 1924, they concentrated their attention against the terrorists in an attempt to break them.

During that period the Japanese feared bombs and guns far more than propaganda and mass movements. By 1924 nearly three hundred of the best and most courageous members of the Uiyeol-dan had been killed by the Japanese, and the organization was demoralized by sacrifices that showed so little result. The majority of the remaining Uiyeol-dan joined the communists and wanted to enter mass political work. Nearly all remaining former Uiyeol-dan members were killed between 1925 and 1927, fighting for the Chinese Revolution. The most spectacular Korean terrorist act after 1927 occurred in Hongkou Park in Shanghai after the fighting with Japan in the spring of 1932. But this was a spontaneous individual act. So far as I have heard, it was solely the idea of two men. The boy who carried out the bombing was only twenty-two years old. He was named Yun Bong-gil. He finished middle school in Korea, then went to Shanghai where he was studying English at the time of the incident.

Bombing at Hongkou Park on April 29, 1932

TERRORISTS SUPREME: KIM WON-BONG & OH SEONG-RYUN

Later I was to become well acquainted with the two best Korean terrorists of all, Kim Won-bong and Oh Seong-ryun. They are today among the most important Korean revolutionary heroes. The Japanese have long dossiers against each of them and would rather catch them than any other living Koreans.

Yun Bong-gil

Kim Won-bong was the classical type of terrorist, cool and fearless and individualistic. He was quite unlike the others I met in Shanghai. Whereas they were very comradely, Kim was silent and refused to participate in athletic exercises. He almost never spoke and never laughed but spent his time reading in the library. He loved Turgenev's *Fathers and Sons*, and read all of Tolstoy. He did not like girls, though they all adored him from a distance for he was a very handsome and romantic figure. Many Korean Tolstoyans became terrorists. This is because Tolstoy's philosophy is full of contradictions that are never resolved, hence the necessity for direct action and struggle in a blind attempt at resolution. I loved Tolstoy all during my early youth but could find no method in his philosophy.

Kim's famous individual performance[76] was in the summer of 1923[77] when he tried to assassinate Governor General Saitō. Dressed like a postman, with seven bombs in his mailbag, he walked into the governor's office in Seoul. A number of high officials who had

Kim Won-bong

THEY WHO LIE IN WAIT

come for a meeting had unexpectedly left just an hour before, however. Kim threw all seven of his bombs[78] into the midst of the remaining group of Japanese and casually walked out of the building.

"What was that noise?" the sentry inquired as he passed the entrance.

"I don't know," Kim replied.

He hid in a little boat on the river for three days, pretending to be a fisherman, while airplanes and police throughout the country searched for him. On the fourth day he went to Andong and on to Manchuria.

When I met Oh Seong-ryun in Shanghai he was about thirty and I was only sixteen, so we did not become intimate at that time. A few years later in Guangzhou, however, he became one of the two dearest friends of my entire life.

Oh Seong-ryun

Kim Won-bong had two distinct personalities. He was extremely gentle and kind to his friends but he could also be extremely cruel. Oh Seong-ryun was not cruel, but he was of a passionate nature. No man whose blood does not run hot in his veins can be a terrorist. Otherwise he could not forget himself in the moment of sacrifice. Kim became the leader of the Uiyeol-dan, and Oh sometimes struggled against him.

Oh had a very strong character and was a natural leader of men. Many followed him loyally, but he also had enemies. Oh liked me and made me his special protégé. After 1926 we worked together as a pair. He was the secret director, I the open leader in our revolutionary work.

Oh was a secretive, quiet man, not open. His whole life was lived in secrecy, and even I do not know the whole of his personal story, though we have been together in the face of death many times. He never believed in words but only in actions. He never trusted men easily but only after long acquaintance. Once he had made up his mind he would not change it easily.

Of medium height and good-looking, but not handsome, Oh had high Mongol cheekbones and thick hair over his wide forehead. He was powerful and healthy. He liked art and literature and had once been a schoolteacher in his home village. He had been influenced by the Russian nihilists and anarchists and joined the Uiyeol-dan in 1918.[79]

Oh carried out many terrorist acts in Korea and Manchuria and was one of the most important planners of a grand "armed demonstration" against Japan in 1922. He and the German, Martin, were detailed for the important task of blowing up the big Yalu River bridge. The Uiyeol-dan planned to destroy eight strategic buildings and assassinate Japanese officials in all big cities. For this purpose they secretly transported two hundred bombs into Korea.

The bombs were shipped from Shanghai in boxes of clothing and consigned to a British company at Andong, on the private steamer of which they were being carried. The Andong company manager was an Irish terrorist whom we Koreans called "Sao."[80] He hated the Japanese almost as much as he hated the British and supported the Korean independence movement enthusiastically at great risk to himself. "Sao" himself went to Shanghai and supervised the deadly cargo. He refused to accept any money for himself and helped Korea only out of sympathy. The Korean terrorists traveled on his boat for several years and hid in his house in Andong when in danger.

The Japanese discovered the plot and made fifty arrests, though they got only ten members of the Uiyeol-dan, and most of the two hundred bombs still lie buried in the Korean soil. "Sao" helped the other terrorists escape on his ship to Tianjin and Shanghai. Soon afterward the Japanese arrested "Sao," and he lost his job. After his release from prison he came to Shanghai, and the Provisional Government had a big mass meeting to welcome him. "Sao" said he was proud and happy to have made this sacrifice for Korean independence. His wife had gone back to Ireland at the time of his arrest, and he soon went away. I do not know where he is now—probably working for Irish independence somewhere. Every Korean loves this Irishman, and he is now a tradition in our revolutionary movement.

Oh Seong-ryun's big personal attempt, however, was in Shanghai when the Uiyeol-dan tried to assassinate General Baron Tanaka in 1924.[81] Tanaka was the main theorist of Japan's program of imperial expansion and the author of the famous Tanaka Memorial.[82] He was deeply hated by all Chinese, Koreans, and liberal Japanese for his reactionary program of conquest. Oh told me the whole story in detail.

The Uiyeol-dan prepared three lines of attack: three men were to be stationed on the bund as Tanaka was to walk from the ship. The first line was Oh Seong-ryun, with a pistol; the second line was Kim Ik-sang, with a bomb; and the third line was Yi Jong-am, with a sword.[83] Each man carried a pistol for self-defense, of course.

Just in front of Tanaka as he walked off the ship was an American woman.[84] When Tanaka was eight meters away, Oh Seong-ryun shot. The American woman was frightened, turned, and threw her arms around Tanaka. Oh had drawn a perfect bead and continued firing in a steady line, so the woman was struck by three bullets in exactly the same spot. Tanaka fell, pretending to be dead, so Oh Seong-ryun thought he had succeeded and made his escape. When Kim Ik-sang saw this he threw the bomb. A British sailor kicked it into the water. Kim Ik-sang ran away, and Yi Jong-am, who could do nothing with his sword, escaped.

Oh Seong-ryun wounded several police following him as he ran and reached Hankou Road from the bund. There he got into a car and threatened the driver, but the driver refused to move, so Oh kicked him out. He tried to drive through the streets, though he knew little about cars. He reached Avenue Edward VII, but there he collided with another car and was arrested by the British.

The British police gave Oh Seong-ryun to the French, as he lived in the French Concession, and the French turned him over to the Japanese consul.

He was kept prisoner on the third floor of the Japanese Consulate in a cell with iron bars on the door and window. In the same room were five Japanese. One was a carpenter and another an anarchist. They were sympathetic with Oh and helped him to escape. A Japanese girl brought a steel knife, and Oh cut a hole around the lock of the door on the advice of the carpenter. One night he and the anarchist opened the door and escaped over the compound wall, wearing the bright red clothes of the prisoner. The other Japanese did not want to make the attempt as they had only short sentences.

Kim Ik-sang

Oh went to the house of an American friend and hid for

three days while the British, French, and Japanese police surrounded and searched every Korean's residence in the whole of Shanghai. His picture was scattered everywhere, and a $50,000 reward was offered.

He escaped to Guangzhou, where he forged a passport and went to Germany. In Berlin a German girl

Korean article about Oh Seong-ryun and Kim Ik-sang's attempted assassination of Tanaka

fell in love with him, and he lived with her family for a year. After he had spent all his money, he went to the Soviet consul, who arranged for him to go to Moscow in 1925. There he was converted to Marxist theories and learned the tactics of mass struggle. He joined the Communist Party and studied at the University of the East.[85]

In 1926 Oh went to Vladivostok and from there to Shanghai. He sent his luggage on to a friend's house, but just as he arrived, his friend's wife warned him that the entire street had been surrounded by a cordon of police. He escaped, but the Japanese got his luggage. They took the photographs of his German sweetheart and his complete set of Lenin, as well as some modern art prints which he always carried with him. Oh was very much annoyed by this confusion.

He went on to Guangzhou to join the revolution, where he became a member of the Central Committee of the Korean Revolutionary Young Men's League.[86] He was my closest comrade during the Guangzhou period and Hailufeng days, and I shall have much more to tell about him later on. I once published some poetry about his escapades.[*]

---

[*] *published some poetry about his escapades*: Although Kim San claims to have written "poetry" about Oh's "escapades," the account he published took the form of a short story. See Appendix I for the first-ever English-language translation of this work, titled "A Strange Weapon." —DH

CHAPTER 8

Reflections on Women and Revolution

AHN CHANG-HO HAD TAKEN a good deal of personal interest in me in Shanghai and wanted to help complete my education. He secured a scholarship for me to go to Nankai University in Tianjin, together with five other Korean boys. When we arrived in October 1921, however, an incident occurred which caused us to refuse to attend the university: a Korean student at Nankai named Kim Yeom entered the running match at the autumn athletic meet. He was a fine athlete and was far in the lead during the race when he heard a Chinese shout, "No wonder he can run so well. He is a running dog of the Japanese." Kim Yeom whirled around in the middle of the race and went over and beat up the Chinese who had shouted this. The faculty was angry at Kim for this, and he was beaten, too, over the incident. Kim and the other six of us withdrew from the school immediately. Later Kim Yeom joined the movies in China and is now considered the "king" of movie stars, while Butterfly Wu ranks as "queen."[87] He is very handsome and sings well and is called Jin Can in Chinese.

We students had lost our scholarships because of pride and did not know where to turn. We decided to go to Beijing. A friend of Ahn Chang-ho gave us money for traveling expenses and tuition, but wanted us to eat at the Xiangshan Orphanage, a charity near Beijing[88] run by Xiong Xiling, while attending school. The other five had no way to get money so they were forced to accept this arrangement. I refused to take charity from the orphanage, however, and wrote a letter to my second brother. It was the first letter I had sent to my family in two years—ever since I had stolen money and run away. My brother replied that I would have to come home and discuss all my affairs in person, after which he might be able to help me. I agreed, and he sent me money to return.

The family was displeased with my years of adventure, and my mother insisted that I should marry. I had always sworn never to take a wife, but to please her and my brother I agreed to become acquainted with a girl she had already chosen. I found that, though very religious, she was pretty, intelligent, and fairly well educated, and she admired me extravagantly for no reason that I could see. In turn, I liked her. She was a typical Korean girl: modest, devoted, loyal. I did not refuse to marry her but agreed to let the matter hang in abeyance until I was out of college. Mother was delighted, and my brother offered to pay my way through medical college, but only on condition that I should complete the course and stop wandering about.

I had learned that one can do nothing effective in the world without some means of earning a living, and that a lack of professional ability handicapped one's revolutionary work as well as one's daily life. There were few doctors in our ranks, and I could aid wounded terrorists and secure their admittance to hospitals. I knew that my future life would be lived in the midst of wounds and suffering and that medical knowledge would enhance my value to the revolution. Also I loved science of any kind, and medicine is one of the most social of sciences and of the greatest value to humanity.

I therefore promised my brother to become a good doctor and went to Beijing Union Medical College, which was one of the best in China. He had begged me to go to Tokyo instead, but I had no intention of giving up my political work during college. Except for a trip to see my friends in Shanghai in 1922, I remained a medical student in Beijing until 1925, when the Guangzhou Revolution called me away. I did well in my studies, but was active the whole time in student work and in the study of political and social science.

❖

During my first year in medical school, I occasionally wrote to my proposed fiancée and would receive very affectionate replies. In 1923, however, I told her frankly that I could never marry any girl, for my life was to be entirely engrossed in revolutionary work and would have to be independent of any ties. I would have no money, and she could never live the hard life that was to be my voluntary lot. She seemed quite broken-hearted—but, nevertheless, only two years later, married someone else in Korea.

From the age of fifteen to the year 1923 I had had no decided opinions on the woman question, though I rebelled against arranged marriage. Those opinions I did have were determined by three influences: Christian idealistic training in respect for women; a natural human feeling for girls of my own age; and the inhibiting underlying thought that in a life of revolution I could never have a domestic life, so that no matter whether I loved a girl very much or not, it would be unfair to her to marry her. Ahn Dong-hui's daughter had first awakened my interest in girls, and after that I was shy and embarrassed in their company but secretly much interested in the opposite sex. In Shanghai there had been many Korean girls, but they were usually much older or younger. I met several at the gatherings of young people with Ahn Chang-ho and Yi Gwang-su and sometimes took them roller-skating in the parks. Ahn Chang-ho taught us not to marry early but to have a healthy, natural friendship with girls in the modern coeducational manner. He believed in keeping such relationships purely platonic, with friendships between boys and girls exactly as those between the same sex. He said that the traditional Oriental separation of the sexes was unnatural and created morbid curiosities and unhealthy attitudes; that it was designed to keep women helpless and an instrument of propagation or amusement only, denying their right to equality and mutual respect. Men must help in freeing women by protecting and guarding their equal status and encouraging them to enter into all activities in partnership with men. Marriage was to be such a partnership, once both were old enough to choose wisely and with an understanding of each other as individual personalities.

I agreed with Ahn Chang-ho, but I was more idealistic and had a tendency to worship from afar. When I became acquainted with the girl in Korea I saw that I could easily learn to like her very much, even though she was not the ideal I had vaguely in mind. I did not then deny marriage absolutely but thought the matter could take care of itself in the future. I was much interested in the general problem, however. There were several pairs of lovers in medical school, and I followed the course of these affairs with curiosity. They usually ended in jealousy and enmity, so I concluded that such love affairs were all nonsense.

Then, when I got into the study of physiology I saw that men's desires and necessities were not the same. The desires and necessities of animals were the same. But men could not make their wants and needs fit each other. And why should they? Rousseau taught the validity of the "natural man," but he influenced me in the opposite direction. The nature of man was not the same as that of the animal. It was natural only to itself. Animal desires are necessary to the animal but not to the man. Man can control his desires and thereby render them unnecessary, I decided. Man existed as such only when he had intellectual will and ideas. In that he was not the same as the animal. His mind existed for the purpose of controlling his body as well as other forces of nature external to himself. Otherwise he failed to measure up to the stature of man as opposed to the beast.

I thought that women were physiologically passive and that their role in life was passive. They wanted peace and fulfillment. They were not active like men, and I did not like this. They were useful for their own purposes but not in a historical period demanding action and sacrifice external to material needs and the family group.

I decided that women and marriage were a biological and economic problem. In time of peace they were important. In time of fighting they were secondary and must be relegated to that position by will. I saw that no man can be independent if married and that to be in love was an even greater bondage. In love a man loses not only his freedom as an individual but also the internal freedom of his own body. Women were weaker than men, and I did not like any kind of weakness. My life was to be lived in revolutionary work and not in helping any woman. In 1923 I decided firmly never to marry and never to place myself in any position where I might become the victim of a love affair. For a long time after this I never talked with any woman and avoided coming into any contact with them whatsoever.

I did strong propaganda among the students in Beijing on this subject, though not all of it was effective. "Man is historical; woman is not. Woman is immediate," I would quote to them. I was an expert on women then—when I knew nothing about them.

"You are worse than a monk. You are a puritan," Kim Chung-chang, the Geumgang-san ex-monk, would say to me.

"What is love?" I would retort, quoting Tolstoy. "Love is only taking another baby's mother for your own child. One man takes a woman to save her from the arms of a cruel man into his own cruel arms."

"Ah, what a fine, clean target you are for some girl," Kim would shake his head sagely. "You have no defense whatever. Don't you know that the only defense against women is more women? You are only keeping yourself vulnerable. I pity you when you fall in love some day. All the heavens will fall upon you. I think you should give up this theory before you are devoured by it. Come with me tonight."

"A great love is better than a mess of little ones, anyway," I would argue. "A great tragedy is not so harmful to a man as piecemeal destruction and demoralization. To be killed is better than to be ruined and still alive."

"There is no more dangerous situation for any man to be in than to be virgin territory for the first woman," Kim would say. "I give you fair warning, for I was once a monk like you. I think that love may be either an injection, a transfusion, or a single blood stream. You can choose between them. I know nothing of real love myself, but I have decided that I must learn something of women."

"After his wife died when he was twenty-five, Hegel refused ever to marry again. If I am no worse at dialectics than he, I shall not complain," I would remark. "To free the mind you must first free the body, even if handcuffs are necessary to do it in the dialectical manner."

"Hegel lived in abstractions. You must live and fight with the material men and women who are the real social forces. If you want to be a virgin ascetic go back to a cliff in the Geumgang-san," was Kim's argument.

But Kim agreed with me then that Korean revolutionaries should not marry. His argument was that you should let love destroy itself and thereby win freedom from it. All our close comrades pledged themselves to the principle of non-marriage because they knew our hard life and economic uncertainties in the future would be burden enough. We all lived together in one group in Beijing and shared our problems in common. Most of us opposed having the others go out at night to nameless places and tried to prevent it. When they came back we said bitterly:

"It costs $6 or $7 a month for food for one of us, yet you spend $10 on women while we are half-starved."

"You have no soul," these students would reply. "You care only for meat, not even for flesh. Is one jin* of mutton enough to satisfy you?"

Our group finally had to take the position that it was a personal problem. If the individual had money enough he could do as he pleased as long as it did not interfere with politics, but we watched those who spent it on such undesirable purposes with hawk eyes to detect the slightest political irregularity and made life unpleasant for them. If anyone should contract a disease, this was to be considered an unpardonable crime against the revolution, so they had to go only to the best places, which were

---

* *jin:* A Chinese measure of weight, corresponding to 1.102 pounds or half a kilogram. –GT

very expensive—sometimes $10 a night—and few could afford to do that often.

"Sing-song girls* are a defense against marriage," Kim would remark. "For this we can thank them. They leave our revolutionaries free agents. The price is not too high."

But I was personally a strict puritan and was never able to rationalize this question. I held that a strong man could and must suppress his body and we wanted only strong men in revolutionary work. Ahn Chang-ho had convinced me of this first, and Tolstoy's ideas influenced me greatly, too. From Tolstoy I learned the philosophy of sacrifice, not only of life, but of desire. I felt that the truth lay somewhere between Tolstoyan asceticism and Rousseau. Tolstoy liked women at first, but after he became creative he had nothing to do with them. I thought to dispense with that first stage and go directly to my work.

---

* *Sing-song girls*: The equivalent of the Japanese geisha. The girls were trained to sing and sometimes play musical instruments for the entertainment of men. Some, but not all, were prostitutes as well.—GT

CHAPTER 9

From Tolstoy to Marx

From 1919 to 1923 Korean students were far in advance of the Chinese in terms of social thinking, partly because of our more pressing need for revolution and partly because of our closer contact with Japan, the fountainhead of the radical movement, both anarchist and Marxist, in the Far East at that time. It was from Japanese translations of Marxism that both Koreans and Chinese first became acquainted with this theory.

Korean students were being trained in Moscow long before any Chinese were sent there. And Korean students and workers and peasants in Russia had participated in the October Revolution, the Civil War,* and the period of intervention. Lenin had turned first to Korea and later to China for the development of Marxist revolution in the colonial lands of the East.

At that time there were eight hundred Korean nationals in Beijing, including about three hundred students. Two rival student groups fought for supremacy—the right-wing Korean Student Association controlled by the

---

* *Civil War*: Here, the civil war being referred to is between White Russia and Soviet Russia. –DH

nationalists, and the left-wing Korean Student Union led by the communists. Each organization kept its membership exactly equal with the other. There was much quarreling over the question of terrorism. The right-wing groups were the pro-terrorist element, while the others opposed this, being followers of the anti-terrorist line of the Communist Party. I joined the Korean Student Union and the Korean Social Science Research Society, also on the left.

The few Koreans in Beijing had seven magazines, probably more than any small group ever had before. All these journals were in the Korean language, and all were edited by student intelligentsia. All fought violently on questions of theory and tactics.

All Koreans wanted only two things really, though they differed in how to achieve these: independence and democracy. Really, they wanted only one thing: freedom—a golden word to those who know it not. Any kind of freedom looked divine to them. They wanted freedom from Japanese oppression, freedom in marriage and love, freedom to live a normal, happy life, freedom to rule their own lives. That is why anarchism had such appeal. The urge toward a broad democracy was really very strong in Korea. This is one reason we did not develop a strong, centralized system of political parties. Each group defended its right to exist and its right to free expression. And each individual fought to the end for his own freedom of belief. There was plenty of democracy among us—but very little discipline.

As soon as I arrived in Beijing in 1921, I began reading Marxism. I studied the *Communist Manifesto* first, then Lenin's *State and Revolution* and a collection of articles called *The Story of Social Development*. Very soon I realized the importance of scientific mass struggle and the futility of coups d'état and terrorist acts. I still admired the heroic sacrifices of the terrorists and liked the free spirit of comradeship among my anarchist friends. But I felt clearly that doom was upon them. In 1922 I returned to Shanghai to be with the Uiyeol-dan and my anarchist comrades again. We drank a good deal of wine, but we were sad, not happy.

Upon my return from Shanghai I had made up my mind that the only real hope of success for Korea was the communist movement. By the winter of 1923 the theoretical foundations of my political beliefs were laid, therefore, though I had no tactics and little experience, and I joined the Communist Youth League[89] that winter.

THE RED MONK FROM GEUMGANG-SAN

It was Kim Chung-chang who made a communist out of me. He guided my theoretical training during that most difficult period in the lives of young Koreans—1922-1925. I was seventeen when I first met him in 1922, and he was twenty-seven. He is still one of my two dearest friends and comrades—the other being Oh Seong-ryun, of whom I have already told.

Kim Chung-chang had the greatest influence upon me of any individual I have ever known. This was not only because of his keen intelligence and superiority generally but because I came to know him at that important formative period of the youthful mind when

Kim Chung-chang

it is most open to influence and new ideas.

I met Kim in Beijing. It was at a student meeting in the Korean YMCA. I had already heard of him, and his personality immediately arrested my interest. He wore dark glasses and looked old for his age. He was a sensitive, highly intelligent type, radiating mental energy, and also very handsome. At this time the struggle between the communist and nationalist tendencies was acute, and Kim was on the communist side. He was the only one well-grounded in theory and always won his arguments.

As soon as we talked with each other, a lifelong friendship was started.

I found Kim Chung-chang to be a most extraordinary person. He was born at Cheolsan or "Iron Mountain" in northern Korea. His father was a very poor farmer, and Kim did farm work as a boy. He was too poor to attend school but learned a good deal from the educated men in the village.

At sixteen, he became a Christian and studied the principles of Christianity earnestly, but they did not satisfy him. So he ran away from home and went to the Geumgang-san of Korea—where he became a Buddhist monk. At the famous Yongmun monastery in the heart of these beautiful mountains, he studied not only Buddhism, but also modern philosophy. There he remained until 1919.

During those years the young monk studied Japanese and read Kant, Hegel, and Spinoza. Hegel was a revelation to him, and he embraced Hegelian idealism with enthusiasm, reveling in its dialectical logic. He was not yet influenced by Marxism.

In 1919 Kim joined the Buddhist Monks' Independence Party, which then had about three hundred members, and published a manifesto on Korean independence. During the March First Movement, he went out to the villages to do propaganda work[90]—wearing his monk's robe, of course. He was then about twenty-four. Arrested in Seoul by the Japanese, he was imprisoned for a year.[91] As soon as he was free, he organized a "lecture group" to continue propaganda work.

Kim Chung-chang in 1919 at Seodaemun Prison

From the Hegelian dialectic, he easily became interested in Marxism, and from his poverty and innate sense of justice he naturally turned toward a belief in social revolution. In 1921 he joined the "Proletarian Federation"[92] and from that time on sympathized with the communist idea.

In 1922, together with five other young Buddhist monks, Kim went to Beijing, where there was freedom to carry on their political work. The six started a literary society, and their magazine was called *Wild Plain* (Hwang-ya). It was devoted to philosophy, poetry, short stories, and literature generally.

During this time, three of the young monks, including Kim, became communists; the other three went back to Geumgang-san, saying that the revolution was all nonsense.

At the same time that I joined the Communist Youth League in the winter of 1923, I helped organize the first communist magazine in Beijing, which we called *Revolution*,[93] together with Kim and eight others. I was one of the three editors of this bimonthly student journal, which was supported by communist sympathizers, left-wing nationalists, and anarchists. It had thirty-two pages. The first issue numbered eight hundred copies, and within six months we had three thousand subscribers. It was sent to Korean students in Korea, Manchuria, Siberia, Honolulu, California, and Europe, and continued publication until 1926. Kim was editor in chief and wrote many excellent essays for this magazine, which influenced my thinking greatly. There was no Korean printer in Beijing, so Kim wrote the whole magazine in his own calligraphy and printed it by the lithograph method on stone. He nearly ruined his eyes doing this work and had to go to the Beijing Union Medical College for treatment.

The next year, 1924,* Kim and I and the other eight organizers of *Revolution* founded the Beijing Korean Communist Party[94] as a branch of the Irkutsk Party system.

In the winter of 1925 Kim decided to go to Guangzhou to do revolutionary work. I wanted to go with him, but we thought it better to take different routes.

TO TOLSTOY: AN ACKNOWLEDGMENT
From my first reading of Tolstoy in middle school until

---

* *The next year, 1924*: During this period I also met several of the earliest Chinese communists, including Shi Cuntong [1890-1970], who was one of the founders of the Chinese Communist Youth in 1920 [actually 1921] and became its first [in truth second] secretary. In 1923 I met Li Dazhao [1888-1927], a leader of the CCP. He used to write for our magazine *Revolution* and often gave us advice and criticism. Later on I knew Qu Qiubai [1899-1935]. —KS

1922, I was a Tolstoyan idealist. Along with that, during 1919 and 1920, I was a nationalist with vague anarchist sympathies, and from 1921 to 1922, I was an anarchist.

Out of Tolstoyanism anything can develop—his is a universal philosophy that can apply to any phase of a man's thinking. It was a logical step toward anarchism, and an equally logical step toward the Hegelian dialectic under Kim Chung-chang's tutelage, then forward to Marxist theory.

I still like Tolstoy, as one loves an old teacher. From 1921 to the Guangzhou Commune in 1927, I carried a volume of Tolstoy in my pocket and read it nearly every day.

Tolstoy has had the greatest total influence in the Far East of any individual, I think, for he has had a broad popularity and following in China, Japan, Korea, India, and elsewhere, as well as Russia. He has had by far the greatest individual influence upon the modern literature of China, Japan, and Korea, followed closely by the other Russian writers. He has for many years influenced both bourgeois and proletarian revolutionaries, as well as the great mass of nonpolitical intellectuals, and even reactionaries, in those countries. He paved the way for Leninism, which has had perhaps the second greatest total influence among elements both for and against it. There is hardly a modern thinker and writer in the Far East who has not been a Tolstoyan at one time or another. I think this universal philosopher will live a long time in history.

Why is this? In my own case I explain Tolstoy in this way: For me Tolstoy represents truth and an approach to universal truth, but not movement. Yet in physics inertia is also a force, is also movement. Tolstoy describes and mirrors reality as a conflict between contradictions. When you understand this dialectical fact of reality, the way is clear for action.

Tolstoy's characters are always in struggle, never

reaching agreement and resolution. Every book he wrote is a study of such dialectical forces. His mind was open and objective, receptive to every fact and change. He mirrored human life and activity as it occurred in the days of his writing, and this picture of Russia was equally true of Oriental countries in their first period of change. I think he would have turned to revolution had he not died too soon. He was always seeking solutions, but was too honest to create them when the reality around him had not yet demonstrated their validity. I often think what a magnificent epic of the October Revolution he would have written had he lived through it. He would have told the whole story in a dozen volumes, with all its dialectical contradictions and struggle, with all its justice and injustice, with all its heroism and weakness, with all its ideals and disillusionments. And I think that such a book would have awakened millions of men to social consciousness as nothing except the fact of October itself has done. No Tolstoy has yet dramatized and described October in terms of human experience, and that is one reason why its total potential has not yet been felt among the masses of the earth. They need an interpreter to bring that great revolution to life and meaning for them.

Tolstoy believed in the equality of all mankind, and he discusses all the problems of man and the nature of his historical development. I like best his *Reader of Humanity*, which I read again and again in four volumes in Japanese translation. This was the book I usually kept in my pocket.

He affirms the validity of the morality of sacrifice and opposes cruelty very much. He is a humanitarian and a lover of mankind. This philosophy has been of vital importance in the awakening of the Orient, where cruelty and selfishness and callousness to suffering have existed for so long. His great contribution has been to awaken his readers to a humanitarian consciousness of the suffering around them and to give them a new idealism. I hated cruelty very much when I was young, and I have seen so much of it that I have learned the great historic value of humanitarianism. Now I no longer hate cruelty. I accept it as a phase of truth. It exists. To like it or not is no longer my personal problem. It is to kill or be killed. To hate the truth is only a diversion of emotional energy. My job is to create justice where cruelty has been. Tolstoy also gave up his hatred of cruelty and concentrated on exposing its existence.

Tolstoy wanted to save the peasants and give land to the farmers. There he touches the basic problem of the Orient. Therefore, his books have a special meaning for Orientals in this stage of their history.

He was an idealist. *War and Peace* demonstrates historical determinism. Yet it demands that man must struggle against this determinism. That is one of Tolstoy's contradictions that proves his grasp of the truth. For me, Tolstoy says that the will is not free. Yet he never denies that the will exists and can be creative in action. He has vision and the long view.

He understood nature and was able to express this understanding for others to grasp. I like nature, especially in its manifestations of change. I accept green nature as it is. Human nature I demand to change, and I believe that this is an attribute of human nature.

Tolstoy was a Spartan, derived from the Greeks. We Koreans all like this. He had dreams—but not too many and not too foolish ones.

He wrote carefully and with deep thought. One thing I liked about him was his idea of study: he never read anything that he wanted to look at only once. And I liked him because he had an honest mind and an honest personality and an honest heart.

Tolstoy was unhappy all his life. In my opinion, he was brave when he ran away just before his death.

Chinese Communist delegates in 1934 listening as Mao Zedong, the chairman of the Soviet Republic of China, gives a report on the progress of the CCP's Central Executive Committee.

PART 3

IN THE RANKS OF CHINA'S

GREAT REVOLUTION

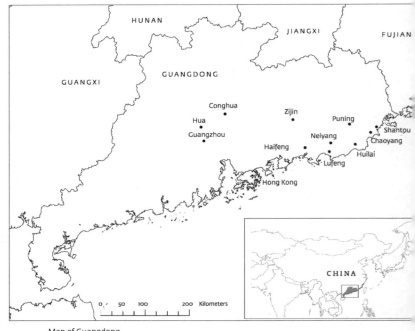

Map of Guangdong

CHAPTER 10

In the Ranks of China's "Great Revolution"

THE COURSE OF my political life has followed closely the general trend of the Korean revolutionary movement. At the time I became a communist, a general change was occurring in all Korean political thinking. The year 1924 marks the sharp curve to the left which the Chinese Revolution took under Sun Yat-sen during his Soviet Russian reorientation.[95] Not only Korea and China but also Japan began to look to the Red Star for guidance.

The Chinese Revolution was rising rapidly. Sun Yat-sen reorganized the Guomindang along the lines of the Russian Communist Party and made an entente with the U.S.S.R. He died in Beijing in 1925, but Guangzhou had become the seat of the new revolutionary sovereignty, and after the May 30th Incident* of that year, affairs moved

---

* *May 30th Incident*: On May 30, 1925 thousands of Chinese workers and students gathered outside a police station in the International Settlement in Shanghai to protest the killing of a Chinese worker and the wounding of others at the Japanese-owned cotton-spinning

speedily. Soviet military and political advisers arrived in Guangzhou, the Huangpu Military Academy* was established to train military cadres for revolutionary work,

Sun Yat-sen (in white with cane at front) opening the Huangpu Military Academy in 1924

and preparation was made for the Northern Expedition to destroy the feudal warlords.[96]

All Koreans, right and left, were delighted with this new upsurge in China, considering it the first step in the emancipation of their own country. Among the first

---

mills and to demand the release of detained students. The British police fired against the demonstrators, killing and wounding many. In response, the Chinese Communists through the labor unions under their influence mobilized students, workers, and small business people to launch a general strike in protest. This in turn caused sympathy strikes in other parts of the country, notably in Guangzhou and Hong Kong (see note 116), fueling a nationwide resistance to foreign imperialism and its domestic partners that is now known as the May 30th Movement. Chinese Communist scholars see the incident and its consequences as evidence of the "high tide" in the CCP-led Great Revolution (i.e. the period from the CCP's 1923 decision for a united front with the GMD or alternately from the May 30th Movement in 1925 to the Guangzhou Uprising in December 1927). By this they mean that the Chinese people became fully conscious of both national and class issues caused by their internal and external enemies. –AJ, MI, DH

* *Huangpu Military Academy*: Better known by its Cantonese name, Whampoa Military Academy. –DH

to flock to Guangzhou to volunteer in the fighting were Korean revolutionaries of all varieties.

When I arrived in Guangzhou in the autumn of 1925, only sixty other Koreans—mostly Uiyeol-dan terrorists—had gathered to fight in China's "Da geming," or "Great Revolution," as it was called. By 1927, over eight hundred Koreans had come to Guangzhou. The flower of our active leadership joined. All were political revolutionaries, and most were intellectuals. About twenty were labor leaders from Japan. Many Communist Youth members came from Manchuria. The average age was about twenty-three. Some middle-school students were fourteen or fifteen, and the oldest among the eight hundred was under forty.

Nearly four hundred men from the Army of Independence in Manchuria volunteered. Over a one hundred came from Siberia, with a history of struggle from the October Revolution as well as years of experience with the Siberian partisans. From Korea proper one hundred arrived. Thirty trained Marxist students came direct from Moscow on Borodin's staff.[97]

All of these eight hundred were sympathetic with the general communist idea, except the majority of the four hundred from the Army of Independence, and some of those were communists. The nationalists and communists came mostly from Siberia and Manchuria. The Korean Communist Youth numbered seventy members.

Made up of so many varied groups, both politically and geographically, no unified leadership could be developed easily. Each group blamed every other for not understanding the situation correctly, and the Chinese Communist Party thought it should give orders to the lot. The eternal curse of cliquism and exaggerated anarchistic democracy in the Korean movement seemed to be nearly as bad as ever. As soon as I arrived in Guangzhou, I set about pointing out the folly of using sect against sect, as that would prevent effective common action.

I was overflowing with youthful enthusiasm and energy and wanted to have a finger in everything. I joined the Chinese Nationalist Party.* Koreans were permitted to join this, but only six of us did so. It was decided that the Korean Communist Party in China should become a branch of the Chinese Communist Party.[98] The Party ordered me into the Korean cell of the Chinese Communist Party, and I became one of its five members.

A SECT TO END SECTS

Three of us set ourselves the task of fighting sectarianism and of forming a mass movement free of cliquism. The other two were Kim Won-bong, at the time considered the "famous No.1 terrorist" and leader of the Uiyeol-dan nationalist wing; and my friend the ex-monk from the Geumgang-san, Kim Chung-chang, who led the group from Beijing. "All of us are revolutionary workers on a basis of equality," we proclaimed.

We prepared the way gradually and in the late spring of 1926 held a meeting for the purpose of creating a central union representing all Korean groups and parties—the Korean Revolutionary Young Men's League. It was very successful and immediately numbered three hundred members. Its elected central committee was made up mostly of communists. It included the founders, Kim Chung-chang and Kim Won-bong. I was a member of the organization committee, which determined membership, and in 1927 was elected to the central committee also.

Kim Chung-chang's pen was soon active, and when the League created its own organ in 1926, called *Revolutionary Action*,[99] he became editor-in-chief, and I was one of the

---

* *the Chinese Nationalist Party*: i.e. the GMD. –DH

sub-editors. Kim wrote the manifestos for the League, and by this time his essays were famous and influential.

Within the League, however, cliques still struggled for hegemony—the Uiyeol-dan nationalists versus the cell from the Chinese Communist Party versus the Shanghai faction from the Korean Communist Party versus the Siberia faction from the Korean Communist Party. Further measures were needed to achieve centralization. Therefore a group of eighty communist members from Manchuria, Siberia, Shanghai, Beijing, and Korea came together, and we organized a secret group known as the "KK"[100]—from the German words meaning "Korean Communists." Our program was to break down all sects, and, when this had succeeded, to dissolve our own "sect to end sects."

It was next decided that it was necessary to create a unified Korean nationalist party. This was done. We saw that this could not be formed in Korea but must develop outside, with the Uiyeol-dan as center. The Uiyeol-dan changed its name to the Korean National Independence Party[101] and elected a new committee of eleven.

Victory over sectarianism was achieved at last. The two open organizations were the Revolutionary Young Men's League and the National Independence Party, while the secret "KK" kept the threads of underlying unity. The "KK" had a direct relation with Borodin and the general staff from Moscow.

The Koreans were very active in all branches of work among the Chinese. Some were advisers, some teachers at Huangpu Military Academy or at Zhongshan University,[102] some on the Revolutionary Military Staff.[103] Others fought in the armies.

In addition to my multifarious political activities, I taught at the Huangpu Military Academy and studied economics at Zhongshan University.[104]

THE FOUR PIONEER BAKS FROM SIBERIA

Typical of the best Korean revolutionaries who came to Guangzhou were Bak Jin and his wife and two brothers. All three brothers had black, black eyes and long thick eyelashes. Bak Jin's eyes blinked when he talked, which gave an impression of earnestness. They were real northern Oriental types, all handsome and stalwart. They filled a room with an atmosphere of power and activity like a Siberian storm from the tundra.

I wanted to get better acquainted with this interesting foursome as soon as I met them. Bak Jin told me about conditions in Siberia, and I asked him to write a report for us on this. I soon learned to love him as my own brother, and he taught me many things about fighting and practical work.

From 1919 to 1921 Bak Jin and his young brothers fought with the partisans in Siberia against the White Guards and the Japanese during the Allied Intervention. The Soviets captured Vladivostok seven times and lost it six times. Bak was in all seven campaigns. In a campaign in 1920 a bullet took out all his front teeth, and he had to wear false ones after that. He had been wounded many times during his life.

Bak's old parents and grandfather died of hunger and cold during the Intervention in Siberia, but when the warfare was ended, Bak and his brothers received land from the Soviets as a reward for fighting so well.

In 1921 a Korean self-government authority was established in Siberia as a department of the Siberian Soviet under the Korean Soviet Committee. There were about 700,000 Koreans in Siberia then. (Today* we estimate that there are 800,000 Koreans in the U.S.S.R.—a large percentage of the whole population of Siberia, which

---

* *Today:* i.e. 1937. –DH

totals about four million,[105] including Russians, Koreans, Chinese, Eskimos, a few Japanese, and some Mongols.)

In 1921 he was elected to the Soviet committee of a district near Vladivostok. One day they were going to a meeting across a frozen river, and one of the young girls fell down on the ice. Bak helped her to her feet. Until that moment he had never once paid any attention to any woman, but during the meeting he kept glancing appraisingly at the girl, who had said, "Thank you." On the way back across the ice he arranged to walk beside her and inquired bluntly if she thought she could love him. The girl was a little surprised, but after a few minutes replied, "Yes, I think I could." Two days later this little romance of the snows ended in marriage. That was the way Bak did things. The pair were very devoted to each other, and their marriage was a model one until Bak's death.

Bak's wife, who had worked in the Red partisan movement and was an active member of the local committee in Siberia from 1921 to 1925, came of an interesting family. Her father was a well-known hero of northern Korea. He was known as the "masked bandit." Thirty times he robbed rich families to get money to support his school for poor children; then, having been captured, escaped from prison, only to die in Siberia.

The KK wanted all the good leadership that came, so we immediately took the Baks as members of our little group. Every Saturday night some of us met together. None of those living in school dormitories or military barracks could afford extra hotel bills, so this one night every week we stayed up from eight in the evening till eight the next morning, holding a political meeting and discussion. We talked furiously the whole time. This is the Korean character—much lively argument and discussion and attempt to demonstrate superior knowledge and ability. Bak Jin would get tired and sleep through a long discussion, then casually wake up and try to carry on where we had left off when he fell asleep, making us all laugh.

"You four are so happy together," I said one day to Bak Jin. "Why is it you don't want a peaceful life now after so much struggle?"

"While the Korean revolution is unfinished, peace is only pain to me," he replied. "Struggle is life. Passivity is death. I like to fight."

Among Koreans there is always a tense struggle for leadership, but Bak cared nothing for this. "Leadership is punishment," he always declared.

But he was a first-rate leader of men. After April 15, 1927,[106] he went to Wuhan to do revolutionary work* and returned to Guangzhou with General Zhang Fakui as an officer of the Jiaodaotuan or Special Training Regiment.[107] His wife became pregnant, and he was very happy, as he thought this was to be his first son. His two brothers were with him as well. During the Commune,** Bak was in command of the gallant "Doomed Battalion" at Lingnan University and was killed there. His loyal wife was broken-hearted and went back to their farm in Siberia with her child yet unborn.

The two younger brothers went to Hailufeng as officers in the Special Training Regiment. What happened to them I shall tell later.

AN ASSASSIN PAYS ME A VISIT

The eighty members of the KK had come from several different places, and there were many enemies and much rivalry among us. One day we lost one of our young

---

* *he went to Wuhan to do revolutionary work:* For more on the significance of Wuhan at this time, see note on p. 152. –DH

** *Commune:* i.e. the Guangzhou Commune. –DH

members named Kim, who was my close friend. He was secretly killed by the Byeong-in Volunteer Unit,[108] because they thought he had given secrets to the KK. To know too many secrets is dangerous for any man in revolutionary work. They also wanted to get rid of me.

A few days later, one of the members of this group came to my room at midnight. The door was locked, and I pretended not to be at home. He waited outside until three o'clock, then went away. Had I opened the door I would have gone the way of poor little Kim. This so-called "Brave Army of 1925" had been organized in Shanghai to oppose both the Communist Party and the Uiyeol-dan. About twenty members came to Guangzhou in 1926. We discovered that they had a plot to kill all the important leaders of the Young Men's League, so the League sent them warnings to leave Guangzhou within a week.

THE "RED MONK" FALLS IN LOVE

From the winter of 1925 to the end of 1927, Kim Chung-chang and I worked together closely in Guangzhou in journalism and in the leadership of the Young Men's League and the communist movement. Then, when the famous Korean terrorist Oh Seong-ryun arrived in Guangzhou in the winter of 1926 from Moscow, where he had become a communist, he joined with us, and we three became intimate friends. Oh came to live with me in the little inn where I stayed. Kim was our political theoretician, Oh was the man of action, and I was their young disciple in all things. I was then twenty-two, Oh about thirty-seven, and Kim thirty-two. I was their "open leader"; they were the power behind the scene.

Oh taught Russian to a military class at the Huangpu Academy. He also wrote essays on the class struggle and national problems and gave talks about the U.S.S.R. He hated poetry and thought I was very youthful because I wrote it sometimes, but, like me, he loved sad things, though he never showed any emotion. He became a member of the KK and was elected to the central committee of the Young Men's League.

In the late summer of 1927 Kim Chung-chang fell helplessly in love, his first love and a very tender one. The girl was a beautiful Guangzhou student[109] at Zhongshan University, very modern and bourgeois. Kim felt that Oh and I considered him a traitor, but he could do nothing about it.

"When you fall in love, it will be a worse case than mine," he said to me, groaning. "You see what happens to a man who has been a monk. It is irrevocable."

Oh and I kept hoping that this love would cure itself, according to Kim's previous diagnosis in Beijing, but it showed no sign of abating.

Kim continued to work as hard as ever, but his enemies accused him of being romantic. Every day he went with his girl to the park at the Place of the Seventy-Two Martyrs.[110] Every single one of his friends wanted him to cut off this girl except myself. I supported him in his "nonsense" and helped the lovers however I could. "A revolutionary is also a man, a human being," I retorted to those who criticized Kim. "Anyway, it will pass. You are all jealous because no girl is in love with you."

I decided that the solution was for the girl to go to Tokyo to school. She and Kim agreed to this, and she went to Japan. But she wrote to her lover every day and after three months was back again—Kim had not replied to her letters for three weeks.

When she could not find Kim in Guangzhou she came to me, greatly alarmed. "He is in Wuhan," I said. "But keep this secret. He will return in a month." Then she wanted to go to Wuhan.

I really envied Kim's happy love affair, though I regretted that the girl was not a real revolutionary. My opinion on the marriage problem changed to read: Love is all right but only with the ideal girl. Kim's girl tried hard to convert me to marriage and introduced many of her friends to me, but I did not like any of them. I taught German to a Korean girl student in medical school in Guangzhou, but when Kim and Oh made the remark that I was falling in love with her, I cut off the lessons immediately.

I MEET BORODIN, TOM MANN, AND EARL BROWDER

In Guangzhou I met all the foreigners* who came to show solidarity with the Chinese Revolution. They were very friendly to the Koreans especially, as we were volunteers, too. I loved "old Tom Man," as we called him. Oh and Kim and I and eight others had our pictures taken with him.

Earl Browder from America was there for a short time too. He looked like a scholar, but his speeches were easy to understand. He talked against American imperialism, and everyone liked him very much.

Borodin I had met earlier. He was middle-aged and stout and did not look like a revolutionary type to us Orientals, accustomed only to fiery youth in the communist movement. But he had a slow, quiet method of organizing things that commanded confidence, and we felt that he had his feet solidly on the ground and admired his grasp of theory and tactics. He was like a rock in a wild sea of

---

* *all the foreigners*: A delegation of the Comintern that included Earl Browder [1891-1973], Jacques Doriot [1898-1945], and Thomas Mann [1856-1941] (the British labor leader, not the German author) arrived in Guangzhou on February 16, 1927 and were welcomed by Chiang Kai-shek and Li Jishen of the GMD. They traveled with the Northern Expedition, arriving in Hankou on March 31, 1927, just before the counterrevolution of Chiang Kai-shek. Mann was one of the most influential labor leaders of his era. Browder was the head of the American Communist Party during World War II. Doriot, a French communist, later became a fascist. –NW

inexperienced youth and enthusiasm.

We took photographs of everyone and were very happy to have so much international solidarity in evidence. A very good communist from Indo-China, educated in France, also came. In 1926 we had organized the "The Oriental League of Oppressed Peoples,"[111] which included the Korean Young Men's League, the Indo-Chinese Nationalist Party, Formosans,* and individual Indians. This organization held a congress. When the Taiwanese delegates returned to their island they were arrested by the Japanese, including Lin Sunji,[112] who is still in prison. He had organized the "Proletarian-Peasant Emancipation League" in Taiwan. In Taiwan then there were many anarchists and communists, and they had a good relation with us Koreans, because we had the same master, Japan. At that time all Oriental revolutionary groups had good relations, but this is not true today.

THE NORTHERN EXPEDITION

The Korean volunteers were noted for their bravery and leadership during the Northern Expedition to crush the warlords. Every Chinese general begged them to join his troops. Most of the Koreans were with Zhang Fakui's "Ironsides," the best army of all.** Others were with Zhu Peide and with Cheng Qian's Sixth Army when it captured Nanjing. The secret of the brilliant success of the Northern Expedition lay in good political work, and Koreans were usually active in this.

---

* *Formosans*: i.e. Taiwanese. –DH

** *"Ironsides," the best army of all*: Here, Kim San is referring to the 12th Division of the NRA's Fourth Army, commanded by Zhang Fakui, which became known for its fighting prowess in part due to its victory in two strategic battles near the Wuhan area in central China during the Northern Expedition. The name "Ironsides" has also been used by Chinese Communists to refer to the Independent Unit of the same Army, commanded by Ye Ting. –DH

It is difficult for me now even to remember the exhilaration and high enthusiasm that all revolutionaries felt during the triumphant onward sweep of the Northern Expedition, which reached the Yangzi valley within six months. On to north China and Korea—our hearts exulted! "Twenty million Koreans are waiting at home and in Manchuria to take up arms against imperialism for the freedom of all Asia," we told the Chinese confidently.

NRA troops during the Northern Expedition

Then came the counterrevolution led by Chiang Kai-shek on the right, and the split between the communists and the Guomindang,* just at the crest of victory when success was within sight. Not only was China split open, the revolution broken, and Korea, Russia, Japan, and other nations split off from revolutionary solidarity, but every individual revolutionary felt himself riven asunder by the

---

* *the split between the communists and the Guomindang:* Part of the strategy of the Northern Expedition was to take control of the great city of Shanghai, a center of wealth and power. This was to be done by coordinating an uprising within Shanghai with an attack from outside the city. Inside Shanghai, the Communists, working with the labor unions, organized an uprising. The troops outside the city were under the control of Chiang Kai-shek. Chiang's decision to turn against his allies, the Communists, was consummated when he gave orders on April 12, 1927 (see note on p. 29) to round up and execute "communists" or or anyone who might be under their influence, leading to what is commonly known as the April 12th Coup ("Shanghai Massacre"). –GT

shock. We Koreans saw a black cloud cover the horizon of our own revolution and could foresee no future moment when it might be dispersed.

When the reactionary Nanjing regime was set up by Chiang Kai-shek against the leftist Wuhan government,* every Korean immediately left the rightist forces and went to Wuhan to support the left.

After the Wuhan government fell, what remained of our Korean group scattered. One hundred of us stayed in Guangzhou to aid in the future recapture of revolutionary sovereignty there. A few in the right wing gave up hope after the Guomindang reaction and returned to Korea or Manchuria. By the end of 1927, two hundred had reassembled in Guangzhou to fight in the Commune.

APRIL 15 IN GUANGZHOU AND AN EXECUTION

I did not leave Guangzhou during the whole 1925-1927 period. On April 15, 1927, three days after Chiang Kai-shek's order for the massacre of the factory workers in Shanghai,[113] the reactionaries in Guangzhou started their "purge." All the workers were disarmed and many arrested. Twenty Koreans were sent to military prison, including communists in the army and in military schools. Only six were in the prison when we opened it during the Commune. All the rest had been executed.

On April 18 I witnessed an incident that made a deep

---

* *the reactionary Nanjing regime was set up...against the Wuhan government*: After the NRA took Wuhan in October 1926, the National Government, which had been in Guangzhou, decided to transfer its capital there. Chiang Kai-shek was opposed to this, fearing that the government would come under the control of Chinese Communists and those GMD leftists who supported the maintenance of the United Front with the communists. This brought about a conflict between the Wuhan government, which was under the control of GMD leftists/CCP, and the government in Nanjing, which Chiang set up in opposition to his political rivals in Wuhan. The conflict came to an end after the coup orchestrated by Chiang on April 12, 1927 (see note on p. 29) and the subsequent decision in July of that year by GMD leftists in Wuhan to split with the Communists. –DH

impression on me. Three Chinese members of the Communist Youth were publicly executed, a girl of sixteen and two boys, twenty-one and twenty-two. They were bound and carried through the streets in rickshaws to be shown to the population before being taken to the

Communists under arrest in Shanghai in 1927

execution ground. Four hundred soldiers followed the rickshaws, and I followed the procession

All three were workers, but they looked like students. They had fine, intelligent faces. The girl, Luo Liumei, was very pretty, with short bobbed hair, thick and glossy black. They had been arrested and condemned to death for doing propaganda work and passing out handbills for the general strike that was being prepared.

The three sang the song of the Communist Youth "Internationale" as they were carried through the streets. They were brave and poised. I never hear that song now without thinking of them.

Hundreds of people followed to the execution grounds, but nobody cried but myself. Tears streamed down my face as I ran along the street, and I didn't care whether the police arrested me as a sympathizer or not. I was very excited because I could do nothing to help them and angry at the callous attitude of the curious spectators. They seemed to think it only a form of amusement. "I can't live in this cruel country," I said to myself. "I can't. I can't. These people are not human."

Suspected communists being rounded up by the GMD in 1927

When the rickshaws stopped, it was three o'clock. The heavy chains were taken off the prisoners, and they walked slowly to the place of execution. One boy's shoe fell off, and he reached down to put it back on, taking a long time to do it. "He wants to live a few seconds longer," I thought as I watched.

All three were calm. You could tell that they were afraid and yet not afraid to die. When they reached the death spot they shouted slogans as ten soldiers lined up to shoot: "Overthrow imperialism and the Guomindang! Long live the Chinese Revolution! Strike down Chiang Kai--."

In the middle of the last slogan they were shot by rifles

not five feet away.

I went up to the bodies and saw tears in the glazing eyes of these brave young people. I stood there for a minute and whispered to them: "I will finish your last sentence: Strike down Chiang Kai-shek!"

I went home afterward and wrote a symbolical poem about having seen myself reflected in the tears in Luo Liumei's eyes after death. I called it "Humanity at Dongjiaochang!"[114]

From April 15 to 18 in Guangzhou many communist and mass organizations were broken up by the reactionaries, and many were arrested to prevent a general strike. The whole leadership of the Workers' Association was arrested, and at Zhongshan University three hundred were taken. Only the three were executed in the public square, but many others were killed secretly. From April 15 to the time of the Guangzhou Commune in December we had the record of the execution of two hundred students of Zhongshan University alone.

Communist sympathizer arrested by the GMD

During those dark days, I saw men sending their personal enemies to death, testifying that they were members of the Communist Party.

GUANGZHOU PREPARES

After the fall of the Wuhan government, the leftist elements gathered forces, and, on August 1, 1927, two communist "Ironsides" commanders led the Nanchang Uprising in Jiangxi Province[115] and started marching south to recapture Guangdong Province as a base for the future revolutionary movement. We waited eagerly for news. This new Red Army was almost annihilated near Guangzhou. In spite of this defeat, it was decided to carry out the uprising in Guangzhou and take the city. Nearby Peng Pai had already organized the first soviet in China, and we were depending upon this peasant movement for support.

General Li Jishen had been in control of Guangzhou since 1926. Now General Zhang Fakui had arrived in the city and was planning to oust Li Jishen from power. On November 17, Zhang Fakui carried out his coup, and civil war between the two armies was imminent. The Communist Party decided to carry out the insurrection as soon as possible to take advantage of the disrupted situation.

Zhang Fakui had brought the Special Training Regiment, made up mostly of radical cadets from the Wuhan Military and Political Academy. This was under communist influence and was to be the backbone of the uprising. Of the two thousand troops in the Special Training Regiment, eighty were our Korean comrades.

Every Korean in Guangzhou joined the Commune uprising except for four women and ten persons who were old residents, and we estimated that we numbered two hundred.

When action began on the night of December 10, the

Koreans from the Academy and from Zhang Fakui's troops* gathered secretly and began the armed struggle, together with the Special Training Regiment. The next morning all the Korean students at Zhongshan University also came to join the fighting.

---

* *Zhang Fakui's troops*: i.e. the communist-influenced "radical cadets" within Zhang Fakui's troops. This is not meant to imply that Zhang Fakui was himself sympathetic to the Guangzhou Uprising. –DH

CHAPTER 11

The Guangzhou Commune

THAT EVENING of December 10, 1927, was one of the most eventful of my life. In my little inn we had a secret meeting of twenty Koreans. Oh Seong-ryun, the famous sharpshooter, was fondling a new pistol as he drowned it in oil. We drew close together in tense expectation, jubilant at the thought of the great mass struggle about to begin. We talked about the chances for success and of how to keep power once we had secured it.

We never mentioned that any of us might be killed within the next few hours but spoke only of how to destroy the enemy. Oh gave us instructions about the handling of a gun.

As we thought of Korea, our hearts leaped forward to tomorrow, for we felt this battle was in defense of our own people too.

Oh and I and a Korean artillery expert named Yang Dal-bu started out for the Special Training Regiment headquarters, which was to be the first center of action. The sentries there had not yet been overpowered, and we had to climb secretly over a wall. It was a dark, moonless night....

Inside the headquarters we found that the leaders of the uprising had just arrived: Ye Ting, fresh from his defeat in the provinces; Zhang Tailei, the famous Communist Youth leader; as well as Xu Guangying and Yun Daiying.

Nearly two thousand cadets stood around, talking in groups, ready for the signal to start.

Twenty or thirty Rightists had already been gagged and bound and placed in one room with a sentry on guard.

We three soon found ourselves surrounded by sixty-seven Korean comrades, including the three Bak brothers. They put their arms around us and welcomed us warmly. I could not speak, so deep was my feeling for the historic moment. I was happy and heavy-throated at the same time.

Zhang Tailei stood on a table and talked to us: "Comrades, tonight we put an end to the old history. Tonight we conquer the last icy mountain in our path forward."

Ye Ting also made a speech and read off the names of the cadets participating. Each group elected its leaders, and the names of the Revolutionary Committee were announced.

Ye Yong was elected as the new commander of the Special Training Regiment, and Yi Yong, a Korean graduate from the Red Academy in Moscow, was appointed by the Communist Party to be Ye Yong's military and political adviser, or Chief of Staff.

In all branches of work, Koreans were put into responsible positions because they were more experienced and many had had good political and military training in Moscow. They acted as a network of Party agents during the Commune, though many Chinese did not know they were Koreans.

The name of the Special Training Regiment was changed to the "Red Army," and several big red flags were brought out to be carried during the uprising.

Ye Ting then gave orders, telling each unit where to go and how to disarm the enemy troops. He was Commander-in-Chief of all the armed forces and head of the Revolutionary Committee in charge of the uprising.

It was necessary to capture the headquarters of the enemy commander, the arsenal, and the artillery station and to disarm the troops guarding the various parts of the city. The workers were to disarm the police and capture the police station. The enemy troops inside the city were much larger than our armed forces, while at Henan, across the Pearl River on the outskirts, were seven of Li Fulin's regiments. Our main forces were only the two thousand cadets and new volunteers of the Special Training Regiment and two thousand armed workers, aside from the soldiers who came over to us from the enemy. We were also depending upon the arrival of peasant detachments from the Dongjiang region, which never came.*

Silence fell over us as the men talked quietly in little groups. Soon we heard the rumbling of many trucks and motorcars at the gate of the compound, bringing the armed factory workers. Then we started out on our various missions.

---

* *peasant detachments...which never came*: The odds against the uprising of December 10, 1927, were heavy. According to one report, in addition to the regiments across the Pearl River, there were five thousand enemy soldiers, one thousand policemen, and one thousand armed gangsters in Guangzhou city. Two days' march away, in the West River district, were about fifty thousand of Zhang Fakui's and Li Jishen's troops. There were also several Chinese and foreign gunboats on the Pearl River, which might be expected to intervene, if necessary, under the excuse of defending Shamian, the foreign concession [known among the foreigners as Shameen]. According to this same report, the armed participants in the Commune did not exceed 4,200. Kim San's story places this at a higher figure, however: two thousand in the Special Training Regiment, two thousand armed workers, and at least two hundred deserters from Dongbei [a region in China's northeast], while four thousand captured rifles were given out while he was in the Department for Arming the Workers (a figure that presumably includes the two thousand given to the workers listed above). As seen from his story, however, two thousand Dongbei soldiers submitted to the revolutionaries without resistance. —NW

ENCOUNTERS WITH THE ENEMY

Oh Seong-ryun and Bak Jin and his two brothers climbed into a truck with the detachment whose duty was to arrest Zhang Fakui and his staff. They surprised the headquarters staff, but General Zhang himself escaped to Lingnan University in his nightclothes and from there into Li Fulin's lines across the Pearl River. Chen Gongbo and Huang Qixiang escaped in the same way.

I went in a car with the Korean named Yang Dal-bu, who was attached to another unit which was detailed to capture Shahe, the big artillery station about ten li away. Yang and a Chinese were in command of this expedition. Yang had gone to school in Moscow and was a fine military man as well as a good secret communist organizer. He was a famous artillery expert, much respected by Zhang Fakui and other Chinese commanders. He had been in charge of Zhang Fakui's artillery during the fighting in Henan Province and had reorganized the whole artillery unit captured from Zhang Xueliang at that time. He did not speak Chinese very well, and I was to act as his interpreter when necessary.

At a distance of six hundred meters the motors were stopped and we moved forward with our guns and swords ready. We had from two hundred to three hundred men, while the enemy post was made up of two tuan, or two thousand soldiers.

We surrounded the post and stood at attention near every door and room. Nobody could fire without orders. When the order came we fired, killing only thirty men. The station soldiers fired in response, but not one of our men was killed. The commander of the post came out and said, "It's no use to fire. Wait!"

Yang knew the commander well and talked with him. This post commander was bound and his men disarmed. The captured rifles were put into the cars and some big guns were dismantled and carried away, while others were brought on their carriages.

Yang knew the mutinous temper of the captured men and that they were not anxious to do any fighting for Zhang Fakui, so he said, "Only fifty men are enough to guard the prisoners. The rest of you must hurry back to the city to help in the capture of Zhang Fakui's headquarters."

The two thousand men were ordered to march back to the city as prisoners, moving slowly along with the big guns. We left our guard of fifty men and went on to other duties.

Yang and I and the leader of our detachment got into a small car and raced back to the city. It was four o'clock in the morning when we arrived. There was intermittent firing, but generally silence over the city.

When we reached the headquarters of the Revolutionary Committee to report, Ye Ting was there and also Heinz Neumann, the German communist,* who didn't know any Chinese. He was the only Occidental foreigner in the Commune. The Soviet consul did not participate in any way.

The police station had been occupied and turned into headquarters for the Revolutionary Committee. The

---

* *Heinz Neumann, the German communist*: Representative from the Comintern in China who wrote under the name "A. Neuberg." He arrived in Guangzhou in 1927 before the Guangzhou Commune, which he directed. He escaped before the debacle when about 5,700 of the Chinese participants were killed. In 1938 in Shanghai he came to call on Edgar Snow. He was very handsome, with direct, blue eyes, and was arrogant in manner. He was not only rude, but hostile, and explained that he was attacking Edgar Snow's *Red Star Over China*. He wrote under the name "Asiaticus" for *Pacific Affairs* and set himself the job of trying to demolish the book. He made the long trip to Yan'an to interview Mao Zedong; he began by attacking Edgar Snow, and Mao did not listen for long. Mao became angry and said: "We know all about Snow; we know he is not a communist; but he was the first to come here to get the news. We also know all about you and your activities. You are wrong to criticize Snow and his book." Mao ordered Neumann to leave Yan'an immediately; Neumann was attacking Mao's policies indirectly by way of Edgar Snow's book and Mao sensed this. Neumann went to the communist New Fourth Army headquarters and there he disappeared, apparently killed, or dead of disease. He was certainly a frightening character, unscrupulous and pitiless in all ways. –NW

workers had been most active in this place, overpowering and disarming the police one by one.

As we reported, a line was drawn on the big map in front of Ye Ting, showing the points taken.

Ye Ting

We went out into the compound of the police station to wait for the arrival of the two thousand prisoners. They appeared at five o'clock and sat down in the street, as the big guns came up in the rear.

"At least we have a few big guns," Yang remarked with satisfaction. He took a flashlight and went out into the street to talk with the captured soldiers, asking them if they recognized him. Yang chose two hundred reliable men whom he knew. They were given guns and ammunition to join in the insurrection.

After this we set out in motorcars for Zhang Fakui's headquarters, which was guarded by the enemy Twelfth Division. By this time every main strategic point on the campaign map had been occupied except this.

General Li Jishen's big house was near the Twelfth Division. As we approached this, Yang said:

"There are many good new guns inside there, just brought from Czechoslovakia on German ships. We must quickly occupy this place and get hold of them."

We tried to take the position by assault. It was well defended, however, and we had to retreat after losing some of our men in the street. Yang and I got into the car again and started back for reinforcements. Just outside this street our two hundred re-armed recruits were awaiting orders.

"Do you men want to join the fight now?" Yang asked them, as I interpreted for him.

"Yes," they all shouted.

"We want all two thousand of you people to volunteer," Yang continued. "But we have not enough guns to give the rest. When we capture guns, both your regiments can fight with us. Come and help us get them."

The rest of the two thousand prisoners were waiting on another street nearby, and they were glad to hear about the invitation.

We drove back to the fighting with the Twelfth Divi-sion, hidden from rifle fire by rice sacks in the windows of the car. The enemy was shooting at us from the gate, and Yang and I stayed at the entrance while thirty men took hand grenades and threw them into the first room of the head-quarters. The enemy retreated but started to throw bombs from the top story, which was very dangerous for us.

"Come back! You'll all be killed," Yang shouted. "Come back into the street again."

We had seven cars in the street and hid behind them as the firing continued back and forth. We retreated again but held both ends of the street.

The enemy took up a machine-gun position in a side street, which swept the main street ahead with bullets. We could not cross this line of fire, so we went back. Yang decided to bring up the big artillery for attack. We went to headquarters, and Ye Ting agreed but said, "Don't harm the houses nearby when you fire."

"All the buildings are close together. We can't avoid hitting some others, I'm afraid," Yang stated, "but I'll try."

Some of the two thousand prisoners pulled one big gun and five shells along the street. When we got back to the scene of action, we sent a letter to our men at the far end of the street to leave in order to escape our fire. By now it was clear dawn. We could see that Li Jishen's house was just in front, and behind it the Twelfth Division head-quarters. Yang saw that it would be impossible to fire only on Li's house and the headquarters. So the German, Heinz

Neumann, came over to discuss the matter.

"Never mind the other houses. Fire!" was his decision.

Yang's first shell tore down the top story of Li Jishen's house, leaving the way clear for a shot at the Twelfth Division. His second shot missed the Twelfth Division, but landed very close by. The third struck the second floor of the Twelfth Division headquarters.

Our troops were then prepared to rush the Twelfth Division and took all the machine guns in the small side street. In the meantime, however, another unit had made a mistake. They had used benzene flamethrowers around the headquarters, and our men could not get through the fire to enter the building. By seven o'clock we had occupied every nearby place except this Twelfth Division headquarters. The surrounding buildings were burning.

The revolution was now in control of all important districts within the city, with the exception of this headquarters, which was near the river. The Henan district across the river was in possession of Li Fulin's seven enemy regiments. No troops had been sent against him when we began action. The enemy troops remaining in Guangzhou who had not been disarmed were only this Twelfth Division and the few soldiers of Zhang Fakui's headquarters staff, together with Li Fulin's seven regiments, and the new Second Division of three thousand men, which had run away to the country at the mountain village of Guanyishan. In the West River areas not so far away were concentrated thousands of troops, which had been recently engaged in the fighting between Zhang Fakui and Li Jishen.

At seven-thirty Yang and I went back to headquarters. Yang was given command of the Artillery Division, made up entirely of the captured soldiers except for some Koreans to strengthen it; and I was given a post in the "Department for Arming the Workers and Peasants."

BY THE WILL OF THE PEOPLE

At nine o'clock a mass meeting of about thirty thousand people with big red flags waving was held to elect a soviet government. I was there. Most of those who came were workmen. A few soldiers who happened not to be fighting at the front participated. There were a great many students and a few spectators, mainly merchants. I saw a sprinkling of girl workers. Those present were all happy and excited. We sang the Internationale and shouted slogans—though the slogans were not spontaneous but initiated by the leaders.

I walked over and stood on the spot where the three Communist Youth victims had been executed several months before and shouted my slogan for them. "Strike Down Chiang Kai-shek!" My pledge to the dead was fulfilled.

The meeting elected eleven officers as a soviet government; the Chairman of the new soviet to be was Su Zhaozheng, a Guangzhou worker who had led the Hong Kong strike in 1925.[116] He was not present at the meeting, as he had left for Dongjiang to organize an army of farmers to rush to Guangzhou and join the workers' uprising. These farmers never came, as they could not arrive in time, and Su had sent a telegram explaining all this. Su Zhaozheng was a good labor leader, and all the Guangzhou workers were his loyal followers.

The slogans of the Commune meeting were: "Land to the Farmers!" "Food to the Poor and the Workers!" "Peace for the Soldiers!"

The program adopted was this: For the workers: an eight-hour

Su Zhaozheng

day, good labor laws, unemployment insurance, and reform of labor conditions; for the peasants and soldiers: land, to secure which all the landlords' land was to be redistributed; for the poor men: guarantee of enough food to eat; for the women: guarantee of the same wages and same legal status as men. There were ten or eleven points, embodying the same principles decided upon by the Sixth Congress of the Comintern.[117]

It was to be a "Workers' and Peasants' Democratic Dictatorship." The "Soviet Government" had its title, but the work was, of necessity, very poor. There was no time to organize soviets of workers, peasants and soldiers, so this was not done.

THREE DAYS

After the mass meeting I took up my duties in the Department for Arming the Peasants and Workers (though no peasants arrived). There were seven of us in charge of distributing arms, of whom I was the only Korean. All guns had to be captured from the enemy troops, and during three days we were able to give out only four thousand. These were insufficient, but we could not get more because we could not occupy the Twelfth Division headquarters where the new arms were kept. Our people had occupied the arsenal, but nobody knew it, as they didn't get communications through in time.

We did not separate the good guns from the inferior ones but let each volunteer choose his own weapon. On the second day, however, I gave the good guns only to the workers connected with the Strike Committee.

The workers gladly joined the uprising, and after the mass meeting hundreds came to the government to ask for arms. A few pounced upon the guns as a new possession and took them home to keep instead of using them to defend the Commune.

Before the uprising it had been estimated that six thousand armed workers could be mobilized, but actually we had less than two thousand. This armed force was called the "Self-Protection Troops" or the "Red Self-Protection Forces."[118]

On the night of the tenth, when the workers had been led by their own leaders, their action had been excellent. On the eleventh, however, the military were put in command, and the workers did not know how to follow their commands and had confidence only in their old leaders. Some even deserted the armed struggle because of this.

After the initial action, when peace and order were restored, the workers saw nothing further to be done, so most of them went back to their homes. This is the common failing of a spontaneous mass army. They forgot that the enemy was quietly biding its time nearby to retake the city unaware.

During the Commune I learned the bitter lesson that the Party must never be a brake on the mass movement. A mass uprising must succeed, no matter how many may be sacrificed on either side. If we do not destroy the enemy, the enemy will annihilate us. To fail is death for all who participate.

This was a mistake of the Commune. On the morning of the eleventh, orders were given to workers not to kill any of the population but only to arrest some reactionaries and bring them for trial.

Less than one hundred persons were killed by the revolutionaries during the whole Commune. Only thirty of the worst reactionaries brought before the Revolutionary Committee for trial were executed. These were all Guomindang officials. No merchants were killed and no rich men, though some were arrested by the workers who had been oppressed by them. Only three women were killed in the street fighting, and these were brought to the government office for identification. I saw a ragged little boy beating the head of one of these dead women with a stone. He was probably a child-slave and she his cruel mistress, I thought.

Had the workers not kept discipline they could easily have eliminated their enemies, but they stood by their orders not to kill private individuals. Contrast such generosity and discipline with the orgy of brutality indulged in by the Reaction three days later, when nearly seven thousand were killed! All during the period of revolutionary sovereignty the city was calm and peaceful.

There were only sixty prisoners in the police station when we retreated on the thirteenth, and not one had been mistreated. As soon as they were freed they got arms and went out into the streets, killing every poor man they could find.

How many soldiers were killed in the fighting at the front was never reported, but it could not have been more than a few hundred, as most of the enemy troops ran away or submitted to being disarmed.

During the Commune there was no student struggle. They did not actually participate either in the mass movement or in the armed struggle, but some of them took guns as ornaments and patrolled the streets. Intellectuals in China usually try to preserve themselves for future reference after the fighting is over. Their attitude of self-preservation annoyed me, and when about fifty Communist Party and Communist Youth intellectuals came to ask for guns, I said to Zhang Tailei: "It's no use giving guns to these people just for ornamentation. We have enough only for real fighters."

Only about fifty individual Communist Party and Communist Youth intellectuals were armed during the Commune. They were incompetent even at trying to arrest people, and exposed themselves in the most dangerous way. When the Reaction came, they ran into houses to hide, where they could be easily surrounded and killed by the enemy. A soldier always runs into the open to escape. Many students and girls were anxious to help, but we had made no provision to utilize them correctly.

A few reactionary students were killed as spies and traitors by the Special Training Regiment during the Commune. The Special Training Regiment itself, of course, was made up, not of professional soldiers, but of student cadets, many of them intellectuals.

❖

Those who showed up best in the struggle were comrades with previous experience in arms and those well grounded in the revolutionary idea. The Workers' Strike Committee did the best work among the civilians and carried on heroically. No women fought in the Commune. But the nurses particularly distinguished themselves.*

None of us had time to eat anything until the evening of the eleventh. On that night I went with Yang and Oh,

---

* *the nurses particularly distinguished themselves*: Because of their devotion to revolutionary work during the Commune, many nurses were treated shamefully by the [GMD's] Reaction when it began. Some died in the streets during the White Terror. Ten of the nurses were arrested in the hospital, stripped naked, and led out into the streets for the public to see, then ordered tortured to death. Their breasts were cut off and their bodies mutilated. This was done by direct order of the GMD authorities, who showed uncompromising, vengeful cruelty. The GMD people were much more cruel than the soldiers. Civilians were given a free hand to kill whomever they desired, and it was they who committed the atrocities. One doctor and several women nurses went with the Special Training Regiment to Hailufeng. Another doctor in the Fourth Army hospital during the Commune, He Zhongmin, came to Yan'an in 1937 to join the Soviet Health Department. –KS

my Korean friends, to the police station, where we found a big jar of wine and cooked a chicken. We invited Heinz Neumann to eat with us. On the night of the twelfth when we went to headquarters to look at the map we saw no change in the situation. The Twelfth Division had not yet been taken. Neither had the Staff Headquarters, nor Henan on the south of the Pearl River.

During the whole silent day all homes had been closed, and only the small food shops were open. I stayed on duty at my department, but the guns had all been given out and I had nothing to do. In the afternoon I went alone to the Fourth Army hospital, where the head doctor was a classmate of mine from Beijing Union Medical College. I had seen the wounded returning from the front with no doctors or nurses to care for them, so decided on my own initiative to win over the nurses for our side. At the hospital I gave a talk to the staff and asked them to vote. All volunteered to join the revolution. I took my friend, Dr. Zhong Ying, to Ye Ting and Zhang Tailei to introduce him and arrange to organize a hospital for the wounded.[119]

Several of us volunteered to help the food department, taking a motorcar around to confiscate rice from the merchants. They gave what we asked, and we took our "gifts" back to aid the fighters. On the way I saw a camera in a big store and suddenly realized we needed pictures to commemorate the Commune. So I went in and asked for it. I think I am the only one who took pictures then. I never saw or heard of any others. But I could not get them printed, so all were lost.

Yang went to the telephone office and the electric light company to organize the workers there and found they were not opposed to the soviet. The Commune got good support from all the workers as soon as they learned the meaning of it, but it took them by surprise.

Yang and Oh and I got into a motorcar in the evening

and went through the streets, giving the password* as we were challenged by the sentries. Yang was very worried because there had been no advance all day, and he felt that Ye Ting was not fully conscious of the terrible consequences which would inevitably result from failure to succeed, for there was no preparation for retreat.

"We Koreans will all be killed," Yang said. "We are too enthusiastic. We are prepared to sacrifice everything. We only know how to march to the front, not how to retreat and save ourselves."

Late that night we Koreans came together to ask who had been killed and wounded and what action had been taken by our Korean group. One of our best Party men, Yi Bin, was dead.**

---

* *giving the password*: The password on the night of the 10th was "baodong" or "armed uprising." On the eleventh it was "suqing" or "clean up." On the 12th it was "Xianggang" or "Hong Kong," which had no meaning except accidentally, as a symbol of running away to Hong Kong, which many did. —KS

** *One of our best party men, Yi Bin*: [A graduate of the Huangpu Military Academy,] Yi Bin [1902-1927] was a good artilleryman who participated in the capture of the airdrome during the Commune. There were ten planes there, but only five were good. We had not a single aviator among us. The Chinese asked the Koreans to supply one, but we had nobody. Yi Bin died near Shamian on the 12th, at the age of twenty-five, while fighting a Japanese gunboat. There were two Japanese gunboats in the Pearl River at Shamian, and on the 12th one of them fired on our lines with machine guns. The Koreans were all very angry and rushed to the bund to fight our old enemy. Yi Bin and Yang Dal-bu and another Korean comrade, Yi Yong, set the artillery up immediately and destroyed the smokestack on the Japanese gunboat with only three shells. The Japanese got scared; lowering their flag quickly, they steamed out of the river. They never came back.

Shamian [commonly known by foreigners as Shameen] is a little island in the Pearl River, only a stone's throw from the Guangzhou bund. It is a foreign concession, where most of the foreigners have their residences. A British warship was anchored there, and some marines landed from the ship and took up their positions behind sandbag barricades, ready to fire, but we did not care. The Central Committee debated whether or not to occupy Shamian and decided not to molest it.

Two other Koreans who had done good work were Kim Hyeong-pyeong, a graduate of the Red Academy in Moscow, and Mun Seon-jae. Both had been officers in the enemy Jingweituan, a newly organized city "protection corps" of two regiments under Zhang Fakui. Mun was a brigade commander. All alone, with his own political work, Mun had persuaded one whole regiment of this corps to turn over to the revolution. Then Kim Hyeong-pyeong helped him reorganize and consolidate these new recruits. Another was a Korean named Yi who had brought about the surrender of the arsenal. Zhang Fakui had only two companies on guard at the arsenal, of which Yi was a lower officer. Yi organized

We got no sleep until the 13th, except for occasional table napping, and were in a state of increasing tension.

On the 13th the Korean Young Men's League held a meeting at Zhongshan University. I was chairman, and Yang and Oh and Kim made speeches. There were twenty present. We decided that we had not been very scientific in our action and that we must take better responsibility for leading all Korean comrades. We arranged to have a motorcycle for common use. We decided who should stay in Guangzhou if the uprising failed, and who should leave. Yang and Oh and I would go with the troops in event of failure.

❖

A sense of failure crept up like a low-lying fog. The Communist Party had very poor organization then and called no meetings or demonstrations. Even on the 13th Zhang Tailei had said to Kim, "Never worry about failing. Think only of winning." He had no preparation whatsoever for retreat—and that was the reason for the great debacle when it came.

Shortly before six o'clock on the 13th I went back to the Department for Arming the Workers. Some Korean comrades reported that Ye Ting had gone to the headquarters at the police station and changed to civilian dress.

---

a secret political movement, arrested all bad elements, and led the whole two companies to join the Commune, so the arsenal was given up without a fight. Yi and his men occupied a factory outside the city after this, but were cut off. They held this place until the 17th, when every man was killed. –KS

[I have been unable to identify the person referred to as Kim Hyeong-pyeong. In the first and second editions, his name was spelled as Kim Ping-hen, and in a Korean edition of this book, Kim Bin-hyeon. Here I have chosen to spell his name as "Kim Hyeong-pyeong," following the lead of MI. Mun Seon-jae's name was spelled in the first and second editions as Meng Sun-tsai. The person being referred to here is possibly Mun Seon-jae, a graduate of the Huangpu Military Academy who had a specialization in political work. –DH (HJS, 539, 585)]

When someone tried to find Zhang Tailei, others said, "No matter—he must have gone to the front."

At headquarters we could find nobody in authority except Yun Daiying, the Secretary of the government. Even Heinz Neumann was gone. When we asked Yun what conditions were like, he merely repeated our question to us. No other important men were left of the Communist Party committee.

About six o'clock Xu Guangying came to headquarters while we were there and ordered everyone to go to Huang-huagang, to the Place of the Seventy-Two Martyrs. He said the British warships[120] were preparing to fire to help Li Fulin and that the British consul had told Li Fulin he could settle the whole thing in twenty-four hours and would then turn the place over to Li. The British troops had already crossed over to Chinese territory from the concession in Shamian, and the Japanese had also landed in the city.

Oh and I went together to Zhongshan University to find our comrades, but could discover nobody. Returning to headquarters we found Yang waiting for us. Then I went to find Kim Chung-chang. I wanted Kim to leave with me and go outside the city with the Special Training Regiment. He wanted me to stay with him and try to hide in his Chinese sweetheart's home. "Go or stay, we must die anyway," we said. We were depressed and unhappy, but I saw that Kim was not so unhappy at parting as I was. "You still have a sweetheart," I said as I left him.

RETREAT TO HAILUFENG

Oh and I went together to the Place of the Seventy-Two Martyrs. Many cars were headed there with men hanging on the sides. There we waited awhile. No important leaders were present except Ye Yong, commander of the Special Training Regiment, and his own regiment.

At seven o'clock we marched with the Special Training Regiment to Daguling Mountain. Next morning we moved on to the town of Panyu. Two thousand tired, confused marchers we were—none had really slept for four nights, and we had hardly enough food to keep ourselves alive. Only a handful of workers had retreated with the Special Training Regiment.

We marched on. Upon reaching Hua Xian* on the night of the 14th, a meeting was held at which Ye Yong said we would stay there to await orders from the Guangdong Provincial Committee and prepare to occupy Guangzhou again. We slept in the xian government compound, and heard mintuan** firing outside the wall. Still no orders from the committee....

By the afternoon of the 15th no news had come, so in the evening we left for Conghua Xian. Next morning at ten o'clock, as we crossed a mountain, we were attacked by mintuan with machine guns. We counterattacked at a run, and the enemy retreated.

Conghua Xian was sympathetic. Even the Merchants' Association sent a delegate to welcome us because they were afraid. They had incense burning before the gods of welcome and firecrackers popping.

We took time here to make a new red flag—we had forgotten to take one from Guangzhou. At a meeting it was decided to go to the Hailufeng Soviet, as there was still no letter from the committee.[121]

We had left Guangzhou on the 13th of December and arrived in Hailufeng on January 7, 1928. During this march we had no important fighting, but we openly asked people

---

* *Xian*: Mandarin word for the unit into which a Chinese Province is divided; comparable to a county. —GT

** *mintuan*: Mandarin word for a mercenary militia hired by Chinese landlords to keep law and order. As is the case with most such words in Chinese, "mintuan" can stand for either the singular or plural and also for individual members. —GT

along the road about directions instead of questioning only friends. In this way the enemy knew our plans and where to wait for us.

Aftermath of the Guangzhou Uprising

The Guangdong people are a very special kind of Chinese. Even the women are lihai.° All the peasants like to get hold of a gun and never hesitate to kill in order to get it. It was dangerous to lag at the rear, as both men and women attacked stragglers to capture their guns. The people along the way took their food and ran to the hills, so we could find nothing to eat.

Along this hard march we were tired, and many were bitter. All were confused and did not know what to think, blaming the committee for sending no orders. But as we neared Hailufeng, spirits rose. Thousands of people from the Hailufeng Soviet came from a hundred li around to welcome us. We sang the Internationale and the Communist Youth Internationale, and all troubles were forgotten....

° *lihai:* Mandarin word meaning "spirited" or "of courageous, fiery disposition." –DH

WHITE TERROR

What was happening in Guangzhou? I did not learn the full story until months later.

The Koreans had a good picture of the last days of the ill-fated Commune because they had no money with which to run away after the 17th and no friends to borrow from. Those who were not killed were spectators to what happened, while the revolutionary Chinese either ran away or were killed. All the house doors and gates of compounds were closed, and the Koreans had nowhere to hide. There were a few Taiwanese willing to aid the Koreans, and three Zhongshan University students hid with them. Kim later told me most of the story; he had stayed safely with his sweetheart's family.

After the Special Training Regiment left Guangzhou, Zhang Tailei led the workers' defensive struggle until his death on the 17th,[122] when the enemy troops occupied the city. Ye Ting had been ordered to Hong Kong by the Party. Nobody knows why the Party failed to give orders at the eleventh hour. It is usually blamed on Ye Ting, but the real reason was simply lack of a coordinated central command.

The White Army began the occupation of the city on the 13th. On the 17th many workers still had their guns, but they were completely surrounded and could not use their arms effectively. The workers fought behind telephone poles, and in small desperate groups. When the White soldiers killed the workers as they ran through the streets, the bourgeoisie came out from behind their doors and clapped.

The workers knew that if they gave up their guns they could not live any longer than it took to make the gesture, so they fought bravely to the very end. On the evening of the 18th the massacre was finished, and the bodies were gathered into motorcars and dumped in the Pearl River.

The Whites killed nearly seven thousand persons from the 13th to the 18th of December 1927. The mass killings occurred on the 17th and 18th. Everyone with a white armband could kill at pleasure. When it recovers power, class hatred is the cruelest passion known to man, and the Guomindang civilians, together with the troops, stopped at nothing. Two thousand rickshaw men were killed. Most of the victims were workers, men, and women. Only a few were students.

THE DOOMED BATTALION AT LINGNAN

One of the most tragic losses was at Lingnan University. At the beginning of the Commune nobody crossed the Pearl River to attack Li Fulin because of the firing of the enemy gunboats. Li Fulin had seven regiments, but they could have been easily overmastered, as they had formerly been bandits and fought only for loot, having no political consciousness. On the 12th, two hundred men, including sixty of our best Korean comrades, wanted to try to take over this position. These two hundred crossed the river and occupied a position near Lingnan University. There they stayed and fought until the 17th. When the Special Training Regiment retreated to the Place of the Seventy-Two Martyrs on the night of the 13th, the command forgot to send the order to retreat to the two hundred men at Lingnan. As a result of this negligence, every single man of the two hundred met his death except one small boy, who lived to tell the story. When we found that no order to retreat had been given to Lingnan, we belatedly sent two Koreans there to give them the news—but they never returned.

Bak Jin was in command of the Korean detachment at Lingnan, and, as he did not know of the general retreat, he ordered all Koreans to stand firm to the end. He was killed in the fighting. His two brothers did not go to Lingnan with him. They escaped to Hailufeng during the retreat.

In 1929 I met the survivor of the gallant Lingnan Two Hundred, a Korean boy named Ahn Cheong.[123] During the Commune he had been a cadet in the Special Training Regiment, though he was only sixteen—there were many boys in the regiment from seventeen to twenty-three. As he told me his story, the tears ran down his cheeks...

"On the 17th I was captured at Lingnan together with the rest of the Koreans. Over fifty of us Koreans and twenty or thirty Chinese were bound and taken to army headquarters for immediate execution. We were strung together with rope like a catch of fish. The Chinese were put into one room, and we fifty-odd Koreans in another. Outside the door we heard the Guomindang commanders order the soldiers to kill everyone in both rooms. The soldiers remained silent and refused to take action. Then the commander said, 'I'll give fifty cents for each man killed.' Still no answer from his men.

"The commander was furious and ordered a machine gun brought up, saying, 'I'll kill all of them myself.'

"Just then the man next to me whispered, 'Your rope has come undone. You can try to escape.'

"I had not noticed that the rope had slipped open on my arms, but it did not take me long to wriggle myself free. There was a long thin rope used to open and close the window at the top of the high room. I hurriedly climbed this, hand over hand, while all the doomed comrades below held their breath with excitement and smiled encouragement.

"I climbed to the roof and lay down flat to hide, then fell unconscious from weakness. From the 12th to the 17th we had not eaten. I was awakened by death cries from my Korean friends, mingled with the steady shooting of the machine gun, which the officer had taken into the room to mow down all the helpless prisoners.

"The moans of the wounded were mixed with curses that we had stayed so faithfully to the end in useless sacrifice of all our best Korean leaders, while the rest of the troops had retreated. Some cried, out, 'Where is Bak?' Other younger boys called out their mothers' names. Then some Chinese came into the room and spoke. I heard a few sharp cries of pain, then silence. I thought the soldiers must be using their swords to hurry the end.

"The Chinese in the other room were taken out into the garden to be killed. The same officer used his machine gun to massacre them also.

"When night came I pulled the window rope out of the window and lowered myself to the ground with it. I took off all my clothes except my underwear and rubbed dirt all over myself to look like a beggar I was famished enough to pass inspection. I escaped to the street and begged food. I couldn't speak Chinese well so pretended to be dumb to hide my identity. I was trying to find some way to cross the river when the police arrested me on the 19th. An hour later a little sampan came down the river with a girl rowing it. The police ordered her to stop and pick me up. They gave her twenty cents to take me away. This was a military district, and they did not want anyone to see what was happening there, so they sent all beggars away. Of course, they never suspected that I was not a dumb beggar.

"I was free! I went to Zhongshan University first to try to find some Korean students there. In the medical school I found three. They gave me $3, all they could find—and some food and clothes. Then I walked along the railway to Kowloon, and on the way some robbers stole all my clothes and money. By now I was a real beggar. When I arrived in Kowloon, the British police arrested me because

I had no clothes on. I pretended to be dumb, and they sent me to a Chinese village nearby. Somebody gave me clothes, and I was set free. I returned to Kowloon. I had no money, so when a Japanese steamer came into port, I stowed away on it."

❖

On the 18th the soldiers surrounded the U.S.S.R. Consulate and bound the consul as well as the vice consul and his wife and three children. The consul wore glasses, and the officer grabbed these and smashed them on the floor in spite.

An American bystander asked the consul for permission to take a movie of the arrest as they left the consulate.

"Yes," the consul agreed, "you may, if you will please get me a new pair of glasses. I cannot see without them. Please go to the German consulate and report this."

The American promised and was told what kind of glasses to order. Later he took the new glasses to the police station where the vice consul and his family had been taken and put into a room to sit on a cement floor, with no food or extra clothing.

In the morning the Chinese took the vice consul away to be executed. He told his wife to give his children a good Soviet education and went calmly. He was killed in the public street so the populace could witness it. They left his body in the street for three days with the phrase on his back "Russian bandit."

The other Russians were freed and ordered to leave within three days. The consul went to the German Consulate, then took a German ship. Believing that the British were largely responsible, the U.S.S.R. protested to the British government and broke diplomatic relations with China.

CHAPTER 12

Life and Death in Hailufeng

ALL OF US FROM the Guangzhou Commune were very much excited to find the Hailufeng Soviet* thriving so well. We had lost Guangzhou, but here in the countryside victory might still be ours.

The Soviet district included all of Haifeng and Lufeng Xian, collectively called "Hailufeng," as well part of Huilai and Puning Xian as well. Neighboring farmers came to look at the new soviet society, wagged their heads in approval, and went back to their villages to organize an armed struggle there.

---

* *Hailufeng Soviet*: This little soviet—the first in China—had been organized by Peng Pai and had come into being on September 9, 1927, two months before the Guangzhou Commune. After it was seen that the GMD was irrevocably counterrevolutionary and that the only hope to continue the struggle lay in the peasant and worker movements, the Chinese Communists decided upon creating soviets as organs for achieving the democratic revolution. The Red Army, created by Zhu De [1886-1976] and others during the Nanchang Uprising [see note 115] on August 1, of which only 1,200 of the original 25,000 troops survived, had marched to the south to establish a base throughout the whole Dongjiang region near Guangzhou, including Hailufeng. Only eight hundred escaped at Shantou [also known as "Swatow" in Cantonese] to join the Hailufeng Soviet, which continued the struggle. Our arrival strengthened their meager armed forces greatly. Hailufeng carried on until May 3, 1928, and did not lose morale until the last days, when the White troops showed clearly that they intended to massacre the whole population, down to the last child, if any resistance whatsoever continued. –KS

We fifteen Koreans were especially interested in everything we saw—we dreamed of leading the same movement in our own country some day. The people in Hailufeng were surprised and pleased to have us fighting with them, and on the day after our arrival had a big "welcome to the Korean comrades" meeting.

When the Special Training Regiment moved on to the front again, only Oh Seong-ryun and I, among the Koreans, were asked to remain in the rear. Oh was made a member of the military headquarters staff and taught in the Communist Party School,[124] where I taught the history of the labor movement and of the Comintern and its activities, and directed propaganda methods. I also had a post in the Party organization department under Zheng Zhiyun, where I worked closely with him and Peng Pai.

RETRIBUTION

I was asked to be one of the seven members of the revolutionary court in Hailufeng because they said that, as I was a foreigner, they thought I would be more objective and just and not influenced by local class hatred and sentiment. I hated this work and tried to escape to the economic committee, so after two weeks they released me. While I was on the court only four were condemned to death, but the experience unnerved me considerably. One of these was an intelligent-looking young man whom the peasants brought to court. There was no proof against him.

"Look at his white hands and face," the peasants said. "There is no mistake. He is a counterrevolutionary landlord's son and a class enemy."

I liked his face, which was open and innocent, and said I thought there was no crime on it and that perhaps he would be glad to join with the revolution against his own father. Peng Pai smiled and took me by the hand.

"You are just as young and innocent as he," he said. "Class justice is not personal but a necessary measure of civil war. We must kill more, not less, in case of question. You don't know the cruelty in Hailufeng under the landlords. If you had seen what I have, you would ask no questions. The peasants are a hundred times less cruel than the landlords, and they have killed very, very few in comparison. The peasants know what is necessary for self-defense, and if they do not destroy their class enemies they will lose morale and have doubt in the success of the revolution. This is their duty and yours."

Peasant gathering in Hailufeng Soviet

When this young man was sent to be executed, his mother and sister took his hands on either side and walked along to comfort him.

I thought of the three young Communist Youth members whom I had seen executed in Guangzhou and could visualize logically that this was only impersonal class justice, but my humanitarian Christian and Tolstoyan training was strong, and I was unhappy. I determined, however, to be strong in my duties and not to let personal sentimentality stand in my way. In the case of the three others, it was not so difficult to condemn them to death, for they were old men with the marks of cruelty and corruption clearly visible on their faces, though we had no proof of recent counterrevolutionary activities. They had formerly been cruel, vengeful landlords. One of them was arrested by the partisans as we were on the march, and they brought him to me to decide his fate in a few minutes. I looked at his flabby hands that had never earned an honest dollar and at the honest faces of the poor, hard-working peasants who had captured him. Class justice was clear enough, but I could not bring myself to condemn him. So I said, "Quickly, gather round in a meeting and let the majority vote on his guilt or innocence." We had only a few minutes to spare, but the partisans halted. The peasants who had arrested the landlord stated the case, and I asked the accused if he had any answer to their charges. He kept his head down and said nothing. The meeting voted unanimously that he was guilty.

How to condemn by looking at a man? For me it was hard. For the local people it was not, but I felt sure that they never bothered to arrest a man whom they did not consider dangerous, for they were as mamahuhu* in this matter as in summary condemnation. During my months in Hailufeng I saw several death lists. These names were checked or dismissed so easily with a flick of the pen that it frightened me, yet I knew that the Guomindang was far worse in these things. The difference was that the Guomindang killed the best and the bravest of China's people, the socially desirable, while the revolutionaries killed the degenerate and the parasites, the socially harmful.

The Red Army in Hailufeng was humane and killed as kindly as possible, with a gun. But the local peasants who had suffered torture under the landlords were not kind to their class prisoners. They preferred to cut off the ears and gouge out the eyes and hang the victims on a tree. Once, after the farmers had besieged the town of Zijin for a month, we occupied it and arrested the magistrate and

---

* *mamahuhu*: A Chinese adjectival phrase meaning "casual," "easy-going," "careless," "negligent," "fair," or "so-so," written with the characters for "horse-horse" and "tiger-tiger." —GT

heads of the Merchants' Association and of the Department of Education. The partisans claimed these men, and, after their deeds had been proven, we turned them over to the farmers, who took thin wire and bound the three together by the thumbs.

The magistrate was a military man, brave and proud. "You peasants can't kill me," he exclaimed. "Only the Red Army has the right to do this." Then he begged the Red Army men to shoot him, for he feared torture at the hands of the peasants.

As I was in the Political Department, I asked the Division Commander to kill the prisoners with a gun, but he said, "No, the farmers have fought for a month for this. These are the people's prisoners, to render justice upon as they like. How many of them have been killed during this month? If you want to know what real torture is, go to the prison in Zijin and ask the walls to talk. The people want to kill only three. If these three had power, they would kill three thousand."

Then I thought again of the three young workers I had seen executed in Guangzhou. It was only human retribution. Those who fail must die. Those who succeed may live.

That night we slept in a Catholic church. There were some books there, and as I had nothing to do, I picked up the Bible and read the New Testament. I wondered what Jesus would have commanded in the name of justice in Hailufeng. "I come not to bring tears but a sword," he might have said. He hated the landlords and moneychangers who robbed the people. He loved what is good and not what is evil. It is good to destroy evil. It is not good to let it remain in power and destroy mankind.

Next day, as we marched along the road, we came upon a large gathering. Everyone was happy and smiling, and the small boys were cheering.

"This is the end of the cruel beast," the people were saying to each other.

"Why do you kill him this way?" I asked faintly, sick with horror.[*]

"Last year this magistrate ordered the leader of our Peasant Union killed in this same way," one of them replied, "and his father and brother were forced to watch it. Now they are handling his case. It is only fair. Let him feel what his victim felt. He is responsible for the execution of a hundred other farmers in Zijin besides. If he caught you now, he would treat you the same way."

I couldn't move. My head was so heavy it dropped on my chest. I felt humanity was a stranger to me. I was not of it.

I thought how much kindness there was among comrades and how much cruelty among enemies. What would a humanitarian like Tolstoy say and feel at a time like this? No doubt he had seen Russian peasants flogged to death. Would he see that it was cruelty to end cruelty? Where was there light to illumine these dark things?

Since that time I have seen many killed and executed, and I am always affected by it. Yet a man fighting in civil

---

[*] *sick with horror*: This was one of two incidents I originally censored out of the story as it was too grisly for me, but it is important to history to understand the cruel revenge ethic in the old tribal-clan society among the peasants. The Red Army was disciplined against torture. In Zijin the peasants were sawing this magistrate in two in a box as gradually as possible, stopping to drink tea from time to time to prolong his suffering. The communists put a stop to such tortures in China after they took power. The other incident referred to a foreign Catholic orphanage. It was believed, in the neighborhood and by the communists, that the eyes of the girl babies were being removed and sold by doctors as "medicine" to cure eye trouble. (Even as late as 1949 there were other instances of this accusation against foreign orphanages, where a high percentage of deaths occurred.) It is important to understand this belief in primitive medicine in old China and to realize that even some communists still found such stories believable, which was one reason they attacked the foreigners. It is possible that some of the Chinese staff did sell the eyes as "medicine" without the knowledge of the foreigners, the principle that "like cures like" being the basis of the primitive medicine. (Indeed, when I was in Beijing, blood was taken from executed persons to cure tuberculosis.) The concept of Christian charity was one the old Chinese could hardly be expected to subscribe to; this was one reason for the animosity against missionaries. –NW

war must formulate his personal philosophy to make such things endurable. I could suffer such a fate more easily than to have to do the same to others, but I do not oppose this. I know that the question is only who is being killed. The ruling class began this killing; they have carried it on for generations. We only fight with their own weapons.

THE CHINESE FAMILY SYSTEM AND THE CLASS STRUGGLE
Feudal remnants were very strong. The city of Guangzhou itself was a center of the arts of civilization, but a few steps out into the nearby countryside brought one into a society as feudal as in an old story book. The family and clan blood system was still strong. The soviets did not break it entirely but gradually weakened it. Each clan was a patriarchal state with the elder as ruler, but inside the family system a bitter division between rich and poor relatives existed. During the armed struggle in Guangdong, the poor and oppressed usually joined the revolution against their rich and powerful family members. In some cases, whole families, rich and poor alike, joined the revolution, while others, rich and poor inclusive, joined the counterrevolution. This was a mistake in revolutionary tactics, and the communists should have insisted upon a class split to ensure true solidarity.

In spite of any family buffers, the class struggle was very intense in Hailufeng. For many years, the landlords had dispensed injustice at their own whim. When the revolutionary movement began to stir in 1925-27, they had been very cruel, and had arrested and tortured to death a great number of people. Old feuds were deep and bitter, and the people bided their time. When the class war broke out in earnest, a few of the most rascally and cruel of the landlords who had committed former atrocities paid dearly for their deeds. The peasants publicly cut off their hands, gouged out their eyes, and mutilated their bodies before death in revenge. Unlike our leniency to the class enemy in the Guangzhou Commune, Peng Pai's line was to let the people dispense justice as they saw it, provided it was the democratic will of the majority publicly executed. Until the Red Army came from Guangzhou he had no armed force for disciplinary measures, anyway, and the people were sovereign in their own right. Only two thousand landlords altogether were killed by the people, however, while after the White occupation and defeat of the soviet at least ten thousand peasants were massacred (nobody knows how many); most of them were women, for female life was considered obnoxious at all times and a revolutionary woman was penalized doubly for daring to assert her right to freedom.

The peasants in Guangdong province are also superstitious, though the revolution was doing fast work in breaking this down. For instance, I remember that when the Communist Youth wanted to destroy some Buddhist idols, the poor peasants rushed out and painted them red, showing them proudly to the Communist Youth delegates. "No, we don't want our Buddhas destroyed. Our gods are revolutionary and support the soviet," they said sagely. "You must destroy only the Buddhas of the tuhao."* Then they painted some of the other Buddhas white, saying that these were the Buddhas on the side of the landlords that deserved punishment.

FIVE BATTLES

The Special Training Regiment had rested for three days after arrival, then gone off to the war front again.

There were several armed forces in Hailufeng: (1) the

---

* *tuhao*: Mandarin word used for "local tyrant." –DH

Fourth Division of the Red Army, numbering two thousand, led by Ye Yong, which was made up of the Political Training Regiment survivors from the Guangzhou Commune[125] and new volunteers; (2) the Second Division of the Red Army, of eight hundred men, commanded by Dong Liang, consisting of survivors from the armies of He Long and Ye Ting after their complete defeat while attempting to capture Shantou several weeks earlier; (3) the Workers' and Farmers' Revolutionary Army, recruited from the local masses; and (4) the peasant Red Guards. Altogether there were usually from seventy thousand to a hundred thousand men in the fighting services, though we had less than ten thousand rifles. All the young farmers joined the fighting, armed or unarmed. There was also an arsenal which made bullets, the machinery for which had been taken from General Chen Jiongming. And some skillful iron workers made iron guns that could shoot two hundred meters. Many of the fighters were armed with these.

Peng's military slogan was "jianbi qingye" which means "strengthen the walls and clear the fields."* Fifty thousand enemy troops had surrounded the soviet nearly two months before they dared attempt to enter Peng's living wall.

Soon after the arrival of the Special Training Regiment, the White armies began to send reinforcements to Hailufeng. Li Fulin, Yu Hanmou, and Li Jishen surrounded the soviet area with troops, but none of them wanted to enter first and be destroyed by us. There were then nearly a hundred thousand troops against our little "Iron Guard" of 2,800 soldiers, supported only by the tens of thousands of mostly unarmed partisans.

The first time the enemy dared enter soviet territory

---

* *clear the fields:* In other words, so that there is no grain left for the enemy. –DH

was when Cai Tingkai came from the west to lead an attack in February and succeeded in occupying Chishi village with two thousand men. Three hundred of the Special Training Regiment rushed to the people's defense. The people shouted and waved red flags as they fought, while women and children on every hilltop furiously flaunted more red flags in the air and screamed encouragement. When the Special Training Regiment arrived, they stood by for a while, smoking cigarettes, waiting to see where the people's ranks would break first, so as to move in where most needed. The enemy broke ranks and scattered, and the Special Training Regiment rushed into the sectors where the people's front had broken, to annihilate the enemy troops. Our people killed five hundred enemy soldiers and the Special Training Regiment lost only three men!

This was a great victory and filled the soviet regions with rejoicing and a sense of limitless power. Cai Tingkai, accustomed to despising the people, had moved in recklessly, without fear of the mass movement.

Yu Hanmou had three thousand troops. His tactics were to sleep on a high mountain in the daytime and go to the front to fight at night—always retreating before dawn. His troops had to carry their food and supplies with them. One day at the village of Gongping, twenty li[126] north of Hailufeng, a mass meeting of thirty thousand people was held. This was on February 19,* and I went from headquarters with Zheng Zhiyun to attend.

While the main speech was being given, Yu Hanmou's troops fired on the meeting. They had come up secretly and surrounded Gongping before any of the people were aware—being off guard because of the enemy's strategy of attacking only at night.

---

* *February 19*: i.e. February 19, 1928.

Thousands were killed by this surprise onslaught. I saw the wounded and dying falling everywhere I turned. Some of the people carried spears, but others had only their knives, which it was the custom to carry always.

The men all ran to the mountain nearby, while the Red Guards mobilized with what guns they had and fought the enemy on a little plain between Gongping and Hailufeng.

I escaped to Hailufeng with Zheng, and that night all Hailufeng—boys, women, even Communist Party intellectuals—armed themselves to punish the enemy for its cowardly deed. They all concentrated for a mass meeting, and Peng Pai raised his slogan: "Use our blood to drown the enemy!" The people liked this slogan, and everyone shouted it enthusiastically. Then we sang the Internationale and other songs and divided into three sections for the attack. We all ran to Gongping as fast as our legs would carry us, including many women and children.

The left column was made up of the Workers' Red Guard. It entered Gongping first and succeeded in making a strong attack. The right column, made up of the Peasants' Red Guard, was broken. The middle was surrounded by the enemy, so the left column came up to the enemy's rear to protect us. I was in this middle column. It was the Communist Party column led by Peng Gui, brother of Peng Pai, and we had two thousand Communist Party and Communist Youth in it.

In the middle of a fierce enemy machine-gun onslaught, a pretty young girl came up and stood beside me with a smile. She was one of the best leaders in the Communist Youth, and we had often worked together, taking an increasing interest in each other. She had considered herself my special girlfriend.

"I have looked everywhere for you," she said calmly. "If you are killed, I want to die with you."

SONG OF ARIRANG

"Lie down quickly," I begged. "You're in the line of fire."

When I turned around a few minutes later to speak to her, I saw only a limp little blue-clad body, blood streaming from her head....

The enemy split us up, and our left and middle were separated from the right. We had no real tactics, only spontaneous mass action. Many times the people rushed forward to the attack in human waves, carrying only their spears and pistols. Always they were forced by the machine-gun fire, which swept our lines, to withdraw. We, of course, had no machine guns.

The left and middle then broke, and the enemy followed hot on our retreat to Hailufeng and occupied a nearby hill. They were afraid to enter the city and struggle in the streets in daytime.

This great people's battle lasted from one o'clock at night to nine in the morning. The enemy had only three thousand trained soldiers with machine guns, and we had most of our seventy thousand partisans in action that night. But we could not "drown the enemy in our blood," though blood enough to do so was shed. We lost at least one thousand and saved three hundred lightly wounded who could run away. Only a few hundred White soldiers were killed or wounded.

We now retreated to a high mountain called Meilong and decided to defend this while planning how to reoccupy Hailufeng and Gongping. By this time the White armies had surrounded the whole Hailufeng district, and the enemy encirclement was closing in upon us. The Red Army of two thousand cadets[*] returned from the east, where it had been fighting during the past weeks.

On March 7 we began the attack to recover Hailufeng

---

[*] *Red Army of two thousand cadets*: Kim San is referring here to the Special Training Regiment he's referred to earlier. –DH

and failed, but were able to reoccupy Shanwei. We had only a few fighters then. The whole Red Army with the Red Guards numbered less than ten thousand, while the enemy had an army at Haifeng that alone consisted of nine thousand troops. The eight hundred men of the Second Division were reduced to six hundred, and of the Special Training Regiment, only a thousand came back. In these two attacks, we lost one-fifth of our armed strength.

Our position was very difficult indeed. By this time all the towns had been lost to the enemy, except Meilong and Shanwei, and we gave up the latter again and returned to Meilong. Enemy cordons surrounded us everywhere, and there was no way to escape, so desperate fighting was the only answer.

In the meantime, Cai Tingkai had moved into Chishi again, and from there came to Meilong to launch his second attack. From midday to the afternoon we struggled at Meilong, and failed. All was finished. . .

In groups of ten or twenty men, our forces dispersed into the nearby villages. The enemy dared not stay in the villages among the hostile population, so always withdrew to safety after attacks. The villages were ours between battles.

After the defeat at Meilong, we decided it was no use to fight with big forces; instead we deployed our men in guerilla warfare. We harassed enemy communications and destroyed all small groups who ventured out to carry rice or supplies.

At night the enemy troops surrounded the villages and in the morning often killed the whole population. For instance, on March 14 and 15, the enemy massacred the whole population of the Qingzao district—two thousand people. They burned all the rice fields and stores, as well as the houses, so we would have no food to carry on with.

LAST WORDS

There was no food left for us by this time. When we lost Meilong and dispersed into small groups, I went to the mountains with a group of Party members. The enemy followed thirty li to destroy us. Whenever we tried to carry our wounded, the enemy caught up, so we had to drop them and run for our lives. After the enemy passed, the people came out and carried the wounded into their houses to nurse them secretly.

This particular mountain was very steep and dangerous, and ordinarily nobody ever attempted to climb it. Two Korean friends, Oh Seong-ryun and Son,[127] were with me, and we climbed up the mountain at the head of the group. I was strong and healthy then, but Oh was heavy and unaccustomed to hot climates. He perspired pitifully. "In the October Revolution in Russia, they never had to climb mountains like this one," he wailed. "Only in China must we be mountain goats as well as soldiers."

That night we strayed into a deserted temple on the other side of the mountain. There were ten of us, and each one searched anxiously for food, turning over every stone in the hope of finding a store of rice beneath. Oh would sound one stone, then I would sound the same one alternately, while we sang an old Korean rice-pounding song. At last, under one hollow stone, we found a small store of rice.

We could find only one old broken iron bowl to cook in, but it would not hold water. So we pounded the rice into flour and made a cake, spreading it on the broken bowl to cook. We could not wait until it was ready but took it away from the fire half-done, and called our friends.

We knew that we must hide or leave, so we said to the rest: "We must all prepare cakes quickly." All night long we pounded rice and cooked cakes. In the meantime, Oh, with an unerring eye for food saw a luckless dog and shot it. It was a black and red chow, of the kind the Guangdong people love to eat. How to cook this treasure? After much discussion, we thought of putting the dog in a hole in the ground and heaping a fire over it. We gathered round the fire and sang and talked. I taught everyone how to sing the song I loved best—the old Korean "Song of Arirang"—and we all wept after we had sung this. The Chinese liked it very much and said they would never forget it.

By this time we were all so exhausted that we had to sleep. It was too dangerous to stay near the temple, so we scattered to hide in the grass like hunted wild animals. We three Koreans slept together, putting Son in the middle to comfort him. Before going to sleep he sang a child's song about the stars. He was a bewildered little boy of eighteen. When we had slept awhile, we awoke ready to face what might come. "How many good friends have you in this world?" we asked each other, and counted them over.

We wrote down our family addresses and gave them to each other. "If you die and I live, what shall I tell them?" we asked.

I wrote to my mother and second brother first, then to Kim Chung-chang and to Jin Gong-mok[128] and Huang Pingchuan. Huang was my best Chinese friend.*

In my letters I said: "I am happy to die here. It is not like dying in a land of slavery. But I wish it were a Korean province as free as our glorious revolutionary struggle has been."

As we moved secretly around the mountain, we met a farmer. He told us our troops had gone to Baisha. We climbed over mountains to reach Baisha. There was no

---

* *best Chinese friend*: In 1930, just before I was arrested, I got Huang a ticket to escape to Japan. He returned in 1933, when I was arrested again. He searched every prison in Beijing but failed to discover my whereabouts. He contracted typhoid in one of those prisons and died five days later on June 8th. If he had had money for good medical attention, he could have recovered. He was only twenty-eight at his death. He had had a scholarship of $80 a month from the Japanese Boxer Fund to study medicine at the Imperial University in Tokyo. –KS [No further information exists on who this friend might have been. –DH]

road, and the way was steep. We had to slide down, grasping at roots and branches to prevent severe falls. At Baisha we separated and went to farmhouses, helping with the work. There we learned that Ye Yong had been killed and that only four hundred of the Special Training Regiment remained.

The villagers kept guards on watch, and when the Whites came, we all ran away. The farmers' goods were few. They picked up their food, pans, and babies and went to the mountains. We did this many times every week. The Whites took from the farmers all the food they could get, and we had nothing to eat but sweet potatoes. For many years after Hailufeng I could not bring myself to eat a sweet potato!

THE BATTLE OF HAIFENG

May 3rd* was our last stand at Hailufeng. One week before, the soldiers had called a meeting of what remained of the Second and Fourth Divisions. All the food was gone. At the meeting it was decided: "If we cannot eat, we die. If we fight, we die. But at Haifeng there is food and money. All we can do is to make one last attempt to return there."

There were only six hundred left to attend the meeting: four hundred from the Special Training Regiment, now called the "Red Army" men, and the rest partisans. During the week, we prepared our guns for the attack. We could eat only once in two or three days, and by May 3 we were famished and weak. Altogether we could mobilize only three thousand men, including the farmer volunteers, with hand weapons for the most part.

On the night before May 3, we each ate a sweet

---

* *May 3rd*: i.e. May 3, 1928. –DH

potato. At 12:30 p.m. we set out. Two cooks, who had formerly been on the strike committee, had just come from Haifeng to find us in order to report that there was $400,000 in the White headquarters, together with four hundred boxes of bullets and plenty of white flour and rice. Our plan was to capture this and run.

By nine o'clock that night we were within thirty li of Haifeng. Oh and Son and I kept close together, and Oh was in command of our column of eighty men. Our duty was to occupy the Party school.* We were part of the Special Training Regiment Fourth Division, which was assigned the task of occupying the town. The Second Division was to occupy Wufuling, a place three li from Haifeng, and to take the middle school, which was used as the headquarters of the Second Division of White troops. The First Division of the Whites was in the town.

The cooks had told us everything. We knew the enemy positions and even the password: "liqi."**

We crossed the river up to our breasts and climbed. Nearing Haifeng, the bravest men volunteered to lead the attack. Three groups of twenty each volunteered from our Fourth Division.

My duty was to help capture the clothes from the sentries at the Party school. Our plan was to pretend we were White soldiers from the middle school headquarters outside the town. For secrecy, we were to use only swords, no guns.

We knew the streets and the disposition of enemy troops, and our eighty men moved in secret until we reached our objective.

We disposed of all the sentries easily. Ten men entered the gate and the others climbed over the wall. There

---

* *Party school*: Here Kim San is referring to a school run by the GMD. –DH

** *liqi*: Mandarin for "strength." –DH

was one company at this Party school, but we took one hundred guns, eight boxes of bullets, and one machine gun, losing only five men. We then quickly surrounded all the enemy troops in one street. Next we broke open the prison and freed two hundred comrades, many of whom were in chains and broken by torture. The people helped them escape.

In less than an hour the whole thing was completed. The peasants had one hundred prisoners to take back—a whole company of troops that had been caught sleeping.

The Whites did not put up much resistance because they expected the garrison at Wufuling to come to the rescue immediately. They closed the doors and contented themselves with throwing hand grenades at us over the walls.

There was no sound whatever from Wufuling, which our Second Division was to have occupied. This worried us. We knew that if reinforcements arrived, we would surely all be annihilated. We decided we could not continue the struggle within the town of Haifeng in view of the danger of an attack from without, so the bugle was blown for retreat.

We marched out of town toward Wufuling. Still no sound. Action to occupy the middle school there had been ordered for 12:30. It was an hour late already.

On arrival we found that the enemy troops had heard the firing in the town of Haifeng and had taken up positions on the hills and at all military points. Our tardy Second Division had just marched up to the foot of the hill. The Whites were very much taken by surprise and because of the darkness had no idea how many men we were.

In ten minutes we started a battle. But, except for the kindly darkness, we were at a disadvantage. When dawn came, the enemy saw how few we numbered and viciously attacked. We ran away, but many were killed and wounded. Our Second Division at the foot of the mountain was almost annihilated—the end of China's first Red soldiers of He Long and Ye Ting.[129]

Son was wounded in the upper part of the leg, and Oh and I carried him nearly twenty li. I was suffering from malaria and had little strength, so it was hard for us to carry him rapidly. Son begged us to shoot him so we could save our own lives.

By the time we came to a village near a high mountain, the firing had stopped. The political workers called a meeting and ordered everyone to escape quickly to the mountains. We three Koreans had fought like demons and were too tired to climb a step. We sat down, feeling ready to die with little Son. Many times we were ordered to climb but could not bring ourselves to do it. We set out to take Son to our secret hospital at Jianyouling not far away. This was under the care of an old-fashioned doctor who used a tree leaf to remove a bullet from a wound, but it was the best we had. There was no modern medicine in all Hailufeng.

On arriving we found that the dry grass huts used as a hospital had just been burned by the Whites. Thirty wounded had been burned alive inside. Only three who could run had escaped death by hiding in the grass. These were captured, and when the enemy found they were two northern Chinese and one Korean, they were taken to Hailufeng. The Korean was Oh's nephew.

Little Son died here from loss of blood. He was too weak even to speak any of his cherished last words.

THE MARCH TO NEIYANG

The Battle of Haifeng was our last attempt. The Communist Party committee futilely ordered that nobody could leave but must prepare for a new struggle. Courage was gone, however, and no cadres remained. Of the survivors of the Special Training Regiment over one-fourth had been lost at Haifeng. Less than three hundred of the two thousand who had left the Guangzhou Commune remained alive, and all of these were famished and ill. Many of the best leaders had been killed—how many nobody knew.

At Jianyouling we gathered together and held a last meeting on the mountain. Little waterfalls fell with a sad tinkling sound, and amid this requiem we bathed our wounds, estimated our dead, and discussed our weaknesses and strengths. We still had no food. We could have taken some during the Battle of Haifeng, had the Second Division done its duty properly, but their failure to capture Wufuling had made us retreat hastily.

At dawn we set out wearily for Baisha, avoiding enemy reconnaissance. There were a hundred of us. At Baisha we were comforted by our friend—sweet potato soup!

We divided into two groups, one made up partly of the Second Division and the other of the Special Training Regiment, and it was decided to go quickly to Neiyang to prevent annihilation by the enemy.

At the meeting in Baisha, the leaders had said that the sick and those who were unable to run would not be permitted to go with the rest to Neiyang, two hundred li distant, so as not to prejudice the chance for the others to get away safely. Many were very sick, some with feet and legs so badly swollen from hiding and marching in the water for days that they could hardly stand. But all insisted on going, because we all knew that any individual left behind must surely die. If they went on the march, at least they would die in the struggle, surrounded by comrades. Therefore, only a few were left at Baisha.

One hundred men left for Neiyang first, followed immediately by three hundred others. It was so dangerous a march that orders were given to kill anybody with a cough who insisted upon coming along. We moved so close to enemy troop that a single cough might have resulted in discovery and the annihilation of all of us, weakened and famished as we were. In all my life I have never seen such self-control. *Not a single person coughed during the dangerous periods of that march, though many had tuberculosis and bad bronchial colds from exposure in the water.*

It took three days to complete the march to Neiyang, and not a few died on the way from wounds and weakness. We hid half-asleep in the grass in the daytime, while swarms of big malarial Guangdong mosquitoes sucked away the lifeblood remaining in the wounded. Like myself, nearly everyone had malaria.

On the third day we came to a big village, which we had to cross by an exposed mountain path. The commanders again whispered the order fiercely: "Not a living son of you may cough! If one of you makes a sound, every one of us may have to pay with our lives. If you cannot control yourselves, you must stay behind. And if any of you are too sick to move fast, you must not attempt to come."

Nobody consented to stay behind.

Many wore white summer clothes, easy to see from a distance, so these were taken off and rolled into small bundles. We crouched on hands and knees at terrible suffering to the wounded and crept along the path slowly so as not to be visible above the tall mountain grass. The leaders put their ears to the ground often and listened breathlessly for the sound of strange footsteps before permitting us to continue our serpentine movement.

Never in my life before had I really wanted to cough, but at one of those moments of deathly silence I experienced the most uncontrollable desire I have ever felt. To be dead or alive at that moment I didn't care. I only wanted to relax the spasm in my throat. I fell flat on the ground clutching at the offender and half-strangled myself until

I was almost too dizzy to rise. But I was victorious over myself. The low column moved on safely, and half an hour later the commander, a Henanese who had taken Ye Yong's place, heaved a sigh of relief and ordered: "Now anybody may cough if he can be quiet about it." We all laughed. It suddenly occurred to me that most of the men had been going through just such an experience as I had all during the three days, and I felt a profound new respect for man's power over his own nature.

We reached Neiyang next morning, and the communists among the local farmers came to greet us.

For many, many weeks we had not tasted rice. Now we ate it as if for the first time in years.

ESCAPE

Neiyang was neither White nor Red, and the enemy had no troops there. The people neither welcomed nor opposed us, so we stayed in the town a week.

During the daytime we ate in the villages and hid in the mountains at night. Over half our men went to Guikeng, thirty li away, and we began partisan warfare against the landlords to get food, as the poor people could not support us. We took from the landlords and distributed to the villagers, so the poor people soon loved us very much.

Every hour we expected enemy troops to come in pursuit, and after a week they arrived. Had it not been for our partisan warfare, they would not have known our whereabouts, perhaps.

In Neiyang itself we had only a hundred men. The enemy occupied all points except the plateau on the very top of the mountain. When the enemy began the attack, some of our men ran to the plateau. Oh and I hid on the mountain in the tall grass. We found a big stone with a spring under it and hid in the water under this stone for a whole day. When it was dark we came out and moved farther along the mountain. The enemy troops were firing into the grass everywhere as we passed by.

In the morning we looked down at the village below. No soldiers were visible. Neiyang, meaning "Inner Ocean," was a beautiful place, with a clear river tumbling down the mountain and the plateau majestic above.

Near the top of the mountain we met some farmers who called us "comrade" and were very kind. We were directed to the secret headquarters of the Farmers' Union in a nearby village of ten families.

Oh and I walked to the door and asked the chief to help us escape to the headquarters of the Communist Party Special Committee at Mutianling in the district of Huilai two hundred li away. A farmer was sent to guide us. We dressed like farmers, carried our food, and hid in the mountains in the daytime, walking fast at night. The farmers relayed us from one village to another. As we crossed Chaoan Xian, our guide said we could move safely in daytime. We met with no incident until sunset, when thirty men and women with swords and guns followed and fired at us. They were people of some White feudal clan and wanted to kill us to seize our guns. Each of us stood behind a stone alternately and covered the thirty pursuers with rifle fire while the other two ran, until we were safely away from danger.

We crossed many mountains that night and encountered an amazing number of snakes, poisonous and hissing. Oh and I were afraid of these creatures, as many comrades had been severely bitten. We had no shoes—no Guangdong farmer wears shoes. Since April we had all been barefoot, and before then had worn only straw sandals.

Oh was much thinner now, and he looked like a haggard old man. I had been strong and in good athletic trim before contracting malaria in April. Two months of marching and fighting with chills and fever racking my body had reduced me to a cadaverous state. Some days I was so sick I walked in a delirium. I learned to sleep as I walked, waking up when I stumbled to the ground on a stone. On other days I felt well again but ineffably weak. Many, many of our comrades were in the same condition or worse. My leg was painfully swollen from beriberi from so many weeks without nourishing food, and I had big watery blisters all over my body, until I could not sit down. For nearly half a year we had been sleeping without shelter in the mountains and marching through the deep water of the paddy fields. It rained nearly every night, and our bodies were drenched in dew from the mountain grass whenever we slept. We had only bamboo hats to keep us dry and no extra clothing whatsoever. I have never recovered from those days in Hailufeng, and my health has been unstable ever since. Even my malaria was not cured until 1929.

After eight days we reached Mutianling. There we found Peng Pai and Zheng Zhiyun. They were living in a cave underneath a big waterfall, which veiled the secret entrance. Peng Pai was very ill. With the relaxation from tension, my sickness came back with a vengeance, and even good old heroic Oh admitted a near collapse. Being a northerner, he had suffered from the hot, damp climate, and his heart and lungs had been affected by the violent action in which he was always dashing about at the front.

❖

On July 23, we felt well enough to attempt going to Hong Kong and arranged to rent a sampan together with four Chinese.

We walked over fifty li the first night and slept secretly

in a village when daylight came. The next evening we continued, and there was still a half-moon when we climbed eagerly into the little sampan. Just as we were about to pull off, a hail of fire began from the shore. Everyone but myself jumped out of the boat and ran. As I leapt up to run I collapsed in a faint of weakness and shock due to my illness. When I recovered consciousness after some time, nobody was in sight, and the firing was far off. "There is no way out this time," I said to myself grimly. I glanced around for the dead bodies but could see none. Then I hid myself in the water with only my nose showing.

I expected to be captured any moment. I had no fear of death by shooting but knew that capture meant torture— they would pull out my eyes and ears and organs until no life was left to suffer. Suicide by drowning seemed the only intelligent thing to do, but hope dies hard. The dim moon was friendly enough. I decided to try to make my way to the village where we had slept the previous night. I would probably faint under torture anyway....

Crawling out of the water on my belly, I wriggled onto the grass. Then I set out for the village. My mind was a blank as I stumbled in the darkness, but it kept asking if Oh were dead or alive, like an obsession of insanity. I don't remember anything about that trip. Apparently I arrived at the house almost unconscious and fell into a stupor for a whole day. The next night a farmer took me back to Peng Pai.

For two days I expected hourly to see Oh's friendly face framed in the spray of the waterfall, but he did not come.

"You may go across country to Shantou," Peng Pai advised. "Then you need not risk taking a boat."

Shantou was two hundred li distant. I waited a little while longer with Peng to regain my strength and in the hope of seeing my dear friend again.

Then one day Peng said kindly: "You may as well make up your mind that they are all dead. It's no use to wait. If Oh does not come today, he will never come."

I never saw Peng Pai again.

Peng Pai would surely have become one of the greatest mass leaders China has ever known, had he not met an untimely death. Nobody I have met in China except Mao Zedong shares equally with him that rare quality of inborn leadership. He created the Hailufeng peasant movement, and his influence spread all through the province, including Guangzhou city. He was the first organizer of the new agrarian revolution and had led the peasant movement for ten years.

Peng Pai came from a very influential family in Hailufeng. He had been chief of the local Department of Education and during his term of office saw to it that the people learned many things not in the official textbooks.

Peng was by nature a man of vision and humanitarianism, with a firm sense of justice. When he inherited his father's big landed estate, he redistributed it to the tenants—a fact of no small importance in encouraging the local tenants to divide the land among those who tilled it. After the purges of April 12 and 15, 1927, he began laying his plans for an armed struggle in Hailufeng, which within a few months resulted in the formation of that first soviet.

I used to meet Peng Pai nearly every day in Hailufeng. He utilized his family's big, modern two-storied cement house as his headquarters, and there we sometimes practiced Japanese together, as he had graduated from Waseda University in Tokyo. He was rather

Peng Pai

short in stature but full of strength and health. His face was long and un-Guangdong-like in appearance, with strong, firm features. He had a very deep voice and stuttered occasionally. Peng was not an intellectual theoretician, and the common man understood everything he wrote and said, but he had always studied hard. He liked to talk over his problems freely with others and always waited for full reports before making decisions. Though he himself spoke quickly and simply, he did not demand short, quick reports from others but let them express themselves naturally.

This soviet government was actually a "democratic dictatorship," and Peng understood how to manage this form of government. He was a revolutionary dictator with plenary powers, but he derived these from the consent of the people. They followed his line by persuasion, not by force. There was no party dictatorship, but rather a single executive who was close to the people and who carried out their will; he led the people, and they followed him. He did not command, but influenced people to vote for his ideas—as a democrat should. If ever one man was in control, Peng was in control of the Hailufeng Soviet, yet he never thought of himself in this light at all, but believed in and jealously guarded the right of majority decision. I remember that one day Peng explained his principles of government to me, saying, "We must centralize all power at one given point. But if this is not based upon a foundation of mass democracy, it will be no firmer than bean curd." In the autumn of 1929, Peng Pai escaped to Shanghai where he was elected chairman of

Hailufeng Peasant Association

the military committee of the Chinese Communist Party's Central Committee. A Hunanese named Bai Xin[130] also went from Hailufeng to Shanghai, where he became a member of that same military committee. The Guomindang promised Bai Xin protection and money to go abroad if he betrayed, so he turned Peng Pai over to the police shortly after the latter's arrival. Peng Pai was executed immediately at the garrison headquarters that same autumn. He died proudly and bravely, never speaking to his captors. Others often begged for leniency or betrayed addresses to save their lives, but Peng Pai met his death as the hero he had always been.

❖

On July 27, I abandoned all hope and set out with a farmer as guide on my way to Shantou. It was another strenuous experience, but on the 4th of August, we arrived safely at the headquarters of the Dongjiang Communist Youth Committee on a mountain near Sanyang.

I spent one night with them, then took a boat to reach Shantou, three hours away. As we neared Shantou I saw with dismay the Guomindang flag and the police at the waterfront. What to do? I was by this time in the habit of either attacking or running away whenever the Guomindang flag appeared. I tried to think what to say and do to avoid arrest, but could summon up no intelligent plan. When we pulled the boat up, however, no attempt to arrest us was made. I have seldom been happier in my life.

That night I slept in the shop of a crippled charcoal burner. The next day, the 6th, I paid $4 for passage to Hong Kong on the *Takayama Maru*, a Japanese freighter. I was still very sick.

"Man dies easily—and also not so easily," I thought.

HONG KONG AND GINSENG

But my curious mixture of good luck and bad was with me still.

I arrived in Hong Kong the next day and went to an inn I knew.

"Why are you sick? Where do you come from? Your Chinese is not good." The clerk demanded suspiciously, sniffing at me as if I were a strange dog.

I said I was selling Korean ginseng* and that near Chaoyang Xian my money, ginseng, and clothes had all been looted by bandits.

"I have no money right now," I pleaded. "Can you wait for payment while I write home?"

He seemed relieved. "Yes, I'll wait. I can introduce you to a Korean ginseng merchant from the South Seas staying here."

I groaned inwardly but had to accept. This generous Korean merchant was named Bak. When he saw me all covered with sores, sick, and miserable, he clucked his tongue and said immediately, "Come to my room, you have no money!"

Bak took me to a public bath and bought me a pair of foreign-style trousers and a shirt for me, costing $10. He even tried to give me his own coat. Then he insisted upon taking me to a foreign-style restaurant to eat, where it cost him $3, and to a movie. We saw *Resurrection*, from the book by Tolstoy. The story caused a depth of sorrow in my heart to flood up, and such a relaxation from my recent experiences that I began to cry. All the tragedy of humanity that I had seen since the Guangzhou Commune —not to speak of myself—called for compassion.

"Are you crying for the heroine or the ginseng?" my

---

* *Korean ginseng*: Ginseng has been used in China and other Asian countries for time unknown as a medicinal herb. Koreans have earned a living finding the root and selling it. Korean ginseng has long had an especially good reputation in China. –NW, GT

companion inquired.

But I could not speak to him.

"Never mind your money and ginseng," he said. "You will not starve while I am here."

Then he took me for coffee and cakes and tried to tell jokes and stories to amuse me.

The next day I went to the secret Communist Party organization of which I had been given the address. I had left my party mandate hidden in my bed at the inn.

I knocked at the door.

Two plainclothes ethnic Shandong policemen reached out and grabbed me. I held up my hands while they searched, finding nothing.

"I am a ginseng merchant," I protested. "A month ago I sold one jin to a Miss Li who lived here, and she only paid for half.* She told me to come today for the rest of my money."

They took me to the police station. For an hour I was questioned by a Sikh and a Chinese.

"Where do you live?"

"At the Taianzhan Inn."

"We'll investigate this," they announced, and demanded that I lead them to the inn.

When we arrived I took them to Bak's room and opened his luggage as if I owned it, while Bak stood by amazed.

"You must tell them the ginseng is mine," I begged in Korean.

Bak didn't talk.

I pulled out two woolen mufflers and announced that one was his and the other mine.

"We both came here together. Mr. Bak went to the south, and I went to Guangzhou to sell ginseng," I remarked.

---

* *jin*: Half a kilogram.

Bak was very confused. "What is this all about? Just tell me something," he asked in Korean.

Then they took me back to the station. Bak followed but was not permitted to enter. Finally an Englishman came, looked at me superciliously and told me to go. I could have embraced him. I had thought my fate was sealed at last. I was so happy I couldn't breathe.

"I wasn't killed in the sampan; I won't be executed here!" I exulted within myself like a chorus.

Bak was waiting in the street. "I have been very worried about you. Is everything all right?"

"Yes, yes, it was nothing," I said airily. "I went to call on a Chinese friend. He had become a thief, so I was suspected. They just wanted to be sure I had no connections with him, that's all."

He shook his head skeptically but said no more.

I fell ill again at the inn, and Bak was very kind. A Communist Party headquarters friend found and visited me and said, "You can find a cheap hospital in Shanghai, and you must go there or you may die. Here it is too expensive. Do you want to go the U.S.S.R.?"

"No," I replied. "I can do good work in China now. It would be better for me to stay."

"Wait here then until you are strong enough, then hurry to Shanghai," he advised.

I wrote to my mother, telling her I planned to go abroad to study and was waiting for a ship to France. This was to let her know I was still alive.

I had lost Little Son's letters to be delivered after his death but remembered his sister's address and wrote to her as I had promised. For Oh I still had hope.

Soon afterward I went to Shanghai with Bak on a ship called the *Zhisheng*. We were caught in a typhoon. I was so weak from seasickness that I could not even rise from bed. In Shanghai, Bak sent me to the Tongren Hospital.

My malaria had come back. When the doctor took my temperature, he sucked in his breath and said, "This is the highest temperature I have ever taken. If it goes down suddenly you will die. This is very dangerous." I lost consciousness and don't remember much about what happened during the next week.

When I recovered enough to read, I found a letter under my pillow from Bak. He had left $30 for me and said he couldn't wait for me to recover but had to hurry back to Korea.

I never saw Bak again.

The hospital cost a dollar a day. I stayed a month, using Bak's kind gift. One day a foreign nurse asked, "Are you a Christian?"

"Yes," I replied, "I used to be when I was a little boy."

Then she gave me an orange every day and was attentive and kind.

CHAPTER 13

Reunion in Shanghai

WHEN I LEFT the hospital in October I went to Shanghai's French Concession to seek out the Koreans who used to live there, but now I could not find any. I knocked at many doors, but no Koreans answered.

Then I went to a Chinese inn that would cost me a dollar a day. I had only a dollar and a few cents in my pocket.

Again and again I searched for my countrymen. No luck. One day, however, as I was eating at a street stall, someone came up and struck me on the shoulder. I looked around and recognized a Korean Communist Youth student from Guangzhou.

"We all thought you were dead," he exclaimed, beaming at me. "We had a memorial for you among those killed in Guangzhou."

That night he took me to see my dear friend, Kim Chung-chang. Kim threw his arms about me like a mother, and I was so overcome with joy that I could not speak for a long time. His wife welcomed me, too. Kim's first question was about Oh Seong-ryun. "He is certainly no longer alive," I told him.

Kim had hidden safely with his sweetheart's family after the Commune. They had been married afterward and had come to Shanghai. There he wrote essays and translated books in order to earn money to help support others. If not for his work, several of our friends might have starved to death in those hard months.

We talked the whole night long. Kim told me all about what had happened in Guangzhou after our retreat to Hailufeng. The Japanese had been furious to discover the number of Koreans who had participated in the Commune and had arrested one thousand of them. Others were turned over to the Japanese in Shanghai. No wonder I could not find any on the streets of the French Concession.

Two days later I found a room near Kim's house and went to see him every day. It took days to talk over all the things we had to say to each other. I was completely broken in health and needed weeks of rest.

One day I was walking aimlessly along the French Concession bund, looking at the Huangpu River bristling with junk masts and ominous with foreign gunboats of every important flag. I looked up and saw a face coming toward me as if in a hallucination. Could it be? The face loomed larger and came before my eyes like a misty image in a dream. A well-remembered horny hand took mine, and two voices whispered hoarsely at the same moment, "I thought you were dead!" We stood transfixed for several minutes, as if our bodies were of the same flesh and blood, and neither could say another word. Then the tears ran slowly down his face. It was the first time I had ever seen Oh show any sign of weeping!

He told me his story. That night in the sampan at Hailufeng, Oh escaped with the boatman when the firing began. He looked around for me many times, then gave up in despair and ran away to save his own life. The enemy troops followed the other Chinese, not Oh and the

REUNION IN SHANGHAI

boatman. They hid under two feet of water in a rice paddy, with only their noses out for breathing. Before light, they walked forty li to the boatman's house, and Oh hid there for a week. He was also very sick at that time. He finally escaped, not through Shantou, but by going to the Haifeng district and on to Huilai, where he escaped observation and took a small steamboat to Hong Kong.

There were several Chinese with him, and at Huilai one was arrested. The mintuan asked this Chinese if he were a communist and when he denied this called in a fortune-teller demanding that he discover the truth. The wise old man looked this young revolutionary over carefully and gave the verdict: "No, he is not a communist now, but in the future there may be danger that he will become one." He was freed on the basis of this judgment, and Oh later met him on the street in Hong Kong.

"Feudalism has its uses in China," said Oh with a grin. "Had the old fortune-teller said he was a communist, he would have been shot immediately."

Oh had come to Shanghai in October, one month after I arrived, and had been unable to find any Korean friends.

The next day I took him to Kim's house. We stayed together there and talked for three days. But it was too dangerous for us to live together, so we each kept a secret room and met at Kim's to eat.

Oh was sick also, with constant backaches and a badly enlarged heart from his Hailufeng experiences, but he would not go to a hospital.

Kim's wife had an elder sister who had been deported from Indochina for revolutionary work. Oh liked this girl and took her every day to the French Gardens. "But she will soon go away, and it will all be finished," Oh said to me. "She is like a drink of fresh water in a desert."

Kim and Oh and I felt very close together in those unhappy days of aftermath in Shanghai. We loved each other with a fraternal spirit as never before. It was as if we had lost everything but our deep friendship, and we wanted to stay together as long as possible, fearing that as soon as one of us were out of sight, death would claim him. The loss of so many of our best comrades in the Commune weighed down upon us like a black doom. Where could we replace these, the flower of the Korean Revolution and the nucleus of our whole party membership? The ghosts of those sacrificed haunted us when we were alone, and we came together again every day seeking comfort and courage in our companionship and pledging ourselves as a solid unit to carry on their work in the future.

More than any other individuals we lamented the deaths of the three brave Bak brothers from Siberia—of Bak Jin, who had died at his post with over fifty other Korean comrades at Lingnan during the Commune, and of the two younger brothers, who had undoubtedly been killed in Hailufeng.

Then, two months after arriving in Shanghai, I received a letter signed with two obviously false names. It said: "We are your comrades from the world of death in the new struggle for life."

The next day I arranged a meeting. When I opened the door, two pairs of black, black eyes behind thick lashes looked in at me. I embraced my lost friends—the two Bak brothers! Thin, tired, and worn, they looked like the ghosts that had haunted my thoughts. How had they escaped from Hailufeng?

They told me that when the Special Training Regiment dispersed in small groups after the defeat at Meilong, they had fought a rear-guard action and retreated. Then (while Oh and Son and I were hiding for a month with the farmers at Baisha and living on sweet potatoes) they escaped to the coast one day in April with twenty others,

including four girls. They took a small boat to the harbor
of Zhufu. There they were arrested by one of Cai Tingkai's
battalion commanders. The other officers wanted to kill
them all immediately, but the commander could not
make up his mind. One of the girls was very beautiful,
and the commander was trying to save her for himself. He
was polite to this girl and talked with her several times.
He seemed really quite anxious to win her good graces,
but she did not respond. Then he discovered she was in
love with one of the men with her and fell into a rage. He
ordered that all should be killed without mercy. The prisoners called a meeting and talked together.

"Do you want to try to save your comrades or see us all killed?" they asked the girl.

She decided to try to save the others by giving good
"face" to the commander and trying to influence him.
She called for him to come again to talk with her. This girl
was brilliant and charming as well as beautiful, and the
commander had really fallen in love with her. He knew
she was a communist, but perhaps he admired her for her
courage. He promised that if she would marry him, he
would secretly send the boat away and save the lives of the
others. She pretended to like him very much for this and
agreed. When he and the girl were married, he kept his
promise, and the boat was given free passage out of the
harbor one night. He had to give the other three girls to
his officers to keep them quiet.

The two Baks stayed in Hong Kong a while, then took
a boat to Shanghai with no further trouble. They now
wanted to go to Moscow for a thorough education to fit
themselves for future leadership.

I heard nothing more about them until 1933, when
I read in a newspaper that they had been killed by the
Japanese in Jilin. They had been fighting with the volunteers in Manchuria, and as they left a secret party meeting

in Jilin City, a spy followed them. Five minutes later the Japanese surrounded the two and shot them both.

What happened to the heroine of the "Zhufu" incident? I had known this girl in Hailufeng. One day in 1930 as I was walking through the streets of Beijing, I saw a thin, pale, unhappy creature, whom I thought I recognized. It was she.

"How did you escape?" I asked, amazed at her tragic appearance.

"The officer kept me for four months, then I told him I wanted to go away for a little while to see my mother as I was ill and homesick. He gave me money to go to Shanghai. I went to see my brother, who is a professor in Shanghai. He shut the door in my face and said, 'I forbid you ever to try to enter my house.' I had no money, and for two months I could find no work. I begged in the streets and nearly starved. Then I entered a house of prostitution but could not bear this life. I went back to my brother and cried, begging for help. He was so shocked at my wretched appearance that he gave me money to go to my home in Henan. There I found my mother had died. My father angrily threw me out into the street again. A friend helped me come to Beijing to enter the Girls' Normal University so I could become a teacher. But I am too sick to work, and I have nobody to help me. The comrades only turn a blind eye toward me now. When I saw that they would not help me after all I had sacrificed, I broke my party relations completely. Now I don't care whether I live or die."

She was nearly dead with tuberculosis. I had no money and no way to help her, so I suggested that she go to the social service department of the Beijing Union Medical College. I was arrested soon afterward and have never heard anything about her since.

This lovely girl was a tragic casualty of the Chinese

Revolution. She had run away from her first husband and from her wealthy family to do revolutionary work. She wrote beautiful Chinese characters and had a fine mind. Her family lost face because she ran away from home and also because of her revolutionary record and loss of morality. They would never forgive her. Because she was weak and helpless and could not work, the Party would do nothing to aid her as they had little money even for active members and had ordered that all members must get work in industry or elsewhere to support themselves. All four of these girls sacrificed everything for the revolution with no thanks from anyone except the men who escaped in the boat through their generosity. I never learned what happened to the other three, but their fate could not have been any better.

❧

At that time there was a political split over the problem of the Korean Revolution. The Korean Party was inside the Chinese Communist Party. The split was over the question of whether the Korean Communist Party should continue its union with the Korean nationalists and work more closely with them or whether it should split with them the way the Chinese Communist Party had split with the Right.

In the Shanghai Committee were three members of the Korean Communist Party Committee, two of whom had escaped from Korea during the mass arrests of one thousand made in March 1928.[131] Most Koreans didn't believe that these two men were any good because they had escaped successfully. Both were intellectuals, and all intellectuals are suspect in crises. We held a criticism meeting in Shanghai over the question of these escapees, and about twenty came. If these two were not trustworthy, their presence in our midst constituted a grave danger. One of these was named Han. I shall have more to tell of him later, when he became my enemy.[132]

Some said the two were good. Many declared that they could not be judged either good or bad as we had no proof either way. Perhaps they could have escaped through the latrine, as they said, but it would not have been easy. I expressed my own opinion that sectarianism was to blame for all such things. Because of the rivalry for personal leadership and the existence of internal sects, it had been easy for the enemy to discover our membership and for their agents to enter our party. Hence the mass arrests in Korea. Our curse was that each individual wanted to be a leader and did not cooperate with the others; therefore every leader suspected every other.

The heyday of the Korean Party, as of the Japanese, was from 1926 to 1928. Then, as in Japan, it was suppressed. During those years many party leaders were journalists, and the Japanese read all papers with a magnifying glass to discover which writers revealed a communist tendency. All kinds of people then wanted to join, including women and students. It was easy to see who was a communist in those days. They were all Bohemians—with long hair and red neckties. They wore old shoes and carefully kept them unpolished in order to appear proletarian, and carried a modern-style thick walking stick. They considered it bourgeois to shave and were all studio Bolsheviks in appearance.

It was considered very smart and fashionable to be a communist, and the girls all admired the members greatly. Many young men joined and broadcast the fact to all the girls in the neighborhood, in order to be local heroes and win feminine admirers. These boys wrote poetry and went often to cafés and sing-song places, where all the girls fell in love with them and refused to take their money. Most of those who wore red neckties and talked loudest of revolution had been refused by the party and were not members. Of course the serious workers did not engage in such frivolity.

After 1928 this romantic period came to a sharp close. Beards still grew long, but there were no feminine admirers to look at them through the prison bars. The merchants lost their red necktie trade but gained it back in shoe polish and shaving equipment. A new period for the Korean Communist Party began in 1928—a coming of age.

❖

Kim Chung-chang was still very much in love with his Guangdong wife, and they were proudly expecting a baby. He wanted me to stay in Shanghai and write books and articles, for he had always had great confidence in my literary abilities, but I wanted action and cared nothing for theory then.

"You must rest and stop direct action for a little while," he advised me. "It is important not to be killed at this time during the White Terror but to prepare for leadership in future work. I can earn enough to keep you alive here while you do theoretical work and study."

"You are too happy," I said to him bitterly. "Marriage has changed you. I can't stop the active struggle now. I want to intensify it."

Marriage really had changed Kim greatly. Formerly he had traveled freely everywhere. Had he not met this girl, he would never have grown roots. Now he was content to sit in his house and write all day long. I felt that my best friend had been taken away from me and was unhappy about it. Two weeks before I left Shanghai, Kim and his wife were angry at me for this attitude. Then Kim came to see me and admitted:

"Yes, you are right. Love really makes a great change in a man. But don't punish me now. When you find a girl, you will be more in love than I am."

"I'll never marry," I declared. "No girl can take the place of my active revolutionary work. You have no freedom. Your wife has a warm heart, but she is not a revolutionary. You should influence her and not let her influence you."

"Yes, you are right," he said. "But you have never tried to influence a woman. It is not so easy."

Just before I left Shanghai, we had a little farewell party in a park. Oh and Kim and his wife and the Baks and Kim Won-bong and others were there. The others would not go back to Kim's house afterward. Only Oh and I went—to "her" house, we said, not "his." We talked together all night, and I stayed to sleep, but Oh went away to his own room.

As I told Kim good-bye, there were tears in our eyes.

"It is nonsense for you to go now. The danger is too great," he said, shaking his head.

❖

In the spring of 1929 I went to Beijing to continue my activities, even though both Kim and Oh wanted me to stay with them in Shanghai as long as possible.

From 1928 to 1931 Kim did journalistic work in Shanghai and translated many books on fascism. He wrote a good book on the colonial student problem and others on different subjects. He has published twenty volumes under different pen names. He is an important theoretical leader of the Korean Revolution. He never liked anything secret and preferred to do open work—that was his nature.

Therefore, he did not want to do active underground work during the White Terror.

In 1931 Kim went to teach in a college in south China. He has three sons now and works very hard in a house full of noise and happiness.

Oh stayed in Shanghai a year. He was depressed and unhappy and sick—and had fallen seriously in love with Kim's sister-in-law, the attractive Chinese schoolteacher from Indochina. In the autumn of 1930, Oh went to Manchuria, and the girl accompanied him, but he sent her back after four months. In Manchuria he has recovered his health and works very hard, traveling in every province and living a difficult, dangerous life. Oh helped reorganize partisan activities in Manchuria and is today the Political Commissar of the Second Division of the Anti-Japanese Imperialism Army there. This army has three divisions. The Second Division is made up entirely of Koreans—seven thousand of them—and is under the control of the communists. The other two divisions are Chinese partisans, with three thousand nationalist Koreans among them. Oh is also a member of the Central Committee of the Society for Korean Independence, which has a broad mass base. He writes to me that the work there is now very successful and that he is at last accomplishing great things. He wants me to join him as soon as I can.

Geumgang-san mountains in Korea, 1936. Photo by Nym Wales.

PART 4

CLIMBING THE HILLS OF ARIRANG

Map of Korea

CHAPTER 14

"A Revolutionary Is Also a Man ..."

WHEN I ARRIVED in Beijing I was made secretary of the Communist Party in Beijing and also a member of the North China Organization Committee, which voted on questions of personnel. All activities were very secret and underground, as they carried the death penalty. I was happy to be back in active work again and full of plans for carrying out our revolutionary activities. Both Chinese and Koreans had confidence in me because of my good record, and things went well. My particular duty was to coordinate all Korean and Chinese revolutionary activities in North China and Manchuria, in addition to carrying out my duties as head of the Beijing Party.[133]

Then I met a girl. It was at an "active members' meeting" of the Party at which I presided. This girl took a leading part in the discussion and seemed highly intelligent and experienced. She distracted my attention all through the meeting, yet through a kind of mutual rivalry her presence stimulated my mind and made me want to create a good impression on her. She was not pretty but had a strong face and was singularly attractive. I seemed to myself to be exceptionally lucid and wise and brilliant that afternoon under this stimulation.

After the meeting the girl came up and introduced herself, telling me her past history. She obviously wanted to become acquainted, and her intelligent eyes were bright with approbation. I immediately threw up all my defenses and was formal and discouraging in manner.

I thought of this Chinese girl constantly for several days but tried to put her out of my mind. After a week I received a message saying that she wanted to discuss some theoretical questions with me and needed help. I ignored the letter and decided definitely never to become friends with her—the potentialities were dangerous. In a few days I received another message with a double meaning. I did not want to be rude and uncomradely, and thought perhaps the wisest thing was to let her know clearly that I was not in the market for love affairs. So I went to see her.

She was frank and honest and perceptive. I admired these qualities very much in anyone. There was nothing coy and coquettish about her. When I told her that I was too busy to talk with her and had no time for personal visits, she looked at me with straightforward eyes and said simply:

"I like you very much. You and I are the same kind of person. I think we would both enjoy being friends. I do not ask that you should be in love with me. Last year my lover was executed here at Tianqiao by Zhang Zuolin, together with Li Dazhao and nineteen other comrades. Since then I have been unhappy, and my life is so empty that I cannot find anything to fill the loss I have suffered. I am not easily interested in any man. If I like you, you may be sure that it is not without meaning for you as well as myself. I know that you care nothing for women. Perhaps that is why I know that our friendship will not be an ordinary one."

I was nervous, and all my old shyness and embarrassment came over me. "You must forgive me," I said, wild with anxiety to escape. "I have never been in love with any girl, and since 1923 I have sworn never to let this problem interfere with my revolutionary work. It is not for personal reasons that I cannot become close friends with you but because of this decision made long ago. Therefore, I cannot see you again as a friend but only through our party business relations.

She smiled, a slow, perceptive smile full of some wisdom that I did not understand: "You have a wild heart that needs capturing. You do not know how much better two can work together in revolution than one. I can help you in your work, and you can help me. Intimate friendship between a man and a girl during the underground life we must lead means psychological stability and deep comradeship—a deeper comradeship than any other relationship can possibly give. You will believe me some day."

"I'll soon go to Manchuria on a dangerous mission," I replied. "If you care for me it will only mean more unhappiness for you. You have had one lover sacrificed. Now you are only asking for a repetition of this experience. If you fall in love with me, you will worry while I am in Manchuria, and this will interfere with your revolutionary work. If I fall in love with you, my mind will not be clear, and I will not be so anxious to risk my life."

"Love does not make a man or a woman a coward. It makes them braver and more determined. If it should make you less courageous, I would despise you for it, and the problem would be solved. Since my lover was killed, I have had no fear of death—either for myself or for another. Life has become less valuable, and courage more. Now my duty to the revolution is greater—I must carry on his work as well as my own. If you die too, believe me, you will not be lost to the revolution. I shall consider my future burden doubled, and I shall not fail. Revolution is not an abstraction. It is made up of living personalities. The personal element is very important. It gives the revolution organic solidarity—loyalty and greater responsibility among comrades. Together we are strong. Separately, you and I are only individuals, not a complete unit."

"Perhaps when I come back from Manchuria—"

"No, that may be too late. Why should you want to die before you have ever loved a girl? A revolutionary is also a man—not a machine. I will go with you if you like. I have no fear of dangerous work. I could be useful and do things you cannot among the Chinese there, for you are a Korean—"

"No, no," I exclaimed in alarm, "that is impossible."

"As you wish, then. If you will send a letter to me, that will be enough. I shall wait for you. I want someone to believe in and think about. If I know that you want me, that will give me more strength, and I shall be less unhappy."

"But I don't want you. You will only be deceiving yourself."

"Yes, you both want and need me. I know this. Don't try to deceive yourself. You are not so stupid as that. You will come back to me. You are merely being selfish with me and depriving yourself at the same time—for no reason. Don't even bother with the letter, then. But your narrow selfishness will not make you a better revolutionary, believe me. That is only a form of left infantilism in questions of your personal life. It is more romantic than being natural."

"Good-bye," I said, with a bow, edging toward the door in terror, for I saw that she wanted me to take her into my arms as a last gesture.

"You are afraid. Don't run. I won't pursue you. Until after Manchuria then. . . ."

Outside the door I drew a long breath and walked quickly along the street, groaning, "Women are impossible."

I spent several sleepless nights trying to crush the new desire that kept rising within me.

"I am worse than a monk, I am a fool," I said to myself. "Why should I die in Manchuria without anyone to mourn for me? Yes, a revolutionary is also a man. . ."

That was what I had said to defend Kim in Guangzhou, and this girl had flung the words back at me.

After Kim's love affair I had decided that love was good only if directed toward the ideal girl. And after my escape from death in Hailufeng and during my illness in Shanghai, I had seen how precious life was and all the things life had to give—food and comfort and friendship and love and security, over short periods of time at least. Almost unconsciously I had built up a vision of the ideal girl with whom I might one day fall in love. Now I brought all these ideas together in mosaic, and Liu Ling fitted them so closely that I felt uneasy. I had decided that this girl must first of all be strong—in idea and body. She must not be weak in face of danger, she must have firm revolutionary determination, and she must be healthy and able to live a hard life without sickness. Second, I wanted to find a girl whose life before she met me had been independent, so that she would not be a burden but a helpmate and so that I would not have to worry about her if I were imprisoned or unable to take care of her. I did not want her to be beautiful, but neither did I want her to be ugly. I wanted her to be scientifically beautiful, with a rhythmic unity of face and body and mind. I wanted her to be beautiful as a whole, not in any part. As a medical student, to me strength and intelligence were beauty—

not surfaces. Beauty of face seemed to be a compensating cover for ugliness underneath—for vanity and selfishness and stupidity. Or perhaps it created these characteristics. And, for me, beauty was action, not passivity. How the girl thought and reacted was to be an essential part of her beauty. She must be flashing with intelligence and fire. Cold intellect was not enough. Then, too—a legacy of my medical days—I wanted to know her family history, because heredity was a part of her that could not be explained away. On this foundation rested all strength and beauty, for if there should be a child, he would inherit only what was there to give him. I was very reasonable, I thought, very scientific. It should not be difficult to meet such a girl—yet I never thought I would find her. My ideal was my protection against lesser temptations.

I did not think the problem of marriage important one way or another if I should find this girl. If we lived together it would be the same as formal marriage. If more convenient to our work, we would not bother. If there were no child, it would be unimportant to marry, probably.

Liu Ling[134] was all these things. She was not even pretty. She was independent, physically strong and attractive, intelligent, warm-hearted, courageous, straightforward, and a good revolutionary. And she liked me. And I liked her. There was only one thing—there had been another lover before me. I had not reckoned with this possibility in my original chart. But I pushed the thought away as nonsense unworthy of a revolutionary thinker.

I felt myself falling into an abyss. To struggle was only to hasten the ungraceful descent. I had the present will power not to see her again but felt that I had not the strength to escape permanently. Love would claim me soon—if that strange uneasiness I was now feeling so uncomfortably were not already the touch of its spreading tentacles. The calm oracular assurance of this girl that I would go back to her was a kind of hypnosis. She seemed to be in league with some mysteries, which one could only dread and not oppose. After Manchuria, perhaps....

CHAPTER 15

Return to Manchuria

I WAS SENT to Manchuria by the Chinese Communist Party to make a connection between the Chinese Communist Party and the Korean Communist Party, as they had no relation at that time. I was also delegated to attend the Korean Revolutionary Young Men's League Congress,[135] which had been called for August 1929 in Jilin. This league was now independent; formerly it had been connected with the Chinese Communist Party.

I went by train from Beijing to Mukden.° This was a dangerous mission, and I had to be very careful. There were two railway stations in Mukden. I did not get out at the Japanese station at Nanmen but went on to the Chinese station at Mukden. At Nanmen, Japanese policemen boarded the train and went through it looking, as we Koreans say, with "poisonous eyes" for anybody suspicious. They paced up and down until we reached Mukden and eyed me curiously, but apparently did not decide I was a Korean or I would have been thoroughly

° *Mukden*: The Manchu name for the city of Fengtian (present-day Shenyang). –DH

questioned. I wore a long gray Chinese gown. Only highly trained secret-service men can tell a Korean from certain tall northern Chinese types mixed with Mongol blood such as are found in Manchuria from Shandong and Hebei. I am tall and look very Korean, but I speak good Chinese and have learned to look exactly like a Chinese scholar. The trick is to put your hands in the long sleeves and to hunch your shoulders forward and walk with a peculiar gait. Koreans are very straight and throw their chests out, while Chinese scholars have always drooped their shoulders forward from the time of Confucius, I suppose. It has been the distinguishing pose of the scholar, along with his long gown.

The Japanese police stop all Koreans or persons suspected of being Korean in stations of the South Manchuria Railway as they leave the train and ask them to "wait." They pull first one then another out of the queues where they are buying tickets or leaving the platform, and speak to them in Japanese by surprise. They are clever in this work.

At the Mukden station I successfully eluded suspicion again. I went first to a public bath and did not take my luggage, which contained secret documents. Then I found an inn and sent the inn boy with the check to call for my luggage. He had no difficulty at all.

At nine o'clock that night the Chinese gendarmes came to the inn and examined me. This is merely a routine custom at all inns and hotels. I said I was on my way to Harbin. They did not suspect I was a Korean.

I wrote a code letter to the Chinese Party organization, the address of which I had been given. I merely said, "Please bring a newspaper. I have not seen one for a long time."

Someone came to call on me and asked if I had sent a letter. He did not carry a newspaper for identification, so

I denied it. We always have to be careful in case the police have intercepted correspondence. Finally he showed me my letter and we both admitted our identities.

We discussed our affairs. The main problem was whether or not the Korean Communist Party should be separate from the Chinese Party. I wanted the Korean Communist Party of Manchuria to be a department of the Chinese Communist Party there and to work together with it as closely as possible.

After three days I went to Jilin, together with a Chinese Party delegate, to attend the Congress and lay plans for future party work. We had to travel eighty li to a village in the mountains. There we met Jang Il-jin, the leader of the Korean Communist Party,° whom I had known in Guangzhou in 1926-27.

At this meeting we pointed out and discussed all mistakes and decided to adopt a new line in Manchuria under which the Koreans and Chinese would cooperate. We Koreans decided that it was a mistake to have directed our fight in Manchuria only against Japanese imperialism and never against the Chinese ruling class or landlords. There were a million Korean farmers in Manchuria oppressed by the Chinese feudal class and working mostly for Chinese landlords. Therefore, we decided to join with the Chinese peasantry and lead an agrarian struggle against the Chinese ruling class as well as against Japanese imperialism, in accordance with the general party line elsewhere at that time. So we organized a new

---

° *Jang Il-jin, the leader of the Korean Communist Party*: This "Jang" likely refers to Han Hae, otherwise known as Kim Jang-chun (1900-1929). A poem written in Chinese in 1930 in memory of Han, titled "Diao Han Hai tongzhi" (Mourning Comrade Han Hae), has been attributed to Kim San by the late Professor Cui Longshui, who translated the poem into Korean. See page 442 in Appendix II for the poem in an English-language translation. Kim seemed to have composed it on the basis of incorrect information about Han, whom Kim thought had died in a prison in colonial Korea. In fact he died of disease in Jilin, China in 1929. –DH (Jeon 2016; Kim 2005; *HSIS*, 533, *Sisa Journal* 1993, 20-21)

"Korean-Chinese Peasants' Union." Until this time, the local Chinese Communist Party had had no peasant organization at all, and no peasants in the party membership, though after 1925 they had organized many intellectuals and city workers into unions. The Korean Communist Party had its unions of peasants and farm laborers, but no city proletariat. The Korean Party now got busy and helped the Chinese to create a peasant organization, and a peasant department that included several Korean members was established in the Chinese Party.

The Congress adopted this new line unanimously. Eighty delegates had arrived. All were eager and full of purpose and political consciousness. Personal differences were forgotten while problems were discussed carefully and objectively. Usually in China we had argued violently after such meetings, and many people had been dissatisfied. At this Congress, the spirit of cooperation and unity was excellent. I was surprised and delighted. I felt that after many years, factionalism had at last been conquered. It was my first experience of a mass movement led by the Korean Communist Party, and it had a very deep influence upon me. There were even seven competent girl farmers among the delegates. I recognized for the first time the full potentialities of the Korean mass movement in Manchuria—our key revolutionary area today. Though I was still absorbed in the Chinese problem as the leading revolutionary task in the Far East, my faith in Korea revived immeasurably, and I felt a hope for my country I had never known before. In 1928 the Communist Party in Korea had been broken by wholesale arrests, and cliques still wanted to dominate each other. Here in Manchuria this phase was over, and the Congress prepared its delegates for unified leadership. The Congress decided that the Korean Revolutionary Young Men's League should keep its independent system, led by the Korean Communist Youth branch of the Manchuria Committee.

This Congress was dominated by the communists, not by the nationalists—an indication of rising revolutionary consciousness. The leaders were Jang Il-jin, Jin Gong-mok, and Ma Cheon-mo,[136] three veterans of the Guangzhou Commune and all good, hard workers. Two of them, Jang and Ma, died from overwork the following year.

After the Congress and subsequent discussions were over, the Chinese delegate went back to Mukden. I stayed in Jilin for two more months to inspect and study all phases of the local situation.

The Korean communists in Manchuria live a harsh, bitter life, and many of them become ill. Even in the winter they must sometimes sleep on the ground in the mountains, in snow or rain. There are so few experienced leaders that they must work very hard and wear themselves out with the strain of constant activity.

During my two months of inspection in Jilin Province, I traveled around every day asking questions and studying the general political and economic problems of Manchuria. I was quite happy to see the revolutionary movement developing so well there.

At that time Koreans in Manchuria were struggling for the right of Chinese citizenship. The Japanese wanted to keep all Koreans under Japanese citizenship. The net result for those who tried to become Chinese citizens was that the Japanese arrested them as Koreans and the Chinese executed them as citizens of their country. (I had become a Chinese citizen in Shanghai in 1922, but dropped this citizenship later.)

From 1924 to 1931 the Korean nationalists had two separate but coordinated governments functioning in Manchuria. One was called the Korean "Government for Justice"[137] and the other was called the Korean "Government for the New People."[138] These two controlled the Korean farmers and schools in their local territory. They printed textbooks and had their own police and courts. The "Government for Justice" controlled seventy thousand people, and its capital was in Xinbin Xian in Mukden. Its leader was Heng Mu-kuan,* a graduate of a Japanese officers' school before 1910. The "Government for the New People" controlled thirty thousand Koreans; its capital was in the north of Jilin Province. It was led by Kim Jwa-jin.

These two nationalist governments opposed the Korean Communist Party in Manchuria.[139] In 1924, the Party had organized the East Manchuria Young Men's League of Communist Youth, which was made up of young peasants and which opposed the nationalists. They organized a few peasant partisans in 1924.

In 1924 the nationalists split into two wings, right and left. One wanted to cooperate with the communists, the other refused.

In 1931 there was much oppression of the Koreans in Manchuria by the Chinese, and the farmers were tired of paying additional taxes to their own two governments, so the two governments closed down. The communists contributed to their collapse, for they opposed both of them, thinking them useless and that a large anti-Japanese union should be created instead. The right wing of the nationalists lost their mass base, and the left wing cooperated with the communist program. After September 18, 1931, when Japan occupied Manchuria, a big partisan movement was started.[140] By 1937 there were only two systems among the Koreans in Manchuria—one communist and one unified nationalist, with the former

---

* *Heng Mu-kuan*: It is unclear who this might be. He might be Yi Cheong-cheon (1888–1957), who graduated from a Japanese army officers school in 1912 and became a leader of the "Government for Justice." –KTS, AJ, MI, MN, GT, DH (*HID* vol. 1, 456; Hwang 2016, 51)

constantly gaining power. In 1937 there was an army of seven thousand Korean partisans under the communists in Manchuria and three thousand under the nationalists.

Before 1931 Zhang Xueliang had utilized these two governments* against the communists. His regime killed many Korean communists from 1928 to 1931. For instance, just before I arrived, forty Korean communists were executed in Helong Xian in east Manchuria. In the capital of Jilin Province, there were eighty Korean communists in prison when the Japanese took over. They released all of them, hoping to use them against the Chinese, and a few turned traitor.

❖

As I walked around their fields and talked with them, I learned much about the individual lives and problems of the Korean farmers in Manchuria and came to feel very close to them. When I had been in Manchuria in 1920 I had observed conditions and sympathized with the farmers, but I was too young to get any grasp on their problems or to feel any serious sense of responsibility for leading them toward final solutions. At that time the only solution offered was to return to Korea after the Japanese had all been kicked out. Now, with my long, full years in China, I understood the meaning both of class solidarity and international cooperation. The Soviet Union I loved like a mother for its leadership in the emancipation of oppressed peoples and classes. The Chinese Revolution I loved as a blood brother whose life and destiny were my own. The Korean Revolution I loved as a child, young and uncertain, whose steps I might help to guide along the pathway of Russia and China before them.

---

* *these two governments*: i.e. the two Korean nationalist governments. –DH

The old farmers, exiled for so many years, listened to me as if in a dream, but the young ones asked about ways and means with eager intelligence and determination. They all agreed that it was no use hoping to return to Korea and that they must lay a permanent basis in Manchuria for struggle against the Japanese and build a union with the poor Chinese farmers for this purpose as well as for breaking down the landlord system.

Because the Chinese farmers realized the improvement in their lives over life in many parts of China, only the Koreans, being the oppressed minority, were revolutionary. The only workers' struggle was among the railway men of the South Manchuria Railway (SMR), which was owned by the Japanese, and the Chinese Eastern Railway (CER), which was owned jointly by the Soviet Union and the Chinese. These were the two big economic organs of Manchuria[141] and controlled its whole economy. The SMR workers were strongly organized* at that time (and still are even today, or so I hear). Yet the lives of workers on the railways were far better than on the farm, so they did not carry on a radical struggle.

In 1929 the Japanese were already preparing steps to occupy Manchuria, and intrigued to split the Koreans and Chinese into hostile camps. The Manchuria government[142] was also guilty of stirring up hatred between the two, which played into Japanese hands. The Korean communists tried to prevent this hostile split, but after 1932 the Korean nationalist independence movement cut relations

---

* *strongly organized*: The Japanese communists were quite active on the South Manchurian Railroad, but in 1930 eighty were arrested, and this broke the whole Japanese Communist Party organization in Manchuria. These Japanese were very brave and devoted to their revolutionary duties. Their work created much encouragement among the Chinese workers, and even after Japan occupied Manchuria, the CCP could not bring out the nationalist slogan because their line then was proletarian internationalism, and they lost an opportunity that was not to recur again. It was the Korean Communist Party that first pointed out that this was left[ist] infantilism and had to be changed to meet the new situation. —KS

with the Chinese and had none except in the objective fact of common struggle.

When winter came I went to Andong on the Korean border to establish relations between the local Chinese and Korean Communist Parties. There I stayed a month and organized a secret cell of twenty men in an ammunition factory. I also organized another cell in Sinuiju Sons.[143] I asked my former friends in Korea to come to Andong to see me, and several of them came. At that time there were only seven communists in Andong.

Andong became very dangerous for me, so I had to leave early in 1930. I had practically no money, though I was spending only $12 a month. My friends gave me some, and the party contributed a little, so I was able to go back to Beijing safely.

CHAPTER 16

A Revolutionary Marriage

AS SOON AS I arrived in Beijing, a message came from Liu Ling asking where we could meet. I replied that it was impossible as it was too dangerous to see any party people immediately after my trip. I had thought of her all during my months in Manchuria—it had been a pleasant thought. But I wanted to put off the moment of surrender as long as possible.

The next day a knock came at my room in the gongyu.[*] Instinct told me who it was. With a pounding heart I opened the door.

"So—you have found me!" I frowned.

I lit a cigarette and tried to appear calm and nonchalant.

"Why not?" she replied, taking off her coat and occupying a chair with a smile of possession. "I received the letter you did not send."

"You are a magician," was my comment.

I was feeling acutely uncomfortable and shy and called the houseboy to order tea.

---

[*] *gongyu*: Mandarin word for a cheap boarding house; nowadays, the term is also used to refer to an apartment. –DH

"Don't pace the floor like a caged creature," she laughed. "I am not so formidable as I look."

"You look very harmless to me," I ventured bravely. It was the wrong thing, and I blushed profusely as she raised her eyebrows skeptically.

My hands shook as I poured out the tea and handed her a spilling bowl.

"You need not try to drown me like a kitten just because I am harmless," she said archly, wiping the tea off her gown.

She put the cup on the table and took mine from me.

"Come here," she ordered, taking me by the hand.

I withdrew my hand silently and retreated to the corner of the room to light another cigarette.

"Must you look ridiculous, like a chimney, on an important occasion like this?" she demanded. "Put down your cigarette long enough to breathe."

"What do you want?" I begged, desperately looking around for a place to sit with some semblance of dignity.

"You know we are in love with each other," she said tensely, coming up and taking my cigarette away as she sat beside me.

She crushed the cigarette under her heel. "Aren't we both alike in being honest and frank? It's no use to pretend. I know you as I do myself."

"What can I say?" I whispered hoarsely.

"There's nothing more for us to say." She took both my hands and held them together warmly.

I knelt down beside her and hid my face on her knees, shaken with emotion.

"It's good to be alive..."

The next afternoon I took her to Beihai.[144] We held hands and walked around in the clear frosty weather, very gay and lighthearted. The passersby smiled, and we smiled back. The world seemed a friendly place full of light and glory. We sat on a bench watching the sunset paint the white Beihai pagoda with bold, brilliant colors like a diligent amateur artist, and I did not notice that my arm around the girl was cramped with cold. It seemed to me that I had never been young and happy before and that a new life was beginning on another planet. Was it only yesterday that I carried the weight of mankind on my shoulders?

That night I wrote a letter to Kim Chung-chang and another to Oh Seong-ryun. "I forgive you all your romantic nonsense," it said. "In fact, tonight I want to forgive everyone and everything. Kim was right about me—only too right." How amused they would be to receive this confession!

We found a room in a gongyu and were very happy together. I thought everything she said was charming and witty, and she seemed to find my remarks brilliant and amusing. Even the smallest details of everyday life became interesting and full of pleasure. Our companionship was stimulating and exciting. My mind seemed keener and my body full of new vitality. All the sickness of Hailufeng seemed flooded away forever. Sometimes I would wake up at night and think it was all a dream—that I must have malarial delirium again.

We lived together blissfully for several months. No gongyu was safe, and we had to move often to avoid arrest, but we did this in the spirit of adventure and bravado. We carried on our revolutionary work, and I decided that Liu Ling was right. Two were a solid unit; one was only an individual. We could comfort each other in moments of depression and share our victories and defeats. Life was natural and healthful and good. Liu Ling was strong and did not appear to mind the hard life and poor food. Poverty seemed like a blessing that made small comforts increase in value and our love precious beyond measure. We had many problems, but they seemed to solve themselves. Liu Ling was my ideal girl.

Then the clouds began to drift over the brightness and clarity. It occurred to me one day that Liu Ling was too much my ideal. For one thing, she was too independent, the prime quality I had demanded. Little things, then bigger things, came up which required decision on one side or the other. At first these seemed rather funny:

"It's only a question of temporary hegemony," I would laugh. "Ours is a revolutionary marriage, but every revolution must determine the question of hegemony sooner or later. I am the proletarian and you are the bourgeoisie, so according to good Marxists, the hegemony must be mine. And of course you are the best little Marxist in the world so you cannot fail to see that."

"Your dialectics are very good," she would say, tweaking my ear. "But your economics are not. I believe in economic determinism, not in abstract dialectics."

Our first major problem was over money. Liu Ling had a job as a school teacher, I had none. I could earn only a little, but I refused to let her pay our expenses and insisted that she live on the bare edge of existence within my means. That was why I called her a bourgeoisie. I did not mind if she spent her own money for her own personal use, but food and shelter were to be on my terms. She said that either I must use one hand to earn a living and the other for revolutionary work, or let her pay the household expenses. I wanted to use both hands for my work and starve if necessary.

Then I found that those very qualities of determination that made her a good revolutionary also made her stubborn and positive in her convictions. Once she had made up her mind, there was no changing it until the last moment when the objective "situation had changed."

"You're worse than the party line," I would say to her.

"You must be flexible and adjust to new conditions before being pushed into it."

But we were a two-man party, and no majority decision was possible. The vote was too often divided equally.

I felt that I was being dominated by the bourgeoisie and this irritated me, for I was also of a positive, proud character. "Fortunately, we are not married, so she can't oppress me very far," I would remind myself.

"I never had much respect for my father's opinions," I told Liu Ling once. "But once he did say an intelligent thing. It was this: 'If a man's life is dominated by a woman, he is a slave two hundred percent. If a woman is ruled by a man, she is only fifty percent a slave."

"We are exactly alike," she would reply to all my criticisms. "Everything you say to me I can also say to you."

She was certainly no burden to me. But to my surprise I found that I did not want her to be so free and competent. I felt that I was myself a burden on her good nature. In fact, I wished sometimes that she would get sick and appear helpless once in a while so I could take care of her.

"You know, I am out of my role," I would say. "I was born to fight for the weak and the oppressed. I am useless for such a competent person as you are."

I thought that perhaps if we were formally married she would be more bound to me and that this would tie all the endless loose strings in our relationship. But I didn't want this either—for then I would be bound myself. Liu Ling wanted us to marry openly, and so did her brothers and sisters, but I could never bring myself to such a permanent decision.

Gradually the frankness went out of our relationship. We became very polite, careful to avoid friction or hurting each other. We gave up trying to solve the basic problems between us and compromised on the little ones. There was much potential trouble under the surface, but we kept the relationship smooth and friendly. If we were to be permanently married, we should have to resolve all issues fundamentally, but we remained individual and free. At first we saw only the good qualities of each other, and afterward all the bad ones appeared below the surface.

I finally decided that there was not much wrong on either side. We were as well matched as anyone short of the impossible. But I was not happy, though I tried not to admit this to Liu Ling. She was anxious to make me happy and really tried hard, but perhaps I asked too much. We were very much alike—yet there was a great difference in training between us. She was Chinese, and I was Korean: she was positive and did not change, yet she accepted me as I was and did not try to change me; I, always the crusader, was ever trying to revolutionize her in small ways and could not accept either her or myself as we were, though I failed to change in things that would have made life pleasanter for us both.

I concluded that it was not in my nature to be happy and that it was a fallacy to seek for happiness. I would undoubtedly be unhappy again with any other girl.

CHAPTER 17

Climbing the Hills of Arirang

ON NOVEMBER 28, 1930,[145] I was arrested in the West City in Beijing.[146]

For almost two years I had carried out my underground duties successfully as a secretary of the Communist Party in Beijing. I had been careful, but my luck could not last.

"UNCIVILIZED" CONDUCT

We were preparing a memorial meeting for the anniversary of the Guangzhou Commune. A Chinese communist and I were planning to attend a secret meeting at a gongyu connected with the Engineering College. Just as we opened the door, we were confronted by six plainclothes policemen who were holding two other comrades under arrest. I slammed the door and ran. They followed and caught me at the gate after a tussle.

I was taken back into the room, as they were waiting to nab more of those coming to attend the meeting. Nobody else came for a long time, so the police decided to move on.

When two of the policemen went out to call a motor car, I decided we must try to fight ourselves free. At least one or two of us might be able to run away. With my eyes and hands I tried to make the others understand. They understood but would not act. I asked permission to smoke a cigarette and called the boy to bring a pot of tea. As the tea was being poured, I threw the lamp at the biggest policeman, knocking him unconscious, then grabbed the hot teapot and threw it at another. The Chinese did nothing to help, or we could easily have escaped. Then the policemen jumped on me, bound my arms to my head and neck, and threw me on the bed. Still not even a sign from the Chinese. They could easily have gotten away.

"Why do you stand there like fools? Are you nothing but cowards?" I demanded. "Why don't you run away?"

"We are civilized!" was the response.

This made me furious. Here were four prisoners and four policemen! "Koreans would never give up like this," I thought bitterly. Even if the police fired, they would shoot only at our legs. Oh, for my old friend Oh of the Hailufeng days!

Despite being so eminently civilized, they were all bound like common murderers. The car did not come, so we walked along the crowded streets to the police station.

When I was questioned, the police asked: "When did you enter the Communist Party and what department are you in?"

"I am not a member of any Communist Party," I declared. "I have no party relation except with the Korean Independence Party. I am a Korean nationalist. I have no time to worry about the Chinese class struggle. I am too busy with our own nationalist movement."

Nevertheless they put heavy chains on me, joining my hands and feet together. I was put into a filthy, narrow room with sixteen men and could not sleep all night. Next to me someone smoked opium all the time, and the sweet smell was nauseating. I sang and talked against the Guomindang to the other prisoners.

"To oppress the Chinese was enough. Now they oppress Koreans, too," I said.

I knew the Chinese character and that they never want any trouble unless they get paid for it, so I planned to make myself as obnoxious as possible in the hope of being got rid of as a nuisance.

The next day I was exhausted from the experience and went to sleep. We were given cornmeal and radish with water, but I threw mine into a filthy corner. The police asked me why I did this.

"I have broken the law apparently, so I was sent here. Now I am also against the prison laws, so what are you going to do with me?"

The next day, when I was examined, I replied "I don't know" to everything.

"For Korean independence, perhaps you also use the Chinese Communist Party?" they suggested. "Why did you go to the Engineering College last night?"

"To visit a friend."

"What is his name?"

I told them the name of a Korean student who actually did attend the school.

Again I threw the food away and next day was too weak to walk.

The police lifted me up, but I collapsed on the ground and refused to talk.

"If you don't answer, your case will not be cleared up. If you answer quickly, we shall finish with it."

I refused to talk and went back to my room for another hunger strike of three days. By this method I hoped to frighten the police into releasing me to avoid trouble for themselves, as they would not easily be able to explain what had happened if I were to die on their hands.

I was so famished for food that I could hardly keep my self-control, but I thought, "If I eat, tomorrow they will torture me." They always tortured to extort confessions. At midnight an officer came in with a Chinese brush and paper. "If you will not speak, then write, and we'll send it to the superior officer. He will either free you or send you to court."

I refused, and as I was falling asleep I heard a policeman say, "He is finished." I rose up and demanded, "What do you mean? That word has many meanings."

"We didn't speak," they answered.

"They can't kill me in this room so easily," I thought. Then alternately, "Yes, they can. China has no law. They can do anything they please."

"In Japan at least there is law," I thought. "Whether you are to be free or in prison and for how long, you always know. But in China death and freedom have little margin between them—nobody knows how it may be judged and on what flimsy evidence. If you have important connections you can be freed easily; if you are a common man you may be executed for nothing." Communism earned the death penalty. I dared not think of all those thousands of young men and women executed in this name—many of whom were entirely innocent.

At last I concluded that what happened to me did not matter—to die one way was as good as any other. Every other day, I ate a little rice gruel, while the guards begged me to eat more.

"Your comrades have already confessed that you are an organizer of the Third International," the police officer said to me one day in an effort to make me talk.

"Whoever told you that lied. You tortured him, and he lied to save himself from more torture. Call him here and let me look at him. Then he will not dare lie," I shouted. "I have no Chinese 'comrades,' but only some friends.

Can the Chinese help the Korean independence movement? No!"

"You are not speaking honestly," he said, and went away again.

On February 1, 1931,[147] at seven o'clock, the judge and two policemen entered my room as I was eating. I put down my chopsticks and waited, but the judge said, "Don't hurry. Eat your food slowly. We can wait."

I knew they could not be taking me to court at such an hour. The policemen had a chain and a box. "Where are they sending me?" I wondered with a sickening feeling.

Out of pride I tried to be calm and continue to eat, but the chopsticks rattled and the food fell out of my mouth. I threw the chopsticks down and demanded: "Where are you taking me?"

"Wait," they replied. "You'll soon understand."

They gave me my fountain pen and watch and asked me to sign for them. I wrote "Correct" in big letters, without my name.

Then I was bound in light chains. I made no further comment. I thought I was being sent to the military headquarters where political executions were expedited secretly. I was making plans to run away, for the two policemen with me did not look very strong. It would be my last chance to escape.

In front of the Police Bureau was a car with a Japanese Legation license* and two Japanese. Many ideas rushed through my brain. I had made no preparation for a story to tell in a Japanese court. I must try to estimate what they knew about me and what to say that would fit in with this reasonably.

"Please," said the Japanese, and I got into the car with one on each side of me.

---

* *Japanese legation license*: i.e. a license from the Japanese Embassy in Beijing. –DH

"How are you feeling?" they asked, truly curious about what I had been through. Tales of torture in Chinese prisons are legendary in Japan. "How did you get along under the Chinese police system? Don't worry now. We Japanese have just laws. In a Chinese prison you are sure to lose your head. Our highest sentence is seven years. You know your own case and what to expect."

I didn't answer. My head whirled with anxiety. I tried to remember all my many friends who had been arrested by the Japanese and to imagine what they had or had not told. Which ones might have spoken about me? How much did the Japanese know? What evidence could they have?

LEGATION EXHIBIT A

"Welcome, Mr. XX." A police officer greeted me at the Legation, calling me by name. He looked carefully at my wrists to see if I had been tortured.

"Have you any lice?

"Yes, I have many colonies of them."

"Ugh, Chinese police are so dirty."

"No, the Chinese police are not dirty, but I am," I commented drily.

"You may have a bath."

They gave me a kimono and took the occasion to look at my naked body, expecting to see bullet wounds or scars from torture. Then they felt the web of my thumb to see if I had used a gun. I had used only a pistol, and they seemed satisfied that I was not a professional soldier. I looked like an intellectual.

I was sent to a small cement cell and given good food and comfortable quilts. I listened to the Hong Kong and Shanghai Bank clock strike the hours.

On the third day, at nine o'clock, the chief of police

came in with an ingratiating smile and said, "We shall talk personally and informally. Whatever you say to me will not be held against you. I want to understand your type of Korean. I promise that nothing you say will become a matter of court record."

"You think I am a child. Do you actually believe I would trust this kind of thing?" I thought.

"My Japanese is very poor," I answered. "For many years I have not spoken it. Since leaving Korea, this is the first time I have talked in Japanese. Therefore I cannot freely express my thoughts to you, unfortunately."

"Your Japanese is excellent," he smiled.

I wanted him to think of me only as a dreamy idealistic student and philosopher.

"When did you begin the study of Marxist theory?"

"After the Chinese Great Revolution failed."

"Before you lived in Beijing, weren't you already a communist sympathizer? Hadn't you already read revolutionary magazines?"

"I have forgotten."

"You say you have studied Marxism for only three years, since 1927. Is this correct?"

"I only knew about it before. I have merely continued a general interest. I am really only interested in the philosophy of dialectical materialism. Dialectics are a good exercise for the brain—even reading Plato and Aristotle is good. I am beginning to think historical determinism is the only good way to understand the course of history. But I am primarily interested in ethics. I don't believe the will of man is free. I am not sure what determines it, but the philosophy of materialism is the most logical explanation I have found—"

I was about to wear him down with a lot of philosophical discussion, but he saw my notion and put up his hand to stop the deluge.

"You don't study the tactics of class struggle? Marxism all bears on this subject. You must know this. Isn't it true?"

"Yes, that is true in a way, but Marxism is also—"

"Do you believe in the practice of Marxist theory then?"

"At present I merely study the theory. When I entered the Chinese movement before 1927, it was because I thought the revolution would surely succeed. Not until April 12 did I ever think to criticize. Until that time I thought the Guomindang and the Communist Party were the same thing—all Chinese were against imperialism and feudalism. When the revolution failed, I thought I had been stupid in merely blindly following others."

He didn't speak for a while but pondered over something. Then he looked up and stared hard at me. How much did he know? I didn't like the amused light in his eyes.

"You swear you are not a Communist Party member?"

"Yes. I am a student of communism, but I am not a member of the party."

"When you finish studying, will you become a party member?"

"Right now I cannot say."

"Will you stir up class struggle?"

"I doubt if I have the power to stir up any class struggle. I have not much faith in my abilities."

"Your tongue is very smooth," he said, and left.

At twelve o'clock I had lunch. In the afternoon the Chief of Police called me. They had many papers and documents spread out.

"Is this your name?"

"Yes, that is my name."

"This report came from the government in Korea.

Apparently you were not killed in Beijing in 1929 as the papers say.* Your father and mother think you are dead. You don't write to them. You should send a letter to your old parents. Isn't it true that communists don't recognize their own parents?"

"I am not a communist. I don't know what they think of their parents."

"Now you must write the truth. We have this big file. Every word in it is about you. Your lies are no use whatsoever and can only harm your case."

I had to write my name and home address, my parents' names, the names of my grandparents on both sides, and all degrees of relatives of the whole family, as well as when and how I was arrested.

"You must now write a full account of your life from primary school until today, telling who was the principal of the school and the names of all the teachers. Was it an old-style or modern school?"

With all their prodding and questioning, it took three days to cover the whole story from primary school to

---

* *killed in Beijing in 1929 as the papers say*: He was referring to an incident that very nearly resulted in my death from a skull fracture. In 1929 Korean nationalists and communists were having an intense political struggle with frequent violent physical manifestations. I was on the duly elected committee of the Korean Union for Independence in Beijing, and when the nationalists within the union called an illegal meeting at Zhongguo College in order to try to take the leadership away from us communists, I went to the meeting with another comrade to see what they planned to do. Without the permission of the chairman I got up and made a speech in which I demanded that all loyal members of the union must leave and wait for our committee to call a legal meeting. An uproar ensued, and the meeting split up. One of the irate nationalists hit me on the head with a heavy teapot and cut me on the nose near the eye with a knife, very nearly a dangerous set of wounds. Unconscious and bleeding profusely, I was carried out—everyone thought I had been killed. I was taken to the Beijing Union Medical College to have some stitches taken in my head and nose. A pleasant woman named Miss Ida Pruitt came in and comforted me in good Chinese, I remember, and I thought her a very good person. In the meantime, all the newspapers in Korea had published the story of my death. –KS
[On November 6, 1929, the Joseon Daily published an article titled "The So-called Beijing Murder Case is a Groundless and Defamatory Story" (Sowi bukpyeong salin sageon eun mugeunhan jungsangjeok heoseol) that included a letter sent by Kim San, using the name Jang Ji-rak, that denounced the reports on the so-called "Beijing murder incident" as groundless and defamatory. –DH]

the time of my arrest. Every day I signed the document that had been written.

When it was finished the chief of police said: "We cannot free you because of two points against you. First, we have proof that you were a member of the Central Committee of the Korean Revolutionary Young Men's League in Guangzhou; and, second, that you have some connection with the Chinese communists."

Then he showed me a report from the Korean court, which had the 1927 confessions of two comrades telling about me, and also a confession from a Chinese comrade who had formerly been chairman of the Communist Party committee of Beijing.

"I am only a member of the Proletarian Cultural League.[148] I have no relation with the Chinese Communist Party. I never saw the Chinese you mention. He is lying to save his own life and make his sentence easier."

"We don't care so much whether or not you have anything to do with the Chinese Communist Party, but I have all the proofs from the Korean court about the League. You can do nothing but bring a guarantor or document proving that you have no connection. Your comrades say you have. How can you repeat 'no, no'?"

Now I saw where the land lay, and this made me happy. I sat silent, feeling calm and unafraid.

"You may as well confess your relation with the League. We cannot believe your statements. If you do this we'll send you to our court. There will be no torture. If you persist in saying no, we can only send you to Korea, where they will get your confession anyway. Then your case will be out of our hands. I want personally to help you, and you may be assured of fairness if you will speak freely. I have handled many Korean cases here in Beijing, but they were all of robbers or ordinary terrorists. None was political. You are my first case of this kind. You are a high type of young man, and you have the brain to consider your actions. Be intelligent in this matter."

Half an hour passed while he smoked and I sat immobile. The Japanese police are clear-minded and very clever and well trained.

Then I said, "I deny the alleged relation."

I signed a confirmation of my life story from primary school to the time of my arrest but refused to sign the statement of my case that he had drawn up.

"Please go back and wait. You will have to be sent to Korea. We cannot handle your case further. In the next day or so you will be sent to Tianjin."

On February 10 at eight in the morning the police said: "You must go to bed early tonight. Tomorrow you will be sent to Tianjin. You have your last chance to call friends or your wife tonight."

"I have no requests to make. Let us consider the thing finished."

That night I was restless and could not sleep. I wrote on the wall, "Here I climb again the hills of Arirang," and signed my name.

Early in the morning I was taken to the police office.

"Your case here is finished. If you really have no relation with the Young Men's League you will soon be free after you get to Korea. If you will be polite and reasonable, we will send only one man to Tianjin with you to save embarrassment."

As they put the handcuffs on me, the officer said: "Excuse me, please, for this. It is regulations." Then he draped a woolen muffler over my forearm so the handcuffs would not show. We drove to the railway station and for the last time I heard the nearby clock strike, like a mournful echo.

We went second class. The plainclothes policeman with me was a graduate of Waseda University and rather sentimental. He showed clearly that he admired me and begged me to give him some poetry of my own composition or tell him how I felt in prison—a Chinese prison experience was something to respect. All Japanese admire a life of courage and secretly respect revolutionaries, no matter how they may hate them. Chinese are more likely to consider you a fool or a paid agent.

"Prison is the greatest college of humanity," I said.

He wrote this down faithfully and looked up at me, pleased with the phrase.

"What did you learn there?"

"I have learned that I have great force within myself. If I had none, why would it be necessary for the authorities to use so much force to oppose me? The state and I are equal."

He liked that too and quoted it carefully.

I gathered that the Beijing embassy policemen had considered me quite an exhibit—feeling face to face with The Revolution in person.

"I like Koreans very much," he remarked confidentially, "though I have never been in Korea. In fact, my present wife is one. You may write a poem for me in your own language, and she will translate it. She will like to keep it."

I said I had no poetry and that I did not feel like composing any at the moment.

"I have never heard the Internationale," he confided a little nervously. "Will you sing a little of it for me? It must be a very beautiful song."

"I haven't any voice for singing the Internationale today," I replied. "It is a song of victory, not of defeat. But I will write it for you in Korean, and your wife can translate it."

I did this, and he folded it neatly and thanked me.

"There is only one song I can sing on a day like this," I remarked.

"What is that?"

"It is an old, old Korean song of death and defeat—the

'Song of Arirang.'"

I told him the meaning of the song and sang it in a low voice as I looked out over the bare, brown fields and thought of the Guangzhou Commune and Hailufeng.

He became very emotional and said it was the most beautiful music he had ever heard.

"Your wife knows that song," I said. "Every Korean has known it for many generations. If you ever hear her singing it to herself you must buy her a new dress and be kind to her."

"I'll never forget it," he promised warmly and called for some beer, which we drank together.

Even the lowest-ranking Japanese officials abroad are well educated. They are the vanguard of the empire. In Korea the policemen are a different type. They are not so polite! In Korea, empire has been won and may be turned over to second-rate administrators as a routine job.

I was actually the first "Korean political case" the Beijing embassy had handled. Nationalists and terrorists they considered "political bandits" and murderers. Previously, the Japanese police had gone directly to Korean houses, arresting the occupants secretly. The Chinese police knew nothing of this. Such prisoners were taken to Tianjin and Korea to avoid local complications.

At the Consular Court in Tianjin nothing happened. The point made was only that according to Law No. 80 of the Twenty-Ninth Year of the Meiji*, anyone dangerous to the Chinese social system was to be deported from China for a period of three years.[149]

THE "WATER CURE" IN SIX DOSES
I was sent by boat to Dalian,[150] where I stayed one night

---

* *Twenty-Ninth Year of the Meiji*: i.e. 1897. –DH

at the water police building. The following morning two policemen escorted me third class on the South Manchuria Railway to Andong, its last stop at the Yalu River. There we stayed one night. The next day some Japanese soldiers took me across the Yalu River Bridge on a motorcycle to the other side in Korea. It was intensely cold, with wind and snow blowing fiercely. My ears were frozen. I could not protect them, as I was closely bound. I was put into a miserable small room at police headquarters. There I had to write the whole long story over again from primary school on. They had the full record from Beijing and Tianjin.

Then my first torture began. One Japanese pumped water into my mouth and nose while another stood by with a pencil and paper to get a confession. They put a tube into my mouth and nose and held my head low by pulling the hair. The pressure was very strong and my stomach swelled up to the bursting point, while I was strangled nearly to unconsciousness.

"You are a bad case. Two of your comrades in prison have proved your relation. Now do you still think you can be freed by lying?" they repeated.

When I became unconscious they sent me to my cell. It was a slimy wet place. I had a fairly private room, but in each of the ten other cells of the prison were packed four to six prisoners. Every day about thirty new men would be brought in and others sent away.

I stayed in this cell for forty days. Six times they gave me the "water cure," pumping it into my lungs and nose until I was unconscious. Several times I could not recover without a long working-over by a doctor, because I was weak and ill anyway. I learned that to breathe a little is better than to try to hold one's breath, as the water runs out more easily. But I would not confess.

One Sunday, when the other officers were on holiday, a

Japanese policeman came in and beat me on the shin with a wooden geta until the flesh was opened to the bone.

"Why do you insist you have no relation when we already know the truth?" he demanded.

"I never saw those two before," I insisted as he showed me the photographs of the two comrades who had betrayed me. "Bring them here to see if they can identify me. I am sure they cannot."

My shin got a bad infection from the beating and was very painful. My nose and lungs bled and pained me constantly.

This water torture harms the lungs permanently if repeated. Sometimes the arteries burst, but the victim does not die. I had a pus discharge from the lungs for a long time afterward and suffered steady pain.

Usually the Japanese torture intellectuals only mentally, not physically. Two policemen make the prisoner stay in one position all night for three nights. When he tires and falls asleep they beat his head and shout. After a long continuation of this, the brain goes sick and the will flabby. When the judge asks the prisoner questions, he has no will left but confesses to anything. Thus the judge gets his true confession—and also many false ones. Often it takes many years to recover from such an experience, and mental derangement results. Many Koreans I have known have suffered this. It is the most dangerous form of torture, yet when a doctor looks he sees no sign. Public opinion is stirred up by physical evidence of torture, but these nervous cases do not attract so much attention.

Korean prisons today are much better than formerly. Since 1928 they have been heated. The food is gijang* and soy bean curd, or sometimes rice—the worst quality of rice after nine siftings.

---

* *gijang*: Korean for "millet." –DH

After a short examination in court, I was sent to a big prison in Sinuiju, the center for all north Korea.

This prison contained over a thousand inmates. A large percentage were partisans from Manchuria. If proved to have killed or aided in the death of a Japanese, such prisoners were executed. If not, a term of imprisonment sufficed. Since 1910 thousands had been executed in this prison—the best Korean fighters for independence and liberty.

As soon as the door had clanged behind me, the men in the cell ran up eagerly and asked if I came from Manchuria. When I said, no, Beijing, nobody spoke to me for an hour. Manchuria was the center of Korean activities; they were not interested in Beijing emigrants. When they discovered the charges made against me, however, they gathered round again and asked many questions.

"Why are so many communists being arrested now?" they wanted to know. "Ah, it is too bad. The communists have much experience, and we should all study their methods and learn from them for the future. If all are arrested, who will carry on the work?"

They wanted solicitously to know what evidence the court had against me and what my sentence was likely to be, and were eager to learn all about China and the political conditions in the outside world.

After seven days I was called into court. I was given a mask of rice grass to wear from the prison to the court so nobody could see me—this was an old custom. Until my case was called, I waited in a small room. There were many phrases written on the walls by former prisoners: "Today I hear the death sentence." "To live twenty-six years or a hundred is all the same. It is only one life. I am not unhappy." "Who comes here must give up all hope." "There is no justice. I am innocent." One man had written, "I will become a gwi,* and when I return I will kill every Japanese in Korea." Another had said, "You have walked here, but you may have to be carried out." There were many curses against the Japanese emperor, the judge, and all Japanese in general. And there were many phrases from the "Song of Arirang." Many names were inscribed with the dates of the death sentences. These sentences were written on the wood with a fingernail or handcuff. Every word dripped with the blood and tears of my poor countrymen. It was like a room in Hell.

When I entered the courtroom I saw two men in red prison clothes waiting near the witness stand. They were the comrades who had given evidence against me.

When the judge turned to these two and asked them if they knew me and if I were a member of the Korean Revolutionary Young Men's League, they answered:

"Yes, he was a member of the Young Men's League. He was elected in the last meeting called in Guangzhou, but he was not present and did not know about it perhaps. We didn't know where to find him and couldn't get in touch with him. We never saw him again and did not know what became of him."

Then my case was dismissed.

At two o'clock on April 1, the prison warder called me in and said:

"The evidence against you is not enough for conviction now, and you will be given your freedom. But do not think this is anything but luck. Your every move will be watched in the future. It is no use to try to enter any group or do any work. We shall know of everything you do. We can excuse the past if in future you do nothing. But your next case will finish you."

---

* *gwi*: Ghost. –DH

All my endurance under torture had been worthwhile. My refusal to confess had saved me.

KOREAN INTERLUDE

I was sick and weak. The prison food had been bad and the cell full of vermin. I had a cough and pus discharge and bleeding from the lungs every day. Because of the broken condition of my lungs, I had contracted tuberculosis, but I did not know it then. Since then I have had tuberculosis and little hope of recovering my natural strength. I, who had been once so athletic and strong, was now a walking invalid—and only twenty-six years old! I was shocked when my nephew remarked on seeing me for the first time, "He is an ugly old man. You told me he was strong and good-looking."

I went back to my home near Pyongyang and stayed two months. During that period I learned for the first time the meaning and devotion of mother love. It made me uneasy to be fussed over and pampered with special food, but I appreciated deeply the spirit in which my mother did this. In recognition of her feeling for me I told her something about my life. She had thought communists and nationalists were the same thing. She sympathized with my struggle for Korean independence and wanted it too. "If Korea were free, you would then come here to live at home with me, wouldn't you?" she asked.

My father was a very old man now, but still worked on the farm. He was as conservative as ever and seldom talked. I was still only an ingrate rebel son to him.

In Korea, when one is released from prison, the public attitude is not like that in China. The Koreans are proud of you and treat you kindly. Even old men and women show their secret sympathies. You have good "face." But in China nobody helps you. Everyone cuts relations if possible, fearing "trouble." Once you are down, nobody wants to help you up. It is considered to be just your own bad luck, and nobody wants to share it with you. For that reason, it takes many different kinds of courage to be a revolutionary in China, and I admire the Chinese greatly for the risks they take. Each individual fights his own battle, not hoping for sacrifice from others when he is in need. Only the communists have a spirit of mutual cooperation and a comradely feeling of responsibility. But there too the old cancer of selfishness eats away the fabric, and you can never be sure how rotten it is. This is the fault of the social system, where human life and death mean little to anyone but the individual, therefore the individual must be doubly selfish to take care of his own interests. If you have power once in your hands, it is automatically cumulative. Everyone is eager to be your friend. If you have no power, you must be a sycophant and will have few friends to work and struggle with you on terms of equality. That is the old Confucian hierarchy of "higher and lower." We had this same thing in Korea, but life was not so cruel there, so the people could be kinder by nature.

CHAPTER 18

Party and Personal Wars

IT WAS JUNE 1931 when I returned to Beijing. Beijing was beautiful in June, with giant acacia trees spreading green masses of color above the dull gray walls that had been so dreary on the winter's day of my arrest. I went to find Liu Ling to tell her of my freedom.

"She was miserable after your arrest," I was told. "When she learned that you had been sent to Korea, she thought you would be a prisoner for many years and went to Qingdao to work. There she was probably arrested by Han Fuju, for a mass arrest occurred at that time. Nearly all of those arrested were executed. She used another name, and we cannot find out what happened to her. We think she cannot be alive now."[151]

I was sick at heart. I walked in Beihai all afternoon, seeking comfort in the gay spring flowers—as gay as we had been that first afternoon so very long ago. Nobody smiled at me this day. A few students stared curiously at the tall, thin figure moving about uncertainly like an invalid from a hospital.

It was always the bravest and best that were sacrificed,

and life seemed to take a special revenge on me and my brief loves. I thought again of Ahn Dong-hui's little daughter in Manchuria; of the sturdy, cheerful young Communist Youth girl in Hailufeng who died fighting for her people. It was not for me to choose a lonely destiny—death was always ready to choose it for me.

ON TRIAL AS A JAPANESE SPY

But this was only my first blow. I noticed that members seemed friendly but afraid to meet me. At first I had no idea why, though it was a natural precaution. Then I discovered that some of my enemies had made secret reports to the party against me—asking how it was that I had been freed so easily from prison in Korea. I had many political enemies, for I was of a decisive, unforgiving character. I was sometimes called a Robespierre for my insistence upon "purity" and incorruptibility to an absolute degree. I had suffered no political troubles of my own, and had little patience with those who deviated even in small ways, always ready to pronounce final judgments from a high seat of righteousness. I had no fear of offending anyone in the name of the party line, and many were the solemn indictments I had dictated against others. Retribution was to fall upon me in the Robespierrean tradition.

I found that this underground campaign against me was being directed by a Korean whom I shall just call Han* and whom I had met once in Shanghai in 1928. He was one of the party leaders who had escaped during the mass arrests in Korea in March 1928 and whom we had accused of untrustworthiness when the case was discussed. I had

---

* *whom I should just call Han*: Many Korean scholars believe this person to be Han Wi-geon (see Biographical Notes). Kim San describes Han as his political enemy in this book, but, according to Kim San's biographer, Kim and Han seemed to have reconciled in Yan'an just before Han's death there in 1937. –DH (Yi 2006)

made it clear that I thought them untrustworthy, not only because their leadership had been objectively bad. I had stated it as my opinion that if they had been imprisoned it was no harm to the movement, because of their stupid sectarian attitude, which made it easy for spies to enter our ranks and betray the whole organization. Over a thousand had been arrested at that time, and I blamed the leaders who had escaped for their objective guilt in this great loss. Han had been bitter and black-hearted about the party attitude, which he considered to have been fostered largely by me. Though my attack had not been personal—indeed I had never been introduced to Han until the meeting in Shanghai—he hated me.

Han had come to Beijing in 1930 just before my arrest and, as I was then acting as secretary of the Organization Committee, he had written me a letter asking permission to enter the Party in Beijing. He had no mandate, and I replied that we must write to the Shanghai Committee for credentials and full reports, and that he would have to wait until we received these. No reply had been received before my arrest, and Han thought I was trying to keep him out of the party and still distrusted him, so he wanted revenge.

In April 1931 he had been accepted by the Party upon the recommendation of another Korean. Now that I had returned, he thought that if I were put back into a responsible position he would not be able to work with me and the Party. His belief was unfounded, for I had been fully prepared to work with him on the condition that Shanghai send credentials, but he did not know that, of course, and thought himself engaged in a life-and-death political and personal feud.

Han had mobilized some Korean nationalists who hated me because I had fought against them previously, and had also convinced several Communist Party members that I was suspect. The implication was that I had written a confession[152] and had been forced to establish secret connections with the Japanese as a spy. Han never openly stated this, but rather implied that there was some secret behind my case.

The Chinese who had known me were on my side and said they did not believe the implication, but wanted to clear it up in order to re-establish confidence. Others were skeptical because of the Koreans who were suspicious of me. I demanded an open trial to settle the thing once and for all.

I was furious at Han for one thing in particular: Though he was the one who had originated the charges, he refused to get proofs of my innocence from the local prison and from Korea. He simply did not want to see me cleared and back in power.

The Chinese Communist Party called a court to settle the case.[153] Members on both sides of the question were present. All were asked to give complete knowledge of me and my record, and any information about my arrest and release. I told the whole account of my arrest and trial in detail. Nothing unfavorable was produced against me. Then the court demanded of Han, the only accuser, why he did not believe me and asked him to show proof of his suspicions.

He could only say, "There is no way to determine his guilt. But we cannot believe in his innocence just because of this."

I explained my previous trouble with Han. Then the court pointed out that nobody had been arrested because of me, and that I had caused no trouble anywhere.

"Yes," Han agreed, "that is true at this moment. But perhaps he is only waiting for a critical time to betray and destroy our organization for the Japanese. To trust him is to open our party to danger."

"You are dreaming," I said to Han. "This is only petty personal revenge. Wait and see."

At the conclusion, the court decided that I was all right and commended me as a good, strong member, stating that for the Koreans to oppose me was wrong and unfair.

I was accepted back into the party ranks without further question.[154] Han was worried because his own position was very uncertain and he felt that others had lost confidence in him because of his unjustified opposition to me, so he did not stop his underground campaign against me, hoping to prove himself correct somehow. He acted as a poison, infecting others with vague suspicions, and those who did not know me well were afraid to become too close with me. Han next started a rumor that I was a Li Lisan man* and therefore not qualified for leadership. This depressed and irritated me.

THE PARTY LINE

There was a critical political situation in party work throughout China. A purge was taking place and a new line being instituted. The "Li Lisanists" were being thrown out, and members were unscrupulously fighting for supremacy, both on the basis of personal rivalry and political problems. The underground nature of our movement made many injustices unavoidable. I was one of many victims of circumstance.

The Chinese Communist Party decided that, as I had

---

* *Li Lisan man*: A reference to Li Lisan (1899-1967), a leading CCP labor organizer known for being very leftist and the leader of the CCP between 1928 and late 1930. At the time Kim San describes, he was being criticized for insisting that the proletariat should lead the Party rather than the peasants. He took the position that the Revolution was at hand and ordered the Red Army in rural military bases to surround and take over the industrial big cities (the "Li Lisan Line"). This strategy ended in failure, due mainly to the fact that the CCP was weak in numbers in those cities. In 1931, Li and his supporters were blamed for these failures and ousted. –NW, MN, MI, DH (BDCC, 512-519)

been one of the most important leaders during the ultra-leftist Li Lisan period, I could not be trusted to carry out the new line faithfully. I objected strongly to being displaced from the leadership, as I was not only prepared to follow the new line but had suffered enough from radical "Putschism"* in Guangzhou and Hailufeng and Beijing to be able to judge these tactics from bitter first-hand experience. But it was a general order from the top, and the local party stated that I must accept this discipline until I could be reinstated. They ordered me to do manual labor in the mines at Zhangjiakou. I submitted, though it was suicide in my sick condition after imprisonment. I could get no job in the mines, however, and found the situation hopeless for party work and too dangerous to attempt. Twice I was nearly arrested because I looked too much like an intellectual, for police supervision was very close. When I made my report, I was told to recover my health and wait awhile. I went to the Niangniang Temple near Yanjing University, where I studied in the library and thought out many problems, both personal and political.

The Li Lisan line had demanded armed uprisings in Guomindang areas and the capture of big cities by the Red Army. It was finally changed in April 1931, and Li Lisan was sent to Moscow for discipline. I had been in prison during most of the controversy, and until this time I had never worried about major theoretical questions but only about matters of local tactics, accepting orders as they came. Now I began to re-examine first principles and to ask questions and seek answers.

After my spy scare and discipline as a Li Lisanist, my mind was confused and disturbed. I could not avoid feeling that part of my trouble came because I was a

---

* *Putschism*: Advocacy of a putsch, i.e. a plotted attempt to use violent means to bring about political change or overthrow a government. –DH

Korean among Chinese;[155] even the communists in China had a tendency toward nationalism. The foreigner is always the first to be blamed. It was a time of general demoralization: the reprisals against the Li Lisan uprisings were very cruel. Thousands of communists were arrested and executed or imprisoned. Others were betrayed and turned over to the Guomindang, or became passive. Still others became Trotskyists* or fascists. Party work became weaker and weaker on the outside, and morale within broke down. The situation was complex and difficult to analyze. There was a swing to the right and a tendency toward surrender. I was extremely worried and anxious to find a clear method to save the party and the mass movement from demoralization. In the end I concluded that our main slogans were correct but that we must vary the tactics to suit different conditions in various parts of the country. There must be some middle ground where common agreement would make it possible to keep solidarity. I proposed that we utilize the democratic slogan in those White areas where uprising was impossible and resulted only in annihilation, and at the same time keep up the struggle for soviets in the Red areas, working toward the equalization of the two different levels of development.[156] The majority of the party voted against this idea, however, and took the line that no democracy was possible during a civil war. What I was suggesting was a form of what was later called the People's Front in White areas, to support the soviet movement in Red areas, thereby mobilizing all potential stra-

---

* *Trotskyists* (or Trotskyites): A reference to Leon Trotsky (1879-1940), a Russian communist leader who vied with Joseph Stalin (1879-1953) to be the leader of the world communist revolution. Chinese Trotskyists were usually branded as "leftist adventurists," "opportunists," or even "reactionaries" because, unlike Stalin, Trotsky opposed the CCP's alliance with the GMD, which he saw as a bourgeois party, not a "bloc of four classes." He argued for an urban revolution by workers, not a rural revolution by peasants, and for permanent revolution as opposed to revolution by stages. —GT, DH

tegic allies instead of alienating them as at present with our open demand for red flags and soviets everywhere. This idea was put into effect in 1935,[157] when it was decided to give up the soviets also.

CHAPTER 19

Fate and Fortune

ARRESTS INCREASED in every province, with the central power competing with the provincial warlords in this. Betrayals increased alarmingly. Even the Secretary of the Communist Party Military Committee in north China betrayed. The party organization in Beijing was broken, and we lost all connections.

I had no work and no money. I developed fevers and became weaker and weaker physically and more and more depressed mentally. Then I went to the Beijing Union Medical College—to the Charity Department. The doctors took an x-ray and told me that my lungs were in very bad condition and that I had tuberculosis, which was spreading rapidly. They wondered how it was that my lungs had become so broken and inflamed. I could hardly tell them that I had Japanese prison torture to thank for this. I still had a discharge of pus and blood, complicated by tuberculosis. I was informed that unless I had absolute rest for many months and was able to get good food and attention I could not live long. I had no money to buy a bowl of rice a day—how could I buy eggs and meat and vegetables and afford "many months of rest"?

The knowledge that I had tuberculosis was a great shock to me. Since Hailufeng I had never been able to regain my full strength, but I had always been so strong and healthy before that I thought it would come back whenever I took time to recuperate fully. I had hoped someday to go to the south to join the Red Army—now this would be impossible. There were several Korean comrades with the Chinese Red Army. I liked open action. I was not happy in secret underground work and in party intrigues and struggles.

Frustrated and bitter, I was filled with anger against everything. This aggravated my physical condition. I could not rest and could not sleep at all. For days I got no sleep and lived in a torture of misery. The gongyu keeper asked me for money every day and wanted to throw me out. I was too weak to walk without dizziness and exhaustion. He suggested that I take opium to rest my nerves and get some sleep so I could earn enough money to pay him! I went back to the Beijing Union Medical College in a rickshaw. The doctors were alarmed at the rapid worsening of my condition and said I should be put in a hospital immediately. They discovered that I had a bad long-standing nervous condition—an inheritance from Hailufeng as well as from my prison experience a few months before. I went back to the gongyu. I would not speak to anyone. I merely played with the dog in the compound and hardly moved around at all. If the gongyu keeper had suspected my identity he could have made a good deal of money by turning me over to the police. I half expected this every day. That would have been one way to pay one's bills.

Then I discovered that my enemy, Han, was still spreading lies about me like a man obsessed. I was infuriated. He was not a man but a snake. I hated him as a thing slimy and unclean. What he had done to me, he would be just as likely to do to others. I wanted to kill him and clean the world of such a creature once and for all. Why not? The thought took form in my mind and seemed to solve the deep sense of frustration and helplessness that overpowered me. And if he killed me, that would be another useful act. He was a powerful man, and I was then weak as a woman. I had been so long accustomed to action that I wanted to strike at something, to struggle physically against myself and the forces around me. I had no psychological mechanism for accepting and resigning myself to the condition of which I found myself a victim.

Carried on by the last strength of desperation and anger, I went to see Han, concealing a sharp knife.

He was at home, alone. I stood in the doorway and looked at him steadily for five minutes. My eyes fascinated him the way a bright point of light hypnotizes a snake.

I moved very slowly over to the table, while he stared at me, paralyzed. With slow determination, I pulled out the knife and laid it quietly on the table between us.

"Within five minutes, one of us is going to kill the other," I said hoarsely.

He did not move.

I waited.

Then I saw tears gathering in his eyes. I knew they were not of fear but of shame and regret. I pitied him and walked slowly out of the room, leaving the knife on the table.

My anger was gone. In its place was only bitter sadness. I did not want to kill anyone. I had only the moral and physical strength to kill myself. Yet I had no gun. Not even a knife. No money to buy poison. Fortunately, one can always starve oneself to death.

The emotional reaction against my attempt at murder

left me exhausted. I lay back on my bed in a delirium of weakness. Suicide by drowning would have been easy, but there was no place in Beijing for this. I thought of the beautiful clear rivers of Korea, where suicide was a pleasure... I who am about to die remember you, Korea, for your beautiful rivers and your lovely green mountains. Your sons are weak, but those mountains and rivers of ten thousand li are strong. They will live when we are all dead in foreign lands. I regret that I cannot bring back my blood to nourish the soil of my birth—even my rotten, tubercular blood, poisoned with despair. I have destroyed myself fighting for you and for the freedom of humanity. Nothing is left but fertilizer for an alien ungrateful land. Even the spirit is dead. I have left only enough to finish myself cleanly and quickly. The will to die is with me still. The will to live has gone. Remember me as I was, friends of those heroic years—full of health and strength and belief and courage. Forget that I did not die in the Guangzhou Commune, in Hailufeng, in Manchuria, in prison. A part of me was killed there, a part lies unburied in every place. Only the heart and the will die here in this filthy room. The rest of me was sacrificed gloriously in battle, and created new hope for you and for mankind....

I fell into unconsciousness, thinking how kind it was of nature to end my suffering so easily in quiet death. A fever warmed my bones comfortably.

I woke up a long time afterward to find the gongyu manager fussing around my bed.

"You've had nothing to eat for days," he said, bringing me food. "You have had a very high fever. I thought you were dying. It's no use for a young man to die like this, even if you want to. Never mind my money. If you will eat and get well, you can leave and go home to your old parents."

He was anxious that I should not die in his house, for

he would have been responsible for the body, and wanted to make me strong enough to go away—where, he did not care.

I think my dormant malaria came back during those few days and the high fever helped to cure me.

The relapse into sleep and unconsciousness had rested my nerves and body, and I felt that the hammering of death in my eardrums had ceased. New, life-giving fluid seemed to be pouring into my veins. Whether I lived or died I did not care. To eat or not to eat was no question. I accepted the food, though I would not have lifted a finger to get it for myself. Gradually a little strength was restored to me, though I was as thin and gaunt as a skeleton.

"Some day I shall repay you for your kindness," I said to the innkeeper. "I shall be able to earn money by doing translation work. Don't worry."

He wanted only to get rid of me, so as soon as I was able to leave, I went to another gongyu. I had long ago pawned all my books and clothes. I owned nothing but what I walked about in. One day someone sent me $20 in an envelope. I think it was Han. I did not care who it was. This was enough to eat for many weeks.

I decided not to attempt suicide again. It was easy enough to die without taking any trouble about it. It was better to be killed by someone else. I had always expected that...

A new philosophy, alien to my nature, seemed to settle over me like cheerful sunlight. Nothing was important. I accepted the fact that I was too weak to solve my many problems. Let them solve themselves. I could not save the Chinese Revolution single-handed. Why be so serious about everything, great and small? Mistakes were inevitable. Perhaps they were even useful in revealing the truth. Perhaps I was mistaken. Perhaps there was no right and wrong. Perhaps whatever *is* is right. Why should a man torture himself with doubts and worry? Are there not enough enemies in the world to do this torture for him? One must gamble with life. One must not fear to lose. One must not care too much if others lose also. History always wins in its own way. What an amazing people the Chinese are! For thousands of years they have been cheerful and content to let life gamble for them. Why change the world? Let the world change you! If no change occurs, that is also good. *Mamahuhu!*

Was I at last succumbing to the Chinese attitude about life and death and struggle? Was I at last being absorbed into this great mass of believers in fate and fortune? What did it matter? One man's luck is another man's misfortune. To sleep and not to dream is good. To eat and not to ask how and why others live. To watch but not to be curious.

I thought that if only I were strong enough I would tramp around the world for ten years, trusting providence to feed or starve me. In either case I would not care. I would sell verses as I went and live in public parks, a poet and a vagabond.

I had been busily engaged in changing the world since the age of eleven. Now the world was changing me. It was reciprocity. Which change was greater I did not care.

It is dangerous to ask questions too close to the truth. It will drive a man mad. It is dangerous to force your truth on others. Perhaps you are wrong. Let them die happy in their beliefs. Do not torture any man's soul with fundamental inquiries. Let him find his answers where he will.

I was gradually coming back to normal and was doctor enough myself to know that my salvation lay in relaxation and relief from worry and political troubles to give the body and the nervous system a chance to recuperate. I did not even read the newspapers, but lay quietly on my bed all day and let nothing disturbing enter my mind.

I bought a book of poetry out of my riches of $20 and at times wrote verses, which I sent to newspapers and magazines. Some of them were accepted, and I earned a few dollars in this way. I wondered why nobody in the party had come to see me. Perhaps they had all been arrested or forced to leave the city. Then one day a young girl comrade came to visit me. She said they had lost connections everywhere and that she did not know what had become of everyone. The party was broken and no activities were possible for a while.

This girl was very kind and came often to see me. She brought me fruit and books. She was much prettier than Liu Ling but undeveloped intellectually. Her lover had been executed the year before, and she was unhappy. This made her take a special interest in helping me—I seemed always to be falling heir to widowed devotion. I like unhappy people. I understand them. Suffering creates character and human feeling. Cheerful, happy people seem like idiots to me. They seem to fly over the surface of life and never to know its meaning. They are not close to the heart of humanity but are remote and isolated. Perhaps that is why they can remain cheerful.

I asked this friend to bring me from the library all the volumes of Goethe, Tennyson, and Keats, whom I enjoyed best. Shelley I preferred not to read; he was a revolutionary romantic like myself, and I wanted to get out of this emotional stage. In middle school I had read over and over again *The Sorrows of Young Werther*. *Faust* I did not understand until now.

I read again the books of Jack London, whom I had always liked. He is the only American writer I know who gives a proletarian interpretation in terms of universal experience. His sentences are simple and strong, and translate well into other languages. His stories about workers are as true for one nation as another. He knows the meaning of poverty and hard struggle, and understands the character of men. In *White Fang*, a dog becomes a wolf as man must also do in order to fight the struggle of life. In London's writings, every cell of animal life is animate and active. You feel vitality and dramatic quality. You feel that he is not an intellectual, but a man of action putting feeling and real experience into his work, and that theme is always failure and renewed struggle. Japanese and Korean workers read London as easily as anyone, and understand him. Through London, a poor worker anywhere learns to feel a kinship and bond of sympathy with American proletarians. I like London better than Gorky. Gorky has good ideology, but he is not a strong man, nor a strong writer like London.

London is positive in his interpretation of poverty and struggle; perhaps that is because his America is the land of opportunity for a worker. Dostoevsky is negative. He exposes the darkness of the human soul through subjective psychology. He admits no positive value to struggle. He could have written exactly the same books about Korea, only the darkness and sadness there are worse than in Russia.

Upton Sinclair I do not enjoy, but everyone in the Far East reads him to get a positive picture of industrial life in capitalist America. He is only descriptive; he contributes nothing to theory. He is broad but not deep, like a searchlight at night. He illuminates surfaces but knows nothing of the hearts of men in the shadows.

Balzac I also re-read at this time. I like his study of the conflict between man's intellect and his passion, and the theme is that man eternally reaches one goal only to search for another.

❖

After a time my physical strength came back, and psychological and mental equilibrium returned with it. I felt a new kind of assurance and stability. My mind became alert again and hungry for action. I felt a great new confidence in myself. I saw that these few months had been a useful influence on me—prison and political struggle, my trouble with Han, my despair and illness. These experiences served to force me into an intellectual coming of age. Murder... suicide... despair—that brief moment was only a bookmark in my life where I found my way. A new chapter lay open before me. All that I needed was to recover my physical health enough to carry on.

I analyzed my past experiences and went through a grueling self-examination. From 1919 to 1924 I had been a student, groping for knowledge and ways and means. During that first stage I passed from one theory to another. From 1919 to 1920, I was a Korean nationalist. From 1920 to 1922, I was an idealist and anarchist, seeking a solid footing to march forward. This I found in the study of Marxism from 1922 to 1924, when I joined the Communist Party.

The second stage of my life was from 1925 to 1928—revolutionary romantic days of action in the Chinese Revolution. Guangzhou, the Commune, Hailufeng. These experiences had broken my health but strengthened my spirit. After that I was thrust into a position of leadership for which I was not fully prepared, but I had developed rapidly. My underground days of leadership in secret activities in Beijing and Manchuria had taught me much. Prison had welded many rough edges into solid form. My murder-suicide-despair days had humanized me and given me a new tolerance and understanding of human nature. I was now no longer a schoolboy, no longer a revolutionary romantic, no longer a party bureaucrat. I was a grown-up human being, equipped with long, hard revolutionary experience, qualified for true leadership in the future. I understood the problems of others through my own. My judgment was balanced and sound—no longer emotional or theoretical but practical and wise, with a solid background of struggle, mental and physical.

As I reviewed my own life and mistakes and wisdom, in comparison with that of others and of the problems before me, I felt a strong, unshakable faith in myself. Since that time I have never lost this. I have had a moral and physical courage and power that have never failed me. I fear nothing. I have absolute confidence in my opinions and abilities. Once I set my mind to a task, I can accomplish it. I can reason and judge in a logical way that convinces me of the correctness of my decisions. Hence I never waver uncertainly or lose direction. I have decision and determination. I can distinguish between immediate things and historical movements. I do not permit small matters to warp my judgment on important ones. I care nothing for difficulties. I cannot be intimidated. When I have made my own decision as to what is correct and true, nothing external can shake it. I have an understanding of the processes of history, which gives me enough grasp of the truth to have positive decisions and interpretations. I have no hesitation in making decisions and giving orders for others to follow when I feel that my leadership is correct. Until I am sure of that, my mind refuses to make decisions. It is like a thing apart from me—a precise mechanism weighing and balancing and moving on, whether I will it or not.

Sometimes I wish that my mind would not be so sure of itself, so positive. But I can do nothing about it. I will not betray myself. I cannot be dishonest. I must carry out the moral and intellectual imperative that propels me forward, no matter what others may think or how much they may disagree with me. I regard this mind as the product of external experience, not as a personal attribute equated only to my own problems. For my personal comfort and happiness, I would rather follow than lead. For the follower there is only one path. For the leader there are always two. The follower is free. The leader is not. The follower can act without responsibility. The leader is burdened with the weight of historical decisions. I am no longer a follower—I was happier when I was. It is my duty to take initiative and leadership—a duty that has been given to me by my experience and that insists upon its performance by an inner compulsion. All those thousands of dead who have not lived to carry out this leadership are like a hand with many fingers commanding me forward. Their knowledge died with them. What I shared of it must live with me and be creative until I too am dead.

A school for Korean immigrants in Longjing, Manchuria circa 1920-30s

PART V

THE KOREAN

NATIONAL FRONT

Map of East Asia

CHAPTER 20

Back to the Mass Movement

IN THE EARLY WEEKS of 1932 I received an invitation from the student body of the famous Second Normal School in Baodingfu to come there to teach. This school had been established by Li Dazhao, one of the founders of the Chinese Communist Party, and had a long revolutionary history. I had friends among the students there, and the student body asked the principal to go to Beijing and ask me to join the staff.

I went to Baodingfu to teach, at the same time helping to organize the student movement as a representative of the party. There were two other leftist teachers at the school.

One day in May,[158] thirty Chinese policemen surrounded the school and brought in a Japanese policeman to arrest me. This Japanese had my picture, which had been taken in prison, and said he was looking for a Korean with a name different from the one I was using at the time. The students ran out and closed the gate, refusing to let me be taken. The principal denied that he had any teacher by that name or any Korean on the staff—he thought

I was a Cantonese from Guangdong. In the meantime the students took me to the hospital and protected me, refusing to let anyone enter. The police believed the principal and at any rate could do nothing, as there was no evidence that I existed, so they went away. The students guarded me in the hospital all night, and the next day found a new position for me at Gaoyang Primary School.[159] Many of them cried when I left. I had made good friends among them. The principal also cried and did not want me to go.

I taught thirty hours a week at this primary school and joined the Anti-Religion League. The school had one training class of fifty students for village normal work. These were all young farmers from sixteen to twenty-seven, and I had warm hopes for them. I taught them history and political science and some philosophy. I had good support from this principal, who was a leftist.

I worked among the local farmers and organized three hundred of them, though only eighty came to meetings. Then a Party delegate* was sent to see me in order to establish a closer connection with the North China Committee. The Party Committee wanted an armed uprising in July. The local mintuan, in command of eighty soldiers, had been a comrade during the Great Revolution, so the party thought the situation favorable.

The local landlords had just brought two hundred pistols from Tianjin to arm new mintuan recruits, and the party wanted my students to seize these pistols and fight. The mintuan commander agreed to this on condition that we should not kill any of his men. He would report that the guns had been stolen by bandits.

I opposed this action because I had a good development under way and knew that if an uprising occurred, all

---

* *Party delegate*: i.e. from the Chinese Communist Party. –DH

our future chances would be destroyed, even if we were successful in seizing the pistols and using them. On my recommendation, that plan was dropped.

Then in August another party delegate, this time from the Hebei Provincial Committee, came to see me and wanted me to organize an armed uprising right away. I still opposed this, but he said: "Anyone who opposes this is afraid and counterrevolutionary. Only an armed struggle can solve the land problem now,"

I gave up my school and went to Beijing to explain the situation,[160] telling the party there of the good progress being made and of the possibilities of expanding the movement as at present, while I was sure an uprising would destroy everything and fail. But the committee did not agree with me, as they had been ordered to start a soviet movement in north China, so it would have to be done.

So I went back to help organize the uprising, though I did not openly join it. Thirty of our men from Li Xian met eight mintuan at Nanxinzhuang who had agreed to cooperate and marched into Gaoyang. There they arrested the chief of police and two of the gentry. After the village was occupied, about eight hundred farmers nearby came and looked on. They joined a mass meeting but did not participate. No mass movement could be mobilized, and after two days, the action had not expanded. The enemy came up to surround the village, and the eight hundred farmers dispersed. In the meantime, the Revolutionary Committee and the friendly mintuan had surrounded the primary school and held all the students prisoner—demanding money from their parents for their freedom. This was in order to buy guns. It was a serious mistake. The students with money were freed, while the poor ones—whose parents were on our side—remained prisoners.

Zhang Xueliang's army had surrounded the village,

and the revolutionary power lost control inside the walls. Nobody could escape. Some tried to hide in the school with the little children. The parents of the students pleaded with the White soldiers not to fire on their children, so the soldiers opened the gate to let all the children out. Some of the revolutionaries and mintuan tried to escape with them, and the Whites fired on them, killing some children and thirty of our men.

All was finished. Martial law was established and no further mass movement or work would be possible in the future. I was sick at heart at the destruction of what I had built up for nothing and at the deaths of the young farmers I had trained.

Beijing had wanted the local railway men and city workers to strike and go to Gaoyang to help, but nobody would do this. Not even a strike could be mobilized. The workers would not participate in armed uprising, though they were anxious for reform slogans.

After Gaoyang, the Party organized similar abortive uprisings in Hebei—in Ningsui Xian, Nancheng, and elsewhere. All failed, and party organizations were broken everywhere. After this we had no movement at all except at Cenan in southern Hebei, where Song Zheyuan afterward destroyed all the partisans in 1935.

I had not agreed with this policy from the first, and when I returned to Beijing at the end of 1932, I put my arguments before the party. They called me a "rightist,"[161] and I became angry and said I would cut my relations with the party completely if the stupid policy were not stopped.

Many in the party were thinking along the same lines and saw the necessity of changing local tactics from armed uprising to open democratic struggle for the farmers and workers and intellectuals together. Together with twenty-five other party leaders, I signed an opinion expressing these ideas for consideration by the party.

The Committee said we were rightists and that we were on the road to Trotskyism and from there to Nanjing.[162] I had translated a book called *Marxism and Religion*[163] by a Japanese, and the bookstore was advertising it in a Trotskyist magazine, so the Committee asked me how this was. I told them I had nothing to do with the advertising of the book, that I had no connections with any Trotskyists nor wanted any, and that I was disgusted with their attitude of throwing labels around promiscuously for no reason. First I was called a Li Lisanist for no reason, then a rightist, and now a Trotskyist. I said it was time they examined the situation for a change and stopped throwing epithets around indiscriminately. The only thing left was to call me a Korean and be finished with it. I privately felt that this one underlay all the others, though I hated to admit it even to myself.

One by one the leaders of the party betrayed* to the Guomindang as they were arrested. Demoralization set in everywhere. Each man distrusted every other, and soon the work was virtually at a standstill. I had foreseen this condition, and it seemed tragically unnecessary that we did not change the line until it was too late, but the heavy mechanism of bureaucracy did not function nearly as fast as in the Guomindang.

I felt that the reason for mass betrayals was political, not individual, and could be removed by changing the line. At the time of the Sixth Congress** everyone was

---

* *the leaders of the party betrayed*: In 1932 a fascist movement with a well-trained system of political police or "Gestapo" was started in China. They borrowed many methods from fascism in Europe, and their work was very effective. Their principal tactic was to demoralize the Party by granting liberty to those they had captured who agreed to become renegades and betray others. The only options given were to repent and confess or be executed. The Third Gendarmes [see note on p. 310] came to Beijing under Jiang Xiaoxian. These were a fascist Blue Shirt group, and Jiang was one of the cruelest and cleverest agents in China. [See note 168.] In their ranks were many communist and leftist renegades, so their espionage work was good. –KS

** *Sixth Congress*: i.e. of the Chinese Communist Party in 1928. –DH

BACK TO MASS MOVEMENT

willing to die bravely, believing the revolution would surely succeed. Later on, however, many were confused and didn't really believe in the party line. Having no conviction, it was easy for them to betray. If you do not truly believe in the line, it is not easy to work hard to realize it at all costs. This doubt existed everywhere from Guangdong to Manchuria. The Manchuria Committee was arrested, and nearly all betrayed—and three hundred Korean communists were arrested in Jilin in 1932. This alarmed me greatly, for I had worked with all those people in 1929 and knew how strong they were then. I sat down and wrote my opinion to the party that the only solution to the problem of betrayal was political. I said that we must again analyze the whole objective situation and consider the opinions of all comrades in order to reach a correct evaluation—then our conclusion will prove either that the line is right or that it is wrong. If the majority agrees that it is right, nobody will then disbelieve, and we shall have a new morale. If wrong, we must admit our mistakes and change the line before we disintegrate entirely. There have been many protests, and the party leadership should heed them before it is too late. This is a disease. The blood is bad. We can't cure it by cutting off a finger. The whole organism has to be revitalized, I concluded.

But the local Chinese leadership paid no attention to this, betraying their mamahuhu attitude. They seemed to think it was fate that turned men into traitors and that nothing could be done about it. They simply multiplied suspicion and fear and did nothing. Soon the leadership was so broken that there was no authority for anyone to do anything—and it was too late. I was unhappy and irritated at this stupidity and slowness, but it did not affect me as before. I had determined never to take affairs beyond my control so seriously again. Mistakes were inevitable—and tragedies follow mistakes. One must do all one can to make others see the mistake and to have it changed; if one fails there is nothing to do but wait for time to open their eyes, and not worry oneself into the grave in the meantime. One must have patience. And in China one must lose the humanitarian fear of sacrificing human life needlessly. One must accept this as part of the objective conditions. It was hard for me to accept this mamahuhu attitude, this carelessness toward human life, because in China revolutionaries are rare—not common like men. The Chinese disregard of the value of human life comes from their concept that China suffers from overpopulation—yet this argument does not hold for revolutionaries, who are few and precious. Every one of us sacrificed needlessly was worth a thousand other men, or indeed ten thousand.

The very men who held to the bureaucratic notion that the line could not be changed were in fact the first to betray, for they had no deep interest in preserving and strengthening the party and the revolution. They merely did their duty as they saw it, taking orders from above and refusing to take responsibility for making recommendations that might have caused them criticism from any quarter. Those who were critical were more loyal to the party than those who did not worry about the line but merely followed orders. Yet all alike were arrested and executed—the executioner does not distinguish between a head full of ideas and an empty one.

There were many inexperienced persons in the communist leadership in the White areas at that time. Already most of the best leaders had been imprisoned or executed, while others had gone into the soviet areas to work, despairing of any movement under the White Terror. Many were young students with hearts aflame but no principles of leadership to guide them. But the good and the bad suffered alike, and the party organization was soon broken almost everywhere, though isolated individuals sought blindly to make connections and to work as best they could.

The Guomindang leaders openly praised Hitler and Mussolini and aspired to imitate them. The reaction was very black indeed. Liberals and even the anti-Japanese movement were suppressed. By this time it was clear to us in the White regions that we would not be able to create a soviet movement despite of having reached the appropriate historical level of development unless the Red Army could overcome the reaction by force. We placed our hopes in the Red Army, but the Guomindang's Fifth Campaign soon began[164] and lasted from 1933 to 1934. Chiang Kai-shek mobilized a million troops and blockaded the soviet regions. The Red Army was having a hard fight even for survival and soon began the Long March to the north.[165] On August 1, 1935,[166] the leadership of the soviet also concluded that a new situation had come about and that we must utilize the democratic slogan to regain our strength and to rouse the anti-Japanese struggle. The Central Committee had been transferred to the soviet regions in 1931, and one by one most of the good Marxist leaders had gone there, while those left behind were imprisoned or killed. From 1932 to 1933, those returning from Moscow* usually also went to the soviets.

Chiang Kai-shek

---

* *returning to Moscow*: Kim San is referring here to a group of Chinese communists trained in Moscow who were sent back to China from the late 1920s to the mid-1930s to take over the leadership of the CCP. Most well-known among them was Wang Ming (see

The information they had about those of us in the White areas* was very limited, and the information we had about them was the same.

Yet great potential revolutionary forces did exist in the White areas, though we had failed to utilize them and to build a mass base.

Biographical Note on Han Wi-geon). These Moscow-trained Chinese communists were usually unfamiliar with local conditions and were in conflict with "indigenous" CCP leaders such as Mao Zedong. –DH

CHAPTER 21

Japanese Prisoner Again and Exile

AT FIVE O'CLOCK on the morning of April 26, 1933,[167] the room boy at the gongyu lodging house where I was staying knocked excitedly on my door and called in:

"The police are here to see you. Open the door, or they will break it down."

Before I could rouse myself from sleep, several policemen forced open the door while others broke in through the window. I stayed in bed and tried to collect my thoughts.

They searched the room and could find nothing. In a few minutes the Blue Shirt plainclothesmen arrived.[168] With them was Zhang Wenxiong,* a renegade member of the

---

* *Zhang Wenxiong* (or Zhang Wenxun): When twenty students were arrested in Beijing during the funeral of Li Dazhao, the founder of the CCP, in 1927, Zhang Wenxiong went into the cell with them, pretending to be a prisoner, too, in order to spy on the students. These students were forced to sign a promise not to enter any political group in future and to oppose the Communist Party. For this they were promised freedom after three days. This document was published in the newspapers. All the students had agreed to sign this repentance, and all but nine were later released, as the judge was not a Blue Shirt and was more just in his actions. Zhang Wenxiong, however, went in and pointed out the nine whom he had discovered to be Communist Party or Communist Youth members while spying on them, and these were not freed.

This Zhang Wenxiong was responsible for scores of deaths and imprisonments. There

local Communist Party Committee, and Si Lingke, another ex-communist. I pretended not to recognize them.

After this they all waited quietly in the room, hoping to surprise any comrades who might come. At eight o'clock there was a light knock on the door, which I recognized. It was a young girl comrade. My heart leaped suffocatingly. The police opened the door and arrested her.

"We'll take these two," one of the Blue Shirts said, "while the rest of you wait inside for any others who may come."

A police van was waiting in the hutong* surrounded by a dense crowd. They stared curiously to see a young girl and

---

was a wholesale drive in Beijing at that time. Many important men were arrested, including the whole Communist Party Committee and the local faction. Most were betrayed by Zhang. For him, causing ten or a thousand to be arrested was all the same. The Party would never forgive him. He was worse than their bitterest class enemy, for he was a traitor. If the revolution succeeded, he would be the first to be killed, so of course he wanted to see the GMD stay in power. Such traitors are worse than the GMD. Their cruelty is criminal in quality, not based on class hatred. They become degenerate and without any moral principles. Nothing has any meaning for them—neither their own lives nor those of others.

Zhang Wenxiong enjoyed arresting communists, young or old, boys or girls, seeking them out with a lust for death and destruction. He could have returned to his home and lived his own life, but his espionage work became a personal duty and a passion. Of course, he would never feel his own life to be safe until every communist was either dead or in prison, so it was a self-defense mechanism too. He received money for his work, but did not need it, as his wife was very rich and owned a match company. He liked the sense of power over human destinies and the knowledge that he could command the forces of evil at will.

This traitor from Zhejiang was about thirty-five years old at that time. He had a fat stomach and full cheeks and little pig-like eyes, very evil in expression. I hated his eyes. They haunted you with their sinister wickedness. His face was not open but secret in type, impassive except for the eyes.

The other traitors usually hid shamefacedly in a room behind curtains and secretly pointed out to the Blue Shirts the Communist Party or Communist Youth members and the young leftist students as they were lined up in the yard opposite. But Zhang walked up openly and accused them like a gloating monster. The poor students shrank back in dismay when they realized that they had confided in this man with the little evil eyes only a few hours before, thinking him an important party comrade and father.

Sometimes comrades also secretly reported their personal enemies or rivals to the police without compunction, in order to have them arrested and out of the way. –KS
[I have not been able to locate the personal information about the figures referred to as Zhang Wenxiong and Si Lingke. Some Korean sources spell their names as Zhang Wenxun and Xu Lingke, respectively, without any reference. –DH]

* *hutong*: Mandarin world for "alley." –DH

myself under arrest.

In the van I told the girl I was sorry to be the cause of her arrest.

"*Buyaojin!*" she replied—"it doesn't matter."

"After we reach the police station perhaps we shall not be able to see each other again," I said. "What should we say now?"

"No more. We have talked before. There you can find some meaning if you have not forgotten."

I saw that she thought she would soon be freed and would be able to help me, as her father was a high government official.

I was without fear. I felt certain that whatever happened would not disturb my equilibrium. The first thought that came to me was of a famous song the Korean terrorists used to sing when they went to Korea for action, knowing that death was close to them. The words were by Im Sa, a modern Korean anarchist poet—[169]

> Two white birds flying into a deep cloud in the sky
> The world below looks as small as an egg. . .
> Now those free wings are locked in a cage—
> Do not wait for the sun to rise!

"I like the song you are singing," a policeman said to me with a grin. "Last night we arrested thirty men, but you are the only one not to be afraid. You must be a real communist without doubt."

I looked at the young girl beside me and smiled. After all, freedom was long and prison short in the life of a revolutionary. You compressed many years into one during periods of action. That was what mattered, not the few years in a cell that one might have to spend now and then. And if prison meant death, that was even shorter.

BLUE SHIRTS AND RENEGADE

At the police headquarters, the Blue Shirt plainclothesman put me in a room with the two members who had betrayed me.

"He is your party comrade," the Blue Shirt said, pointing to Zhang Wenxiong. "When I leave, you must talk with him. We have you on our list, and we know all about you. The questions I am going to ask are merely to see if you tell the truth or not."

Then he asked me many questions in front of the two members. This was to make it difficult to lie effectively, as the prisoner knows the two have betrayed him. Others besides these two had also betrayed and given names to the police. The Blue Shirts forced every betraying communist to lead them to the arrest of at least two other members to secure their own release. Before their release, they had to promise openly not to continue to do Party work. This open renunciation, which was usually published in the papers, was meant to make it impossible for the members to do party work ever again, as all other members would then distrust them. This was the new fascist tactic.[170]

When the Blue Shirt left me alone with the two members who had chosen to betray me, Zhang Wenxiong turned to me and said:

"I have seen your opinion written for party consideration signed with twenty-five others. Do you think the party can now agree to it?"

"I never gave any opinion to the party. I have only been teaching school to earn my living."

"What is your present opinion on the China problem?" he persisted.

"I don't know. I never study the China problem now," I replied. "I am only working on Korea."

"To work in the political movement one must have freedom. It is no use to be in prison. We recover our liberty and by this are able to carry on the revolutionary work. Otherwise, we shall either be executed or imprisoned indefinitely," Zhang stated.

He meant that I should join with the Blue Shirts and the Guomindang.

"You are a political man," I replied. "I am only a common person now. My liberty is merely a personal question. It will not help any political movement. I am not working in any party."

"Have you decided then?"

"Decided what?"

"To die?"

"Do what you please with me."

"Those are dangerous words. Be careful."

Day after day passed,[171] and I had no idea what they meant to do with me.

❖

During the weeks of my detention, from April 26 to June 15,* about fifty communists were brought into the prison. Nearly forty repented and betrayed. Each would be forced to betray two other comrades to the police to secure his own release. Anyone who went out of the prison was a traitor, and two police would follow him until his quota of two members had been arrested. After that he was free, and no more spies would be sent with him.

Such betrayals and weakness of moral fiber had been increasing for two years, but I had never realized the

---

* *from April 26 to June 15*: Kim San asked me to change the dates and places of his arrest and prison experiences so as not to provide proof in case of future trouble. I changed the place from Beijing to Tianjin, and vice versa. He was arrested May 1, 1933, in Beijing, where he was questioned, not in Tianjin. On July 20, 1933, he was taken from Tianjin to Tanggu, on the way to Dalian and Korea. –NW

extent of the condition until now. I organized a secret meeting in the prison to discuss the reason for these mass betrayals, which looked like defeat at the end of a struggle. We discussed what was wrong with the Party line and what tactics to use in court or under duress, and how it was never permissible under any circumstances to sign a repentance or to betray or cause the arrest of other comrades. We must die rather than admit to our party connections. What was at stake was not the fate of the individual leaders but the whole morale and discipline of the movement. Should not-good members betray those who had been expelled or were untrustworthy to save their own lives for the vital work that must go on? No! What was at stake was not an idealistic principle but the whole question of how to preserve the integrity of the revolution. The end could not justify the means, for means and ends were inseparable; one was created organically by the other.

Seeing all these betrayals made me sick at heart with a physical revulsion. I felt that the character of human life was bare of anything beautiful and splendid. I lost faith in humanity, and my confidence in the Chinese Communist Party was shaken. Mistakes, injustices, stupidity, cowardice, one can forgive. But how can one forgive treachery? I wondered if the Koreans would do this under like circumstances. They would betray from personal hatred but not from weakness and cowardice, I thought. Would the Japanese? The Russians? The Europeans? Was it something deep in the Chinese character that even revolution could not change? It was contrary to my whole life's belief that any race could be condemned apart from any other. I knew there had been betrayals in every country, but I could not believe they matched these in China. It could not be a racial characteristic. It must be that there was some weakening because of a breakdown in political morale that these comrades were no longer willing to sacrifice for the slogans under which we were struggling.

This experience was very valuable to me. It gave me complete confidence in my own courage and moral integrity. I had tested myself and found that I was strong to the end and would never betray. I resolved never to resort to any questionable means to gain my ends, no matter how important that end might be. Never would I betray friend or personal enemy. I would kill my enemy with my hand, but I would never destroy him by betrayal to others. What moral right had we of the revolution to win if we had to do so by treachery? We must create individuals better and finer than the class enemy, and rottenness in leadership would destroy our end. It was better to die honestly, even though our tasks remained unfulfilled, rather than to try to survive by treachery and intrigue.

I determined in that cell in Beijing in 1933 always to be true to myself and never to care for any man's lies or treachery. I would not fight treachery with treachery. If I could not win on my own terms, failure would be honor and victory for me. In a secret movement it is easy to betray and to gain political position through intrigue and careful lies and evasions. But no man who must resort to this deserves to be a leader, and no party that does not purge itself of this will survive. Internally or externally, the logic was the same. Leadership must be honest and straightforward, or it destroys not only its following but itself. Whether I believed in a thing or not, I would not sabotage it by treachery. I would fight it openly and honestly. Truth is always on the side of the progressives. Lies only serve the reaction. We need no lies to win. History is on our side, and history does not lie.

How exultant was the Guomindang at these betrayals! This alone made them unforgivable.

❖

On May 31 all those who had repented were ordered to go to the city government, where there would be newspapermen to publish their confessions and some Guomindang and student delegates to hear them. This was a propaganda stunt by the Guomindang to demoralize the communists and their supporters. Some of the prisoners made speeches against the communists and their supporters. Others lied and said they had been important party members and now wished to support the Guomindang. The Blue Shirts asked them to do this to indicate that the party leadership had betrayed.

When I went out into the courtyard, I saw all those who had repented having their hair cut and putting on clean clothes to go to the city government. They would be free tomorrow.

The Blue Shirt leader and Zhang Wenxiong came up to me and said, "This is your last chance. You need only to go to the city government and repent, then you can get your liberty too. The newspapermen will take your picture and write down your speech of repentance, and you can walk away a free man."

"I have no opinion to give to any newspaperman," I said dryly. "I think I have no reason to go."

"When this opportunity is passed, you will never again be free," the Blue Shirt said to me. "I do not want to harm any young men. I want to save them. What will happen to you later I cannot guarantee."

"Then you can save your Chinese young men and be proud of it," I said bitterly. "I will be very happy not to be saved by you."

"Your wife will be released soon, but you will be a prisoner. She will follow another man."

"For the last time, she is not my wife," I spat out.

Was it idealistic and foolish and quixotic to refuse to do this? Would it not be the only intelligent thing—to make a public repentance and gain freedom to work again? It looked a simple thing. But I had made my resolution—never to betray myself, my party, or any other man. It might be a foolish gesture, but it would be true to myself, and that was the rock on which my moral security rested.

I walked slowly back into the cell. There were only six of us left. Four were young students. Was I still a revolutionary romantic like them, throwing away my liberty, perhaps my life, for a beautiful gesture? No matter, I would do it....

In the meantime, the parents of my friend came. They gave money to secure her release. The police agreed to let her go, but she asked the judge about my case and said she would wait a few days so we could be released together, and asked her parents to help me. She thought this might influence the judge. Her father was furious.

"You can wait ten years in prison! What use is it to take you out with such ideas!" he stormed.

She finally had to accept her release before any trouble came up.

EXPERT INQUISITOR

On June 15,[172] the police came in and said, "You will leave here today."

I signed for my belongings and walked outside where a big car was waiting, with five policemen as guards. I thought they might be sending me to the Japanese consul—but no Japanese were present. I then became very worried, as I decided I was being sent to the Third Gendarmes' headquarters,* perhaps to be executed. This

---

° *Third Gendarmes' headquarters*: This was the terror of the students in Beijing. But during

place was the Blue Shirt center and carried out many secret executions of revolutionaries. The last thing I saw as I left was the smug face of Zhang Wenxiong, those little eyes looking on mockingly as if he had not been robbed of this victim yet.

I did not notice where we were going. When the car stopped I was pleasantly surprised to see the familiar Japanese Legation before my eyes.

The Japanese officials gave the police a receipt for my "body"!

All the officials looked new to me, but one of them recognized me. "Ah, you look so old now!" he exclaimed. "In three years you have become another man."

It was true that I looked very bad indeed, especially after my six weeks' detention. All the thoughts in my mind during those years were written on my face, I suppose.

They asked me where and why I had been arrested and other questions.

"In my room," I replied. "I have many friends. Who is communist and who is not, I don't know. I do not ask this question."

"You lie," they said. "But how is it you are arrested when you are an important committee man? In Japan it is not easy to get the communist chiefs. It is only easy to get the foolish boys who write slogans everywhere. You did not repent like the rest of them, no?"

Then they gave me the newspaper, which had a whole page of repentances and speeches by those who had been arrested at the time I was.

"The Chinese communists are brave men compared with

---

the Xi'an Incident on December 12, 1936 [see note 20], the leftists took their revenge. The Third Gendarmes were at that time acting as Chiang Kai-shek's special bodyguards in Lintong. When Chiang Kai-shek was captured, most of the Third Gendarmes were killed. The commander, Jiang Xiaoxian, was shot as soon as his identity was learned. He was bitterly hated for his sadistic cruelty. –NW

other Chinese," the ranking police official remarked. "But they are also *Chinese*. When it rains the Chinese get together; when the rain stops, they disintegrate again. That rain is money. The communists like money just as well as any other Chinese. If Nanjing* pays them well, the communist leaders will all sell out just like anybody else. Ha, ha, ha!"

"Why were you arrested—do you know?" he pursued. "Apparently your comrades got themselves arrested just to get money from the Guomindang. You are a profitable commodity wanted by the Guomindang now. What's the matter, wouldn't they pay for you?"

On the second day the head of the Korean Department of Police came to see me. He spoke Korean, and I was alarmed. Any Japanese who lives long in Korea is a hard taskmaster, and those who have risen from the ranks to high positions are very cruel. They have the imperialist psychology combined with the domineering quality of the parvenu. Those fresh from Japan are much better and more humane.

"Pay attention," he said brusquely. "The man who handled your case in 1930 was kind to you. You think it is our duty, no? You have not forgotten he was easy with you then. I hope you have also not forgotten who helps you out of Chinese prisons. Now you will have none of this. I have been in the Police Department for twenty years, and this political subject is my special line."

He narrowed his eyes, and his face flushed with anger for no reason at all. Yes, he was the cruel type.

He started to ask me questions, but before I could answer he kicked me several times on the shins with his heavy shoe and pulled out a handful of hair. I refused to speak a word. Then he beat my ears to a bleeding pulp with a ruler. He could do nothing more so he sent me back

---

* *Nanjing:* i.e. the GMD. –DH

to my cell, saying, "I am going to Tianjin tomorrow, and I will take you with me and handle your case there. You will be sorry for this stubbornness."

The situation in Beijing then was very tense between the Chinese and Japanese because of the recent fighting with the Chinese Twenty-Ninth Army. Apparently, I was going to be sent away immediately.

I was so angry and weak that I collapsed on my bed from nervous exhaustion.

The next morning at nine o'clock I was handcuffed and escorted to Tianjin by a plainclothesman whom I had not seen before. He talked with me on the way, discussing books, philosophy, and general cultural problems quite intelligently. What was the best book to learn Chinese, he inquired. Ah, it is so difficult a language.

At the East station in Tianjin a motorcar was waiting, and I was taken to the Japanese Consulate.

The Vice Consul, a young lawyer, was the judge in the Court of Examination. He asked me only my name, address, age, occupation, and such and sent me to the "gaimushō"[301] prison. This was a small one-story place. In it were three Koreans and five Japanese. The Koreans and four of the Japanese were heroin cases while the other Japanese was accused of fraud.

After two days I was summoned out of my cell—to be confronted with my inquisitor from Beijing, who had come separately on the train.

"Now we can begin again," he commanded gruffly. "Sit down here and write out everything you have done since you left prison in Korea in 1931, to continue this document."

He had my complete file in front of him, and the report I had made in 1930.

---

[301] *gaimushō*: Japanese word for "Foreign Office" or "Ministry of Foreign Affairs." It is used here ironically. —GT

Question after question: Why, why, why? Why did you come back to Beijing? Why did you go away again? Why do you change jobs and houses so often?

I wrote down enough to carry the report up to that very day.

"You are a member of the Chinese Communist Party, no?"

"No."

"Every Korean in Beijing knows you are a communist. Are you two men? I don't think so." His face was drawing into crueler and crueler lines.

"Why do the police arrest you, then, if you are not a Red?"

"A member of the China League of Left-Wing Writers[173] was observed coming to my house."

"Are you also a member of this?"

"Yes."

"You are not a communist? Answer the truth."

"No. I am not a communist."

"Then why do you enter this League?"

"So that this group will introduce me to new contacts and get me jobs doing translation work and teaching. You have to belong to some group in China or you cannot get new work to earn a living. They helped me go to other towns to get jobs, too."

"Do you know the program of this China League of Left-Wing Writers?"

"Yes."

"What is it?"

"They have three slogans—against imperialism, for the overthrow of Nanjing, and the protection of the Red Army."

"Is this league open or secret?"

"I don't know. They never discussed this. Both, I guess."

"No slogan against Japanese imperialism?"

"It is a cultural group, not a political one."

"Everything you say is a lie, there's no truth in any of it. There is no cultural group in China that was not formed for political purposes."

Then he struck my face and pulled my hair sharply.

"Don't look at me as if I were the foolish man who handled your case in Beijing before. He didn't understand the character of the Koreans. You can't be kind to a Korean."

He kicked me on the shins and below the kneecap viciously.

I walked quickly out of the room and into the next, where a number of people were standing. I demanded to see the chief of police. Someone pushed me back into the room.

I was furiously angry and refused to speak a word. My inquisitor pulled out several handfuls of hair and beat my face again and again.

"Speak! Has this league an anti-Japanese slogan?"

I said nothing.

"The man who was kind to you here before hoped you would not continue to oppose Japan if he treated you decently. You thought he was a fool and that you were very clever, didn't you?"

He rang the bell and sent me to the cell with a guard.

The next morning at nine o'clock I was called in to see him again.

"Decide my case now," I said in cold scorn. "I have no further replies to make to a man such as you."

When court opened session, I was tried before two judges, but there was no important evidence against me, except that I had broken the order not to return to China for three years after my arrest in 1930. Therefore, according to the Second Article of Meiji Law No. 80, I was subjected to one month in prison and a fine of 20 yen. For lack of money, I had to work out the fine at the rate of two yen a day.

I put on the red clothes of the prisoner and was set to work digging earth. During these two months in the "gaimushō" eighty-six Korean prisoners came and went. I made friends with one of the policemen, a Waseda University graduate, who gave me a package of cigarettes every day and was eager to learn about Marxism.

The morning of July 30, I was sent to Dalian. On the train to Mukden some Japanese soldiers gathered in a knot and asked me questions about the Red Army in China. They had learned I was a communist suspect, and we talked together for four hours. They demanded that the police open my handcuffs while I ate lunch, saying it was "a shame to treat a fine intelligent man in this common manner."

In Korea I again went through the long weary rigmarole of investigation, but finally I was released.

"I now sign the order for your release," the judge admonished. "But because you were ordered not to return to China for three years after 1931, you will be forbidden to leave Korea until that period is up, which will be January 1934. You have committed no new offense, but we must insist that you observe this order."

I was so ill that I had to spend a month in the hospital. My family and relatives were very friendly and proud of me. They only asked that I should be more careful in the future and never spoke a word against my political beliefs.

In January I left for China again. On the train to Dalian, the blinds were kept down, and there was firing along the way. The partisans were keeping merry vigil along the railway line. In Beijing I lived at a friend's home in the Western Hills for a while.

CHAPTER 22

Two Women and Marriage

AS SOON AS SHE LEARNED of my release from prison, the girl who had been arrested because of me[174] came back to Beijing to search for me. She had been away with her mother for a while.

The look in her eyes as she came into the room was disturbing. Was I to be involved in this troublesome woman question again?

We talked of my prison experiences and of inconsequential things. But she had more to say than this.

"My parents have asked me about you," she said with embarrassment. "I mean, they wanted to know just what our relations were."

"Oh," I said. "I'm sorry. I can explain to them that we have never been anything but good friends. I hope they have not been suspicious of you because of me. I have caused you enough trouble."

"But I don't want them to know this. I told them you were my husband. Then my father asked when we were married, and I said we had not bothered to get married. He was so angry that he threatened to beat me, and if not for my mother, would have thrown me out of the house and disinherited me completely. He will hardly speak to me now."

I was amazed. "But why did you tell them this lie?"

She did not answer, but looked down shyly. Then in a half-voice: "I love you. I want to be married to you......"

I was too surprised to speak. I walked over to the window and looked out nervously.

"If you do not want to marry me, I will be a wife to you just the same," came the quiet little voice. "I think you will learn to like me someday. I can help you. I want to try to make you happy and well again. You are so very sick now. I care for nothing else. It will make me happy only to be near you."

A warm flood of emotion tumbled over me. My heart lifted in gratitude that this unselfish, loyal little person should want to share the poverty and sorrows of my life and ask for nothing in return. Human nature was mocking me again with its reviving splendidness, just when I had harshly thrust aside its ugliness and lost faith.

I walked back to her impulsively and held her hand to my lips.

"You are a sweet and lovely child. It makes me happy just to know that such a person as you exists in the world." My words were earnest with sudden truth.

She drew her hand away with a smile and ran out the door.

Marriage? I had not thought of such a thing. I had once dreamed of finding a woman to love forever. But I had not thought of marriage for its own sake. I would never find that woman. She could not exist. Why not try to create her in the image of my dream?

This girl was very young and could be molded to my will. There would be none of my trouble with Liu Ling, the dominant one. This one would not disturb my soul, but neither would she disturb my mind. She was not too pretty to be sweet and kind. She was strong and healthy. And she was good. I could make of her the perfect revolutionary wife, build up her mind and knowledge.

Here was loyalty, generosity, honesty, goodness. Where were more beautiful attributes to be found? I was sick through and through of what I had experienced of betrayal and cruelty and selfishness. Loyalty seemed to me to be the most precious quality of humankind.

I had nothing to offer this girl—yet was not my life richer than one of comfort? It would be spiritually splendid, though without material pleasures.

What was the family that it had persisted throughout every stage of history? Was it not a valid relationship?

The knowledge that here was someone loyal to me in a dark moment enfolded my tired, sick body like a warm blanket on a winter night. It relaxed aching muscles and troubled heart and mind.

But I would not marry until we understood each other thoroughly. I told her all my problems and troubles and tried to break down her enthusiasm. The result was only to make her more devoted than ever.

"You and I will not be happy," I said frankly. "Marriage cannot be successful until the whole pathological condition of society around us has been changed. The only happiness we can expect will be in the work we do together in revolutionizing that society. I do not believe that any intelligent pair can be happy in this present world. I know I cannot. Only on the recognition of this fact can we build any sound relationship. If our marriage is not miserable, we shall be lucky. If it is, no matter. We can try, anyway, if you are willing to accept the objective conditions as they exist. I must be free at all times. I cannot be bound. Neither do I wish to bind you, for that is also an attachment for myself. I shall have to go away often and leave you, and then you must take care of yourself entirely. Perhaps we can only live together a few months and that will be the end."

"You make it sound very dismal," she replied. "Perhaps we should not get married."

"Free love is only an illusion," I said. "'The chains of the whole world bind us. The social relationship is basically the same, or no true relation exists at all."

And so we were married.[175] We rented a little house at Xizhimen with four rooms. My friends came to see us, and we lived a fairly normal married life for several months. I tried to relax my mind and rest my nerves and body in preparation for the future.

How to live? Always the pressure of earning money. I secured a job tutoring in a rich family. I taught three children three different classes for $30 a month. It was difficult. Spoiled and selfish, they threw their books around and were rude. They wanted me to do their mathematics to give to the teacher in school next day. This cheating I refused to do and gave up the job.

I next did some writing but could find no place to sell it. I did translation work[176] and let a Chinese publish the translations under his own name for which I received $1.50 for every thousand words.

Then I had a bright idea. I would learn to teach dumb children. Many children of rich families in China are deaf or dumb, and in all China there are few places for them to learn. With such a job I would have freedom for my own work. I sent to Japan for seven textbooks and studied them. In three months I was able to teach. I practiced on a boy for three weeks, and it was successful. Then I secured a position in a family for several months, but the parents would not cooperate, and I felt the whole thing was futile.

My wife thought this all nonsense. Why not do mass

education work? She asked. I was interested in this and had studied Latinization,* which was just then beginning in China.

I was sick of fraud and deception and penurious minds and pocketbooks, and in the winter of 1934 we went to Shijiazhuang[177] where I edited a daily paper for a month at a salary of $40, then got a job teaching at a school. I soon began to use my Latinization in a railway workers' family school, and it was very successful. In 1935 I began political training classes in the railwaymen's union, as well as helping at the school. I became well acquainted with these workers and built up a good organization. "No propaganda for any party!" was our slogan, and we kept the organization open and legal. In May 1935 it was well organized, and I placed it under the North China Committee of the Communist Party directly. My little wife had helped in this work, and I was very proud of her rapid development in revolutionary activities. She also had a job teaching school.

In the spring of 1935,[178] I decided to go to Shanghai to renew my contacts with the Korean revolutionaries. For ten years I had been working in the Chinese Revolution, and I was eager now to be more active for my own country. My wife stayed in Shijiazhuang.

Kim Chung-chang came from Guangxi to meet me, and we talked over all our problems and ideas. When I told him that I was married and almost domesticated, he would not believe me. He questioned me closely about my wife, then shook his head and sighed:

"I have met only one girl in all these years who might be your equal, and she is here in Shanghai now. Why did you

---

* *Latinization*: That is, romanization, which the Yan'an authorities began promoting the use of in 1937. The official romanization system of Chinese in China, called "pīnyīn," is now widely used by most scholars and media, though the Wade-Giles system is still used in Taiwan and by some other scholars.—NW, GT, DH

compromise? Here I have been hoping to arrange the great love of the century."

"I don't want to meet her," I replied. "I love my sweet little wife dearly. I have forgotten all those immature fancies I once had. She is far more than my equal in loyalty and generosity and goodness."

I refused to be introduced to Kim's marvelous discovery, and he was much chagrined.

"I have three sons, and I am a hopeless middle-aged model of domestic happiness," Kim argued. "But you are still free and only thirty years old. You can aspire to anything. And you are sad and lonely in spirit. You need a companion, not a child-wife to comfort your ego with devotion."

I plunged into discussions of political questions with many Korean and Chinese comrades in Shanghai and forgot about Kim's notion. Then, one afternoon at a secret meeting of some Chinese party comrades, I was deep in talk with a friend when I looked up to see a pair of luminous brown eyes concentrated on me. They belonged to a beautiful Chinese girl sitting across the room. I stopped in the middle of my discussion and stared at her, spellbound. She smiled at me in an amused manner and turned her eyes away.

"That is Miss Li," my friend observed. "She is one of our best comrades, very intelligent and competent. You may trust her completely. She is superb in dangerous work and has never failed."

He called her over and introduced us. She joined the conversation with brilliance and displayed a natural wit and charm that nearly took my breath away. I felt suddenly very old and shabby and tired. She made me realize that I had been half-buried in myself and my problems for a long, long time.

I had never before seen such poise and assurance as only

a woman conscious of superior beauty and intellect and charm can have. I thought morbidly how very tragic it would be if such a lovely creature should meet the fate of the others I had admired. I wanted to withdraw my fatal admiration, as if it carried the stamp of death for her.

Miss Li paid no particular attention to me, save for sudden witty thrusts that threw me off balance. I could not reply to her except in heavy serious phrases that sounded academic and professorial. I had forgotten that one could be bright and gay as well as revolutionary. Here was fearlessness that laughed at fear and at itself alike. Beside her self-confidence, my own hard-won and long-tested courage and belief in myself seemed stodgy and unalive. I had no love of life, therefore no fear of anything. Death was meaningless. For her, life and death and all things were full of meaning and purpose. She could never be wounded but only killed. Within me was a half-dead mass of dark scar tissue of wounded spirit and pride and defeat. I had been sensitive to every small destruction until the nerves no longer responded. My ego had been expansive and open, subject to battering and bruising from all sides. Hers was smooth and compact and encased in a bright shield that could not be easily penetrated.

Why did all women look at me in that amused way? Was I so harmless, and so easily harmed? The superior attitude of this one particularly irritated me. My ego rose in self-defense. This time I would not be pursued. Neither would I run away.

But Miss Li showed no sign of pursuing me. She made it amply clear that pursuit was to come from the other side. Good—then the situation was saved.

When I went away that afternoon, I wrote a long devoted letter to my wife and told her how much our marriage had helped me to recover stability and equilibrium and how happy the thought of her always made me feel.

The reply was disconcerting. How shrewd women are! It said: "I am unworthy of you. You are far superior to me. I have tried to develop, but I am still too young. I have always been afraid you would meet some other girl. Perhaps you have already met her. Do not consider me if you are in love with someone else. You are sad, and I feel that I can never make you happy as you deserve to be. Really, it is true that I care only for your happiness, and I shall not be sorry if you find it elsewhere. You are more important to me than myself. I shall still love and admire you, and we can be friends anyway."

I resolved never to see Miss Li again and to be loyal to my wife at all costs. One thing I was sure of—my own will power. Whatever I determined, I would do.

Nevertheless, I was several times in her company through our common activities, though I maintained my strict reserve. Soon it occurred to me that there was a conspiracy afoot in Shanghai. I demanded of Kim to know if he were acquainted with Miss Li and if she were the same girl he had "discovered" for me.

"Yes," he confessed. "But she does not know anything of my idea. I merely told her about you casually in rather glowing terms. I am sure she is already in love with you. You are a glorious pair."

"Indeed!" I exclaimed. "This is the finish, then. I am going to send for my wife."

That same afternoon Miss Li happened to be at a secret meeting. It was the custom for members to leave at different times to avoid police suspicion. Somehow, Miss Li and I were left together alone in the room. I could hardly go away first.

"I expect to stay in Shanghai some time," I remarked. "I have just written to my wife to join me here."

"Oh," her face was tragic. "Are you married—I mean, really married?"

"Yes, in the old-fashioned way, too, very much married."

"Somehow I didn't expect you to be. I'm sorry. I mean—one meets so few persons that one wants to marry, don't you think?"

"I have made only one concrete attempt myself," I replied, trying not to appear nervous.

"I have rather been waiting for some tall, handsome stranger," she laughed gaily.

"I waited, too, but not quite long enough."

"Was it a mistake?"

"No. I found something very precious, anyway."

"Is that enough?"

"Yes. It is something good that I value and will never destroy. I will never hurt my little wife. So long as she is loyal to me, I will not break her happiness. We cannot be together long anyway. I will soon go away on a trip from which I don't expect to return."

"Do you enjoy torturing yourself?"

"Yes. It is better than torturing another."

"Then good-bye for the moment." Her eyes were very bright, but I could not see the tears.

I walked home, depressed and miserable, feeling a little quixotic and foolish.

I did not need to reflect that I lacked a special kind of human companionship. I needed someone to change and influence me, to break my will and criticize my opinions, to congratulate me intelligently when I was right and help me to see when I was wrong. I needed someone who was strong and superior. Or did I? Why confess an insufficiency even to oneself? It was enough to recognize a lack without admitting a need. Why stir the ashes of a forgotten dream...?

All my Korean comrades tried to induce me to leave my wife. "You will never find such a girl again," they pleaded. "You are silly. Your young wife will soon forget, but you will never forget Miss Li."

"This is romantic nonsense," I insisted. "What is wrong with all of you? You should be a little more grown up after all these years."

My wife arrived a few days later from the north. It did not take her long to discover Miss Li, but she was happy that we had nothing to do with each other. A few months afterward I planned to go away on my trip to the northwest.

"You may be a widow for several years," I told her. "I intend to go to Manchuria to fight with the partisans after this trip."

But she pledged to be faithful to the end.

CHAPTER 23

The Korean National Front Against Japan

IN THE SUMMER AND AUTUMN of 1935 nearly all the important Korean revolutionary leaders gathered secretly in Shanghai to discuss our problems. We examined our role starting from the Guangzhou period and made an exhaustive study of conditions in Korea, Manchuria, and Japan, as well as in China.

During my time in Korea from August 1933 to January 1934—only three months of which had been spent out of prison—I had wasted no time in acquainting myself with every phase of the local political and economic situation. Now in Shanghai, after getting further information from comrades who had worked in every country of the Far East, I sat down and wrote a long analysis of the Korean Revolution and the tasks remaining before it. This report had considerable influence upon the Korean leaders. After much discussion, we decided that a new revolutionary situation had come about, and that we must prepare to meet it.[179] The principal conclusion was that we should now take the leadership in the fight against Japanese imperialism instead of scattering our energies in this or that internal struggle.

We counted the small number of experienced veterans left in our ranks and decided that they must join together in a cohesive unit and take active leadership of the Korean Revolution proper. We wanted more results, more influence, and the movement in Korea and Manchuria had become very important after September 18, 1931.* Manchuria, not China, was now the center of the Korean movement, and all Korean revolutionaries were anxious to go there. Many, like Oh Seong-ryun, had already gone, and a number had already been sacrificed, such as the Bak brothers.

After 1927, we had only the Chinese Communist Party among Koreans in China—no separate Korean communist organization existed.[180] We now voted to reorganize our party members into an individual Korean unit, which could rally round it all Korean revolutionaries—nationalist, anarchist, and others—and prepare a national front. All Korean communists in China with whom we could make contact were consulted and unanimously agreed with this policy, promising to join. The nationalists, who had always criticized us communists for having lost ourselves completely in the Chinese movement for so many years, were very pleased and agreed to work with us and to let us have a fraction within their party.

To have one Korean here and one there in the Chinese Party was of little use. We decided that we must join together for common action and safeguard the Korean Revolution instead of sacrificing only for China directly. Since 1932,[181] the Korean Communist Party and our

---

* *September 18, 1931:* The date when a bomb was set off on train tracks near Mukden. Fighting temporarily broke out between Japanese and Chinese forces, eventually leading to the complete takeover of Manchuria by Japan by early 1932. This marked the beginning of Japan's military occupation of China, which would continue until 1945. Commonly referred to by some scholars as the Manchurian Incident or the Mukden Incident, while in China, it is referred to as the September 18th or 9.18 Incident. –GT, DH

Manchurian Communist Party had been independent, for the Chinese did not study the Korean problem and had little understanding of it.

"We can no longer afford to lose ourselves like salt in water," we agreed. "We must join China as one force to another, not as lost individuals. We must bend our energies quickly toward building and preparing the Korean movement for action in the future, for Japanese imperialism is moving very fast."

On August 1, 1935, the Chinese Communist Party and the Red Army and the soviets issued their manifesto offering an anti-Japanese United Front with the Guomindang, and we Koreans immediately began the formation of our own National Front to cooperate with the Chinese.

We created in Shanghai the "Korean League for National Liberation."[182] I was elected a member of the Central Committee, which also included nationalists and three anarchists, as well as other communists. The program of this league was to achieve the success of the bourgeois-democratic phase of the Korean Revolution by establishing a free republic on the basis of the anti-Japanese struggle. Our principal points provided for the overthrow of Japanese imperialism and the confiscation of its vested interests in Korea; the guarantee of democratic civil liberties and the right to an education for the Korean people; reform of livelihood conditions and the abolition of oppressive taxes; the nationalization of public utilities and monopoly enterprises (all under Japanese control at present); and friendly relations with all nations and states sympathetic with Korean national emancipation.

With this league as a nucleus, we then set about forming the Union for the Korean National Front, and its program of action[183] was formally drawn up in July 1936.[184] The leaders then went back to Korea, Manchuria, Japan, and other parts of China to mobilize support for this program. The fifteen articles in this program provided for the union of "all the people of Korea who agree with the principle of Korean independence, irrespective of social class, party, political or religious belief." Korean-owned enterprises were to be protected, and Japanese interests in Korea to be opposed. The class struggle was to be arbitrated and subordinated to the national struggle, but all workers directly under Japanese imperialist control were to be "organized without restraint." Broad economic reforms and mobilization of the widest possible mass movement were to be encouraged, including equality for women. A great common front was to be formed* against the fascist aggressors with the Chinese anti-Japanese movement, the U.S.S.R., the anti-fascist People's Front of Japan, and with the whole world peace front.

❧

In August of last year** I was elected by the Korean League for National Liberation and by the Korean communists as a delegate to the Chinese soviet districts in the northwest. The Chinese Communist Party made the connection for me, and I set out on my hazardous journey alone, pretending to be a Chinese during my travels.

At that time the capital of the Chinese soviets was in Baoan, a village in the far north of Shaanxi Province. The civil war and blockade[185] were still active against the soviets, and it was very dangerous to try to smuggle through the lines, I waited in Xi'an. Then the secret Red Army messengers arranged for me to pass through

---

* *a great common front was to be formed:* See Appendix II for more background on the fascinating extent and depth of the reforms that were planned at the time, and then compare them with what has or has not occurred since and how the world has changed—and whether the reforms suggested continue to hold any value for the future. –GT, DH

** *last year:* i.e. 1936. –DH

to Yan'an, which was in the hands of Zhang Xueliang's Northeast Army from Manchuria. I had to walk secretly from Yan'an to Baoan over difficult mountain paths and without food or shelter. This experience weakened me and caused my tuberculosis to become active, so I was very ill along the way and could hardly summon enough strength to continue my journey. It took me many days to reach Baoan, and when I arrived I collapsed and could not move from my bed for two months. I was so near death that I did not expect ever to rise again.

Edgar Snow had entered the soviet districts a few weeks before my arrival. He was in Baoan, but I did not see him because of my illness. He was the first foreigner to break through the blockade in the northwest, and I was the next.

After the Xi'an Incident in December 1936, the Red Army took over Yan'an, and the capital was transferred here from Baoan. Still weak from my illness, I moved to Yan'an with the others.

As soon as I was well enough, I was asked to teach a special class for the staff of the Military Committee.[186]

There are only two Koreans in Yan'an now—myself and a young student named Yi,[187] who accompanied the troops during the arrest of Chiang Kai-shek at Lindong and who came to Yan'an to study at the academy after the Xi'an Incident. At the front, General Peng Dehuai had as his chief of staff a Korean named Mujeong.

In order to train cadres for the coming struggle, many Korean revolutionaries from China are now going to Manchuria, which will be our base of partisan operations until a favorable time comes for action within Korea proper. Others are infiltrating into strategic positions with the Japanese so as to be ready when the time comes. We are being very careful and scientific in this preparation in order to guarantee a great final victory where so many small failures have been. My duty now lies in the leadership of this new movement, and for that task, I must summon and coordinate all the experience of the past.

I heard from my wife that our son has been born. Since the war with Japan began, I do not know what has happened to my wife and child.*

---

* *my wife and child*: Both survived. As mentioned in note 174, Kim's wife was named Zhao Yaping. The name of the son she had with Kim San, born on April 20, 1937, is Gao Yong-guang (more commonly known in South Korea as Go Yeong-gwang). His mother did not tell him that his father was Korean until he was twenty-seven years old. His last name Gao is his mother's second husband's surname. In 1980, he read a copy of the Chinese translation of *Song of Arirang* and through this came to know his father. When he learned his father had unjustly been condemned to death as a "special agent of Japan" and a "Trotskyist," he initiated a petition to the CCP to prove his father's innocence. Mr. Gao was actually the second of Kim San's two sons. According to a Korean source, a man named Zhang Gaoli from Shandong Province, who was looking for information about Kim San in the early 1970s, was also Kim San's son. (Yi 2006, 606-607) In fact, Kim mentioned to Nym Wales that he had two sons but didn't know what had happened to his first son, who had been born out of wedlock to a woman in Hailufeng who considered herself Kim San's "special girlfriend" during a three-month period. (Yi and Mizuno 1991, 259) –GT, DH

Top row: Yi Dong-hwi (L), Peng Pai (R). Middle row: Kim Won-bong (L), Kim Chung-Chang (R). Bottom row: Kim Ik-sang (L), Oh Seung-ryun (R).

EPILOGUE

"Only the Undefeated in Defeat..."

MY WHOLE LIFE has been a series of failures, and the history of my country has been a history of failure. I have had only one victory—over myself. This one small victory, however, is enough to give me confidence to go on. Fortunately, the tragedy and defeat I have experienced have not broken but rather strengthened me. I have few illusions left, but I have not lost faith in men and in the ability of men to create history. Who shall know the will of history? Only the oppressed, who must overthrow force in order to live. Only the undefeated in defeat, who have lost everything to gain a whole new world in the last battle. Oppression is pain, and pain is consciousness. Consciousness means movement. Millions of men must die and tens of millions must suffer before humanity can be born again. I accept this objective fact. The sight of blood and death and of stupidity and failure no longer obstructs my vision of the future.

The tradition of human history is democratic, and this tradition is the equal birthright given to all men. But some do not claim this birthright, and others steal it from them. Water can drown or save a man. Human society today is not a village pond but an angry flood. One must learn to swim. From the age of fourteen to this moment I have never left the water. I have given myself up many times, but I am not yet destroyed.

I have learned that there is only one important thing—to keep one's class relation with the masses, for the will of the mass is the will of history. This is not easy, for the mass is deep and dark and does not speak with a single voice until it is already in action. You must listen for whispers and the eloquence of silence. Individuals and groups shout loudly; it is easy to be confused by them. But the truth is told in a very small voice, not by shouting. When the masses hear the small voice, they reach for their guns. The mere urgent whisper of an old village woman is enough. True leadership has keen ears and a guarded mouth. To follow the mass will is the only way to lead to victory.

For the individual to struggle against superior power is only futile tragedy. One must organize equal force against force, and if this cannot be mobilized, action must wait and not engage in adventurism. Parties and groups and large bodies of men make many stupid mistakes leading to disaster, and I have participated in many such blunders, but mistakes are an inevitable part of leadership. You may see this mistake, but until you can win the following of the majority you have no right to leadership. To be in advance of your time does not qualify you for leadership but only for propaganda work and criticism. Lenin was the greatest democratic mass leader of our day because he followed the masses and pushed them. He did not pull them along by a string.

Yet the minority must be protected, for it is the initial instrument of change, the child and father of the majority. To stifle it is only to breed a monster. And it is the duty of every man to fight for his belief. To be false to himself is to be false to his class, his party, and his revolutionary duty. There is no place for cowardice in revolutionary leadership. No man has the right to leadership who has not strong beliefs and confidence in his own judgment. Moral courage is the essence of the revolutionary ethic. When a revolutionary submits to being deprived of his right to exercise freedom of opinion, he is failing in his duty. And no mind is free which oppresses others. Monoliths are not built of broken stones and the weakest quality clay. They can be made only of living men and strong minds, and no mortar can hold them together except the cement of free association. Without this democracy even the feeblest clay will one day turn to dynamite. A keystone is not an arch. Without support from both right and left, it will collapse. When voluntary following turns to fearful obedience, disintegration begins.

It is not easy to be morally brave in a political party; it is easier to follow, and to shirk responsibility. To be alone on a mountaintop is pleasant; to be alone among comrades is to be lonely indeed.

The quality of moral strength, however, lies not in stubborn stupidity but in the ability to change with changing conditions. The growth of the human mind seems to be limited. At a certain point it remains static and can no longer reach out and grasp new realities but softens into a childish nostalgia for some October long past. "Old Bolsheviks" would do well to be interred gloriously with their Lenins before the next generation trims their stubborn whiskers in derision.

One must accept the vote of a given majority—but whether that majority is right or wrong, that is another question. A Lenin may be right and the whole party wrong. But when a solitary Lenin happens to be right it is because he represents the majority will of the masses, not because he is an infallible individual personally. And when the party is wrong, it is wrong because it no longer represents the mass majority under it. Where democratic expression exists, the problem of leadership is easy. Where it is suppressed, it is dangerous and difficult. A true democratic mass vote cannot make a wrong decision; the problem is how to realize this vote. The line between right and wrong is a fluid one. In times of rapid historical change, what is right one day may be wrong within a week. The mercurial changes within a mass movement are proof of the correctness of mass judgment, for they truly reflect change, which is the essence of truth. Truth is relative, not absolute; dialectical, not mechanical. The swing from Right to Left and back again is in itself a process of reaching a correct evaluation. And that swing is also in itself a factor producing change. Men learn and reach correct judgments only by experience. To test a certain line of action is not to make a mistake but to take the first step toward discovering the correct line. If that test proves a certain line to be wrong, the test itself was correct, was an experiment in search of correctness, and therefore necessary. There are no controlled conditions in the great laboratory of social science. You cannot throw away a test tube and start again with the same given elements. There is only one test tube, and its compound changes qualitatively and quantitatively as you watch. Everything you do or fail to do goes into that mixture and can never be retrieved.

    I have not always reasoned in this way. Until 1932 I sat like a judge, mercilessly condemning "mistakes" and beating recalcitrants into line like a drill sergeant. When I saw men killed and movements broken because of stupid leadership and stupid following, a fury possessed me. I could not forgive. When Han and another Korean party leader were on trial in Shanghai in 1928, I did not care whether they were spies and traitors, but I felt earnestly that they deserved any punishment for their objective criminal stupidity in having a party organization so weak that the Japanese could arrest a thousand men in a few days.

I was an idealist. I judged the actions of men by their intelligence. Now I know that a man is composed of many things besides a brain. A revolutionary leader does not work with human skulls, to be lined up Right or Left. He works with the material of human life, with all its animal and vegetable characteristics, with all its variable and imponderable attributes. He works with the human spirit, so hard to crush, and with the human body, so easily destroyed. Often the body must be destroyed to waken and free the spirit of others. The execution of one man like Li Dazhao or Peng Pai may mean the awakening of a million.

For myself, I no longer condemn a man by asking what is good or what is bad, what is right or what is wrong, what is correct or what is mistaken. I ask what is value and what is waste, what is necessary and what is futile, what is important and what is secondary. Through many years of heartache and tears, I have learned that "mistakes" are necessary and therefore good. They are an integral part of the development of men and of the process of social change. Men are not so foolish as to believe in words; they learn wisdom only by experiment. This is their safeguard and their right. He knows not what is true who learns not what is false. The textbook of Marxism and Leninism is written not in ink but in blood and suffering. To lead men to death and failure is easy; to lead men to victory is hard.

Tragedy is a part of human life. To rise above oppression is the glory of man; to submit is his shame. To me it is tragic to see millions of men blindly give up their lives in imperialist wars. That is waste. It is tragic to see them utilized to oppress each other. That is stupidity. It is not tragic for men to die consciously fighting for liberty and for the things they believe in. That is glorious and splendid. Death is not good or bad. It is either futile or necessary. To be killed fighting voluntarily for a purpose in which you believe is to die happy. I have seen so much waste of human life, so much futile sacrifice ending in failure, that it has not been easy for me to reach a philosophical justification for this. But one thing I always remember—the revolutionaries died happy in their sacrifice; they did not know it was futile.

One man's happiness is another man's sorrow. I claim no right to it.

Nearly all the friends and comrades of my youth are dead, hundreds of them: nationalist, Christian, anarchist, terrorist, communist. But they are alive to me. Where their graves should be, no one ever cared. On the battlefields and execution grounds, on the streets of city and village, their warm revolutionary blood flowed proudly into the soil of Korea, Manchuria, Siberia, Japan, and China. They failed in the immediate thing, but history keeps a fine accounting. A man's name and his brief dream may be buried with his bones, but nothing that he has ever done or failed to do is lost in the final balance of forces. This is his immortality, his glory or his shame. Not even he himself can change this objective fact, for he is history. Nothing can rob a man of his place in the movement of history. Nothing can grant him escape. His only individual decision is whether to move forward or backward, whether to fight or submit, whether to create value or destroy it, whether to be strong or weak.

Opposite page: Kim San in Yan'an, 1937. Photo by Nym Wales.

Nym Wales in 1937 with Manchurian soldiers in front of wall near Yan'an that reads "Welcome to the Red Soldiers to come over to the Government [GMD] side"

Postlude

BY NYM WALES

KIM SAN ASKED me not to publish this manuscript until two years after telling me the story at the end of 1937.* Since then I have heard indirectly that he went to Manchuria through the dangerous guerrilla lines in north China in order to work with his friend Oh Seong-ryun and the Korean volunteers, but whether he is now** dead or alive I do not know.

In 1938, his friend, Kim Won-bong, the former famous terrorist, organized in central China a Korean Volunteer Corps to fight against Japan.[188] These several hundred Koreans are commanded by Kim Won-bong, who is also secretary of the Union for the Korean National Front and of the Korean National Revolutionary Party. A publicity booklet of this group that I've received states that their greatest duty is "the consolidation of all revolutionary elements abroad and at home in preparation for a struggle of the entire Korean people against the Japanese."

My husband, Edgar Snow, interviewed several of the Koreans in this Volunteer Corps in Hankou in 1938 and told me there was much difficulty in getting support from the Chinese National Government. The Guomindang was not enthusiastic about having such fiery leftwing revolutionaries fraternizing among their troops, apparently fearing the political consequences. Soon afterward, however, the corps was dispatched to the front to fight, and a number of Koreans have deserted the Japanese

---

* *Kim San asked me not to publish*: Nym Wales kept her promise and published the first edition of this book in 1941 with the John Day Company. She concealed Kim San's real name, Jang Ji-rak, until 1961, when she compiled her "Notes on Korea and the Life of Kim San." It turns out, Kim San was killed upon the orders of the CCP on his way to Manchuria. See this edition's Afterword, "Kim San after 1937," for more on this. —DH

** *now*: i.e. when this postlude was written, which was around 1940 and 1941. —DH

armies to join. There have been many cases of sabotage against the Japanese by Koreans, and they are an invaluable part of the Chinese espionage service. Korean conscripts* take every opportunity to desert. In February 1939, about seven thousand Korean troops mutinied near Guangdong and killed their Japanese officers. Such cases are not infrequent.**

The Koreans have become much more active during recent months. In June 1940, the Korean Independence Party, an amalgamation of the Korean Nationalist Party, the Korean Independence Party, and the Korean National Revolutionary Party, was formed in Chongqing.[189] Among its members are included "six different organizations of overseas Koreans in the United States."

In September 1940, it was reported that the Provisional Government of the Republic of Korea, which never technically ceased to exist since its Shanghai days in the early 1920s, had been revived in Chongqing.[190]

On September 17, 1940, the headquarters of a "Korean Independence Army" was inaugurated in Chongqing under command of fifty-three-year-old General Yi Cheong-cheon, a Korean graduate of the Japanese Military Academy who had been a captain in the Japanese Army before 1919. The meeting was presided over by Kim Gu, the Finance Minister of the Korean Provisional Government and Chairman of the Korean Independence Party. This is a conservative group, and the new Independence Army was officially sponsored and given financial support by Generalissimo Chiang Kai-shek. According to

---

* *Korean conscripts*: i.e. to the Japanese army. –DH

** *Such cases are not infrequent*: In an article in *Asia Magazine* for June, 1939, entitled "China's Japanese Allies," Edgar Snow tells of the Japanese and Korean volunteers assisting China. –NW [In fact, the Korean Volunteers Corps was assigned non-combatant missions by the Chinese National Government. This greatly disappointed many Korean volunteers and caused them to move from GMD-controlled areas to Yan'an, which was under CCP control. –DH]

The Union for the Korean National Front commemorates the founding of the Korean Volunteer Corps by Korean socialist organizations in Hankou, China on October 10, 1938. Kim Won-bong, wearing hat and leather strap across his chest, stands behind the miltary flag. Kim Chung-chang (alias of Kim Seong-suk), wearing glasses, stands in the front row. Provided by the Ministry of Patriots and Veterans Affairs.

the announcement,* General Yi's headquarters will be in north China, and the army will recruit Korean guerrillas in Manchuria and try to get Korean deserters from the Japanese armies. General Yi "also counts on the Koreans in the Soviet Far East Red Army to join the colors." Apparently this conservative group also intends to take over Kim Won-bong's volunteers, for it has been announced that "Korean soldiers and officers now fighting in the various Chinese units will be transferred to the Korean Independence Army."

A federation of Taiwanese revolutionaries was also formed in Chongqing in 1940, and the leaders announced that "Taiwanese revolutionists have started many uprisings in Taiwan. Japanese-owned mines were bombed, oil

---

* *announcement*: China Information Committee, Chongqing, September 23, 1940. –NW wells set on fire, and railways wrecked."

Very little information has come out of strictly censored Korea proper since the war between China and Japan began, though occasional reports indicate that all is not well. No doubt they are, according to plan, waiting for a "favorable moment." In September 1940, however, there was a report of a new anti-Japanese non-cooperation movement among 200,000 Christians, an echo of March First in 1919.

I was in Seoul in 1936 when the new governor-general, the famous General Minami Jirō, arrived. Since then he has been very busy defending "the Achilles heel of the Japanese Empire" and building a base for war industry and transport in Korea. In August 1939 he announced that "the Japanese government is concentrating its energy and attention upon the onerous task of blending Japanese and Koreans to make a harmonious whole. Remarkable is the progress made in this respect since 1940 or thereabouts, when the Koreans were immensely alienated in feeling from the Japanese." The intention is to assimilate and "Japanize" the Koreans and to make the country a part of Japan's internal economy. This is an unfruitful and expensive business. Military expenses for Korea usually amount to over fifteen million yen annually, and even in 1935,

Kim Gu (on left), Kim Won-bong (on right), and others in Chongqing at the 22nd anniversary commemoration of the March First Movement in 1943

206,214 persons were arrested. In that year there was a regular police force of 19,409 and an auxiliary force of 200,000. Partisans from Manchuria frequently "cross the Yalu River" and inflict losses on the Japanese.

The Japanese own 17% of all the cultivated land in Korea, and 85% of the peasants are either landless or part-tenants. The working class gets half the wages given to Japanese. Here is an explosive mixture.

The suppression and exploitation of Korea are probably greater than any other modern colony has suffered. These have served to prevent any mass armed uprising on the peninsula so far, but the important fact about Korea is its strategic position—it is still "the dagger pointing at the heart of Japan." There is no doubt that the Koreans will be one of the key factors in the overthrow of the present Japanese system, and that fairly soon. Let us consider the position: According to Kim San there are from fifty thousand to seventy thousand regular Korean partisans among the million exiles in Manchuria, and ten thousand volunteer troops. There are 800,000 sovietized Koreans in Siberia. The working class in Korea numbers one million with 300,000 industrial workers. Even in 1937 there were 300,000 recalcitrant Korean workers in Japan, and more have been imported since due to labor shortages.

The story of the constant Korean struggle against Japanese domination is a very heroic one when one considers the pressure under which this has been maintained. As compared with the colonial movements in India, Java, Indo-China, Taiwan, and Burma, for instance, it has been very persistent and active, though most of the armed attacks have been launched from Manchuria. As tested in Korea, Japanese colonial policy has been far from an example of enlightened imperialism. It has created the most unhappy country in the East.

ENDNOTES
BIOGRAPHICAL NOTES

ENDNOTES

[1] *a power she scarecely expected*: The following paragraph from Totten's original essay originally followed this sentence.

> At present, this book in its Japanese translation has probably done more than any other single volume to destroy prejudices among young people in Japan against Koreans, prejudices inherited from the days when Japan colonized Korea. In America the role this book can play is even greater: it can help make Americans aware of the plight of Koreans in the first place. The popular apathy and ignorance of Americans concerning the division and occupation of Korea, and the war that grew out of that, left them unprepared to see through the myths and distortions that served as pretexts for bringing them into an even bigger and more tragic war in Vietnam in which the American government also stepped in to keep the country divided and to hold one part under American dominance. Focusing on the human condition, a book like this not only breaks down the stereotypes of 'gooks' and 'communists' but also awakens constructive interest in what 'independence' and 'revolution' mean to those involved in the struggles to achieve them.

[2] *always in his ears*: Totten's essay originally concluded with information that has been superceded by more current research about Kim San that can be found in the Appendices at the end of this edition. The original ending read as follows:

> In order to protect his identity and safeguard his life, Kim San asked Helen Snow not to publish Song of Ariran for at least two years after their conversations and to refer to him only by the name 'Kim San,' a pseudonym invented for the book (though he had used many aliases before). Since she last saw him in Yan'an in 1937, she has had no word from him or about him; he did indicate that he intended to go to Manchuria, but whether he went or not is unknown. Nor does she know even if he is still alive.
>
> Only in her 'Notes on Korea and the Life of Kim San,' which she wrote for the Nym Wales Collection at the Hoover Institution, Stanford University, in 1961, did she publicly reveal that Kim San confided to her his real name: Chiang Chi-rak (Jang Ji-rak). She knew him in Yan'an as 'Chiang Ming (Zhang Ming).' He revealed also that he had used the Korean name '[Yu] Han-San' ('Cold Mountain') during the Guangzhou Commune and the Chinese name 'Ying Kuang [i.e. Yanguang]' for literary purposes.
>
> With this clue, Dr. Dae-sook Suh, a specialist on the Korean Communist movement now at the University of Hawaii, was able to discover the name 'Jang Ji-rak' in a Japanese police record of 1928 whom Dr. Suh has identified as a Korean nationalist. Unfortunately, Dr. Suh has been unable to find further material concerning this person in the 1930s or subsequently.
>
> Nor has the Japanese publication of Song of Ariran shed further light on the identity of Kim San despite the inclusion, in the very popular second edition of 1965 (Ando Jirō, translator, Ariran no Uta [Tokyo: Misuzu Shobo, 1965])° of the photograph of himself which Kim San gave Helen Snow in Yan'an.
>
> Perhaps someday the mystery of Kim San's identity may be cleared up. But in some ways it is nice not to know. It lends the man a kind of immortality, like Odysseus sailing off into the West to new adventures at the end of the Odyssey, living on in the tales left behind in the heroism of his deeds.

° The first edition of this translation was published by Asahi Shobo in October 1953. The revised edition with footnotes added with the help of Kang Tok-sang is now in its ninth printing and has evidently had a tremendous impact in Japan, especially on Koreans there. –GT

³ Totten's essay originally included this acknowledgement:

> I would like to thank Helen Foster Snow for inviting me to write this. In preparing it, I consulted a fellow member of the Tokyo chapter of the Committee of Concerned Asian Scholars, Angus McDonald, who suggested some changes and helpfully did some of the rewriting himself. I also incorporated suggestions from Susan Pharr, David Conde, and Herbert Bix. For permission to use footnoted material from the revised Japanese edition, I would like to thank Mr. Obi Toshihito of the Misuzu Shobo of Tokyo.

PRELUDE

⁴ *Yan'an*: City in China's Shaanxi Province that served as the revolutionary base of the Chinese Communist Party (CCP) from 1937. During the Sino-Japanese War (1937-1945), it was the capital of the CCP's Shaanxi-Ganxu-Ningxia Border Region Government. Often called the "holy place" of the Chinese Revolution because of its role in the 1949 birth of the People's Republic of China (PRC) under the leadership and revolutionary principles of Mao Zedong. –DH

⁵ *Chinese soviets*: The widespread use of the word "soviet" (Russian for "council") began in the Russian revolutions of 1905 and 1917-18 when the Soviets of Workers, Peasants, and Soldiers were formed as "governments by committee." The first Chinese soviet was formed in Hailufeng in 1927 (see note on p. 18), but the first Chinese Soviet Republic was established later in Jiangxi Province in 1931 and is commonly called Jiangxi Soviet. The "Chinese Soviets" referred to here are those in Yan'an in 1937, areas under the control of the CCP's "Border Government" mentioned in note 4. In Mandarin, "soviet" is pronounced "suweiai." –GT, DH

⁶ *Military and Political Academy*: Based in Yan'an, this institution—first established by the CCP in 1933 as the Workers and Peasants Red Army Academy and renamed the Chinese People's Anti-Japanese Military Political Academy (Zhongguo renmin kangri junshi zhengzhi daxue) after the emergence of the Second United Front in 1937—recruited students from throughout China with the goal of nurturing a revolutionary cadre through study, production, and battle. It eventually produced some 200,000 graduates. –MI, DH

⁷ *the armed struggle has been carried out from Manchuria*: Because Manchuria (current-day Liaoning, Jilin, and Heilongjiang Provinces in China, known as the "Northeastern three provinces") lies just across the border from Korea, it provided an ideal base for launching military attacks on Japanese occupation forces there. Most who migrated to Manchuria also engaged in cultivating farmland, educating the children of exiled patriots, and organizing military training centers. In 1931, the Japanese took over Manchuria and established the Manchukuo (Manshūkoku in Japanese), a Japanese "client state," setting up the last Emperor of China, Puyi (1906-1967), as its head. –GT, DH

⁸ *Beijing*: Although earlier editions of the book used the older spelling of the city's name, "Peking," Beijing will be used through this edition, as it is more familiar for contemporary readers. At the time being referred to in this passage, Beijing ("Northern Capital") had actually been renamed Beiping ("Northern Peace") by the National Government of the Guomindang (GMD, Nationalist Party). This happened because the GMD, which had finally unified China in 1928 and was at the time occupying the city, had proclaimed Nanjing ("Southern Capital") as its seat of government. After 1949, the city was again called Beijing by the newly victorious communist government. –GT, DH

9 *won a contest in the Olympics*: Because Korea was a colony of Japan from 1910 to 1945, Son Gi-jeong ran as a member of the Japanese Olympic team. In celebration of his gold medal, Korean-owned newspapers published a photo of him with the Japanese flag on his chest whited out. The Japanese colonial government immediately banned papers that had published the altered photo. Official Olympics records showed Son's gold metal as a win for Japan until 1999, when the South Korean government succeeded in getting the records changed so as to recognize that the feat was accomplished by a Korean and not a Japanese marathoner. –MI, GT, DH

10 *King Shan*: I have not been able to identify who King Shan was and if he was Korean. A Korean translation of *Song of Arirang* provides Kim Chan as the person's Korean name without a reference (Wales and Kim 2005: 36). –DH

11 *Shadows of the White-Clothed People* (Baek-ui dongpo ui yeongsang): Though this manuscript by Kim San has never been found, the title was used for a Korean-language edition of *Song of Arirang* published in China in 1986 by Liaoning minzu chubanshe. A Chinese-language translation of *Song of Arirang*, published in Hong Kong in 1977, was titled *In the Ranks of the Chinese Revolution* (Zai Zhongguo geming duiwuli). –DH

12 *since the Civil War in 1927*: i.e. the Chinese Civil War, which began when the GMD turned against the CCP, with which it had maintained an alliance (a "United Front") since 1924. –DH

PART I
CHAPTER 1: RECUERDO (MEMORIES)

13 *in 1919*: Here Kim San is connecting his decision to leave for Tokyo to study to the failure of the pro-independence demonstrations earlier that same year on March 1, 1919, called the March First Movement, which led to massive reprisals by the Japanese colonial government. –DH

14 *the lines of foreign intervention in Siberia*: After the Russian Revolution of 1917, the Allied Powers, including the U.S. and Japan, decided to send military forces to Siberia with the goal of supporting the anti-revolutionary forces (i.e. White Russia) against the revolutionary forces (i.e. Soviet Russia) during the civil war there. Japan did the majority of the fighting there against the Red Army of Soviet Russia. As it turned out, the Japanese military dreamt of a Siberian empire extending as far west as Lake Baikal, and the American troops came with the objective of containing the Japanese. The Japanese in particular helped the White Russians try to crush the revolution happening there. As the Japanese intervention dragged on, however, it became increasingly unpopular in Japan, and the stock of the Japanese military went down to its lowest ebb. The "Allied" (actually Japanese) intervention lasted from 1918 to 1922. –GT, DH

15 *a year of political crisis in China*: Reference to the internal military and political conflicts and divisions among the GMD leaders between those who supported and opposed Chiang Kai-shek, coupled with Japan's invasion of Manchuria. –DH

16 *Yi Dynasty*: Another name for Korea's Joseon Dynasty (1392-1910). Derived from the surname of the Joseon Dynasty's founder and the kings who succeeded him, this name is used primarily by Japanese scholars and in Japan. –GT, DH

17 *the earthquake in 1923*: A reference to the Great Kantō Earthquake that struck the Tokyo area on September 1, 1923, resulting in the loss of between 100,000 and 200,000 lives, and the destruction of 570,000 dwellings, roughly three-fourths of all those in Tokyo.

(Gordon 2003, 140) According to Korean and Chinese sources, Japanese police, soldiers, and vigilante groups killed over six thousand Koreans (and approximately seven hundred Chinese) in the aftermath of the disaster on the basis of false rumors that the Koreans were plotting, in collaboration with Japanese socialists, to incite social unrest by poisoning wells, committing robbery, or using bombs to commit acts of terrorism. –DH

[18] *Rice Riots of 1918*: These started on July 23, 1918 when a fisherwoman in Toyama Prefecture who could no longer stand the spiraling rise in the price of rice threw a stone through the window of a rice merchant. This touched off riots that spread to thirty-six prefectures and resulted in thousands of arrests and the calling up of military forces. It also helped lay the basis for the subsequent so-called Taishō democracy period, which falls roughly during the reign of Emperor Taishō (1912-1925). It is also interesting to note that when talking about the riots, Kim San does not mention the "burakumin" (special community people), often referred to derogatorily in Japanese as "eta," which roughly translates to "trash," since the burakumin were likewise set upon and beaten during this crisis. Nor does he touch upon the struggle of leftists in Japan in general at this time. For an account of this "special community people" in Japanese left-wing movements, see Totten III 1966, 364-377 and *passim*. –GT

[19] *took the occasion to arrest…as "communists"*: Reference to the large-scale arrest of Korean communists by the Japanese in Korea that began in Seoul in February 1928. Most of those arrested belonged to the so-called Marxist-Leninist Party (ML Party, also known as the Third Korean Communist Party (see note 54)). –DH

[20] *before the Xi'an Incident in 1936*: i.e. before the arrest in Xi'an of Chiang Kai-shek by his own military commander, Zhang Xueliang, who undertook this step in order to persuade Chiang to work together with the Chinese communists, bringing the civil war to an end in an effort to resist Japan. This incident led to the formation in 1937 of the second United Front between the GMD and the CCP. Afterwards, Chiang took Zhang prisoner, eventually bringing him to Taiwan under house arrest. Toward the end of Zhang's extraordinarily long life, he was freed and moved to Hawaii where he died. –DH

CHAPTER 2: KOREAN CHILDHOOD

[21] *members of the Korean Independence Party*: This seems to refer to those who generally favored modern reforms rather than the preservation of traditions. The actual Independence Party collapsed much earlier than Kim San's birth in 1905. –DH

[22] *could read a little Korean, which is easy to learn*: That is, his mother could read hangeul (hangul), the Korean alphabet developed in 1443 that gradually came to be used throughout Korea under the Joseon Dynasty, though the use of Chinese characters continued to be widespread in official documents and among the yangban, the traditional aristocratic ruling class of the dynasty. –GT, DH

CHAPTER 3: DECLARATION OF INDEPENDENCE

[23] *a Christian school of about three hundred students*: Many scholars believe the school Kim San matriculated at was the Sungsil School in Pyongyang, which was established in 1897 by an American Presbyterian missionary. –DH

[24] *March 1st, 1919*: Reference to the demonstrations that launched the March First Movement. (See note on p. 34.)

[25] *the help of President Wilson and the great powers at Versailles*: At the conclusion of World War I, President Woodrow Wilson gave a speech where he declared the right to national self-determination from colonial powers as part of his Fourteen Points speech about the requirements for a lasting peace. The belief in Korea at the time was that in light of Wilson's remarks, the U.S. and the other Allied Powers of Europe who'd gathered at Versailles in 1919 to finalize the terms of the post-World War I peace agreement would support Korea's bid for independence. This belief led to the demonstrations on March 1st, 1919 that have been subsequently memorialized as the beginning of the Korean Independence Movement. –GT, DH

[26] *to give part of Shandong to the Japanese*: A German military base had been based in Qingdao, a city on the Shandong peninsula, before World War I. During World War I, Britain offered this area to Japan in order to induce Japan to side with the Allies against Germany. When the 1919 Versailles Peace Conference confirmed this transfer after the war, it ignited the fire of nationalism, resulting in the student demonstrations in Beijing on May 4, 1919 that developed into what is known as the May Fourth Movement (see note 34). –GT, DH

[27] *the betrayal from Versailles*: Contrary to the expectations of those Koreans who had participated in the March First demonstrations, the result of the Versailles Peace Conference was that Korea would remain a colony under the Japanese. –GT

[28] *Cheondogyo*: Translates to "teaching of the Heavenly Way." Originally known as the Donghak (or Tonghak, meaning "Eastern Learning") movement, this religious movement led to an armed uprising of peasants in 1894 that swept southern Korea, threatening the Joseon Dynasty. –GT, DH

[29] *Taiping Rebellion in China*: Containing revolutionary elements that were inspired in part by Christianity, this massive armed rebellion that began in southern China lasted from 1850 to 1865 and almost succeeded in overthrowing the Qing Dynasty. Led by Hong Xiuquan (1814-1864), it sought to establish what Hong called "the Heavenly Kingdom of Great Peace." –GT, DH

[30] *their lands had become smaller and smaller every year*: Many Koreans, including peasants, small landowners, and Buddhist priests, lost their lands, purportedly for not having registered with the Japanese colonial government in a timely fashion after having been sent notices to do so. Since many Koreans, particularly peasants, were illiterate, they did not understand what the notice was about and, in some cases, never even received it. –DH

[31] *these two incidents*: The Suwon incident (better known as the "Massacres at Jeam-ri") occurred on April 15, 1919. Many people were shot as they ran out of the burning church, and twenty-nine died immediately. Several foreigners witnessed this, including Frank William Schofield (1889-1970), a Canadian missionary and veterinarian teaching at the Severance Medical School in Seoul, who continued to testify about what he had seen to the outside world in an effort to support Korea's independence. For these efforts, he was later buried in the Korean National Cemetery in Seoul. –DH

[32] *Korean Daily News* (Daehan maeil sinbo): A Korean-language newspaper founded in 1905. Its president, an Englishman named Ernest Bethell, employed independence activists such as Yang Gi-tak (1871-1938), who was the general manager there, Bak Eun-sik (1859-1926), who worked as an editorial writer, Shin Chae-ho (see Biographical Notes), and others. As such, the paper played a large role in the patriotic enlightenment movement, and when Korea was annexed by Japan in 1910, it, along with other papers

and journals, was ordered to cease publication. In the first edition of *Song of Arirang*, Nym Wales mistakenly called this the *Korean Independent News*. –MI

[33] *Oriental Daily News*: Throughout the book, this newspaper is referred to by both Kim San and Nym Wales as the *Oriental Daily News*, but it is more commonly translated these days as the *East Asia Daily* (Dong-a Ilbo). –DH

[34] *May Fourth Movement in Beijing*: On May 4, 1919 students from universities in Beijing began demonstrations to protest against the warlord government then in power there in Beijing for its humiliating acquiescence to the terms of the Peace Conference in Paris, which included Japan's takeover of the German "sphere of interest" in China, that is, the Shandong peninsula (see note 26). The demonstrations on that day were to develop into a much broader and longer lasting cultural and political movement based on anti-(Japanese) imperialism, and is now known as the May Fourth Movement. –DH

CHAPTER 4: TOKYO SCHOOL DAYS

[35] *Bak Geun*: No detailed biographical information about this person is available. –DH

[36] *Korean Young Men's Independence Party*: Reference probably to the Korean Young Men's Independence Group (Joseon cheongnyeon dongnip dan), established in 1918 by Korean students in Tokyo. –DH

[37] *Washington Conference a few months before*: This military conference of nine countries was held in Washington D.C. from November 12, 1921 to February 6, 1922. During it, U.S. and Japan agreed to limit the number of battleships they possessed using a 5:3 ratio based on tonnage. More commonly known as the Washington Naval Conference. –DH

CHAPTER 5: CROSSING THE YALU RIVER

[38] *Kropotkin...had influenced me*: Reference to Peter A. Kropotkin, a Russian anarchist. See Biographical Notes.

[39] *seven hundred li*: A distance of approximately 217 miles.

[40] *$30...$130*: It is unclear whether Kim carried dollars or whether these numbers are an estimate in dollars of other foreign currency. –DH

[41] *Sanyuanpu*: An area in Manchuria just across the Yalu River from Korea that was viewed by the Japanese military authorities as a threat and labeled as being under communist influence. At the time of the Japanese annexation of Korea, Koreans under the influence of the New People Society (Sinminhoe), a militarized anti-Japanese self-government group established in 1907 by Ahn Chang-ho, moved to Sanyuanpu and established schools to teach agriculture and the nationalist ideology of the Sinheung (literally, "Newly Burgeoning"). From 1923-24, the area became a base for the Korean Army of Independence. Sanyuanpu is now considered to be part of the city of Tonghua in Jilin Province. –GT, MI, DH

[42] *No. 1 feudal landlords*: The term "feudal" is being used loosely here. Likewise, "No. 1" simply means the most powerful of the landowners. –GT

[43] *military school at Hanihe*: This military school at Hanihe in Manchuria, translated throughout the book as the "New Development School" is known in Korean as the

Sinheung (literally "Newly Burgeoning") Military School. Originally called Sinheung Middle School, it began as part of the agricultural and ideology schools in Sanyuanpu that are described in note 41. Though it was already teaching military subjects, its name was not changed to the Shinheung Military School until 1919. At that time, it appointed as military instructors Yi Cheong-cheon (1888-1957), who would in 1940 go on to become the commander of the Korean Restoration Army (Gwangbok gun), as well as others who had graduated from the Japanese Army Officers School (Nihon rikugun shikan gakkō). Some two thousand graduates were eventually produced by the school, whose objective became to achieve independence for Korea, before it was disbanded by Japanese military forces. –MI, DH

44 *hundreds of thousands of others in Siberia*: By the end of WWI, there were significant Korean populations in cities such as Vladivostok, Irkutsk, Chita, and Khabarovsk, and Korean farms existed throughout Siberia. –DH

45 *Manchus permitted the Chinese to enter*: The Manchus conquered China in 1644, establishing the Qing Dynasty, which lasted until 1912. During this period, the people of the sparsely populated Manchuria were divided into "banners" that served as social and military organizations, and Manchuria itself was kept as a hunting reserve that Han (Chinese) people were not permitted to enter. –GT, DH

46 *occupied Hunchun*: The Japanese Consulate General in the Chinese-controlled city of Hunchun in Manchuria, right across the Tumen River from Korea, was attacked twice, in September and October 1920, and a number of guards were killed. On the grounds that this was the work of Korean independence forces, the Japanese dispatched troops to an area called Jiandao, where many Koreans had settled, to clean them out. However, according to recent studies, it is now thought by some scholars that the raid on the Japanese Consulate General was in fact staged by the Japanese themselves. –MI, DH

47 *the Japanese massacred the civilian population, killing over six thousand Koreans*: The Japanese who invaded Jiandao fought a fierce battle against the Korean independence troops at Qingshanli in eastern Manchuria's Helong Xian, after which the independence forces moved north, crossing into Siberia. Although Kim San describes Japanese forces as having killed six thousand people, other sources report the numbers killed as closer to three thousand Koreans and more than two hundred incarcerated. As a result of this Jiandao Incident, the Korean independence movement was temporarily brought to a complete standstill. –MI, DH

48 *What happened to...my first schoolboy love, I never could find out*: According to a Korean source, the pastor's real name was Ahn Dong-sik and the fourteen-year old daughter was named Ahn Mi-sam. The latter survived and later changed her name to Ahn Ji-suk. As of 1993, she was living in Seoul. –DH (Yi 2006, 606)

CHAPTER 6: SHANGHAI, MOTHER OF EXILES

49 *Jo Un-san*: No further information about this person has been found. –DH

50 *Korean People's Association* (Shanghai daehanin georyu mindan): The Korean People's Association, which was based in Shanghai's French Concession, was the successor of the Overseas People's Friendship Association (Shanghai gyomin chinmokhoe), which was founded in May 1919 and consisted of seven hundred Koreans living in Shanghai. Though ostensibly an organization for self-sufficiency and mutual aid, it was actually an inde-

pendence movement organization set up to support the Korean Provisional Government both financially and in terms of personnel. –MI

[51] *Korean Independence News*: What is referred to here as the *Korean Independence News* was begun by the Korean Provisional Government in August 1919 under the name *Independence* (Dongnip). As described in note on p. 61, it was started in secret due to the impossibility of publishing a radical newspaper within Korea at the time. In October of the same year, its name was changed to *Independence News* (Dongnip sinmun). It ceased publication in 1925. After the Provisional Government moved from Shanghai to Chongqing (see note 190), it resumed publication and continued to do so until 1943, this time in Chinese, though with the same title. –MI, DH

[52] *Inseong School*: Established in Shanghai in 1916 as a Christian school, the Inseong School became a public school managed by Koreans living there. In 1935, the school, which stimulated a sense of national consciousness in its Korean students, was permanently closed due to pressure from Japan. –MI, DH

[53] *began in August 1919*: These preliminary meetings for the founding of the Korean Provisional Government actually began in April 1919, rather than in August, as is sometimes claimed. The founding date of the Korean Provisional Government is now considered by the South Korean Government to be April 11, a little over a month after the demonstrations that marked the beginning of the March First Movement. –AJ, DH

[54] *the first Korean Communist Party*: The history of Korean communism is a long and complicated one to describe. What Kim San is referring to here is the Korean Socialist Party (Hanin sahoedang), which was begun in Khabarovsk in June 1918 by Yi Dong-hwi. After moving to Shanghai, he changed the organization's name in 1921 to the Korean (Goryeo) Communist Party, also known as the Shanghai Korean Communist Party or the Shanghai faction. Another group, founded by Russian-born Korean Bolsheviks, used the exact same name (i.e. the Korean [Goryeo] Communist Party) but was based in Irkutsk. While various socialist and communist parties had been set up since 1918 by Koreans in China and Siberia, the Korean Communist Party was not officially set up inside Korea until 1925; it was recognized by the Communist International (Comintern) the following year. Yet another group, the Marxist-Leninist Party (ML Party), began in Seoul in February 1928, and is also known as the Third Korean Communist Party. –GT, DH

[55] *Tokyo Imperial Military Academy*: Yi Dong-hwi was actually a graduate of the old Korean Military Academy in Seoul. –GT, DH

[56] *commander-in-chief*: Here Kim San was somewhat misinformed. According to other accounts, Yi was a major in the Korean Army when it was officially abolished in 1907. Nevertheless, soldiers continued to rally around him surreptitiously. –GT

[57] *"Irkutsk Party"*: Either Kim San or Nym Wales evidently got the two factions mixed up here. What is described as the "Irkutsk Party" was in fact their competitors, the Shanghai faction. (See note 54.) –MI, DH

[58] *four years before a Communist Party was set up in China*: Kim San should have said "three years," because the CCP held its first "Congress" in July 1921. –GT

[59] *500,000 rubles*: Nym Wales originally wrote "$500,000." Other sources usually say rubles. –GT

[60] *People's Delegates Congress*: In the beginning of 1921, Ahn Chang-ho and others proposed

a "Korean People's Delegates Congress" (Gungmin daepyohoe) to redirect the independence movement at a time when the Korean Provisional Government was weakening due to internal squabbles. Kim Rip and other communists supported this. It took time but the Congress opened in Shanghai in January 1923. As Kim San explains, the Congress fell apart in June 1923 because the "reformists" and the people who wanted to start something new could not reconcile their differences. –MI

[61] *in 1924...Kim Rip was shot*: The correct date of Kim Rip's assassination was February 6, 1922. –DH (*HSIS*, 65)

[62] *died in 1928 at his home near Vladivostok*: Yi Dong-hwi did not die in 1928, as Kim San thought, but lived on till 1935, when he passed away from sickness in a Korean "colony" on the outskirts of Vladivostok in January 1935. –GT, MI, DH

[63] *After 1924*: This should probably read "After 1922", since this presumably refers back to the assassination of Kim Rip, which took place in February 1922. –DH

[64] *carried his point*: Two sentences that originally concluded this paragraph have been omitted from the text: "Ahn was a member of the 'Three Days' Cabinet' in Korea about 1900 and was forced to escape after its fall. Later he returned and started the *Korean Independence Daily News* in Korea, which was eventually changed and taken over by the Korean government." The reason for this omission is that AJ found no evidence that Ahn was involved in that incident, which actually took place in 1894. Ahn was a student around that time at a school in Seoul set up by an American missionary. This may be one of the many apocryphal stories that have collected around his name. –GT, DH

[65] *in 1910*: Ahn Chang-ho first visited California in 1900. –DH

[66] *Shanghai War*: What is here referred to as the Shanghai War is fighting that took place in Shanghai between Japanese and Chinese forces in January and February of 1932 in the wake of the Manchurian Incident (see note on p. 328). –GT, DH

CHAPTER 7: THEY WHO LIE IN WAIT

[67] *went in for direct action against the Japanese*: The most spectacular instance of direct action undertaken by Koreans living in Shanghai during that period occurred in the Hongkou Park Incident described in note on pp. 94 and 103. –GT

[68] *One was the Uiyeol-dan*: What Kim San recalls subsequently regarding the Uiyeol-dan is not entirely correct. It is not certain whether these deviations from historical fact were deliberate or not, but when they do occur, a note is provided by the editors. –MI, GT, DH

[69] *Red Flag Society*: According to various sources, the Red Flag Society was a secret armed organization established in 1923 (i.e. not 1919 as Kim San states) in either northern Manchuria or Vladivostok in connection with either Yi Dong-hwi and the Shanghai Korean Communist Party or the Comintern. Its aim was to carry out anti-Japanese activities, the assassination of pro-Japanese Koreans, communist propaganda activities, etc. –DH (Kim 1997, 113-114, 116)

[70] *"Friends of Korean Independence" movement*: The League of the Friends of Korea (Han-guk chin-u hoe) was organized in response to an appeal to support Korean independence made to the American public by Philip Jaisohn (Seo Jae-pil [1864-1951]) in September 1919 in Philadelphia, Pennsylvania. The League included among its members Senator Floyd W. Thomkins and over a hundred others. It set up branches in a number of cities and published the English-language *The Korea Review*. –MI, DH

71 *directed by Martin, a German*: According to Kim Won-bong's first biographer, he initially contacted three foreigners and selected a German to make bombs, but was not happy with the skill level of the German. Kim Won-bong was later introduced to a Hungarian named "Majaal" who worked closely with the Uiyeol-dan and produced excellent bombs that were shipped to colonial Korea. Kim San might have changed the Hungarian's name and nationality here to protect his identity. –DH (Bak 1947, 97-108)

72 *first started in Korea proper*: The first anarchist organization in colonial Korea was probably the Black Labor Society (Heungno hoe), organized in Seoul in 1923. –DH

73 *Black Youth League*: There are few records of the Black Youth League (Heuksaek cheongnyeon dongmaeng), but its Beijing branch is believed to have been the first Korean anarchist organization in China (i.e. not "in Korea" as Kim San states), and was possibly established by Shin Chae-ho. Korean anarchists in Japan began with the Black Wave Society (Heukdo hoe)—later the Black Friends Society (Heuk-u hoe)—which was organized in Tokyo in 1921 by Bak Yeol (1902-1974) and others. In 1925 the Black Flag League (Heukgi yeonmaeng) was about to be launched, when it was discovered and dissolved by the Japanese police. –MI, DH (Hwang 2016)

74 *Anarchist Federation*: This organization, founded in Beijing in April 1924 by Yi Hoe-yeong (1867-1932) and others, was called the Korean Anarchist League and published the *Justice Newspaper* (Jeong-ui gongbo). In 1928 the members of this organization reorganized themselves into the Korean Anarchist Federation in China and published a Korean-language periodical called *The Conquest* (Talhwan). That same year they joined anarchists from China, Vietnam, Taiwan, and India in forming the Eastern Anarchist League. –DH (Hwang 2016)

75 *I joined the anarchist group*: The Uiyeol-dan was not an anarchist group per se. According to many scholars, however, it adopted anarchist principles such as direct action into its activities. –DH

76 *Kim's famous individual performance*: At this point Nym Wales evidently thought Kim San was talking about Kim Won-bong, when actually he was talking about another person named Kim Ik-sang, an Uiyeol-dan member who, under the direction of Kim Won-bong, attempted to assassinate Saitō Makoto (see Biographical Note; referred to by Kim San as Baron Saitō), then General Governor of Korea, though he failed (see note 83). –GT

77 *the summer of 1923*: This incident actually occurred on September 12, 1921. –GT, DH

78 *threw all seven of his bombs*: According to Korean sources, Kim Ik-sang threw three bombs. –DH (Bak 1947, 55-74; Kim 1997, 74)

79 *joined the Uiyeol-dan in 1918*: Other sources say that Oh joined the Uiyeol-dan in 1920, which seems more likely given that the Uiyeol-dan itself was founded in 1919 (see note on p. 34). –DH (*HSIS*, 285; Yi 1973, 260)

80 *called "Sao"*: Reference to George. L. Shaw (1880-1943). See Biographical Notes.

81 *in 1924*: Here again Kim San is mistaken about the date. The assassination attempt actually took place on March 28, 1922 while Army General Tanaka Giichi (1864-1929)—referred to by Kim San as "Baron Giichi"—was on a trip to Shanghai. The Uiyeol-dan had decided this was a good chance to carry out their plans to assassinate him. –KTS, MI, DH

82 *Tanaka Memorial*: This document was reportedly drawn up in 1927 for a meeting presided over by Tanaka Giichi, Japan's prime minister at the time, at which Emperor Hirohito was presented with plans concerning Japan's policies regarding China and East Asia. Back

then the Tanaka Memorial was thought to be "a blueprint for Japan's conquest of Asia and the world," but this view has since been largely discredited. –MI, DH (Gordon 2003, 353n17)

[83] *Oh Seong-ryun...Kim Ik-sang...Yi Jong-am, with a sword*: Accounts verify that the alleged prospective assassins of Tanaka were Oh Seong-ryun, Kim Ik-sang (1895-1943), and Yi Jong-am (1896-1930), all members of the Uiyeol-dan. Both Kim and Oh were arrested immediately, while Yi was arrested in 1925 in Korea. As Kim San explains, Oh was detained in the Japanese Consulate but escaped. Yi died in prison in 1930, and Kim Ik-sang was convicted by a court in Nagasaki of participating in both this plot and the attempted assassination of Governor General Saitō (see note 76). Though originally sentenced to death, his sentence was later reduced to twenty years of detention. Released after having served his term, he was allegedly assassinated by a Japanese police detective. –KTS, MI, DH

[84] *American woman*: W.J. Snyder, the woman who was shot to death, had been on a world tour trip with her husband, H.A. Thompson, who was wounded in the assassination attempt. –DH

[85] *University of the East*: This refers to the Communist University for the Toilers of the East (Kommunisticheskii Universitet Trudiashchikhsia Vostoka, abbreviated KUTV), an institution set up by the Comintern for the purposes of training Asian revolutionaries. Many Koreans studied there. –MI

[86] *the Korean Revolutionary Young Men's League* (Han-guk hyeongmyeong cheongnyeon yeonmaeng): Also referred to in the text as the Korean Young Men's League or the Young Men's League. The likely precursor to the Association of Korean Revolutionary Comrades in Guangdong (Liuyue hanguo geming tongzhihui), which was organized in June 1926 and led mainly by Uiyeol-dan members with the goal of uniting and promoting the skills of the Korean revolutionaries in Guangzhou. The Association's members numbered between two and three hundred. In April 1927 Kim San was elected one of the nine members of its Central Committee and was placed in charge of its propaganda activities. –MI, DH (Kim 1997, 165-168)

[87] *Butterfly Wu*: The English name of Hu Die (1908-1989), a popular Chinese actress in China in the 1920s and '30s. –DH

CHAPTER 8: REFLECTIONS ON WOMEN AND REVOLUTION

[88] *a charity near Beijing*: In fact, the orphanage was in Xiangshan not in Hsi Shan (Xishan) as Nym Wales wrote in the original text. –DH (GCMR, 489)

CHAPTER 9: FROM TOLSTOY TO MARX

[89] *Communist Youth League*: Founded in 1921 as the Socialist Youth League of China (Zhongguo shehuizhuyi qingniantuan), its name was changed in 1925 to the Communist Youth League (Gongchanzhuyi qiigniantuan). More colloquially referred to as Communist Youth throughout the book. –DH

[90] *to do propaganda work*: Kim Chung-chang became acquainted with some of the leading figures of the March First Movement during his stay at what some scholars say was Yongmun Temple and others Bongseon Temple. –DH (HHH, 37-40)

91 *imprisoned for a year*: Kim Chung-chang was actually in prison for two years and released in April 1921. —DH (*HSIS*, 84)

92 *Proletarian Federation* (Musanja dongmaeng hoe): An organization set up in Seoul in January 1922 mostly by former work-study students who had studied in Tokyo. Known as the first radical group in Korea, its mission was to liberate the propertyless classes. (Kim and Kim Vol. 2 1986, 33-36). —DH

93 *Revolution*: Not much is known about this magazine beyond its name ("Hyeongmyeong" in Korean). —DH

94 *Beijing Korean Communist Party*: In an interview, Kim Chung-chang recalls founding the Creating-One Party (Chang-il dang) in 1924 (and publishing *Revolution*) with Jang Geon-sang (1883-1974) and Kim San as a sub-organization of the Irkutsk Korean Communist Party. Jang Geon-sang, however, calls the organization "the Revolutionary Comrades Society" (Hyeongmyeong dongji hoe). No matter what its official name might have been, Kim San seems to remember it as the Beijing Korean Communist Party. —DH (*HSIS*, 84; *HHH*. 61-65, 174)

PART III
CHAPTER 10: IN THE RANKS OF CHINA'S GREAT REVOLUTION

95 *during his Soviet Russian reorientation*: This refers to a reorganization of the GMD along soviet lines and concepts such as, for example, "democratic centralism," that was initiated by Sun Yat-sen in 1923. This was meant to help transform the GMD into a disciplined revolutionary party, and, as a result, strengthen Sun Yat-sen's position as the party's undisputed leader. At this time, the emphasis of the GMD shifted towards recognizing the importance of workers and peasants. Subsequent to this reorganization, Chinese Communists were allowed to join the GMD while continuing to maintain their CCP membership and the first United Front between the two parties was launched soon thereafter. —DH

96 *Northern Expedition to destroy the feudal warlords*: A military campaign undertaken by the National Revolutionary Army (NRA), operating under orders from the National Government of the GMD, whose objective was to unify China by overthrowing warlord rulers in collaboration with the CCP. Known as "Beifa" in Mandarin. —GT, DH

97 *Borodin's staff*: Reference to Mikhail M. Borodin, Soviet advisor to the National Government of the GMD. See Biographical Notes. —DH

98 *should become a branch of the Chinese Communist Party*: What Kim San is referring to here is the "one communist party in one country" principle in "the Communist International Regulations," which was adopted by the Comintern on August 29, 1926. Because of it, Korean Communists in China could not set up their own party in China but had to join the CCP. —DH (Murata 1981, 369, 373)

99 *Revolutionary Action*: According to a Japanese source, the organ's name was *Revolutionary Movement* ("Hyeongmyeong haengdong" in Korean and "Geming yundong" in Mandarin). —DH (Kim 1997, 168)

100 *"KK"*: Koreanische Kommunisten. —DH

101 *changed its name to the Korean National Independence Party*: The only known source that refers to the Uiyeul-dan changing its name is the memoir of Yu Ja-myeong (1894-1985), an

Uiyeol-dan member and anarchist, who recalls that the Uiyeol-dan changed its name to the Korean National Revolutionary Party (Joseon minjok hyeongmyeong dang) in Guangzhou. It is unclear why Kim San calls it the Korean National Independence Party. –DH (Yu 1999, 149; Kim 1997, 186)

[102] *Zhongshan University*: Founded in 1924 and originally named Guangdong University, this university was named after Sun Yat-sen, also called Sun Zhongshan, following his death in 1925. The number of Korean students enrolled at the university ranged between forty-seven to fifty-seven in 1926 but decreased to twenty-eight in 1927, due mainly to their participation in the Northern Expedition, which began in July 1926, as well as the breakdown of the GMD-CCP United Front in 1927. –DH (Cui 1994; Chang 2005)

[103] *Revolutionary Military Staff*: It is unclear what Kim San is referring to here. –DH

[104] *studied economics at Zhongshan University*: Kim San seems to have started out in 1925 at Zhongshan University as a medical student but by the following year he had enrolled as a fourth-year student in law and politics. –DH (Cui 1994, 119-122)

[105] *totals about four million*: According to figures found by MI, 167,400 Koreans were living in the Soviet Far Eastern area in 1926, so this 700,000 figure seems like an exaggeration. On the other hand, Korean scholar Chong-Sik Lee shows the number of Koreans in Manchuria in 1934 was 719,988. (Lee 1978, 54). Kim San might have confused the number of Koreans in Manchuria with the number of Koreans in Siberia. –MI, DH

[106] *April 15, 1927*: This date — three days after Chiang Kai-shek's massacre of the communists and workers in Shanghai on April 12, 1927 — is when GMD military leaders such as Li Jishen started their own "purge" of communists and communist sympathizers in Guangdong. –AJ

[107] *Special Training Regiment*: Though this is not a literal translation of "Jiaodaotuan," Nym Wales uses the two terms interchangeably, more often than not preferring the Chinese name. Throughout the book, however, "Special Training Regiment" will be used, as it is easier for most readers to recognize and remember. –GT, DH

[108] *Byeong-in Volunteer Unit*: A Korean right-wing terrorist unit in Shanghai. The original text gives the name of the group as "Ping Yin Yi Tung Tui". "Ping" ("Byeong" according to Korean pronunciation) refers to the third of the ten Heavenly Stems, and "yin" ("in" in Korean) refers to the third of the twelve Earthly Branches, so the word "byeong-in" refers to the year 1926. "Yi Tung Tui" ("Yiyongdui" according to the Chinese pinyin romanization system, or "Uiyongdae" in Korean) can be translated as "volunteer unit" or "army." Kim San later refers to this organization as the "Brave Army of 1925," possibly out of some confusion about the year. –GT, DH

[109] *the girl was a beautiful Guangzhou student*: This woman, whose name was Du Junhui (1904-1981), would go on to marry Kim Chung-chang. According to a Chinese source, Kim Chung-chang became close to Du while teaching Japanese to her prior to her studying abroad in Tokyo. He recommended that she study Marxism, internationalism, and the theory of class struggle, and as a result, her consciousness of the world and of revolution rapidly matured. After 1949, when Kim returned to Korea, she remained in China. –MI, GT, DH (Jin 1990, 135)

[110] *Place of the Seventy-Two Martyrs*: Constructed in 1918, this monument memorializes the dead gathered from among those who carried out an armed uprising in Guangzhou in April 1911 that functioned as a prelude to the 1911 Revolution, which overthrew the Qing Dynasty and brought about the Republic of China. –MI, GT, DH

¹¹¹ *Oriental League of Oppressed Peoples*: More accurately translated as the United Society of the Eastern Oppressed Peoples (Dongfang beiyapo minzu lianhehui). Organized during the period when the Chinese Revolution was being developed from 1926 to 1927, it was composed of delegates from China, Korea, India, Taiwan (Formosa), and elsewhere. –MI, DH (Mizuno 1992)

¹¹² *Lin Sunji*: Unclear who this was. This person's name does not appear on the list of the organization's members. –DH (Mizuno 1992, 318)

¹¹³ *massacre of the factory workers in Shanghai*: Part of the strategy of the Northern Expedition was to take control of the great city of Shanghai, a center of wealth and power. This was to be done by coordinating an uprising within Shanghai with an attack from outside the city. Inside Shanghai, the Communists, working with the labor unions, organized an uprising. The troops outside the city were under the control of Chiang Kai-shek. Chiang's decision to turn against his allies, the Communists, was consummated when he gave orders on April 12, 1927 to round up and execute "communists" or anyone who might be under their influence, leading to what is commonly known as the April 12th Coup ("Shanghai Massacre"). –GT

¹¹⁴ *Dongjiaochang*: The name of a public field in Guangzhou where political/military gatherings or ceremonies, including executions, were held by the GMD and its National Government. It was turned into a sports stadium in 1932 and is now called Guangdong Provincial People's Stadium. –DH

¹¹⁵ *two Communist "Ironsides" commanders led the Nanchang Uprising in Jiangxi Province*: The "two Communist Ironsides commanders" described by Kim San are Ye Ting and He Long. They led the Nanchang Uprising, the first uprising undertaken by the CCP after the break-up of the United Front between the GMD and the CCP. This symbolized the CCP's strategy at the time of emphasizing an urban-based revolution (see note on p. 274 on Li Lisan). Some thirty thousand troops previously in the NRA participated in this along with other CCP members. These Communist soldiers were eventually organized into and renamed the Red Army of the CCP. In 1931, Jiangxi Province would be the site of the first Chinese Soviet Republic, commonly called Jiangxi Soviet, (as opposed to the first Chinese Soviet, which was in Hailufeng). –MI, DH

CHAPTER 11: THE GUANGZHOU COMMUNE

¹¹⁶ *Hong Kong strike in 1925*: One of the "sympathy strikes" that followed the May 30th Incident (see note on pp. 139-140), the Hong Kong strike was a general strike of Chinese workers and peasants precipitated by the killing of fifty-two and the wounding of 117 Chinese by British and French soldiers with machine-guns at a demonstration in Guangzhou on June 23, 1925. Hong Kong was immobilized as more than 100,000 workers evacuated the city and moved on Guangzhou. –GT

¹¹⁷ *Sixth Congress of the Comintern*: The Sixth Congress met from July to September 1929. What Kim San probably means here is that what was ultimately decided upon at the Comintern in 1929 had already been adopted at the Guangzhou Commune in December 1927. –MI, DH

¹¹⁸ *"Self-Protection Troops" or the "Red Self-Protection Forces."* The Mandarin name for the Self-Protection Troops is "Ziweijun" and the Mandarin name for the Red Self-Protection Troops is "Chiweidui." –DH

¹¹⁹ *to organize a hospital for the wounded*: Kim San seemed to have used his medical knowl-

edge during the Guangzhou Uprising. He Cheng (named Dr. Zhong Ying in the text), a Chinese participant in the uprising and Kim's classmate from the Beijing Medical Union College, recalls seeing Zhang Zhiluo (Kim San) running with a medical kit on his back towards where the shootings were most intense, and was as a result deeply impressed with the enthusiasm a Korean comrade had for the cause of China's liberation. –DH (He 1985, 117-118)

[120] *British warships*: In order to control piracy, major foreign powers kept warships patrolling the Yangzi River, the center of British influence in China, as well as around Hong Kong. –GT

[121] *there was still no letter from the committee*: This lack of communication during the Guangzhou Uprising might have had something to do with the inability of the communists to communicate accurately among themselves. Arif Dirlik has suggested that there were divisions over language, class consciousness, perspectives, and so on among the workers and radicals participating in the uprising. (Dirlik 1997) Nie Rongzhen (1899-1992), a graduate of the Huangpu Military Academy, remembers that he had to flee to Hong Kong after the failure of the Guangzhou Commune without knowing the orders from the CCP since he, as a Sichuanese, couldn't understand the Guangdong language spoken among the workers and communists in Guangzhou. –DH (Nie 1983, 86)

[122] *until his death*: Kim San states that Zhang died on December 17th, after the defeat of the Commune, but he was actually killed during the fighting on December 12, 1927. –DH

CHAPTER 12: LIFE AND DEATH IN HAILUFENG

[123] *Ahn Cheong*: No further information about this person has been found. –DH

[124] *Communist Party School*: Reference to the Dongjiang Party School, which Kim San and Oh Seong-ryun had been appointed to as members of the school committee when in Hailufeng. –DH (Zhang 1988, 218)

[125] *Political Training Regiment survivors from the Guangzhou Commune*: Kim San appears to be referring here to the Special Training Regiment who survived the Guangzhou Uprising. Later, he will also describe this as the "Red Army of two thousand cadets." –DH

[126] *twenty li*: A distance of little less than seven miles. –DH

[127] *Son*: In the first edition, Nym Wales spelled this person's surname as Sung, but according to a Korean translator of *Song of Arirang* as well as Kim San's biographer in South Korea, this person's surname was Son. –DH (Wales and Kim 2005, 275 and *passim*; Yi 2006, 296 and *passim*)

[128] *Jin Gong-mok*: The person referred to here is most likely Kim Sang-seon (1901-?), whose other aliases include Jeong Gong-mok (Ding Gongmu in Chinese). "Jin" is the Chinese pronunciation of the Korean surname "Kim." Kim Sang-seon originally came to Beijing to study but went to Guangdong in 1926 and enrolled as a student at the Huangpu Military Academy. In 1927 he moved to Wuhan to enter the Wuhan branch of the Central Military Political School. He joined the Korean Communist Party in Shanghai in 1928, and the following year became director of the Organization Department for the Party's General Branch in Manchuria. In 1930 he participated in setting up the Minorities Committee under the Manchurian Provincial Committee of the CCP. He was arrested by the Japanese police in 1931 and sentenced to eight years in prison in Seoul. He was released in 1941. –DH (*HSIS*, 476)

[129] *China's first Red soldiers of He Long and Ye Ting*: Reference to the remnants of the first-ever CCP troops that fought against the GMD in the Nanchang Uprising, mobilized by He Long, Zhou Enlai, and Ye Ting. –DH

[130] *Bai Xin*: No further information about this person has been found. –DH

CHAPTER 13: REUNION IN SHANGHAI

[131] *mass arrests...made in March 1928*: Concerning the large-scale arrests of 1928, when different factions were vying for dominance, it can be said that in Korea, the Korean Communist Party (Joseon gongsandang), strove to broaden its organization after its founding in April 1925, with the intention of leading the labor movement and setting up a people's united front, but it suffered from four waves of oppression from authorities. Internal factional struggles grew, and by the latter half of 1928, the party was suppressed. After that, the "ML" (Marxist-Leninist) faction, the Seoul faction, and other factions sought to revive and rebuild the Party, but a real resurrection was not possible until 1945. (See note 54.) –MI

[132] *he became my enemy*: Many scholars believe that the person named Han was Han Wi-geon (1896-1937), who participated in the 1919 March First Movement as a student leader in Seoul. See Biographical Notes.

PART IV
CHAPTER 14: A REVOLUTIONARY IS ALSO A MAN

[133] *my duties as head of the Beijing Party*: Kim San was briefly (from April to May 1930) in charge of the Organization Department of the Beijing City Committee of the CCP. At the end of May he left for Tianjin for a mission. –DH (*ZGBZZ*, 69-70)

[134] *Liu Ling*: Scholars have discovered that the actual name of this woman was Qiu Shu-rong. For more on her, please see Biographical Notes.

[135] *the Korean Revolutionary Young Men's Congress*: This "Congress" possibly refers to either the one held in May 1928 in Jilin by the Korean Youth Alliance in China (Jae jungguk hanin cheongnyeon dongmaeng) or the one held in May 1929 in Jilin by the Korean Communists there to reorganize the Korean Communist Party. Given what Kim San explains below, it is likely the former but could also be a mixed story of both. –DH (Kim and Kim 1986 vol. 4, 269-284; *HSIS*, 23, 170-171, 273, 521-522, 533)

CHAPTER 15: RETURN TO MANCHURIA

[136] *Ma Cheon-mo*: The person described as Ma Cheon-mo possibly refers to Ma Cheon-mok (1902-1931), who was a member of the Special Training Regiment in 1926 in Guangzhou and who joined the Manchuria General Bureau of the Korean Communist Party's Marxist-Leninist faction in 1929. The following year, Ma dissolved the Bureau and joined the CCP. He died in a Chinese prison. –DH (*HSIS*, 170-171)

[137] *"Government for Justice"* (Jeong-uibu): Formed in 1924, this government brought together the various Korean nationalist organizations in Manchuria. The chairman of its Central Executive Committee was Yi Tak, who later apostatized after the Manchurian Incident of 1931 (see note on p. 328). The other main leaders included Kim Dong-sam (1878-1937) and Yi Cheong-cheon. It dissolved because of internal squabbling in 1929. –KTS, AJ, MI, MN, GT, DH (*HID* vol. 1, 456; Hwang 2016, 51)

SONG OF ARIRANG

[138] *"Government for the New People"* (Sinminbu): Formed in 1925 in an area due north of the northernmost tip of Korea in China's Jilin Province, this organization engaged in a number of activities, including the creation of a military school, until its demise in 1929. In the first (John Day) edition of this book, Nym Wales called this group the "Chan Yi Fu" or "Government for Truth" (Kim San must have translated the meaning of "Chan yi" or "Cham-ui" for Nym Wales as "truth"). However, "Cham-ui bu" was in fact the name of the "General Staff Headquarters" (see note 139). It is obvious that Kim's description of this group refers to the "Government for the New People" (or "Sinminbu") so this has been substituted above. —KTS, AJ, MI, MN, GT, DH (*HID* vol. 1, 456; Hwang 2016, 51)

[139] *These two nationalist governments opposed the Korean Communist Party in Manchuria:* In addition to the Government for the New People and the Government for Justice, there was another group called a "General Staff Headquarters" (Cham-uibu), which was organized in 1923 under the Korean Provisional Government and dissolved in 1928. These functioned as "democratic organs of civic government" and also "organs of military administration exercising jurisdiction over the training of resistance forces and their deployment in the armed struggle against Japan." —KTS, AJ, GT, DH (Lee 1984, 365)

[140] *a big partisan movement was started:* After the Manchurian Incident in 1931, Korean partisan activities came to be divided into the pro-Korean nationalist Korean Revolutionary Army (Joseon hyeongmyeong gun) and the pro-Chinese Communist Red partisans. The Korean Revolutionary Army was organized into military troops serving the Nationalist Government (Gungmin-bu) that operated in south Manchuria subsequent to the dissolution of the "Government for Justice" and the "Government for the New People" in 1929. After 1930, the Korean communists joined the CCP, organizing armed anti-Japanese struggles and also successfully creating a soviet district in which they organized guerrilla forces. These communist partisans, under the leadership of the CCP, formed the Northeast People's Revolutionary Army (Dongbei renmin gemingjun) in 1934 and the Northeast Anti-Japanese Allied Forces (Dongbei kangri lianjun) in 1936. The majority of the soldiers in the 1st and 2nd Army Units of these forces were Koreans. —MI, MN

[141] *two big economic organs of Manchuria:* At the turn of the 20th century, the Russians built the Chinese Eastern Railway, which ran across Manchuria. In order to counter Russian influence and to establish their own economic base in the area, the Japanese built the South Manchuria Railway. This eventually led to the 1904–1905 Russo-Japanese War, which was fought in Korea and Manchuria. —GT

[142] *Manchuria government:* Reference to Zhang Xueliang, who was the warlord in control of Manchuria. —DH

[143] *Sinuiju Sons:* Apparent reference to a company. In the original editions of this book, it was referred to by the Japanese romanization of the Korean place-name, i.e. Hsinkiju Sons. -DH

[144] *Beihai:* Reference to Beihai Park. —DH

CHAPTER 17: CLIMBING THE HILLS OF ARIRANG

[145] *November 28, 1930:* The date of Kim's first arrest is unclear. Kim says here November 28, 1930, but a Korean source says November 20, 1930, while Chinese sources say December 9, 1930. Dates throughout this account of his arrest and torture are not necessarily accurate, and were perhaps deliberately obsfucated to protect Kim San's activities. Please refer to the Chronological Account of the Life of Kim San in Appendix I for the latest schol-

arship on an actual timing of dates and details where they are available. –DH (Yi 2006, 398; Cui and Jin 1992, 206; Cui 2015, 356-357)

[146] *West City in Beijing*: Better known today as Beijing's Xicheng District. –DH

[147] *On February 1, 1931*: According to sources, the date on which Kim San was transferred to the Japanese Embassy in Beijing and then to the Japanese Consulate in Tianjin was actually January 7, 1931. –DH

[148] *Proletarian Cultural League*: Kim San could be referring here to the Korean Proletarian Artists Federation, commonly known as KAPF. However, this could also be a reference to the Chinese League of Left-Wing Writers, which had connections to the CCP. –DH

[149] *was to be deported*: According to records, this judgment was given on January 14, 1931. In a picture possibly taken at the Japanese Consulate in Tianjin after his trial, Kim San appears wearing a piece of large paper on his upper body, on which is written the verdict that he will be barred from staying in China for a period of three years from January 14, 1931. See photo on p. 384. –DH

[150] *Dalian*: Previously known as Lüshun. –DH

CHAPTER 18: PARTY AND PERSONAL WARS

[151] *she cannot be alive now*: According to a recent Korean source, Liu Ling was in fact still alive at the time. Her real name was Qi Shurong. See Biographical Notes for more details. –DH (Yi 2006, 357, 607)

[152] *I had written a confession*: According to various sources, Kim San did indeed write a confession for the Chinese police in December of 1930. –DH

[153] *called a court to settle the case*: This apparently took place in June of 1931. –DH

[154] *accepted back into the party ranks without further*: Given what Kim San says below about his relationship with the CCP, it seems that he was not expelled from the CCP at this point, but must have been temporarily suspended for a period of time, during which he was probably arrested again in 1933. His second arrest and release might have been the very reason for his eventual expulsion from the CCP. –DH

[155] *my trouble came because I was a Korean among Chinese*: A case that is comparable to Kim San's is that of the Chinese Communist Gao Kelin (1907-2001), who was the secretary of the Military Committee of the Beijing City Committee of the CCP from April to May 1930, when Kim San was serving as director of the same committee's Organization Department. Gao was also arrested in Tianjin after June 1930 but was released after six months in prison. According to Gao, after his release, he was contacted by the Provincial Committee of the CCP, rested for a while under orders from the Party, and finally returned to the same position, this time in the Hebei Province Special Committee. (Gao 1987, 66-75) Considering Gao's case, Kim San might well have thought that he was not being fairly treated by the CCP. –DH

[156] *working toward the equalization of the two different levels of development*: What Kim San seems to be proposing here is a more diversified approach that would emphasize promoting a movement against Chiang Kai-shek's dictatorship in GMD-controlled areas ("White areas"), in alliance with democratic forces such as intellectuals and students, while continuing class struggle in those areas controlled by the CCP ("Red areas"). –DH

[157] *in 1935*: Apparent reference to the CCP's "August First Declaration," which called for stopping the civil war between the GMD and the CCP and establishing a united front to resist Japanese aggression. See notes 20 and 166. –DH

PART V
CHAPTER 20: BACK TO THE MASS MOVEMENT

[158] *In May*: Again, these dates do not accord with what has been documented through other sources. –DH

[159] *found a new position for me at Gaoyang Primary School*: Kim San is documented as teaching at this school in March 1932. –DH

[160] *went to Beijing to explain*: Sources say this happened in July 1932. –DH

[161] *called me a "rightist"*: Sources say that on August 27, 1932, Kim San was accused of being a "Trotskyist" for his criticism of the CCP's decision to launch an uprising in Gaoyang Xian. –DH

[162] *to Nanjing*: The implication is that those who signed were becoming "reactionaries," since the headquarters of the GMD and its National Government's capital were located in Nanjing. See note on page 152. –DH

[163] *Marxism and Religion*: The book Kim San is describing was probably *Marxism and Atheism* (Marukusushūgi to mushinron), by Sano Manabu (1892–1953), a leader of the Japanese Communist Party who later converted to support the Japanese Emperor. Originally published in Chinese in 1927, Kim gave it the title *On Atheism* (Wushenron), and published it in April 1929 under the pseudonym Zhang Beixing. Under the same pseudonym, Kim San translated another book by Sano into Chinese, publishing it in August 1932 just prior to his being accused of being a Trotskyist, with the title *Outlook on the Life of Feuerbach, Marx, and Lenin* (Feierbaha Makesi Leining de renshengguan). –DH

[164] *the Guomindang's Fifth Campaign soon began*: More properly known as the Fifth Military Campaign to Suppress Bandits, this was one of a series of military campaigns launched by Chiang Kai-shek to suppress communists, who were called "bandits." Attacks by his Nationalist Army against the Jiangxi Soviet (see note 115) that was the Red Army's base were made in four waves starting in 1930; all ended in failure. The Fifth "Anti-Bandits" Encirclement started in 1934 and utilized the building of pillboxes to block off the soviet area, then tightened this ring, squeezing the Red Army and the soviet and placing them in great danger. In order to break out, the Red Army and the soviet made the surprising move of initiating the Long March from Jiangxi Province to Shaanxi Province under the banner of "Moving North to Resist Japan." (See note 165.) –MN, MI, DH

[165] *the Long March to the north*: An epic retreat from Jiangxi Province to Shaanxi Province by the CCP and its Red Army that lasted for more than a year from 1934 to 1935 and covered approximately six thousand miles. It was initiated to break through Chiang Kai-shek's military encirclement of the Jiangxi Soviet. During the march, Mao Zedong emerged as the undisputed leader of the CCP. –DH

[166] *August 1, 1935*: Kim San refers here to "the August First Declaration," which was issued jointly by the Government of the Chinese Soviet Republic and the Central Committee of the CCP on August 1, 1935. It called for stopping the civil war between the GMD and the CCP and the establishment of a "united national defense government" that would resist Japanese aggression. This declaration symbolized a shift in the CCP's policy line from class struggle to national struggle and led to the formation of an anti-Japanese (second) United Front. –MN, MI, GT, DH

CHAPTER 21: JAPANESE PRISONER AGAIN AND EXILE

[167] *April 26, 1933*: Sources indicate that Kim San was actually interrogated by Beijing police on May 1, 1933. –DH

[168] *Blue Shirt plainclothesman arrived*: Reference to the Blue Shirts Society (Lanyishe), a secret group in the GMD primarily composed of graduates of the Huangpu Military Academy whose aim was to support and consolidate the dictatorship of Chiang Kai-shek through the use of fascism, terrorism, Confucianism, and even GMD-controlled, top-down mass movements (notes on pp 297 and 302-303). –DH

[169] *Im Sa, a modern anarchist poet*: I have been unable to identify this anarchist poet, but he may have been an Uiyeol-dan member. –DH

[170] *the new fascist tactic*: Indeed, a former member of the Beijing Branch of the China League of Left-Wing Writers (see note 173) remembers that after the arrival of Jiang Xiaoxian in Beijing in 1933, large-scale arrests of communists and their sympathizers took place in which those arrested were forced to repudiate their Communist Party membership and publicly declare their anti-communist stance to many newspapers. This massive repudiation by those arrested occurred in part due to the widespread belief at the time that in order to continue their revolutionary work, it would be better for them to survive, no matter how, rather than to be executed or imprisoned for life. –DH (Li 1990, 164-165)

[171] *Day after day passed*: While detained by the Chinese police, Kim San seems to have written (in Chinese and dated May 21, 1933) "My Confession" using one of his aliases, Li Tiean. In this, he describes himself as being from Guangdong and admits that he joined the CCP as well as the GMD in Guangzhou. He also reasserts the position he'd been maintaining for the previous two years: that he had not joined any political party; that he had deeply studied philosophy, religion, history, and economics, as well as the political and economic problems of China; and that he had opposed the rash policies (the "Wang Ming Line"; see biographical note on Han Wi-geon) of the CCP, the GMD's policy of non-resistance towards Japan, and the state of internal militarist conflicts in China. –DH (Yi and Mizuno 1991, 444-446)

[172] *On June 15*: Some sources say that Kim was taken to Tianjin on June 6th. –DH

[173] *China League of Left-Wing Writers*: Established in March 1930 in Shanghai with the participation of, among others, the authors Lu Xun (1881-1936), Mao Dun (1896-1981), and Qu Qiubai (1899-1935). It promoted a movement for revolutionary literature and was generally under the leadership of the CCP. For example, its north branch is included in the official organizational history of the CCP in Beijing.–MN, GT, DH (ZGBZZ, 120-123)

CHAPTER 22: WOMEN AND MARRIAGE

[174] *the girl who had been arrested because of me*: Although her name appears in at least one Chinese source as Zhao Eping (Cui and Jin 1992, 208-209), it is now known that the name of the woman who later married Kim San was Zhao Yaping. See Afterword in Appendix I for more details. –DH (Kwon 1986, 53-61; Yi and Mizuno 1991, 441)

[175] *we were married*: Sources say this took place in January of 1934. Xizhimen, where they subsequently settled, is a neighborhood in Beijing. –DH

[176] *I did translation work*: During this period, he seemed to work as "proxy writer" and published books such as *Politics Economy Geography* and *The Third Cultural Crisis*. –DH

SONG OF ARIRANG

177 *in the winter of 1934 we went to Shijiazhuang*: In spring or early summer of 1935, Kim San is recorded as having left Beijing for Shijiazhuang in Hebei Province and helping Song Kuangwo edit *Commercial News* (Shangbao). He is also said to have roomed with Wang Yizhen, at the time the president of Communication (Jiaotong) Bank. –DH

178 *spring of 1935*: In fact at the end in 1935. –DH

CHAPTER 23: THE KOREAN NATIONAL FRONT AGAINST JAPAN

179 *we must prepare to meet it*: Around this time, many Korean socialists, including anarchists, as well as socialism-oriented radicals began to discuss the possibility of making use of the "new revolutionary situation"—i.e. that Japan had invaded China and that many Chinese, in response, were demanding a united struggle against Japan. Agreeing that a victory by China over Japan would bring about the liberation of Korea from Japanese colonialism, they believed that they too must be united, regardless of any differences among themselves regarding ideology, political positions, and so on. Similar to the idea of the Chinese United Front, their idea of a national front prioritized national struggle over class struggle for the immediate common goal of national liberation. –DH

180 *no separate Korean Communist organization existed*: As explained in note 98, the Comintern adopted the principle of "one Communist party in one country" in 1926. –DH

181 *Since 1932*: Historian Mizuno Naoki questions this statement, since the Korean Communist Party in Korea was destroyed in 1928, and after 1930, Korean communists in Manchuria joined the CCP. But what Kim seems to be referring to here is not that Korean communists gained organizational independence but that they made the decision to adopt an independent strategy based on the national conditions of Korea. –DH

182 *"Korean League for National Liberation"* (Joseon minjok haebang dongmaeng): Formed between the fall of 1935 and the beginning of 1936 by Kim Chung-chang, Bak Geon-ung (1903-?), a graduate of the Huangpu Military Academy, Kim San, and others. –MN, DH

183 *its program of action*: See pages 414-419 in Appendix II for more background on the fascinating extent and depth of the reforms that were planned at the time, and then compare them with what has or has not occurred since and how the world has changed—and whether the reforms suggested continue to hold any value for the future. –GT, DH

184 *in July 1936*: The idea to form the Union for the Korean National Front (Joseon minjok jeonseon yeonmaeng) had been discussed since summer 1936 among leftist Koreans in China. They finally founded this organization in November 1937 with the participation of the Korean League for National Liberation, represented by Kim Chung-chang; the Korean National Revolution Party (Joseon minjok hyeongmyeong dang), represented by Kim Won-bong; and the League of Korean Revolutionaries (Joseon hyeongmyeongja yeonmaeng), represented by Yu Ja-myeong. –MN, DH

185 *blockade*: i.e. by the GMD.

186 *the Military Committee*: Presumably the same "Military and Political Academy" referenced by Nym Wales in her Prelude. See note 6. –DH

187 *a young student named Yi*: According to a Korean report, this boy's real name was Seo Hwi (1916-1993). After 1945, he became a deputy director of the Central Committee of the Workers' Party of Korea in North Korea but was expelled from the Party under Kim Il Sung (1912-1994) during the "Yan'an faction" expulsion in the 1950s and took refuge in China in 1956. –DH (*HSIS*, 238-239; *Sisa Journal* 1993, 21)

POSTLUDE

[188] *a Korean Volunteer Corps to fight against Japan*: This was originally called the International Brigade. –DH

[189] *an amalgamation...was formed in Chongqing*: This actually took place in May 1940. –DH

[190] *had been revived in Chongqing*: In 1940, the Korean Provisional Government moved to China's wartime capital, Chongqing, where Kim Gu organized military units to recover the Korean homeland and fight against the Japanese. After the surrender of Japan in 1945, American occupation forces refused to recognize this Korean government-in-exile as the authentic government of Korea, though they did choose to support Syngman Rhee (see note on p. 93) because of his pro-American background and position, naming him the first president of South Korea. –DH

BIOGRAPHICAL NOTES

AHN BYEONG-CHAN (1854-1922): A lawyer who attempted to defend Ahn Jung-geun (see Biographical Note on Ahn Jung-geun) after the latter assassinated Itō Hirobumi in 1909. After the March First Movement, Ahn Byeong-chan organized the Great Korean Youth Troops (Daehan cheongnyeon dan) in Andong, and later became a member of the Irkutsk faction of the Korean Communist Party. In January 1922 he attended the Far Eastern Peoples' Congress in Moscow. He was on his way back, carrying money from the Soviet government, when he was murdered by the anti-Bolshevik White Army in Russia (i.e. not by "robbers"). –MI, DH (*HSIS*, 266)

AHN CHANG-HO (1878-1938): One of the most famous leaders of the Korean independence movement. Popularly known by his nom de plume, Dosan. He participated in the Independence Club (Dongnip hyeophoe) after its founding in 1896 and set up the San Francisco-based Cooperative Association (Gongnip hyeophoe), which later changed its name to the Korean National Association (Daehanin gungminhoe). In 1907 he returned to Korea and developed a patriotic consciousness-raising movement by becoming a leader of the New People Society (Sinminhoe). See note 41. He became active in educational work and founded such schools as Osan (a center for March First Movement activities), and Daeseong, both located in Korea's Pyeong-an Province. Just before Japan's annexation of Korea, Ahn fled abroad and continued his activities in America and China. But in 1932 he was arrested and sent back to Korea, where he was thrown into jail for a time. In 1937 he was again arrested in Seoul, but because of sickness, he was released on probation in December of the same year. He died on March 10, 1938. –MI, AJ, GT, DH (*HID* vol. 2, 1145-1146)

AHN JUNG-GEUN (1879-1910): Remembered as a patriot and martyr by Koreans for his assassination of Itō Hirobumi (1841-1909), the main architect of Japan's colonization of Korea, during the latter's visit to Manchuria in October 1909. Ahn was apprehended by the Japanese and executed on March 26, 1910, at a prison in Manchuria at the age of thirty-one. –AJ, DH (*HID* vol. 2, 1142-1143)

AHN, PHILIP: Film actor whose father was the Korean independence activist Ahn Chang-ho.

BAK JIN (1887-1927): The real name of this figure was Bak Yeong, though he also used other names, including Bak Seung-nam, Bak Mong-gak, and Bak Geun-seong. Having participated in the 1919 March First Movement and other military struggles against the Japanese, he moved to Russian territory, where he joined the Bolshevik Party and served as leader of its Korean unit. In 1923 he was elected to the Soviet Committee of Far Eastern Peoples and later was elected its head. Toward the end of 1926, he headed for Guangzhou with his two younger brothers and his wife and was enlisted in the Special Training Regiment (see note 107). As Kim San goes on to relate, he was killed in the Guangzhou Uprising in December 1927. His brothers' names were Bak Geun-man and Bak Geun-su. –MI, DH (*HSIS* 119; Yi 2006, 204)

BORODIN, MIKHAIL MARKOVICH (1884-1951): Mikhail Borodin was sent by the Soviet Union to Guangzhou in September 1923 as a political advisor to assist Sun Yat-sen with the formation of the first United Front between the GMD and the CCP. After Sun's demise, Borodin continued to serve as "supreme political advisor" to the National Government during the Northern Expedition. After the GMD's split with the CCP in July 1927, he went back to the Soviet Union and died in 1951 in prison, two years after his arrest under Stalin's rule. –GT, DH

CHEN GONGBO (1892-1946): One of the founding members of the CCP, though he later joined the GMD. While a member of the GMD from the late 1920s to the early 1930s, he became a key leader for the leftists against Chiang Kai-shek's military dictatorship. During the Sino-Japanese War, he joined Wang Jingwei's collaborationist government in Nanjing, and was in favor of peacefully resolving the military conflict with Japan. After Wang's death in 1944, Chen became chairman of the collaborationist government. He was tried by the GMD for the crime of high treason and was sentenced to death after 1945. –MI, DH (BDRC vol. 1, 196-201)

CHEN JIONGMING (1878-1933): An early governor of Guangdong Province. He sided with Sun Yat-sen and controlled the province by force. Later he withdrew his support of Sun, and in 1923 was driven out of Guangdong; his remaining forces were finally subdued by the GMD-led Revolutionary Armies in 1925. –MI, DH (BDRC vol. 1, 173-180)

CHENG QIAN (1882-1968): Commander of the Sixth Army and of the Fourth Route Army during the Northern Expedition. In the 1930s, he served as chief of the general staff and governor of Henan Province under the National Government, but joined the People's Republic of China after surrendering to the Chinese Communists in August 1949. (BDRC vol. 1, 280-284) –DH

CHOE NAM-SEON (1890-1957): A historian and writer involved in the March First Declaration of Independence in 1919. For this, he was arrested and imprisoned. Choe's later career is controversial, since he participated in the Japanese colonial government-sponsored editorial board for the History of Korea and served from 1938 to 1943 as a Korean history professor at Kenkoku University in Manchuria, which was founded by Japan. Because of these activities, he is now counted among those pro-Japanese traitors who supported Japan's pan-Asian expansionist ambitions and invasion of China. –MI, GT, DH (CIS 3, 688- 691; HID vol. 2, 2243-2244)

DONG LIANG (1896-1932): Former labor movement activist in Shanghai, graduate from the Huangpu Military Academy, and participant in the Northern Expedition. An important communist military officer, he also participated in the Nanchang Uprising and the Hailufeng Soviet. –DH (Xie 1988, 266)

GAO YONGGUANG (1937-): The son of Kim San. Born on April 20, 1937, he is more commonly known in South Korea as Go Yeong-gwang. For more on him, see note on page 332 and the Afterword. –DH

HAN FUJU (1890-1938): GMD military officer and Governor of Shandong Province from 1930 to 1938 who was arrested and executed by the GMD government for his failure to resist against Japan as well as disobeying orders, retreating of his own volition, forcing opium upon the Shandong people, and more. –DH (BDRC vol. 2, 51-54)

HAN WI-GEON (1896- 1937): Participated in the 1919 March First Movement as a student leader in Seoul. To avoid imprisonment, he fled to Shanghai, where he helped set up the Korean Provisional Government in April of that year. Later he became a student in Tokyo, but in 1924 he returned to Korea and became a reporter for the *East Asia Daily* (Dong-a Ilbo); at the same time he joined the underground Korean Communist Party and became its Propaganda Section Chief. Fearing for his safety in 1928, he again fled to China. In Shanghai, he helped to rebuild the Korean Communist Party. He was a member of the Korean Communist Party's "ML (Marxist-Leninist) faction" (see note 54) and became the head of the Propaganda Section of the CCP's Hebei Province Committee when he joined the CCP in 1930. The following year, under the pseudonym "Li Tiefu," he criticized the "leftist line" of the Central Committee of the CCP, subsequent to which he broke relations with the CCP. Because of this, Han is better known in China as Li Tiefu. As Li Tiefu, he advocated for what became known as the "Tiefu Line," which opposed the "leftist adventurism" of the Soviet-trained CCP leader at the time, Wang Ming (1904-1974), author of what is usually called "the Wang Ming Line," which was at one point criticized by Mao Zedong as "dogmatism" that followed the Comintern line of revolution without taking into account the Chinese national conditions. In 1936, Han returned as Secretary of the Hebei Province Committee of the CCP. In May of the following year, he made his way to Yan'an, but died there of tuberculosis. In 1940, the "Tiefu Line" was approved by the CCP as being correct and legitimate. –MN, MI, DH (*HSIS*, 525-527; Dong et al. 1986)

HAN HAE. See Biographical Note for Kim Jang-chun.

HAYAKAWA SESSUE (1886-1972): Japanese actor who became one of the biggest silent film stars in 1910s and '20s Hollywood. –DH

HE LONG (1896-1969): He played an important role in the CCP-led Nanchang Uprising on August 1, 1927, though he actually joined the CCP after it. He was "one of the foremost Red Army commanders" and later became a vice-premier in the People's Republic of China. -DH (*BDCC* vol.1, 297-303)

HUANG QIXIANG (1898-1970): The commander of the NRA's Garrison Headquarters at the time of the Guangzhou Uprising. Later he came to oppose Chiang Kai-shek and chose to become a member of the National Committee of the Chinese People's Political Consultative Conference. In 1949, he joined the People's Republic of China (PRC). He held several offices in the PRC. –MI, DH

KIM CHUNG-CHANG (1898-1969): Pseudonym of Kim Seong-suk, who is better known in China under yet another name, Kim Gyu-gwang ("Jin Kuiguang" in Mandarin). Having been a monk for three years, Kim participated in the 1919 March First Movement, for which he was arrested and spent two years in prison. He came to Beijing in 1923 and was involved in organizing the Creating-One Party (Chang-il dang), a Communist Party branch connected to the Irkutsk faction. He also joined the Uiyeol-dan. He became a student at Zhongshan University in Guangzhou and in December 1927 participated in the Guangzhou Uprising. Kim Chung-chang was one of the leading figures in the establishment in 1937 of the Union for the Korean National Front, which Kim San also joined. As a way of supporting the idea of a national front, Kim Chung-chang joined the Korean Provisional Government in 1942. After his return to Korea in December 1945, however, he cut off relations with the Provisional Government and throughout the 1950s and '60s stood with progressives against the dictatorial South Korean regimes of Syngman Rhee and Park Chung Hee, a stance that resulted in him being repeatedly arrested and prosecuted. (*HSIS*, 84-85; *HHH*, 29-156; Du 1985) –MI, DH

KIM IK-SANG (1895-1943): As written in note 83, Kim was arrested immediately and convicted by a court in Nagasaki of participating in both this plot and the attempted assassination of Governor General Saitō (see Biographical Note on Saitō). Though originally sentenced to death, his sentence was later reduced to twenty years of detention. Released after having served his term, he was allegedly assassinated by a Japanese police detective. –KTS, MI, DH

KIM JANG-CHUN (1900-1929): Also known as Han Hae. He died of disease in Jilin, China in 1929. See Appendix II on page 442 for the poem in an English-language translation, written originally in Chinese and attributed to Kim San in memory of Han, titled "Mourning Comrade Han Hae" (Diao Han Hai tongzhi).

KIM JWA-JIN (1889-1930): Organized and subsequently became Supreme Commander of Korean troops fighting for independence as what he named the North Route Military Command (Bungno gunjeongseo) in 1919, in which capacity he fought the Japanese army in several encounters, notably at the famous Battle of Cheongsan-ri ("Qingshanli" in Mandarin). In 1929, in response to increased Communist activities in Manchuria, he worked together with Korean anarchists in Manchuria to organize the United Society of All Korean People (Hanjok chong yeonhaphoe). He was assassinated in 1930 by a Korean communist. –KTS, AJ, MI, MN, GT, DH (*HID* vol. 1, 456; Hwang 2016, 51)

KIM RIP (1880-1922): One of the officers of the Korean Socialist Party founded and headed by Yi Dong-hwi in June 1918 in Khabarovsk (i.e. what would come to be known as the Shanghai faction). When Yi went to Shanghai in 1919 to become the Korean Provisional Government's premier, Kim Rip became his secretary. Though he is described here as bringing funds from Moscow in the winter of 1923, this actually took place in December 1920. Kim was assassinated in February of 1922 in the midst of a conflict with the Korean Provisional Government over the use of these funds. –MI, GT, DH (*HSIS*, 64-65)

KIM WON-BONG (1898-1958): A well-known socialism-oriented independence fighter and leader of the Uiyeol-dan, he worked with both Korean communists and Chinese nationalists between 1927 and 1935. In the mid-1930s he participated in the Union for the Korean National Front, and later went to Yan'an, where he continued his anti-Japanese military activities with the CCP. He returned to Korea in December 1945 after working as a National Committee member in the Korean Provisional Government but soon joined the North Korean government in 1948 as its Minister of National Censorship. In the late 1950s, he was purged from the North Korean government. Also known as Kim Yak-san. –DH

KIM YEOM (1910-1983): Better known in China as Jin Yan (i.e. not Jin Can as stated in the text), Kim Yeom's real name was Kim Deok-rin. In 1921 he moved to Manchuria with his father, a pro-independence activist, and in 1927 was able to get into the world of motion pictures in Shanghai. Under the auspices of the left-wing movie-production movement, he developed a good reputation for his performances in many pre-1945 Chinese silent films. He remained in the People's Republic of China (PRC) after 1949 and continued to star in many movies. –MI, DH

KROPOTKIN, PETER (1842-1921): Considered "the most important anarchist theoretician to have widespread influence in East Asia" and someone who "left the deepest influence on Koreans' interest in and conversion to anarchism." Known for his argument that mutual aid rather than conflict and competition constitutes the primary factor in the evolution of humanity. –GT, DH (Dirlik 2015; Hwang 2016, 15 and *passim*)

LI DAZHAO (1889-1927): One of the first Marxists in China and a key founder of the CCP. He was also known as a leader in the New Culture Movement for his writings published in *New Youth* (Xin qingnian). In 1924, Li played an important part in the formation of the United Front between the GMD and the CCP, but in April 1927 he was arrested inside the Soviet Embassy compound in Beijing by the warlord government of Zhang Zuolin and executed. –MI, DH (BDCC, 527-530)

LI FULIN (1877-1952): Military commander tasked with the suppression of the Guangzhou Uprising. He got his start as a "local rebel" and was a member of the Revolutionary Alliance organized in 1905 by Sun Yat-sen with the goal of overthrowing the Qing Dynasty. By the time of the Northern Expedition, he was the commander of the NRA's Fifth Army. –MI, DH

LI JISHEN (1886-1959): Leader of the Guangdong military clique who took part in the National Government. Having been made Chief of Staff of the General Headquarters of the NRA, he was tasked with the defense of Guangzhou against the Communists in the Guangzhou Uprising. He later participated in several movements to oppose Chiang Kai-shek. When the People's Republic of China was established in 1949, he became one of the Vice Chairmen of the Central People's Government, much as he had been Chairman of the GMD Revolutionary Committee, which sided with the Communists and was eventually accepted into the new Chinese Communist government in 1949. –MI, DH (BDRC vol. 2, 292-295)

LIU LING: Her real name was Qi Shurong, and she was a student at Beijing Women's College of Education (Beiping nüzi shifan daxue). She is also known to have used other names including Liu Ling and Qi Xiaochen. Having learned that Kim San died in 1938, she married again in 1946. –DH (Yi 2006, 357, 607)

MUJEONG (1905-1960): Mujeong's full name was Kim Mu-jeong, but he was commonly known by his first name. He joined the CCP in 1925 and also took part in the Long March as an operations unit leader. After graduating from the Red Army College, he became Commander of the Artillery Regiment of the Eighth Route Army in 1938. In 1941 he organized the North China Korean Youth Federation, and the following year, the Korean Independence League. He was the Commander-in-Chief of the Korean Volunteer Army at the time of Korea's liberation in 1945. During the Korean War, he became Commander of the Second Army Group of the Korean People's Army (i.e. the North Korean army) but was purged and died in 1951. –AJ, GT, MN, DH (HSIS, 172-173; Suh 1967, 221, 225)

OH SEONG-RYUN (1900-1947): Also known as Ham-seong ("Xiansheng" in Mandarin) and Jeon-gwang ("Quanguang" in Mandarin). The stories Kim San relates in the book pertain to Oh's activities in the 1920s as a member of the Uiyeol-dan and the CCP, which Oh joined in 1927 in Guangzhou. In the 1930s, Oh's activities were concentrated in Manchuria, where he joined the CCP-led armed struggles against the Japanese and also helped organize in June 1936 the Association of Koreans in Manchuria for the Recovery of the Fatherland. In January 1941, however, he surrendered to the Japanese Army and subsequently collaborated with the Japanese by becoming an adviser to the Security Department of Manchukuo. Accounts differ as to his death. After Japan's surrender in 1945, he was either arrested and beaten to death by the communists for his collaboration or he died of disease in 1947. –MI, DH (HSIS, 284-285; Yi 1973. 256-280)

PENG DEHUAI (1898-1974): One of the key commanders of the Red Army, Peng fought against the GMD's "Anti-Bandits Military Campaigns" in the early 1930s (see note 164). Peng was also a venerated veteran of the Long March (see note 165), during which he served as Commander-in-Chief of the Red Army's Third Army Group. During the

Sino-Japanese War (1937-1945), he served as Vice Commander in Chief of the Eighth Route Army under Zhu De. After the establishment of the People's Republic of China in 1949, he held important posts such as the Vice Premier of State Affairs and Minister of Defense. Peng led the Chinese Forces in the Korean War (1950-1953). In 1959, he opposed Mao Zedong by criticizing the Great Leap Forward, and thus lost his status. –MN, DH (BDCC, 727-737)

PENG PAI (1896-1929): The founder of the first soviet government in China, organized in Hailufeng (see note 5 and note on p. 18) in Guangdong Province in November 1927. "One of the earliest members of the Chinese Communist Party," he is described by the CCP as someone who "devoted himself to the organization of peasantry" and also as "one of the greatest revolutionary martyrs." (BDCC, 720-724) –DH

RHEE, SYNGMAN (1875-1965): A pro-American, American-educated, staunch anti-communist, Syngman Rhee believed American aid was necessary for Korea's independence and poured his energies into diplomatic and propaganda activities. Elected president of the Korean Provisional Government, he was able to gain support from some quarters in the United States, and eventually returned to Korea to become the first president of the Republic of Korea (i.e. South Korea) in 1948. Twelve years later, in 1960, having become a dictator himself, he was forced from office by the student-led "April 19th Revolution" and fled to Hawaii, where he died in 1965. –MI, GT, DH

SAITŌ MAKOTO (1858-1936): a Japanese naval commander, was appointed Governor General of Korea in August 1919 and again in August 1929. As Kim San goes on to describe, the appointment of Saitō in 1919 signaled a change in the Japanese government's colonial policy in Korea from one of military rule to one of cultural rule. In 1921, an Uiyeol-dan member attempted to assassinate Saitō but failed (see notes 76 and 83). He was eventually assassinated on February 26, 1936, not by Koreans, but by young Japanese army officers who considered him too pacifist and bourgeois when giving advice to the Japanese emperor. –MI, GT, DH

SEO HWI (1916-1993): After 1945, he became a deputy director of the Central Committee of the Workers' Party of Korea in North Korea but was expelled from the Party under Kim Il Sung (1912-1994) during the "Yan'an faction" expulsion in the 1950s and took refuge in China in 1956. –DH (HSIS, 238-239; Sisa Journal 1993, 21)

SHAW, GEORGE. L. (1880-1943): Referred to by Kim San as "Sao". Shaw, who had a Japanese wife, owned a trading firm in Andong called the Yilong Company (Yilong yanghang) and was a secret supporter and sympathizer of the Uiyeol-dan. –MI, DH (Kim 1997, 121-130)

SHIN CHAE-HO (1880-1936): Independence activist, historian, and anarchist. One of the people who helped found the modern study of the Korean nation and Korean historiography. In 1923, he penned the Uiyeol-dan's Declaration of Korean Revolution, in which he emphasizes a revolution to destroy "exploitation and social inequality" based on direct action by the masses. This shows the Uiyeol-dan's shift toward anarchism. –AJ, MI, DH (Hwang 2016; Graham 2005, 373-376)

SON BYEONG-HUI (1861-1922): The third patriarch of the Donghak Movement, and one of the signers of the 1919 March First Declaration of Independence. –MI, GT, DH (HID vol. 1, 967-968)

S O N G I - J E O N G (1912-2002): The gold medalist marathon runner from the 1936 Olympic Games in Berlin. Because Korea was a colony of Japan from 1910 to 1945, Son Gi Jeong ran as a member of the Japanese Olympic team. –MI, GT, DH

S O N G Z H E Y U A N (1885-1940): At the time being described in this book, Song was Commander of the National Government's 29th Army and Chairman of the Government of the Hebei-Chaha'er Political Council. –MN, DH (BDRC vol. 3, 189-192)

S U Z H A O Z H E N G (1885-1929): "One of the few men of proletarian origins to achieve a senior position" in the CCP and an organizer and leader in the Hong Kong Seamen's Strike of 1922 and the Guangdong-Hong Kong Strikes of 1925-26. After the CCP-GMD split, he went to Moscow in 1928, where he attended the Sixth Congress of the CCP and was elected to the Politburo of the CCP. He died in Shanghai after returning from Moscow. – MI, DH (BDCC, 771-773)

S U N YAT - S E N (1866-1925): Also known as Sun Wen or Sun Zhongshan. A key leader of the 1911 Republican Revolution that overthrew the Qing dynasty and established a republic in China. He briefly served as the provisional president of the republic after the success of the revolution and later founded the GMD. He is called the "father of the nation" in Taiwan and the "forerunner of the democratic revolution" in China. –DH (BDRC vol. 3, 170-189)

X I O N G X I L I N G (1867-1937): A Chinese government official who served both the Qing Dynasty and the new Chinese republic after 1911. In the 1920s and '30s, during the latter years of his life, he devoted himself to doing charity works and helping refugees. –MI, DH

X U G U A N G Y I N G (1898-1984): A participant in the Nanchang Uprising and, during the Guangzhou Uprising, the Chief-of-Staff of the Workers and Peasants Red Army (Gongnong hongjun). –DH

Y A N G D A L - B U : An officer responsible for training people how to use Soviet-made canons at the Huangpu Military Academy. He also used other names including Yang Dae-bu and Yang Dae-bo. –DH (Kim 1997, 165, 179)

Y E T I N G (1896-1946): A key military leader in the CCP-led Nanchang Uprising, which gave birth to the Red Army, (see note 129 and note on p. 182) and also the Guangzhou Commune. After the failure of the Commune, Ye stayed abroad until 1938, when he was given command of the New Fourth Army in central China during the Sino-Japanese War. But when GMD forces made a surprise attack against the New Fourth Army in 1941, he was taken into custody by them. After his release in 1946, he was killed in a plane crash along with some other CCP leaders –NW, MI, GT, DH (BDCC vol.2, 1011-1016)

Y E Y O N G (1899-1928): Joined the CCP in 1927. Participated in both the Nanchang Uprising and the Guangzhou Uprising. After the failure of the Guangzhou Commune, he was arrested and executed in August 1928 by the GMD forces. –DH

Y I B I N (1902-1927): A graduate of the Huangpu Military Academy, Yi Bin was a good artilleryman who participated in the capture of the airdrome during the Guangzhou Commune. He died near Shamian on the 12th, at the age of twenty-five, while fighting a Japanese gunboat. –KS

YI DONG-HWI (1873-1935): He was a major in the Korean Army at the time of its abolishment in 1907 by the Japanese, and in 1910 he joined the anti-Japanese group the New People Society (Sinminhoe). In 1911 he was among 105 Koreans arrested for anti-Japanese activities in Manchuria. He fled to the Russian Far East near Vladivostok, arriving well before the Russian Revolution, and became a leader of Korean exiles there. In 1918, Yi formed the first Korean Socialist Party with Bolshevik support. This was later renamed the Korean (Goryeo) Communist Party and associated with the Shanghai faction of the Korean communist movement. Already renowned in Kim San's boyhood, he would go on to influence Kim San directly when the latter went to Shanghai and met him there. Yi died in 1935 in Vladivostok. –GT, DH (Suh 1967, 6-21ff; *HSIS*, 327-329; *HDI* vol. 2, 1542)

YI GWANG-SU (1873-1935): Better known by his penname, Chun-won (Cumings 1997, 156), poet and writer Yi Gwang-su penned the Declaration of Independence, which was announced by Korean students in Tokyo on February 8, 1919. Soon thereafter he escaped to Shanghai, where he stayed until March 1921. It was around this time that Kim San met Yi Gwang-su in Shanghai. In Shanghai, Yi became editor of the *Independence News* (Dongnip sinmun) where Kim San would eventually work. He returned to Korea, where, in 1922, he put out the thesis titled *On National Reconstruction* (Minjok gaejoron), which was seen as a conciliatory stance toward Japan, causing consternation among many Korean patriots. In November 1938, Yi declared his support for Japanese rule. Because of this, he is now listed as a "pro-Japanese Korean," meaning national traitor. During the Korean War (1950-1953), it is said that he was taken to North Korea. –GT, DH (*CIS* 2, 744-755)

YI JONG-AM (1896-1930): The alleged prospective assassin of Tanaka Giichi and a member of the Uiyeol-dan. Yi was later arrested in 1925 in Korea, and died in prison in 1930. –KTS, MI, DH

YI YONG (1897~1954): One of the military commanders in the Korean armed struggles in Siberia and Manchuria against Japan. He participated in both the Guangzhou Commune and the Hailufeng Soviet. In 1931 he was arrested by the Japanese and thrown into the notorious West Gate (Seodaemun) Prison in Seoul. After the defeat of Japan, he held high posts in the Democratic People's Republic of Korea (North Korea). –MI, DH (*HSIS*, 353-354)

YU HANMOU (1891[6]-1981): A Guangdong Army commander in the GMD. After the war with Japan ended in 1945, he became Chairman and Commander in Chief of Guangdong Province. He fled to Taiwan with the GMD in December 1949 and played an important role in the GMD government. –MI, DH (*BDRC* vol. 4, 61-62)

YUN BONG-GIL (1908-1932): An independence fighter widely respected by Koreans for his audacious April 1932 bombing at Hongkou Park in Shanghai, which killed or wounded three high-ranking Japanese military commanders and a Japanese diplomat. Arrested and tried by a Japanese court, he was shot to death in Japan in December of the same year. –DH

YUN DAIYING (1895-1931): Well-known communist intellectual and a key figure in both the Nanchang Uprising and the Guangzhou Commune. Before the Guangzhou Commune, he was a member of the Central Committee of the CCP and the political instructor at the Huangpu Military Academy. After the break-up of the first GMD-CCP United Front, Yun became active underground in Shanghai, where he was arrested and executed by the GMD in 1930. –DH (*BDCC* vol.2, 1026-1029)

ZHANG FAKUI (1896-1980): A leading Guangdong military commander. Zhang participated in several movements to oppose Chiang Kai-shek and was a supporter of Wang Jingwei (1883-1944), Chiang's political rival who led the GMD government in Wuhan in 1927. –DH (*BDRC* vol. 1, 56-61)

ZHANG TAILEI (1899-1927): Organizer in 1921 of the Socialist Youth League of China (Zhongguo shehuizhuyi qingniantuan), which changed its name in 1925 to the Communist Youth League (Gongchanzhuyi qiigniantuan). Commissar of the Army and Navy under the CCP's command during the time of the Guangzhou Commune, he is considered one of the leaders of the uprising, and is referred to as "the martyred hero" in the history of the CCP. –DH (*BDCC* vol.1, 49-52)

ZHANG XUELIANG (1901-2001): Zhang Xueliang became a military commander for the GMD after inheriting control over Manchuria from his father, the notorious warlord Zhang Zhuolin. Known as the Young Marshal, he worked closely with Chiang Kai-shek in the arrest and execution of communists. He is also famous for his role in the Xi'an Incident (see note 20). –GT, DH (*BDRC* vol. 1, 61-68)

ZHANG ZUOLIN (1873-1928): A notorious warlord in Manchuria who controlled Manchuria from the 1910s until he was assassinated by the Japanese on June 4, 1928, after which his son, the "Young Marshal" Zhang Xueliang, succeeded him. –DH

ZHAO YAPING (?-1989): Kim San's wife. After 1949, Zhao worked as vice-principal of the School for Women Cadres in Beijing and also in the Ministry of Forestry. She remarried in 1945 a man with the surname Gao (Yi and Mizuno 1991, 488-489, 506) and died in 1989. (See note 174.) –DH

ZHENG ZHIYUN (1901-1928): Close associate of Peng Pai's. Zheng joined the Research Society for Socialism (Shehuizhuyi yanjiu hui), which Peng organized in 1921, and the following year joined the Socialist Youth Corps. Particularly active in the peasant movement, Zheng was an important contributor to the Hailufeng Soviet (see note 5 and note on p. 182.). –DH (Xie 1988, 265-266)

ZHU PEIDE (1889-1937): One of the military commanders of the NRA during the Northern Expedition. Served as governor of Jiangxi Province from 1927 to 1929. (*BDRC* vol. 1, 453-457) –DH

ZINOVIEV, GRIGORY (1883-1936): A Bolshevik revolutionary and close associate of Vladimir Lenin's. During the 1920s, he was the head of the Comintern. –DH

1905년 경북 용천에서 빈농의 아들로 태어난 金山. 본명 張志樂은 20세 때 '인간 해방과 항일 투쟁의 비책을 배우기 위해' 중국공산당에 입당했다. 그는 33세 때 반혁명 간첩혐의를 받고 중국공산당 근거지 延安에서 억울한 최후를 맞기까지 '조선 독립'을 위해 헌신했다.

조선독립군 군관학교(신흥학교)를 최연소로 졸업한 김 산은, 이후 상해에서 이동휘·안창호·이광수를 위해 일하기도 했으나, 그가 죽을 때까지 가슴에 품은 뜻은 언제나 시베리아·만주 지방의 조선족 유민 2백만명을 규합하여 일본으로부터 조국을 되찾는 일이었다.

장지락과 함께 〈아리랑〉을 쓴 님 웨일스는 그를 가리켜 '현대의 정신을 소유한 인물'이었다고 술회한다. 그런 그가 단테적 심리를 졸업하고 톨스토이즘과 아나키즘을 거쳐 마르크시즘에 도달한 것은 당시 상황에서는 당연한 일이었다.

30년, 33년 두번이나 일본 경찰에 체포된 뒤 당과 동지들까지도 '고문에 못이겨 변절했으리라'고 의심하자 그는 극도의 정신적 혼란을 겪은 것으로 기록되어 있다. 그러나 이 기간에 그가 소외감 속에서 이루어낸 저술 번역 작업은 거의 기적에 가깝다.

중국에서 투쟁했던 10여 년간 장지락의 이동 경로를 따라가노라면 한 인간이 이토록 성실하게 자기 생애를 이끌어갈 수 있을까 감탄하지 않을 수 없다. 그 자신 "나는 한번도 행복한 적이 없었다"고 말한 바 있으나, 행동하는 지성인으로서 장지락의 생애는 그만큼 치열했다.

그러나 37년 님 웨일스라는 탁월한 기록자가 연안에 나타나지 않았다면 장지락은 그의 다른 우수한 동지들처럼 흙진에 묻혀 사라졌을 것이다. 장지락의 웅장한 생애가 기록된 〈아리랑〉이 처음 세상에 나온 것은 41년 뉴욕에서였다. 님 웨일스가 남편 에드거 스노의 〈중국의 붉은 별〉과 경쟁이라도 하듯 써내려간 원고를 〈대지〉의 작가 펄 벅이 보고 출판한 것이다. 그러나 정작 조국은 지난 50년간 그를 외면해 왔다. 북쪽에서는 항일투쟁 업적을 독점하려는 김일성에 의해, 남쪽에서는 냉전 이념에 의해 매몰된 것이다.

그러나 56년전 중국 공산혁명의 근거지 연안 동굴에서 엮어진 이 장편 서사시는, 시대와 민족을 뛰어넘어 서서히, 그리고 부단히 복원되어 왔다(26~27쪽 연표 참조).

〈시사저널〉은 연변·북경·고베·도쿄를 잇는 현지 취재를 통해 장지락의 사후, 그의 업적을 재조명하고 복원하려 애써온 사람들을 추적했다. 이것은 시대가 요청하는 일이기도 하다. 김영삼 정부는 임정 요인 유해를 송환하기 시작했고 한완상 부총리 겸 통일원장관도 "사회주의 혁명가들을 재평가해야 한다"고 밝히고 있는 때이다(〈시사저널〉 제202호 참조).

북한에서도 최근 소극적이나마 장지락의 투쟁 사실을 인정하고 있음이 이번 〈시사저널〉 취재를 통해 밝혀졌다. 이밖에도 〈시사저널〉은 그가 동지의 죽음 앞에 바친 長詩 〈[illegible]〉를 찾아내고, 님 웨일스의 〈Song Of Ariran〉이 발간된 지 5년 만에 한국에서도 〈신천지〉에 전문 번역 연재되었다는 사실을 밝혀냈다. 〈편집자〉

1934년 북경 서산의 김 산.

김 산의 詩 〈시사저널〉 최초 발굴

[illegible]의 동지를 조문하여 ([illegible])
30년 6월27일 오후 2시 남대문 감옥에서 사형

아! 희생한 지여
희생한 지여
꽃꽃이 거로누워 희생한 그대여
그대는 벌써 암흑의 세월을 떠났구나
고통은 그대의 마음을 침습하였지만
그대의 피로써 최후의 전투를 진행하였다
이 침혹하고 원수에 씌인 감옥은
그대의 처참한 나날을 소모하였다
이 피 비린 마수가 가득한 사회는 그대의
미약한 생명마저 무참하게 교살하였다

아! 희생한 지여
희생한 지여
눈 감고 보지 않는 희생한 그대여
현실 사회의 압박에 견딜 수 없기에
그대는 부득불 반역의 길에 나섰다
부르조아의 악취를 벗어나기 위해
그대는 부득불 일어서 반항하였다
사람이 사람 피를 빨아먹는 걸 증오하여
부득불 혁명의 붉은 기를
날리게 되었다
그대는 사회 반역자이다
그대는 끝내 인간 감옥에서 희생하였다

(8절의 마지막 구절)
그대 편안히 고이 잠드소서
우리의 날들은 내일에 있으니
[illegible] 그대여! 내 긴장된 마음으로
인터내셔널의 노래를 높이 부르며
그대를 보내노라

Portrait of Kim San in 1934 from an article in *Sisa Journal*

AFTERWORD

Photograph of Kim San in 1931 with handwritten notes about aliases. Bottom left: Zhao Yaping, Kim San's wife. Bottom right: Gao Yongguang, Kim San's son.

KIM SAN AFTER 1937
DONGYOUN HWANG

KIM SAN'S DEATH AND RECENT "RESURRECTION"

After having finished three months of interviews with Nym Wales (Helen Foster Snow) in August 1937, Kim San seems to have remained in Yan'an until October 1938, when he was ordered by the Chinese Communist Party (CCP) to leave for Manchuria. Since he knew Manchuria had already been serving as "the center of the Korean [liberation] movement," he must have expected that this "key revolutionary area" and "base of partisan movement" for Koreans would be the place from which "a great common front" could "be formed with the Chinese anti-Japanese movement."

He never made it there. In October 1938, while on his way, it seems he was shot to death. The order for his execution most likely came from Kang Sheng (1898-1975), who was at the time in charge of security and intelligence for the CCP in Yan'an.[1] Various sources also implicate Kang as the person behind a report written in 1937 about Kim that concluded that he was a Trotskyist and a "special agent" ("tewu" in Mandarin) of Japan. No details are known to us as to how and why such a report was commissioned, what evidence of Kim's activities and alleged "crimes" might have existed, or what further information about Kim's death there might be, since the relevant CCP documents have not been made available.[2]

Since his death in 1938, Kim San has suffered long periods of obscurity in both North and South Korea as well as in China. Despite his dedication and contributions to the Chinese Revolution as a CCP member, he was ousted from the ranks of the Party and his name erased from

---

[1] Kang Sheng (1899-1975) was one of the most important members of the CCP specializing in intelligence and security work. In 1938, he was Director of the Social Department (Shehui bu) and also of the Central Intelligence Department (Qingbao bu), the CCP's chief security organs in Yan'an at the time. He died in 1975, but his role in the excessiveness of the Cultural Revolution caused him to be posthumously expelled from the CCP. Other sources have pointed to Gao Gang (1902-1954) as the person most likely to have ordered Kim San's execution. Gao was commander of the Shaan-Gan-Ning Border Region's Peace Preservation Corps and also secretary of the CCP Committee for the Shaan-Gan-Ning Border Region from 1938 to 1942.

[2] The late Professor Cui Longshui of the Party School of the Central Committee of the CCP (Zhonggong zhongyang dangxiao) in Beijing is the only person to have accessed the relevant documents in the CCP archives in Beijing as far as I am aware.

its history, no doubt in large part because of his purported crimes. For the family he left behind—his wife (Zhao Yaping) and son (Gao Yongguang)—this resulted in political as well as personal suffering, most notably during the Cultural Revolution (1966-1976), when both were placed under surveillance and sometimes interrogated. In North Korea, Kim's name disappeared from histories of Korean communists and accounts of the fight for Korean national liberation. When, after the Korean War (1950-53), Kim Il Sung (1912-1994) initiated a purge of those Korean communists (known as the Yan'an faction) who, like Kim San, had made Yan'an the base of their pre-1945 activities, any possibility of recovering the history of Kim San in North Korean became even more difficult.

In South Korea, however, Kim San's name was not entirely forgotten — at least not in the immediate aftermath of Korea's liberation in 1945. Starting in October 1946, a serialized version of the first English-language edition of *Song of Ariran* (published in 1941 by the John Day Company with the subtitle *The Life Story of a Korean Rebel*) was translated into Korean and published in the South Korean magazine *A New World* (Sin cheonji). *Song of Ariran*'s first Korean translator, Sin Jae-don, recalls in his introduction to the series how his blood had "boiled" with excitement when he first came across Kim San's account in Shanghai (Sin 1946, 268). But many who read the work in South Korea initially believed Kim San to be a fictional character. This—combined with the banning of all commemorations honoring pre-1945 socialist or communist independence activists during the anti-communist dictatorships of Syngman Rhee, Park Chung Hee, and Park's militarist successors—meant that both *Song of Ariran* and Kim San were soon all but forgotten in South Korea as well.

It took about forty years for Kim to make his return to public memory. In China, the process began in 1978, two years after the end of the Cultural Revolution, when Kim's son, Gao Yongguang, submitted a petition to the CCP's Central Organization Department requesting a re-examination of his father's "spy" case and the reinstatement of his CCP membership. Mr. Gao sent letters requesting help with his petition to both Hu Yaobang (1915-1989), a former student of Kim San's at the Chinese People's Anti-Japanese Military Political Academy in Yan'an (see note 4) who had subsequently become the director of the

CCP's Central Organization Department, and Ye Jianying (1897-1986), who had participated in the 1927 Guangzhou Uprising with Kim. Five years later, in a letter to Mr. Gao dated January 27, 1983, the CCP's Central Organization Department came back with its findings, which describe the death of "Comrade Zhang Ming" (i.e. Kim San) as having been caused by "a falsely charged case" that "occurred under a particular historical condition." Based on this, the CCP decided to restore Kim San's honor and reinstate him once again as a member. Accordingly, all charges against Kim San for being a "special agent" of Japan and a Trotskyist were dismissed.[3]

The name and story of Kim San first began circulating in Japan, thanks to a Japanese-language translation of the 1941 English-language edition of *Song of Ariran* by Ando Jirō that was published in 1953 by Asahi shobō (and subsequently revised and re-published in 1962 by Misuzu shobō). But as had been the case in South Korea, many in Japan believed Kim San to be a fictional figure. In the late 1970s, however, at around the time Kim San's son was petitioning the CCP for a re-examination of Kim's case, writer Yi Hoe-seong, historian Mizuno Naoki, and journalist Kim Chan-jeong—all of whom were based in Japan—became involved in a quest to unravel the mystery of Kim San's identity. By the 1980s, their combined efforts had succeeded in verifying that the Kim San of *Song of Ariran* was an actual historical figure. This research ultimately resulted in an edited volume about Kim San by Yi and Mizuno that includes interviews with Kim San's wife and son in Beijing (conducted by Kim Chan-jeong), as well as with Nym Wales herself (by Yi Hoe-seong). Also included in this landmark text of Kim San scholarship were: a Japanese translation of "Notes on Korea and the Life of Kim San," an unpublished manuscript by Nym Wales that included additional stories about Korea and Kim San; a research article by Mizuno on Kim San; and a Japanese translation of a short story originally written in Chinese by Kim San titled "A Strange Weapon" (Qiguai

---

[3] In the official letter titled "On the Redressing Decision about the Problems Regarding Comrade Zhang Ming" (Guanyu Zhang Ming tongzhi wenti de pingfan jielun), dated January 27, 1983, the CCP's Central Organization Department gives more information about the two charges that led to the decision to "send him [Kim San] back home" (meaning to kill Kim). This letter, which was sent from the Central Organization Department of the CCP and addressed to Gao Yongguang, states that Kim San was accused of being a "special agent" and a "Trotskyist." The letter is available in Korean translation. (Yi 2006, 15, 599-602).

de wuqi).[4] With the publication of this edited volume, many scholars and individuals finally became convinced that not only had a person named Kim San existed, but that he had left behind a wife and son who were, as of 1988, still living in Beijing.

On the Korean peninsula, Kim San's name was never entirely forgotten, thanks to the 1946 translation that had appeared in *A New World*. During the the 1960s and '70s, in dark days of Park Chung Hee's military dictatorship, the book began circulating in secret within the intellectual circles of journalist Lee Young Hee, who had brought the Japanese edition of the book from Tokyo to South Korea (Lee 2005). The publication of the second English-language edition of *Song of Ariran*, published in 1972 by Ramparts Press with a forward and notes by the late Professor George O. Totten III, also helped to further South Korean interest in Kim San. But it was not until 1984 that Kim was able to "return alive" to South Korean consciousness. That was the year the first Korean-language translation of the 1972 Ramparts Press edition of the book came out from DongNyok Publishing. Though this first official Korean-language publication of the work remained banned until 1987, copies were successfully circulated, and through these, Koreans were able to learn about Kim's fight for Korea's national liberation and in the Chinese Revolution. In 1986, Hakmin-sa, another progressive publisher, published Nym Wales' "Notes on Korea and the Life of Kim San," basing its translation off of the Japanese translation of the work by Yi and Mizuno. Throughout the late 1980s and 1990s, more and more journalistic reports on Kim San began appearing, fanned by the growing democratization movement. South Korean broadcasting companies even aired documentaries about Kim San, honoring him as an independence fighter who had joined the struggle against Japanese colonialism. A book written about Kim in 1993 by Baek Seon-gi finally placed Kim San and his life in the context of the Korean national liberation movement. Although not the product of rigorous historical research, Baek's book marked the beginning of scholarly interest in Kim by South Koreans.

Kim San's return to public awareness in South Korea was made offi-

---

[4] These "Notes" by Nym Wales are available at the Hoover Institution of Stanford University: The Nym Wales Papers Collection # 58002, Box/Folder # 27. For Kim San's short story in English translation, see Appendix II.

cial when the Ministry of Patriots and Veterans Affairs of the South Korean government decided in 2005 to confer upon him a Patriotic Medal in the Order of Merit for National Foundation, which his son, Gao Yongguang, received on his behalf. In North Korea, Kim San was honored by Kim Il Sung in the latter's 1992 memoirs, which describe Kim as "an international warrior" and one of the "thousands of communists and patriots" who "devoted themselves to the Chinese Revolution" (Mizuno 1995, 36).

KIM SAN'S LIFE IN REGIONAL PERSPECTIVE

Kim San's short life can certainly be described as "raw human drama,"[5] but *Song of Arirang*'s account of it is also perhaps one of the best extant first-hand accounts of how the intense interactions among radicals circulating in the region occurred in such locations as Tokyo, Shanghai, Guangzhou, and Yan'an. These locations where radical thought and activity were concentrated shifted historically in accordance with regional and national circumstances. In the early part of the twentieth century, Tokyo and Shanghai served as crucibles within which radical cultures were forged and radical discourses on revolution and anti-imperialism articulated. And in the mid-1920s and 1930s, Guangzhou and Yan'an emerged as centers for revolutionary and socialist activities. While such interactions among radicals from all parts of the world produced common discourses and joint activities, they were also often shaped by the identification and articulation of particular national circumstances and needs. Kim's story exemplifies this complex process of radicalization and accommodation, with regional and transnational contexts registering as significantly as specific national contexts. In nation-based accounts of the rise of radicalism/socialism in Korea, for example, the impact of transnational exchanges are usually marginalized or, in many cases, not even included. Instead, nationalism (i.e. the Korean independence movement) is often given priority and credit over radicalism and socialism.

What is interesting in this regard is Kim's own description of his "political life" as one that "followed closely the general trend of the Korean revolutionary movement." His transition from thinking of himself as

---

[5] George O. Totten III, "Foreword," in Nym Wales and Kim San, *Song of Ariran: A Korean Communist in the Chinese Revolution* (San Francisco: Rampart Press, 1972), p. 9.

a radical nationalist to identifying as an anarchist, then as a communist, and finally, a communist willing to prioritize nation-based needs, can be viewed as corresponding to the "general trend" of the Korean independence movement and more broadly to the ways in which other radical movements in the region were influencing and transforming each other. Kim's story thus tells us about identifiable elements of East Asian regional interactions in the history of Korean socialism and the Korean independence movement, demonstrating the importance of transnationalism for the formation of national discourses.

Analyzing his own past experiences, Kim spoke to Nym Wales as having gone through three stages in his political and ideological transformation. His revolutionary life began in the fall of 1919 when he went to Tokyo, "the Mecca for students [from] all over the Far East and a refuge for revolutionaries of many kinds." Many Asian students such as Kim went to Tokyo in search of a modern education, hoping to learn from their Asian neighbor's success as a newly emerged world power. While engaged in this pursuit, they often became aware of the problems of capitalism prevalent in Japanese society. This critique of capitalism, combined with an anti-imperialist consciousness, often resulted in a profound radicalization, one that was further facilitated through interactions, both direct and indirect, amongst themselves, with other foreign students, and with Japanese radicals and socialists. It is in this sense that Japan can be said to have functioned as "the fountainhead of the radical movement in East Asia." Tokyo in particular was a place where many Asian radicals and revolutionaries, including Japanese socialists, were concentrated, at least until the Japanese government's 1925 promulgation of the Peace Preservation Law. Kim San's experience of radicalization there was thus not unique; as he points out, many communists, both Korean and Chinese, including Peng Pai, were "Japan-returned students."

After a brief stay in Tokyo, Kim San became determined to set out for Moscow, "the primary source of the 'new thought.'" During his constant movement throughout East Asia, Kim describes himself as having "passed from one theory to another," "seeking a solid footing to march forward." A radical nationalist in the period when he was traveling from Tokyo to Manchuria to Beijing, he turned to anarchism in Shanghai, "the new center of the nationalist movement" for Koreans and began to participate in direct actions against Japanese colonialism, associating himself with a number of independence activities, whether initiated by nationalists or anarchists. While in Shanghai, he describes himself as having been "thrown into a maelstrom of conflicting political ideas and discussions." In 1923, he finally found his own "footing" there "in the study of Marxism."

The following year, Kim headed south to Guangzhou, which the Guomindang (GMD, Chinese Nationalist Party) had made its base of operations after forming an alliance after 1924 with the CCP and the Comintern. Guangzhou had as a result become known as what Kim describes "the seat of the new revolutionary sovereignty"—that is, a place where many revolutionaries from all over the world gathered. Even the terror-oriented Uiyeol-dan proclaimed its transformation into a revolutionary party while in Guangzhou. It is thus unsurprising that while there, Kim San, along with Oh Seong-ryun, Kim Chung-chang (Kim Seong-suk), Kim Won-bong, and the Bak brothers, decided that the most effective way to regain Korea's independence was to fight for the liberation of all oppressed peoples. It is in this spirit that Kim San joined the CCP and decided to fight for the Chinese Revolution along with other like-minded Korean comrades.

In the second stage of his life, which begins with his arrival in Guangzhou, Kim San describes himself as a "revolutionary romantic" who prefers taking action to studying and examining the reality at hand. During this period of excitement and daring, he engaged actively in the Chinese Revolution. However, the massacre of communists in April 1927 by the GMD in the midst of the Northern Expedition, coupled with the subsequent failure of the Guangzhou Commune in December of the same year, signaled the retreat of the radical movement in China. It was at this point that Kim San found himself becoming increasingly bewildered by the gap between the ideals of the communist revolution for human liberation and the reality of the anti-communist political climate at the time. During the period from 1929 to 1934—a time when he was engaged in secret CCP activities in and around Beijing as well as briefly in Manchuria—he was arrested twice. These were difficult times for him, resulting in what he describes as "murder-suicide-despair days." Ironically, however, such hardships "humanized" him, giving him "a new tolerance and understanding of human nature." He was "now no longer a schoolboy, no longer a revolutionary romantic, no longer a party bureaucrat." He had, rather, become "a grown-up human being, equipped with long, hard revolutionary experience, qualified for true leadership in the future" and convinced that his "judgment" was "balanced and sound—no longer emotional or theoretical but practical and wise with the solid background of struggle, mental and physical."

The Japanese invasion of Manchuria in 1931 and then north China in the ensuing years once again shifted the political landscape, unleashing a tide of nationalism in China. By the time Nym Wales encountered Kim San in 1937, Yan'an, which had already been functioning as the center of Chinese national struggle, was becoming known as a new gathering place for communists and radicals in the region. During the Yan'an period (1937-1947), the CCP was no less nationalist than internationalist. Given these constantly shifting circumstances, it's not surprising that Kim tells us throughout the book of his struggles with a tension between the work he is doing for the Chinese Revolution—his uncompromising dedication to which caused some Koreans to call him "a traitor"—and his own hopes and ambitions for Korean national liberation from Japanese colonial rule, which at times alienated him from the Chinese communist cause.

This tension between his nationalist goals and the transnational message represented by the Chinese Revolution seems to have been resolved in the final stages of his life as recorded by Nym Wales. By the time the two met in Yan'an, Kim had already begun to shift his attention away from the specific goals of the CCP and towards the Korean national front. As he himself states, he "wasted no time" in acquainting himself "with every phase of the local [i.e. Korean] political and economic situation" and making efforts to "inspect and study all phases of the local situation." The outcome of these studies was his decision to consider Korea's colonial condition and prioritize its independence. Without independence, after all, there was no possibility for a worldwide revolution, much less a new society in Korea. This shift, however, did not mean that he had abandoned the transnational goal of human liberation and freedom, nor that he no longer supported the Chinese Revolution. Rather, in the wake of Japan's invasion of China, he found himself adapting yet again to changes in the "revolutionary conditions." In short, now that Japan was a common enemy for both China and Korea, their respective national struggles against it were to be prioritized over class struggle.

Subsequent to the decision by the Comintern to place Korean communists under the leadership of the CCP, Kim must have realized that Korea's national goal of independence would inevitably be subordinated to China's efforts against Japanese imperialism. It could very well have been at that moment that Kim San began to consider himself "salt in water"—refusing to be engaged *only* in the Chinese Revolution and its goals, and choosing instead to pursue a nation-based revolution that sought to unify all Koreans, regardless of class differences, in the fight against Japan. Whatever the case may be, Kim San would have been eager to leave Yan'an and to join his Korean comrades in Manchuria, where he could fight the Japanese on behalf of Korea. It is possible that Kim suggested such a nation-based strategy to CCP leaders while in Yan'an in an attempt to garner their support. It is also possible that this roused suspicions among CCP leaders that he was trying undermine their leadership or attempting to sabotage Chinese efforts to have Koreans unite with them in the fight against Japan. The charges that he was a special agent of Japan and a Trotskyist—which ultimately led to his death in 1938 as he was headed to Manchuria— might have had something to do with this.

KIM SAN AS A TRANSNATIONAL KOREAN REVOLUTIONARY
Some scholars once believed Nym Wales' account of Kim San's life and activities to be "largely exaggerated" with "distorted" historical facts (Suh 1967, 271 n36). Indeed, several of Kim's contemporaries publically wondered if he could even be considered "a prominent revolutionary," claiming that he had not been as active as other more well-recognized Korean communists, and even pointing out that he had "never participated in Korean Communist Party activities in China" (Yi and Mizuno 1991, 475). Such assertions de-emphasize the meaning of Kim's life and activities. It may well be true that portions of the book have been "exaggerated" and/or "distorted," but any such exaggerations or distortions that exist are likely to be at least somewhat unintentional, as Kim was not, from his vantage point in 1937, in a position to see the whole sweep of the Chinese Revolution or of Korean communist activities in China. Furthermore, any intentional distortions could very well be ascribed to the need to conceal Kim San's true identity and activities—a necessary caution in order to protect his own life as well as the well-being of the organizations with which he was affiliated.

As for the idea that Kim might not have been as "prominent" as other Korean revolutionaries: while this might be true, it is also true that few if any other first-hand, on-the-ground accounts of this period exists, certainly none told with such vivid detail and from this particular Korean perspective.

Today, scholarly evaluations of Kim San's life, especially those undertaken in China or in South Korea, tend to take place through a filter of nationalism. After Kim San's verdict was reversed in 1983 and he was reinstated as a CCP member, Korean-Chinese (Chaoxianzu) scholars in China began to portray him as "an unflinching warrior," "a sound revolutionary," and "a revolutionary martyr" who possessed the "internationalist spirit" for the sake of "China's human liberation project." (Kwon 1986, 66; Luo 1987, 1354) Such evaluations consider Kim's life and activities almost exclusively within the context of the CCP-led Chinese Revolution. Kim San's name now appears with some regularity in published memoirs and histories of the CCP and its local branches in Beijing and Shijiazhuang. According to these accounts, Kim was "a loyal proletarian warrior" and "a loyal revolutionary" who, as a Korean, remained faithful to the CCP. (Cui and Jin 1992, 202).

On the other hand, in South Korea, where Kim San has emerged as a national patriot who fought for Korea's liberation from Japanese colonialism, there is rarely any mention of his deep affiliations with communism and the CCP. Kim appears mostly in the context of a historical recounting of the Korean independence movement, where he is described either as "a fighter for national liberation" or an "ill-fated independence fighter" (Yi 2006, 25). Since the 1993 publication of Baek Seon-gi's book about him, Kim San's evaluation in South Korea has been largely positive. Similarly, as mentioned earlier, North Korean accounts of Kim San list him as an "internationalist warrior" and "patriot."

This range of evaluations is quite revealing. As the activities of Kim San's short life demonstrate, the breadth of ideas that many radicals and colonial intellectuals in East Asia grappled with when trying to mediate between national consciousness and transnational aspirations was vast. Certainly it was more complex and varied than one might think from the respective national versions of Kim San's story. His revolutionary experiences—which include episodes relating to all three East Asian countries and the ups and downs of their respective revolutionary movements—was already being characterized in 1951 as what one Korean researcher of China based in Japan describes as "a bird's-eye view of the whole Far East." (Kim 1950, 64, 66) By reading about Kim San's life and activities, we are able to grasp at once the transnational aspects of radicalism in East Asia as well as its nationalist origins in the many colonies and semi-colonies there.

As he himself declares, Kim San loved the Soviet Union "like a mother for its leadership in the emancipation of oppressed peoples and classes" and the Chinese Revolution "as a blood brother whose life and destiny were my own." But at the same time, he never forgot to love the Korean Revolution "as a child, young and uncertain, whose steps I might help to guide along the pathway of Russia and China before them." What we see in him is thus neither exclusively nationalist nor simply internationalist aspirations; he was instead a transnational revolutionary whose longing for human liberation combined both his national consciousness and his transnational aspirations. In this regard, some have even suggested that Kim San be called "Korea's Che Guevara."[6]

But if Kim San was not just a Korean independence fighter nor simply an international warrior in service of the Chinese Revolution, neither was he "a noble romantic intellectual revolutionary" (Lee 2005, 12). We might instead call him, somewhat contradictorily, a transnational Korean revolutionary who, armed with his own concrete revolutionary experiences in China, fought for universal human liberation and, at the same time, practiced a nation-based approach to the question of the Korean revolution. During the many years of his unconditional fight for the Chinese Revolution, his goal of national freedom never faded away. Yet he continued to yearn for the emancipation of "the oppressed nations" and peoples of the world. As he himself explains, "I have destroyed myself fighting for you and for the freedom of humanity." Spanning as it does so vast a swathe of early twentieth-century East Asian radicalism, the story of Kim San's revolutionary life and activities deserves to be shared widely, rather than contained and constructed by any one country.

---

[6] "Buhwal haneun han-guk ui Che Guevara 'Kim San'," (Resurrecting Korea's Che Guevara, 'Kim San'), *Ohmynews* (July 27, 2005) http://www.ohmynews.com/NWS_Web/view/at_pg.aspx?CNTN_CD=A0000270861 (Accessed March 14, 2016)

EDITOR'S ACKNOWLEDGMENTS

This new edition has been made possible mainly thanks to the passion and enthusiasm of the late Professor George O. Totten III, who spent his final years re-editing and updating this book but was unable to complete it before his passing in 2009. When Professor Sunyoung Park of the University of Southern California and Ms. Sunyoung Lee, the Publisher of Kaya Press, asked if I might be willing to help edit and shape this edition, I felt honored. In working to complete this book with additional editorial and other materials, I have benefited greatly from the scholarship about Kim San and *Song of Arirang* that has been building up since the 1980s in South Korea, Japan, and China. I would particularly like to thank the many individuals who have helped me with encouragement, information, and/or materials in three East Asian languages, though I alone am responsible for any shortcomings and errors that remain in the book. To name them: Arif Dirlik, Kim Sung Bo, Yim Sung Mo, Mizuno Naoki, Kim Taek Ho, Hong Jung Sun, Han Hong-gu, Quan Helü, Sin Ju Baek, Song Hyewon, Lee Junhee, Yi Han-gyeol, Kim Yeon-Gap, Kee Mee Yang, Sung Wooje, Yi Won-gyu, Kwak Jong-gu, Nohno Koji, Malgorzata "Gosha" Domagal, and the library staff at the National Library of Korea. Chung Li, my research assistant deserves my special thanks for her help in preparing the maps in this edition. My thanks also go to Hayun Cho and Evelyn Shih for their wonderful translations of Kim San's literary writings. I would like also to express my appreciation to Yvonne Cha for her crucial help and suggestions at the final stages of publishing this book.

I want to make a special note here to express my deepest appreciation, with sadness, to Arif Dirlik for writing the new foreword to this edition of *Song of Arirang*. In doing so, he kept his promise to me during his final months, at a time when he was too physically weak to do any other writing. His intellectual integrity, analytical insights, and critical thought, as well as his generosity with inspiration and support, will all be missed.

APPENDIX I

Kim San's Aliases and Pennames

A Chronological Account of the Life of Kim San

KIM SAN'S ALIASES AND PENNAMES
COMPILED BY DONGYOUN HWANG

Despite all of the research that has been undertaken about Kim San since the very first publication of *Song of Arirang* and its subsequent translation into Korean, Japanese, and Chinese, a great deal of information about him still remains unknown to us. One of these enduring mysteries has to do with Kim San's actual name. In order to conceal his identity while doing clandestine work, he used more than twenty aliases and pennames. But in her "Notes on Korea and the Life of Kim San," Nym Wales broke her silence on the matter. People now believe Kim San's name to be Jang Ji-rak (Chang Chi-rak in the old Korean romanization system). Bolstering this view is the fact that many of Kim's friends and comrades in China and Korea also remember his name as being Ji-rak.

However, a photo of Kim San discovered in China (see page 384) seems to question this assumption (Baek and Hong 1998). The photo, which serves as a mug shot of sorts, was most likely taken in January 1931 at the Japanese Consulate in Tianjin, where Kim San was detained after his first arrest by Chinese police in November 1930. In the photo, Kim appears wearing a large piece of paper on which his name, home address in Korea, the verdict handed down against him, and the date of the picture have all been handwritten in Chinese characters and Japanese katakana. The photo thus identifies his name as Jang Ji-hak and his home address as 289 Hajang-Dong, Bukjung-myeon, Yongcheon-gun, Pyeong-an bukdo, Korea. Underneath the photo are five other names that have been used by him, handwritten in Chinese characters, including Jang Ji-rak.

Given this new evidence, it seems quite possible that Jang Ji-hak might be the actual registered (i.e. legal) name reported by Kim San's parents to the authorities for inclusion in their family register after his birth in 1905. It is also quite likely that the Japanese police in Tianjin would have relied upon this official family register, a legal document they could easily have obtained in Korea, in order to identify him. Nevertheless, all extant evidence and testimonies attest to Kim San's family and friends calling him "Ji-rak," not "Ji-hak." It thus seems quite likely that Kim himself preferred to go by this name.

At this point, the only way to definitively answer the question of Kim San's birth name would require finding and verifying his family register (hojeok), which was presumably made during the last years of the Korean Empire (1897-1910) or during the Japanese colonial period (1910-1945), and which might quite possibly still be preserved in North Korea.

ALIASES USED BY KIM SAN

		Korean Romanization	Chinese Romanization
한국유	韓國劉	Han Guk-yu	Han Guoliu
장북신	張北辰	Jang Buk-sin	Zhang Beichen
장북성	張北星	Jang Buk-seong	Zhang Beixing
장지학	張志鶴	Jang Ji-hak	Zhang Zhihe
장지락	張志樂	Jang Ji-rak	Zhang Zhile
장지락	張志洛	Jang Ji-rak	Zhang Zhiluo
장명	張明	Jang Myeong	Zhang Ming
김산	金山	Kim San	Jin Shan
류명	柳明	Ryu (Yu) Myeong	Liu Ming
류자재	柳子才	Ryu (Yu) Ja-jae	Liu Zicai
우치화	于致和	Wu Chi-hwa	Yu Zhihe
이철암	李鐵庵	Yi Cheol-am	Li Tiean
유청화	劉淸華	Yu Choeng-hwa	Liu Qinghua
유춘화	劉春華	Yu Chun-hwa	Liu Chunhua
유금한	劉錦漢	Yu Geum-han	Liu Jinhan
유금명	劉錦明	Yu Geum-myeong	Liu Jinming
유금평	劉漢平	Yu Han-pyeong	Liu Hanping
유한산	劉寒山	Yu Han-san	Liu Hanshan
유정화	劉情華	Yu Jeong-hwa	Liu Qinghua

PENNAMES USED BY KIM SAN

		Korean Romanization	Chinese Romanization
북성	北星	Bukseong	Beixing
염광	炎光	Yeomgwang	Yanguang
황야	荒野	Hwang-ya	Huangye

A CHRONOLOGICAL ACCOUNT OF THE LIFE OF KIM SAN

BY DONGYOUN HWANG AND GEORGE O. TOTTEN III

This chronological biography is based largely on the information to be found in *Song of Arirang*, written by Helen Foster Snow (Nym Wales) and Kim San, as well as different sources originally published in Korean, Chinese, and Japanese. Dates, times, and details are often changed from what is described in the book. Given the confidential nature of Kim San's life and activities, not all of the specified dates can be fully verified without access to documents only available in the People's Republic of China and North Korea. Therefore, we have chosen to put them in brackets to indicate the possibility of differing accounts that may be revealed at a later date. Please see bibliography at the end of this book for more on these sources.

1905 [March 10] Kim San is born at 289 Hajang-dong, Bukjung-myeon, Yongcheon-gun, Pyeong-an bukdo, Korea, an area where, historically, people with the surname Jang (Andong) have been concentrated.

1910 Late August. Kim San goes to church with his mother, where he sees people crying and lamenting after the announcement by Japan that it has colonized Korea.

1911 Sees Japanese police beating his mother, who was unable to get a vaccination for him in time at a clinic. This is his first encounter with a "real" Japanese. He notes that at around this time, Yi Dong-hwi, an independence movement fighter, becomes his hero.

1912 Begins elementary school.

1918 Is admitted to Sungsil School, a Christian middle school in Pyongyang.

1919 [March 1] Participates in the March First Movement in Pyongyang.

[March 7] Is arrested and detained for three days.

Summer. Goes to Tokyo to study and prepare for his college entrance exams.

Fall. Returns to Korea.

Winter. Decides to run away from home to study in Moscow,

but civil war breaks out in Siberia. Unable to complete his trip, he decides instead to walk about 700 li (350 kilometers) through Manchuria to Sanyuanpu, Liuhe Xian in Jilin Province so he can train in a Korean nationalist military school.

1920 January. Arriving in Sanyuanpu, ends up staying at the house of a teacher named Ahn Dong-hui. Meets Ahn's daughter, Mi-sam.

March. Is admitted to the Sinheung (Newly Burgeoning) Military School in Hanihe, Tonghua Xian, in Jilin Province in China, where he studies for three months.

Winter. Arrives in Shanghai, where he finds work as a proofreader and typesetter at the *Korean Independence News* (Dongnip sinmun). At night, he learns English and Esperanto at Inseong School, where he meets Yi Dong-hwi, Ahn Chang-ho, and Yi Gwang-su. He also joins the Young Korean Academy (Heungsa-dan) and declares himself a "nationalist." At around this time, he finds out that his mentor Ahn Dong-hui and his family have been murdered by the Japanese and that Ahn's daughter Mi-sam is missing.

1921 Meets Oh Seong-ryun, a member of the Uiyeol-dan, and joins the Uiyeol-dan. He identifies himself at this point as an "anarchist."

October. Through Ahn Chang-ho's introduction, he enters Nankai University in Tianjin, though he soon decides to withdraw from school and go back to Beijing, where he stays briefly at the Xiangshan Orphanage before returning home to Korea. Reads the *Communist Manifesto* and Lenin's writings.

1922 Spring. Returns again to Beijing from Korea and enters Beijing Union Medical College. Joins the Korean Student Union, a leftist group of Korean students. Travels to Shanghai, where he interacts with Korean anarchists and Uiyeol-dan members before returning again to Beijing.

1923 Winter. Joins the Communist Youth.

1924 Winter. Helps Kim Chung-chang (Kim Seong-suk), Kim Won-bong, Jang Geon-sang, and others organize the Creating-One Party (Chang-il Dang), which some scholars say may have functioned as a branch of the Irkutsk faction's Korean Communist Party. Involved in the publication of its official organ, *Revolution* (Hyeongmyeong)

Invites Li Dazhao, one of the founders of the Chinese Communist Party (CCP), to contribute writings to the *Revolution*. Also makes the acquaintance of early CCP members, the writers Shi Cuntong and Qu Qiubai.

1925 Fall. Arriving in Guangzhou, enters Zhongshan University as a second-year medical student.

November. Is hired at the Social Sciences Academy in Beijing, a group established by progressive Koreans there. Because he is still living in Guangzhou, however, he is unable to accept the job.

Winter. Joins the Guomindang (GMD) and becomes a member of the Korean Nucleus of the CCP.

1926 Late Spring. Establishes the Korean Revolutionary Young Men's League (Joseon hyeongmyeong cheongnyeon yeonmaeng) in Guangzhou and is elected a member of its Organization Committee.

June. Joins the Association of the Korean Young Comrades in Guangzhou.

Summer. Becomes vice editor-in-chief of the Korean Young Men's League organ, *Revolutionary Action* (Hyeongmyeong haengdong in Korean; referred to as *Revolutionary Movement* by a Japanese source) under editor-in-chief Kim Chung-chang. Establishes the KK Group, and becomes acquainted with Bak Jin and his brothers. Meets up again with Oh Seong-ryun, who has come to Guangzhou from Moscow. Also teaches at the Huangpu Military Academy.

August. Makes the acquaintance of Mikhail Borodin.

September. Changes his major at Zhongshan University from medicine to law and politics.

1927 February. Meets Thomas Mann, Jacque Doriot, and Earl Browder in Guangzhou.

April. Is elected as a member of the Central Committee of the Korean Revolutionary Young Men's League and joins its Propaganda Committee, a separate branch from the Organization Committee to which he was elected earlier.

[April 18] Witnesses the GMD and the police in Guangzhou killing young Chinese students including Luo Liumei after Chiang Kai-shek's April 12 massacre of communists and workers in Shanghai. Writes a poem titled "Humanity at the Dongjiaochang."

May. Receives a letter from home telling him that his second brother has died.

[December 10] Arrives at the Headquarters of the Special Training Regiment (Jiaodaotuan) with other Koreans. They join a contingent of sixty-seven Koreans who are already there. Together, they participate alongside Chinese communists in the Guangzhou Commune.

[December 11] In conjunction with Yang Dal-bu, occupies the artillery position at Shahe and helps to attack troops under the command of Zhang Fakui. Is put in charge of the Department of Arming Peasants and Workers after a soviet government is proclaimed in Guangzhou. Invites Heinz Neumann from the Comintern for dinner at the newly occupied Police Bureau.

[December 12] Meets He Cheng, a classmate from Beijing Medical Union College, who helps deliver necessary medical supplies. Also introduces He to Ye Ting, who assists in setting up a field hospital.

[December 13] Participates in a Korean Revolutionary Young Men's League meeting at Zhongshan University at which next steps after the failure of the Guangzhou Commune are discussed.

[December 14] Arrives in Hua Xian with other Commune participants after having retreated from Guangzhou. Accompanied by an anonymous female communist.

[December 16] Arrives in Conghua Xian, northwest of Guangzhou and is welcomed by the people of the Hailufeng Soviet.

1928 [January 5] The men reorganized from the Guangzhou Uprising into the Fourth Army of the Workers and Peasants Red Army arrive in Haifeng Xian under the command of Ye Yong.

[January 7] Kim San arrives at the Hailufeng Soviet.

[January 21] Under the name Zhang Beixing, serves alongside Oh Seong-ryun (Xiansheng) as a member of the School (i.e. Academic Affairs) Committee of the Party School that has been recently set up by the Dongjiang Special Committee of the CCP. In this capacity, creates teaching plans and syllabi that include such topics as the Outline of Leninism, the Construction of Soviets, the Second International and World Revolution, the History of the CCP, Military Knowledge, Propaganda Skills, etc. He is also appointed to the Judicial Trial Committee.

February - June. Takes part in five different battles to defend the Hailufeng Soviet. Contracts malaria.

[May 3] After failing to reoccupy Haifeng Xian, the Red Army is dissolved.

[July 27] Kim San arrives in Neiyang and sets out for Shantou, having barely escaped death multiple times subsequent to the Red Army's defeat.

[August 4] Arrives at a fishing village near Sanyang.

[August 6] Takes a Japanese ship to Hong Kong. Once in Hong Kong, makes the acquaintance of a Korean ginseng merchant who helps him.

September. Makes his way back to Shanghai.

October. Is reunited with fellow Ui-yeol Dan members Kim

Chung-chang (a.k.a. Kim Seong-suk) and Oh Seong-ryun in Shanghai.

November. Opposes Han Wi-geon's entry to the CCP.

Returns to Beijing.

1929 March. Testifies as a witness at the trail of the former Uiyeol-dan member who assassinated Bak Yong-man. Is attacked at a meeting of Korean nationalists in Beijing and suffers a serious head wound as a result, resulting in his hospitalization.

April–May. Using the name Liu Qinghua, is placed in charge of the Organization Department of the CCP Beijing Branch.

[April 1] Using the pen name Zhang Beixing, translates Sano Manabu's *Marxism and Atheism* (Marukusushūgi to mushinron) into Chinese, publishing it as *On Atheism* (Wushenron).

End of May. Is sent to Manchuria to make connections between the CCP and the Korean Communist Party.

[May or August] Attends a meeting of the Korean Peasants Alliance in Manchuria. Travels secretly throughout the area in an effort to strengthen the alliance of Korean organizations there in preparation for an anti-Japanese front.

October 26. The *Joseon Daily* publishes a report saying that Kim San was killed at the nationalist meeting that took place in Beijing in March where he was attacked and wounded.

November 6. A letter sent by Kim San disputing the report that he's been killed and disclosing his name and mailing address in Beijing is published in the *Joseon Daily*.

[Winter] Carries out a secret mission near Andong.

1930 January. Returns again to Beijing where he meets up with and eventually moves in with Liu Ling. The two live together for several months.

March. His short story, "A Strange Weapon" (Qiguai de wuqi) is published in the periodical *New East* (Xin dongfang). He organizes a student demonstration in commemoration of the March 18, 1926 Massacre of Beijing students.

June. Writes a poem entitled "Mourning Comrade Han Hae." Together with Liu Ling, teaches CCP members at a training center in Xiangshan. Goes by the name Liu Zicai.

[November 20 or December 19] Is arrested in Beijing and interrogated by Chinese police. Writes a confession for the Chinese police.

1931 [January 7] Is handed over to the Japanese Embassy in Beijing and then transferred to the Japanese Legation in Tianjin.

[January 14] Is ordered by a Japanese consul to leave China and not return for three years. Is then sent to Sinuiju in Korea for further interrogation.

[February 20] Traveling through Dalian and Andong, he arrives in Sinuiju, where he is detained by the Japanese police and tortured, resulting in permanent damage to his lungs.

[April 1] After denying all charges against him, he is released. Returns to his familial home in Korea.

June. Travels to Beijing where a man named Han gives a false statement accusing him of being a spy for the Japanese. His CCP membership is possibly suspended. Hides at the home of Kim Gi-chang to escape possible arrest by the Chinese warlord government in Beijing. Is ordered by the CCP to go to Zhangjiakou to do manual labor but is unable to get a job there and returns to Beijing.

Winter. Meets a Chinese woman named Zhao Yaping, and, under her care, recovers from tuberculosis, which he contracted after having been tortured. Writes a poem in Chinese titled "Comrades, We Have to Fight" (Tongzhimen, women yao zhandou).

1932 January. Pretending to be Cantonese, teaches at the Second Normal School in Baodingfu and is almost arrested. Starts a secret underground organization of teachers and staff at the school.

March. Teaches at an elementary school in Gaoyang Xian, where he organizes peasants.

July. Is ordered by the CCP Hebei Province Committee to carry out an armed uprising in Gaoyang Xian, but refuses.

[August 1] Publishes yet another book by Sano Manabu that he's translated into Chinese, publishing it under the title *The Outlook on Life of Feuerbach, Marx, and Lenin* (Feierbaha Makesi Leining de renshengguan).

August. attempts to start a peasant uprising in Gaoyang Xian as ordered by the CCP, but fails. Afterwards, submits a letter of opinion in which he criticizes the CCP's decision to launch the unsuccessful uprising.

Fall. Returns to Beijing where he translates writings on feudalism in the Japanese politics, the power of the German president, etc., which he publishes under the penname Huangye in *International Translated Reports* (Guoji yibao).

December 12. Publishes a translated writing titled "A Recent State of Mrs. Lenin" (Leining furen de jinzhuang) in *The National News Weekly* (Guowen zhoubao) under the penname Huangye.

1933 [May 1] Is interrogated by the Beijing GMD police after having been arrested along with his companion, Zhao Yaping.

[May 7] Is accused of being a Trotskyist within the CCP. Going now by the name Li Tiean, writes a confession in which he denies having joined any political party.

[May 21] The GMD police discovers that Li Tiean and Liu Qinghua are both aliases for Kim San and decide to hand him over to the Japanese Consulate.

[June 6 or June 15] Arrives at the Japanese Consulate in Tianjin.

[July 20 or 30] Is sent to Korea where he is interrogated by the Japanese police and imprisoned. Upon his release, he is cared for by his family.

1934	January. Goes back to Beijing and soon marries Zhao Yaping. Earns money by teaching and working as a proxy writer, writing books such as *Politics Economy Geography* (Zhengzhi jingji dili) and *The Third Cultural Crisis* (Disanci wenhua weiji).

1935	Spring or Early Summer. Goes to Shijiazhuang, where he helps to edit *Commercial News* (Shangbao) while living at the house of a friend and teaching Japanese in the guest room of the president of Jiaotong (Communication) Bank.

September–October. Establishes a CCP branch at Pinghan Railway Fulun School and encourages Wang Shuliang, Kang Ruihua, Tao Xijin, Zhu Lian, and others, to join the CCP. Sets up a Shijiazhuang Operation Committee within the CCP.

December. Organizes a demonstration of students and workers in Shijiazhuang in support of the December 9th Movement.

End of Year. Travels to Shanghai, where he meets with Kim Chung-chang (Kim Seong-suk) and Bak Geon-ung and, in response to the CCP's "August First Declaration," discusses the possibility of establishing a League for Korean National Liberation, in which communists, anarchists, and other Korean nationalists could all participate.

1936	April. Goes to Nanjing.

June. Becomes acquainted with Jeong Yul-seong, the composer of the CCP's People's Liberation Army's marching song.

Summer. Participates in the Union for the Korean National Front and drafting "Program of Action of the Union for the Korean National Front." Elected as a delegate to the Chinese soviet districts in the northwest by the newly established Korean League for National Liberation. Joined at around this time in Shanghai by his wife, Zhao Yaping.

[August 1] Leaves Nanjing for Baoan, where the CCP Central and the Red Army's Headquarters are based.

October. Arrives in Baoan. Is now using the name Zhang Ming.

December. Moves with the CCP to Yan'an and begins teaching Japanese economics at the Anti-Japanese Military Political Academy.

1937 January. Continues to teach physics, chemistry, mathematics, Japanese, and Korean at the Anti-Japanese Military Political Academy in Yan'an.

[January 21] Writes a poem titled "My Fatherland, Korea" (Wode zugo, Gaoli).[1]

April. Using the name Zhang Ming, attends the Meeting of CCP Representatives in the Northwestern Region in Yan'an. Meets with Seo Hwi, whom Kim San describes in the book as "a young student named Yi and the only other Korean in Yan'an at the time."

[April 20] Receives a letter from his wife, Zhao Yaping, reporting that she has borne him a son. In his reply, he asks her to let his son know that he is Korean and to raise him to become a soldier.

June 18. Begins interviews with Nym Wales (Helen Foster Snow), wife of Edgar Snow. These will take place over the course of seventeen meetings that last until late August.

1938 [August 18] The CCP's Shaan-Gan-Ning Border Region Security Bureau submits a report stating that Zhang Ming (Kim San) is a spy of the Japanese invaders and must "be sent back to home," meaning that he must be executed.

Early October. Kim San is ordered by the CCP to go to the war front.

[October 8] Kang Sheng approves Kim's execution as a Trotskyist and Japanese special agent.

---

[1] See Cui Fengchun 2015, 365-368 for this poem in Chinese. Cui states with no further explanation that this poem was written by Kim San under the penname Qiangshou (literally "strong beast") and was published in *Liberation Daily* (Jiefang ribao) on January 20, 1937. However, because this newspaper was first published in Yan'an in May 1941, it has been difficult to confirm Kim's authorship of this poem. I am grateful to Professor Mizuno Naoki for bringing my attention to Cui's paper. –DH

[October 19] Kim San is executed on his way to the war front in Manchuria.

1939   Writing in Baguio in the Philippines, Nym Wales turns her interviews with Kim San into a book manuscript.

1941   The first edition of *Song of Arirang* is published in New York by the John Day Company as *Song of Ariran: The Life Story of a Korean Rebel*.

1946   October. The first Korean translation of *Song of Arirang* is undertaken by Sin Jae-don and serially published in the magazine *A New World* (Sin cheonji). The series continues until January 1948.

1953   October. The first Japanese edition of *Song of Arirang* is published in Tokyo by Asahi shobō.

1972   June. Second edition of *Song of Ariran* is published by Ramparts Press with Foreword and Notes by George O. Totten as *Song of Ariran: A Korean Communist in the Chinese Revolution*.

1977   April. The first Chinese-language edition of *Song of Arirang* is published in Hong Kong.

1978   Gao Yongguang, the son of Kim San and Zhong Yiping, approaches the CCP to ask that it make an official statement reversing the charges made against Kim San.

1983   January 27. The CCP Central Committee officially announces the reinstatement of the honor of Zhang Ming (Kim San) and his party membership.

1984   September. The first Korean edition of *Song of Arirang* in book form is published by DongNyok Publishing under the title *Arirang* with no subtitle.

1987   February. The first mainland China edition of *Song of Arirang* is published by Lioaning minzu chubanshe in a Korean-language edition under the title *The Shadow Image of the White-Clothed People* (Baek-ui dongpo ui yeongsang).

1991   May 28. Yi Hoe-seong and Mizuno Naoki publish *Notes on* Song of Ariran: Kim San and Nym Wales ("Ariran no uta" oboe gaki: Kimu San to Nimu Ueruzu) with Iwanami shoten.

1993 Kim San is brought up and evaluated as "an internationalist warrior" and "a patriot" in *With the Century* (Segi wa deobuleo), the memoirs of North Korean leader Kim Il Sung.

September. The first Chinese-language edition of *Song of Arirang* to appear in China is published in Beijing by Xinhua chubanshe.

2005 The South Korean government awards Kim San (Jang Ji-rak) a posthumous Patriotic Medal, which Gao Yongguang receives on behalf of his father.

2017 December 13. During his state visit to China, South Korean President Moon Jae-In introduces Gao Yongguang in a formal reception for Koreans in China as the son of Jang Ji-rak (Kim San), "the Man of Will (jisa), who dedicated himself to the independence of his fatherland and the Chinese Revolution."

APPENDIX II
WRITINGS BY KIM SAN

The Basis for the Korean National Front

Program for Action of the Union for the Korean National Front

A Strange Weapon
(Short Story)

Mourning Comrade Han Hae
(Poem)

THE BASIS FOR THE KOREAN NATIONAL FRONT

KIM SAN

This piece was taken from Kim San's "Analysis of the Korean Revolutionary Movement," which was originally included in the first John Day edition of this book but excluded in the second Ramparts Press edition. Kim's writing is not printed in full here because of the many inaccuracies it contained. In the following excerpted piece, Kim San clearly sees Japan's invasion of Manchuria and north China beginning in 1931 as a sign of changes in revolutionary conditions not only in China but also in Korea, which necessitates the formation of a national front in Korea for all classes to be united. –DH

A new period of history in the Far East began when the Japanese occupied Manchuria on September 18, 1931. For Korea this was an important change. It was the signal for Japan to create tight monopolistic control of the whole economy of Korea—as a part of the Japanese war economy. Big capital came to Korea from Japan and broke the native bourgeoisie, which had formerly cooperated with the Japanese, hence this class too turned against the Japanese. This did not occur quickly but gradually, and in 1935 the nationalist bourgeois politicians of Korea were the first to raise the appeal for the unity of all classes and parties against Japan. At the same time, the intensified industrialization of Korea has strengthened the potential power of the proletariat. In their hands is now a vital part of Japan's war industry—an Achilles heel at which to deal a blow against the conquerors when the time comes.

In preparation for her conquest of China and the whole Far East, Japan has tried to utilize Korea as a base from which to launch this expansion. After the conquest of Manchuria in 1931, the Japanese slogan was "Industrialize Korea." They dared to have this slogan because they planned to transfer their market from Korea to Manchuria and considered Korea already safely a part of Japanese home economy. When General Minami Jirō became Governor General in place of General Ugaki Kazushige, he called a conference in Seoul in August 1936 to organize a new program for the intensified industrialization of Korea. All local Japanese capitalists, and a few Koreans as figureheads, were in attendance. The conference decided to build a cotton industry in southern Korea and a sheep-raising and wool industry in the north. They also planned to develop and take over all mines (including the few remaining American-owned gold mines) as rapidly as possible, which has been done.

The further plan was to build new railways—there are now almost

5,000 kilometers of railways in Korea—and to increase exports from Korea in order to get capital for this industrialization. Korea now exports to Manchuria rice, fish, sugar, ginseng, iron, rubber shoes (made with rubber from the South Seas [Southeast Asia]), stockings, and a little cloth. Her principal export to Japan is rice—averaging about 9,000,000 tons a year—and lumber (for houses and paper-making), not to speak of the human labor exported, and students, especially revolutionaries.

Japan decided that Korea was to be no longer a pure colony but an industrial region for Japanese capital to exploit on somewhat the same terms as in Japan proper. In 1937 the Hayashi Cabinet in Japan designed a five-year plan for the industrial development of Korea requiring 1,400,000,000 yen in capital, compared with a similar need of 2,900,000,000 yen for Manchuria. Altogether the Hayashi industrial program called for a total of 6,900,000,000 yen for Japan, Korea, and Manchuria.

Because of the increased pressure on Korea since 1931 and the industrialization of the country, the revolutionary power in Korea has grown rapidly for several years. The intensified Japanese control and exploitation of all classes is welding them together into a national front, and the objective situation gives more and more relative internal power to the proletariat and dispossessed classes. This dynamic will bring about socialist changes. There is no other solution to the national problems.

PROGRAM OF ACTION OF THE UNION FOR THE KOREAN NATIONAL FRONT

KIM SAN

This is also taken from Kim San's "Analysis of the Korean Revolutionary Movement" and was included in the second Ramparts Press edition of *Song of Arirang*. The program of action presented here was drawn up in July of 1936, as described by Kim San in the chapter titled "The Korean National Front." The final, official version of this document differs slightly from this one and can be found in the inaugural issue of the *The Korean National Front* (Chaoxian minzu zhanxian), published on April 10, 1938 (p. 19), as well as in issue No. 4 (May 25, 1938, p. 24). This journal, published in Chinese, was an organ of the Union for the Korean National Front. —DH

I. To unite together all the people of Korea who agree with the principle of Korean independence, irrespective of social, class, party, political, or religious belief, and all organizations and individuals, men and women, old and young, in order to achieve a successful struggle for the emancipation of the whole nation.

II. To protect all native industry and commerce, and develop agriculture, at the same time opposing all Japanese capital, industry, and commerce in Korea and all forms of collaboration with such Japanese imperialist enterprises.

III. To determine, by fair arbitration between the owners and workers in national industry and commerce and between landlords and tenants in agriculture, a minimum subsistence wage and maximum working hours for workers and a maximum rent for tenants, in the meantime ceasing class war and encouraging class cooperation during this period.

IV. To organize without restraint all workers, farmers, professionals, and wage earners and all employees of Japanese imperialism, whether in public or secret enterprises or in state administrative and legislative positions.

V. To encourage a broad reform movement to improve the economic life of the nation and to awaken the national consciousness to the struggle for economic rights, in the meanwhile absolutely opposing Japanese immigration and the policy of sending Koreans to Manchuria.

VI. To encourage a broad movement to demand the rights of citizenship and the protection of human rights in order to awaken the whole nation to a struggle for democracy, at the same time opposing Decree No. 7 [i.e. "the law for the protection of the social system" that was promulgated by the Japanese to suppress the Korean national movement and provided for "cultural policy"] and the cruel policy of taking away the people's freedom.

VII. To create and expand a movement for the development of national culture and education in order to develop traditional national culture and absorb the new culture, in the meantime opposing the policy of deceiving the people and keeping them under the surveillance of "cultural policy."

VIII. To protect the people's chosen national religions and permit them to develop freely (Christianity, Buddhism, the Cheondogyo, Confucianism, and the Tang Chün Chao) and encourage these religious sects to stop quarreling and struggle together for the common freedom of belief, meanwhile permitting them to unite together against the religion imposed by the Japanese as an instrument of imperialism (Shinto, the Tenrikyo, etc.) and oppose superstitious and backward tendencies (the Taiyi jiao [Tae-eul gyo], Fu T'ien Chao, Kung Yi Chao, etc.).[1]

IX. To unite together the whole system of education, teachers with young students, and to generally build all kinds of educational and cultural organizations to promote the idea of emancipation and national culture, at the same time using the method of strikes by students and teachers and all other methods to oppose the Japanese imperialist ideas that are pouring into the educational system in order to enslave the minds of the people.

X. To positively protect and help the movement for the equality of women, granting the freedom of marriage and divorce and opposing laws against women's rights for the inheritance and ownership of property; and to give women equal rights—to all occupations, to education, to holding political office, and to freely participating in social movements—by opposing the Japanese law of so-called "social morality," which oppresses women.

XI. To form a union with the Chinese national anti-Japanese front and

---

[1] I have been unable to identify some religions referred to here in the Wade–Giles system of Romanization of Chinese. —DH

with the anti-aggressor front of the U.S.S.R., at the same time opposing Japan's advance against the U.S.S.R. and seizure of China.

XII. To definitely support the anti-Fascist people's front of Japan, and to form a close relation with this.

XIII. To create a great common front between the peoples of China, the U.S.S.R., Japan, and Korea, and to become the center of all the nations of the Orient directly under the oppression of Japanese imperialism in order to organize a vast anti-aggressor and peace front in the Orient.

XIV. To form close relations with the world peace front against the Japanese, German, Italian, and other Fascist aggressors.

XV. All Koreans abroad in other lands must agree to the following:

(1) Each and every group, party, and individual abroad, irrespective of political or religious beliefs or occupation, shall unite under the anti-Japanese principle and take responsibility for carrying out special important duties as part of the whole national united front according to the particular conditions in the different countries and districts where they may reside.

(2) All Korean workers, students, and merchants in Japan must unite together and positively participate in the Japanese anti-Fascist people's front, while at the same time uniting closely with the national front in their own homeland.

(3) The whole body of revolutionary Koreans in China—all groups, armed forces, and individuals—must unite together and actively assist the Chinese anti-Japanese united front, while at the same time realizing their special duties as follows: (a) Organizing and giving revolutionary education to the forces for Korean independence within this Chinese anti-Japanese united front; (b) In Manchuria, the Korean Revolutionary Army, the Korean Communist Party, the Red partisans, and all Korean troops among the Chinese volunteers, must unite together as a unit around a common program while keeping their separate national character within the cooperative Chinese anti-Japanese federation of armed forces and in the meantime making an effort to enlarge and strengthen these Korean armed forces; (c) those Korean hirelings who come to different parts of China as instruments of Japanese imperialism are

also under Japanese oppression (including those forced to deal in opium, prostitution, smuggling, etc. in order to earn a livelihood), and we must use a special method of leading them to turn against their Japanese imperialist employers when the time arrives.

(4) All Koreans in the U.S.S.R. must unite together to become a part of the whole united front and at the same time realize their special duties such as the following: (a) All Koreans must receive military and political training, and at the same time organize a Korean Volunteer movement for future action; (b) They must positively develop high military leaders to send to the Korean revolutionary troops moving about in China; (c) They must give material help to the Korean revolutionary movement to aid the comrades imprisoned, wounded, sacrificed, or otherwise in need.

(5) All Koreans in America and Europe and elsewhere must unite together and become a support to the Korean national united front, and must send money and do propaganda and try to assist their country through the mobilization of international support and sympathy.

A STRANGE WEAPON

YANGUANG

Kim San, using the penname Yanguang, wrote a short story about the attempted assassination of military general Tanaka Giichi by Oh Seong-ryun and others and Oh's subsequent escape from the Japanese Legation in Shanghai. Written in Chinese, it was published under the title "A Strange Weapon" (Qiguai de wuqi) in *New East* (Xin dongfang) Vol. 1, No. 4 (1930). *New East* was first published in Beijing in January 1930 by the Research Society for the Problems in the East (Dongfang wenti yanjiu hui), an organization whose stated mission was "to make efforts for the liberation of the Eastern peoples and to promote the equality of the humans of the world." (Mizuno 1990, 360) This short story was subsequently translated into Japanese and Korean (Yi and Mizuno 1991, 367-405; Yi and Mizuno 1993, 181-219; Kim 1990, 336-357). It is translated here into English for the first time. –DH

1

A major incident took place in 1923 on the Huangpu River waterfront in Shanghai.

2

Ever since the poisonous dragon of capitalism smashed through the cradle-like borders of feudal entities, the people have found themselves so harassed by it that they can no longer even dream of peace and happiness. Produced in England, it traipsed across Germany before moving on to America. It rejoiced; it delighted. It rejoiced in being the greatest hegemon in the world, whom no one dared to resist. It delighted in being the son of God, before whom the powerful were forced to prostrate themselves in displays of devotion, and on behalf of whom the masses were exploited, amplifying its power and influence. It was its own master, its needs the only thing that mattered. It paid no attention to the fact that its progeny, though filial, were cursed with lives shortened by syphilis or tuberculosis. It viewed the masses as mere chattel; once they'd been forced to do whatever it fervently desired, it was of no consequence if they died miserably, one by one, wherever they had finished their tasks. All that meant was that it would no longer have to gaze upon their thin, sallow, accursedly ugly faces; it would no longer have to hear the sound of their agitated, inarticulate voices, voices it regarded as unfit to mingle with the elegant sounds of poetry. The world would then feel as if it were built from bricks of happiness and filled with the fragrant, the sweet, the beautiful, the joyful. At this thought, it became immeasurably proud and immeasurably bold. No longer satisfied with the tracks it had left throughout all of Europe and as far as the American continent, it used its ponderous, ox-like body to smash through the door of Asia. There it became pregnant again. Giving birth in Japan, its descendants began to multiply!

Those spawn are today's Japanese imperialists.

Having embarked upon this path of capitalist imperialism, Japan has been obliged by filial duty to carry out its goals and objectives, and so has begun snaking out its tongue once again in search of human flesh. Taiwan was the first to be eaten; Korea was the second. Your nation came next. From the outside, China might seem somewhat lacking in vigor, but it contains many great essences within.

Still, given sheer gluttony and gaping mouths of the Japanese imperialists, they must have ingested malignant toxins along with everything else. This is indeed the case. Many such potential pathogens have been consumed, and if they were all to erupt at once, they will be dangerous.

Below is an account of one.

3

Seven years ago, three people regarded as rebels by the Japanese imperialists escaped to Shanghai. One was named Yi [Yi Jong-am], another Kim Ik-sang, and the third was named Oh Seong-ryun. All three were dedicated Korean youths of middle-class economic status or higher whose families had enjoyed generations of scholarly renown. Their parents' only wish was for them to pursue further schooling that would set them on a path to official promotion and future wealth, thus bringing honor to their family names. It was, of course, a great blessing to have been born into circumstances that could give them such comfortable lives, and for this they were duly grateful. Their parents' hopes for them, which sparkled like light and pulsed with a special power, spoke to them in the crisp wind and the quiet waters that ran through their school campus, exhorting them to seek fulfillment in their classrooms and their books. These three youths had, from childhood, often received this kind of implicit guidance from their parents, and each, in his own way, sought to follow the thread of it by distinguishing himself from the multitudes of his compatriots.

Every day, when the three went to school, their eyes would shine with golden sparks of hope and the radiant dreams of youth. Thanks to something that had been decided in a previous life, they had been born to this position of privilege. The world was their oyster. They felt as if they were standing high atop a beautiful wall from which they were looking down, while everyone else could only gaze up at them furtively or lower their heads and sigh in shame.

But when unfortunate reality crashed down upon them, it drowned them like a deluge!

Just as they were hard at work pursuing beautiful flowers of hope, the poisonous dragon of Japanese imperialism shifted its glance and caught sight of Korea, which had until then been living quietly like a fatted lamb. And, like a hungry demon that gnashes its teeth when it glimpses a banquet, it charged over to devour the tasty morsel bursting with fresh nutrients and protein.

The violent currents unleashed by this poisonous dragon plunged all of Korea into a mess of mud and debris, flooding everything indiscriminately from the loftiest realms of the palace to the lowliest of farms. Our three devoted Korean youths also fell victim to the death and destruction that followed this deluge. Despite struggling in the flood waters for a long time, they remained in the land of the living, golden sparks of hope still gleaming within their breasts. They were saved by the waves of the Yellow Sea. Washing up the mouth of the Suzhou River, they were able to crawl quietly onto the banks of the Huangpu River.

This, to them, was a rebirth!

Looking back at the masses of people from their homeland whom the deluge had drowned, they rejoiced to still be alive.

It's sheer luck that we were able to reach the banks of the Huangpu River, they thought. *We three are the only ones left; this is certainly something worth celebrating!* But then they thought of their happy families, their loving parents, their dear siblings, their friends and relatives—all vanished now like smoke. Everything had been spattered with blood and mixed with mud: the splendid streets where they had once shared leisurely walks with lovers; the natural beauty of the countryside; the vibrant, aromatic flower gardens. Their homeland, shorn of all freedom and bereft of the clean, delicate grace of their compatriots, had become a lamb under the foot of an iron lion. Thinking this, six eyes shed sparkling, golden tears. They sang out:

> Oh Huangpu River! Oh Huangpu River!
> Huangpu River whom we love most dearly! Huangpu River whom we can never forget!
> Your smile of clear waves, dark and deep; your smile filled with deep pity!
> You saved us from the wild and violent torrents, you let us hide, nestled deep in your arms,
> And now you've delivered us safely to shore.
> Just so: your compassion, your benevolence, your heart brighter than the moon—
> How shall we, oh how shall we commemorate you, thank you, and praise you?

> Oh, Huangpu River! Oh, Huangpu River!
> Huangpu River whom we love most dearly! Huangpu River whom we can never forget!
> How did you know that we were birds without a nest, fish without water?
> How did you, with your compassionate heart, your pitying smile, know to save us from the endless, violent torrents, the crazed waves?
> If you hadn't rescued us,
> We would undoubtedly have perished in those malevolent, out-of-control waves.
> How could we even imagine walking back and forth on the paradisiacal banks of the Huangpu River
> Much less conversing with you today?"

> Oh Huangpu River! Oh Huangpu River!
> Huangpu River whom we love most dearly! Huangpu River whom we can never forget!
> You are like a God on earth.
> You saved us:
> Ah, what a beautiful city, what a flourishing city!
> —Alas, more's the pity, more's the pity!

How could we, birds without a nest, fish without water,
Bear to live here?

We remember: our countrymen beset by disaster.
We remember: our families, parents, brothers, sisters,
  and lovers.
We remember: the cars and horses lined up outside the
  gates of our family homes.
We remember: our splendid cities, our beautiful
  mountains, lakes, and gardens.
This, all of this, has been drowned, consigned
  to oblivion by the violent torrents of the poisonous
  dragon.
What further need have we of life?
What further need have we of life?

Huangpu River! Huangpu River!
Oh, Huangpu River, whom we love most dearly! Huang-
  pu River, whom we can never forget!
You truly are a God on earth!
Oh, God, thank you for saving us!
Perhaps, in your benevolent love, you let us live so we
  could save in your stead anyone still struggling in the
  violent torrents!
We accept this charge, we accept, we accept! We swear
  to be your brave and loyal followers,
We swear to save those countless countrymen beset by
  disaster!
We allow our hot tears to join the flow of your body,
  causing it to slowly swell, sending it forth to charge,
  ferocious, upon the lair of that poisonous dragon, to
  purge it with a cleansing flood.
Oh! Oh, God! Ease your mind, we will never be disloyal.
We will battle for your benevolent love, we will battle
  for our families, parents, brothers, sisters, relatives,
  friends, and lovers! We will battle for our homeland
  with its history that spans over four thousand years!
Now we depart! Now we prepare for battle!"

4

After escaping from Korea, they settled in Shanghai for quite some time, agonizing every day over how to avenge their homeland. Gathering together young Koreans who were living in Shanghai, they formed the "Righteous Group of Korea"—a weapon they wanted to forge into the solid mass of a bomb that could destroy the whole of Japan and its territories, erasing it from the face of the earth. They would neither be happy nor feel their task was complete until they were able to kill every Japanese wretch wearing a kimono. Every day, from dawn until they entered their dreams, not a single moment passed when they were not plotting how to slaughter the enemy.

One day, they came across a piece of news in the papers: the Japanese Army Minister Tanaka Giichi (hereafter, Tanaka) would be coming by ferry from Tokyo to Shanghai on official business on X [sic] day of X [sic] month. The three youths were very happy when they read this. Shrinking away from the attention of others, they began to make plans: one would carry a knife, another would carry a bomb, and the third would carry a gun. Oh Seong-ryun grabbed the gun, saying, "I will shoot first; one of you will have a knife, the other will have a bomb. If the gun misses, whoever has the bomb will throw it at the target. If we are close to the target, whoever has the blade will strike." After Oh spoke, Kim took up the bomb, so the knife fell to Yi. With this distribution of duties now complete, they found a recent photograph of Tanaka and prepared to go to the Huangpu River and wait at the place where ships from Japan docked upon arrival. It was already afternoon when they finished their preparations, so they headed out to the riverbank. As they walked, they thought: *Sinful Tanaka, you are unsurpassed in your contributions to the empire! Your crimes are known to the whole world! You occupied our homeland and ordered your soldiers, more vicious than jackals, to slaughter our people! Now the time has come for you to rest, to die filled with regret from our firepower, our glinting knives! During your time on earth, you murdered indiscriminately, killing for fun! You even destroyed so many of your own people in Japan, people who had nothing to do with us! And now, abandoning all restraint, you've strewn the corpses of our comrades across our fields, staining the rivers with their blood! Have you no conscience that can be troubled by your indulgence of such a murderous, bestial hobby? Whether or not you repent, we have been ordered by God to send you, evil thing that you are, off to your punishment in hell in the name of Justice. Oh Tanaka, Tanaka!*

Your crimes are innumerable! This torrential spot on the banks of the Huangpu River will be the last place you shall ever walk! If not for God's mercy, even death by ten thousand blades would be too good for you!

Filled with righteous indignation, the three youths walked along with smiles on their faces. Before they knew it, they had reached the riverbank. There they saw Japanese soldiers standing at attention like jackals, and Japanese police surveying their surroundings like dogs hunting for prey. Fear crept up on one of the youths: *With so many military and police personnel here, is this mission to assassinate Tanaka a foolhardy one?*

Meanwhile, the brave Oh Seong-ryun was busy considering the best strategy for how to open fire on Tanaka. Turning to look at his companions, he noticed that Yi was looking a bit shaky and felt a rush of anxiety and resentment. *Wretch who shirks battle! Go if you want to!* Oh thought to himself. *Get out of here. As for me, I've pledged to fight the enemy to the death!*

But just as a great rage against Yi was beginning to build up inside him, a loud toot announced the arrival of ship XX [sic], which had just anchored. Refocusing, Oh and his comrades watched the ship's many passengers board a small boat that headed noisily towards land. Oh Seong-ryun hurriedly fished out the photograph of Tanaka from his satchel and hid it in his palm, surreptitiously matching the face pictured there against the disembarking passengers. Tanaka, who had the swagger of a bully when walking the halls of bureaucracy, was now, when in public, intent on hiding himself within the crowd. Seeing Tanaka's repulsive face, his extravagant clothes, his body stinking of blood, filth, and guilt, Oh was driven almost mad with hatred.

Bang! Bang! Bang! Oh Seong-ryun fired three shots in a row.

Turning around, he asked Kim, "What happened? Did I hit him? Hurry... hurry... Throw the bomb! Hurry!"

Kim lobbed the bomb with a *swish*.

"Whoa, look! A British sailor tossed it into the river before it could explode!" Oh shouted in a panic. "Hey! Contemptible British sailor! Why did you do that? Are you just a lackey for that running dog of Japanese imperialism?

"Why even bother asking? The British navy is the lackey of British imperialism, and just as imperialists join with other imperialists, imperialist lackeys form alliances with other imperialist lackeys!"

Shifting his focus, Oh then asked, "Comrade, tell me quickly, is Tanaka dead or not?"

"Dead, dead. He must be dead. You fired three shots, and they seem to have landed. Look! Isn't that him lying on the ground over there next to that beautiful Western lady?" Kim answered, pointing at the scene.

"Is he dead? Is he truly dead? Then we've succeeded! For the moment at least, we have avenged our homeland! Oh no, Comrade Kim! The police are coming, let's get out of here!"

As he spoke, Oh turned around to search for Yi so they could all make good their escape, but he had already disappeared. Oh ran towards Kim. "Where is Yi?" he asked, his face filled with resentment despite his panic.

"Him? Don't even mention him. I knew from the beginning that he was less than enthusiastic, and after you fired the gun, he immediately ran off," Kim replied.

"Contemptible! Cowardly! Disloyal, inconstant, false revolutionary! How could he have run away at the very moment the battle was about to begin! Very well, let us make haste and escape. Look! That youth in Western clothes who was standing next to that lady's corpse is charging this way. I'm afraid he's coming after us. Let's shoot at our pursuers... Hurry! Run! Hurry!"

"Go! Go! Go! Hurry! Hurry! Hurry!"
Bang! Bang! Bang!

5

Having shot three times, Oh Seong-ryun assumed Tanaka must have perished from the bullets. Little did he know that the person he had hit was not in fact Tanaka, but rather the daughter of American tycoon XX [sic], who had been on her way to Shanghai for her honeymoon. While in Tokyo, she and her young husband had heard that the XX [sic] ferry to Shanghai on X [sic] date of X [sic] month would be carrying Tanaka. Greedy no doubt for the additional comforts they assumed a ship carrying a person of Tanaka's status would provide, they decided to book the same one. Tanaka, who had somehow learned that the young woman was the daughter of an elite capitalist in America, welcomed the newlyweds.

The young couple had disembarked in step with one another, walking hand in hand and shoulder to shoulder. Tanaka had walked forth into the welcoming crowds as well, following close behind the young bride, as if intoxicated by her and determined to follow her to her quarters. Then unexpectedly, she crumpled to the ground. With a *Bang! Bang! Bang!*, a red-hot bullet passed through her body, turning it cold and grey, and whizzed by his own, grazing him. He immediately lowered himself to the ground and lay there without moving, pretending to be dead. He knew someone was trying to assassinate him. *The heavens favor me too much*, he thought. *No one can kill me.* Eventually picking himself up, he ordered his subordinates to capture the culprit, then made his way to the Japanese consulate with an armed escort to rest and recover.

By this time, Tanaka's soldiers and the police and the young husband were all chasing valiantly after Oh and Kim, who were fleeing as fast as they could. Seeing their pursuers close in on them, Oh again opened fire with a *Bang!*, and one of them crumpled to the ground. Whenever Oh caught sight of the enemy about to shoot, he would dodge and weave, the red-hot bullets falling impotently around him or, better yet, striking someone else. He continued to shoot behind him with a *Bang! Bang! Bang!* until, all told the dead and wounded numbered in the dozens. But at long last, having run into a dead-end alley in the French Concession, he stopped and allowed himself to be arrested with dignity. Afterwards, he was escorted away to the Shanghai Municipal Prison. There he was reunited with Kim Ik-sang, now a fellow captive. In the end, both brave, battle-worthy youths were captured and taken into public custody.

That evening, they spent the night in a state of shock! But believing that Tanaka had perished from their bullets, they felt proud and happy. For them, Tanaka's death was merely the first success in their mission to avenge their homeland and reinstitute Korean sovereignty. They imagined it to be the first step on a journey to recover the happiness of their former lives surrounded by the warmth and kindness of their families and beloved friends. They thought: *Even though we've been arrested—even if they execute us—we can find comfort in the fact that we have done our homeland and comrades proud. Once our national sovereignty has been restored, the whole country will unite to commemorate us.* Thinking this, their imprisonment did not weigh heavily upon them. *You bastard, Tanaka*, they thought to themselves. *You thought no one could dare to even pinch you, but now we've forced you to bid farewell to the world. What formidable foes we've proven ourselves to be!* Thinking such thoughts, a hint of a smile would appear on their faces.

The next day, Oh and Kim learned from their prison guard at the city jail that were to be transferred to the Japanese consulate. The guard, who was Vietnamese, recognized the unbearable grief and melancholy that had caused the two comrades, exiles without nations, to commit these spectacular crimes of revenge. He thought: *We Vietnamese have become the enemy's beasts of labor, their murder weapons. Next to men such as these, we should feel ashamed.* How could he be so weak-willed as to have become the servant of a mortal enemy? What could he do to achieve something akin to what these two imprisoned Korean patriots had accomplished? He began to feel depressed. The more he considered the two valiant, heroic patriots, the more he felt a sense of admiration mixed with envy and even tendrils of compassion. So he decided to speak to them: "Oh great Korean patriots, respectable and beloved youths! Your assassination of Tanaka was spectacular and honorable beyond compare! And yet..." The guard stood outside their jail cell, his face showing signs of genuine emotion.

"But what?" Oh and Kim asked together.

"But you are in great danger. The enemy you thought you assassinated is not dead."

"What? He's not dead?" Oh and Kim exclaimed, taken aback. After a moment, however, they insisted with great confidence that Tanaka had indeed been killed. They pressed the Vietnamese soldier for further information, suspecting that he was lying to them.

"It's true! He's not dead," the Vietnamese soldier said solemnly.

Oh and Kim continued to stare at him in silence, unconvinced.

Seeing that they were not going to believe him, the Vietnamese soldier found a copy of that day's newspaper and cut out an article. Its headline read "Tanaka Survives Assassination Attempt." Reading through the clipping, Oh and Kim realized that what the Vietnamese soldier had told them was the truth. Again, they were dumbfounded.

But just at that moment, the order to send the two criminals to the Japanese consulate arrived. "You must think of a way to escape!" the Vietnamese soldier whispered as he took them from their cell.

His words made Oh and Kim realize that they had completely misjudged their prison guard, who had taken such great pains to bring them the news he did. They wanted to thank him, but the prisoner escort was giving them evil looks and they were not permitted even a moment's delay.

6

The Japanese consulate in Shanghai is located on the banks of the Huangpu River, so its façade looks as if it's being cleansed day and night by the unending flow of the mighty Yangzi River. Designed and built in a western style, it is as modern and solid as any western building and stands just over fifty meters tall. Consulate officials live on two of its four floors, which are decorated in a trendy Japanese style that combines Chinese and Western curios in a particularly harmonious show of hybridity. The first and fourth floors of the building are, however, remarkably different in character. The first floor houses those willing to serve as slaves and beasts of burden for the Japanese. Needless to say, the furnishings there are considerably inferior to those on the second and third floors. The fourth floor is reserved for prisoners. It contains barely anything at all in the way of furnishings beyond some metal mesh that separates the space into a single large cell with another smaller cell within it. It was to this fourth-floor prison that Oh Seong-ryun and Kim Ik-sang were being transferred.

Ever since reading the newspaper article about Tanaka still being alive, Oh's and Kim's emotions had alternated between waves of disbelief and anguish and frustration at their own incompetence. Why had they been unable to kill this Japanese devil more vile than a beast? If only they'd been successful, anything, no matter what—even dying!—would have been worthwhile. *But somehow we couldn't finish him off! And now we're going to be taken to the Japanese consulate, where he is sure to humiliate us! Alas, alas! What useless creatures we are!*

A dozen fierce-looking soldiers had arrived to escort Oh Seong-ryun and Kim Ik-sang out of public custody and into a vehicle. Guards from the city jail kept the two under strict surveillance while they were being transported. Oh and Kim were still so preoccupied with regret about their incompetence that they were sartled to lift their heads and find that they had already arrived at the doors of the Japanese consulate. They had only a moment to process their surprise before being rushed inside by consular guards whose eyes were full of rage and whose mouths were full of filth. Looking upon these beast-like guards, the two wanted to tear them to pieces. But remembering how they had fumbled their chance and subsequently lost their freedom, they could manage only bitter smiles.

Oh Seong-ryun was promptly banished to the small cell on the fourth floor. Kim Ik-sang was for some reason judged to be a lesser criminal and thus imprisoned separately, a development that Oh felt like a stab to the heart.

Oh's small cell was located in a corner of a larger cell, surrounded by walls woven from metal mesh. One side had a window, revealing a leaden blue sky that was particularly beautiful in its neatness and unity. Three other prisoners in the outer cell greeted Oh with smiles as he stepped into his smaller inner cell, but he found himself unable to say even a word in reply.

The days went by in a blur for Oh, time passing like flowing water. Looking at the metal web of the prison walls and the bars that framed the window, Oh realized that his imprisonment was merely the first stop on a path that would end in death. From time to time, he would peer out the window to watch the waves of the Huangpu River as they rose and fell. Sometimes one wave would be smashed to pieces by another, which would then continue to flow on quietly, as if demonstrating the transience of human life. This filled him with sorrow. At other times, he would be filled with rage at the cruelty of humans: *Why do humans act like beasts and kill one another? Even me. Why did I take up a gun and kill those people?* Considering this question quietly for a moment, he answered his own question. *If these pernicious Japanese crooks had not occupied my homeland, what quarrel would I have with them? If that ruthless Tanaka had not ordered his minions to massacre my people, making homeless exiles out of youths such as us—youths with some degree of courage, youths unable to tolerate the idea of just sitting by and watching the destruction of our homeland, the slaughter of our people—how would I have ever been able to steel my heart to shoot him? And yet, if my homeland were powerful, not only would it be impervious to the bullying and humiliation of Japan, but the Japanese people, encouraged by our homeland's power, would want to collaborate with us. If only it were possible for Japan and Korea to be dubbed the two strong thumbs of Asia! Then I would never have viewed Japanese people as enemies, much less gone on to commit such a crazed and violent act!* Having considered all this, he finally and truly understood that this was a world in which humans killed humans and the strong killed the weak. He wanted to crumple it into a small ball and smash it to pieces on the ground, but he also knew that even this was a complete fantasy. The only way to create equality among the nations of the world would be to obliterate all those who were cruel and violent, people who liked to "kill for the fun of it." Only then could the world be safe and peaceful once more. So not only did he not regret attempting to assassinate Tanaka, he felt certain there was no other option. His only hope of recovering his homeland and getting revenge for his murdered compatriots was to continue in the same manner!

As he entertained such thoughts in his jail cell, his heart roiled constantly like boiling water. He was not in the least concerned about the likelihood of a death sentence. He thought instead of Tanaka: *After this incident, Tanaka must be plotting new, vengeful schemes to kill my compatriots.* He thought, too, of the prison guards who treated him and all the other prisoners as if they were tigers or wolves who might escape their cages, and of the three Japanese prisoners who had welcomed him with smiles when he first entered the prison cell. They were all members of a cruel nation. He would give anything to be able to strike down the prison gate and run out and kill them all—and then, if escape were impossible, to fire the gun at himself. Killing himself would be better than suffering the humiliation of execution at the hands of Japanese crooks! He entertained such thoughts from dawn to dusk, and again from dusk to dawn. Whenever he was not asleep, he nursed a rage against the three Japanese prisoners. At times he did so unconsciously, at other times deliberately, but always in secret. Sometimes he would unwittingly glance up at the Japanese prison guards, who were soldiers, and whom he hated even more. During this period, he felt that all Japanese people, regardless of age and gender, were evil, and that they were all born enemies of the Korean people. If he had been able to escape at this time, he would most certainly have shot any Japanese person on sight. Alone in his small jail cell, he felt exceptionally lonely. And this loneliness led to depression and sadness.

One of the three prisoners in the larger cell was named Katō, the second was Katō's brother-in-law, and the third was purportedly a carpenter.[2]

Katō had been accused of being an anarchist, and his brother-in-law

---

[2] *Katō*: This person's real name was Tamura Chūichi, and he was not an anarchist. The other two Japanese names are unknown. –DH

had also beenarrested and brought in by association. The carpenter, who had been arrested on suspicion of fraud, was most likely a selfish proletarian. As if in acknowledgement of their common fate, these three Japanese prisoners had expressed a certain respect towards Oh Seong-ryun ever since he'd arrived. It was a pity that none of them understood the Korean language and that Oh Seong-ryun didn't know any Japanese. But after more than ten days, Oh Seong-ryun found himself developing a sense of sympathy for their common plight, especially since they were all prisoners in a foreign land. He unconsciouslyallowed a more welcoming expression to appear on his face. When this happened, Katō answered with a friendly expression. He showed his respect for Oh by extending one upraised thumb as if to say, "You're really something!"

Seeing that he was being praised, Oh Seong-ryun couldn't help but feel his anger towards all Japanese—an anger that had inflamed his hatred of Katō—begin to subside. In this way, after more than a month of living side by side, the two began to get closer and closer.

One day, just before dusk, Oh Seong-ryun was running through a multitude of possible escape plots in his mind. He could see that all four walls of his small cell consisted of metal mesh and would thus be impossible to breach. In despair, his thoughts turned once again to suicide. *Wouldn't that at least be better than allowing those Japanese bastards to humiliate me?* he thought. He thrashed at the metal mesh wall to see if it would break, but not only was he entirely disappointed, his arm also began to ache with a sharp pain. He sank back into a glum stupor. As he hung his head, in no mood to think further or to even look through the window at the azure sky, a fragrant wind came into the cell, carrying with it the sound of a flute. This jolted him into a state of anxiety.

Where is that flute music coming from? Wondering this, he turned around in search of the music's source and heard a sound that was at once sharp and fine and bright and filled with warmth. It burrowed its way into the jail cell and into the ears of everyone there. Clever Oh Seong-ryun deduced that the flute player outside must have some connection with someone on the inside. Just as he was turning his attention to the three denizens of the large cell, the one whose appearance and manner stood out a bit from the rest replied "Hai!"[3]

The person who'd called out was Katō. Although Katō didn't understand the Korean language, he knew the trendy modern language of English, and because Oh Seong-ryun had also paid attention to such foreign trends, Katō was able to tell him in English: "The person outside playing the flute is my younger sister." He gestured towards the man standing next to him and said, "This is my sister's husband."

Hearing this, Oh Seong-ryun immediately stood up and approached the window to take a look outside. Who should appear but a young woman dressed in a kimono, wearing geta sandals on her feet and thick powder on her face. She smiled at him from the roof of the building across the street. Oh's mind, which had been clouded by depression for the past month, was transported into a state of freshness and ease by her winsome smile.

A burst of gobbledygook Japanese came out of Katō's mouth as he shouted over Oh's head. Then another even shriller burst of gibberish flew past Oh.

These sounds flew back and forth several times, reducing Oh Seong-ryun to silence. When he saw that the beautiful young woman had at last disappeared from her perch, he turned around to ask Katō what she had said. During the conversation that followed, Oh learned the crimes for which his fellow cellmates had been indicted, the heaviest of which had been committed by Katō, who had already been sentenced to a year in prison. Katō's brother-in-law had been sentenced to half a year, and the carpenter, who had been convicted of fraud, only had three months to serve before he would be released. After explaining this, Katō added: "The weather is too hot right now, and everyone is parched, so I have sent my sister to buy pears. When she comes back, we shall all have pears to eat."

Soon after, the flute sounded again, and they knew that the pears had arrived. When Oh Seong-ryun peeked out the window to take a look, he saw the young woman smiling back at him, holding pears wrapped in a handkerchief.

When the prisoners heard that the pears had arrived, they were all overjoyed. But they fell silent when they considered the difficulty of

---

[3] *Translator's Note:* "Hai" means "yes" in Japanese. Japanese katakana characters are used in the original to indicate a different language spoken.

A STRANGE WEAPON

bringing the pears up to their floor. Thinking of the fruit, they could only look at each other ruefully and salivate.

They pondered this problem for some time, pounding their heads with their fists, but were still unable to come up with a plan for getting the pears. It was Oh Seong-ryun who came up at last with a strategy for resolving the situation. He put his plan into motion by using his hands— handcuffed though they were—to slowly pull out one thread at a time from his woven sleeping mat. He then tied a chopstick to the resulting string and tossed it out the window so that the woman could tie the package of pears onto the chopstick, which he then tugged back. As anticipated, he was able to grab the pears, but the metal bars on the window made it impossible for him to pull the bundle through. Grabbing the string with one hand, he used three fingers from his other hand to bring the pears in one by one, passing each one down to the three hungry prisoners in the larger cell. At the very end of this process, he felt something wrapped in the handkerchief. Looking at it more closely, he was surprised and elated to find that it was a small knife. *With this small knife, I can kill a few hundred Japanese crooks, and even if I can't do that, at least I can take my own life to avoid being humiliated by them.* Worried that the three Japanese prisoners might discover that he had hidden something, he used his body to keep the knife out of the other prisoners' lines of sight, hiding it away carefully.

Thanks to Oh Seong-ryun's ingenuity, the pears had arrived safely. None of the three Japanese prisoners would have had any idea how to get those pears into the cell. They had been full of sympathy and respect for him beforehand, but they were now utterly impressed by his intelligence and generosity as well. All this shone from their smiling faces like spring flowers. Katō, who was the most taken with Oh Seong-ryun's intelligence, gave him the most pieces of pear to eat.

As Oh slowly ate, he was already beginning to plot how to make the best use of the small knife.

Day after day, he plotted in secret. He no longer felt his incarceration to be a source of suffering. *One of these days*, he thought, *I will overcome these inhospitable circumstances.* And so his stay in his cell was filled with anticipation.

7

By April, the heat of the sun in the southern regions was already beginning to press upon the senses. Those living in Shanghai were required to bathe at least once a day. This had become a general rule, and no exceptions were permitted. Thus the prisoners were also given a chance to bathe. By the grace of some God—for they could think of no one else to thank—they were brought every evening to purge their bodies of filth with blessed waters. This nightly routine was the one respite allowed them, and they accepted this baptism with piety.

But somehow God's love was only enough to appease the easily satisfied. After some time amongst the washed, the stubborn and incorrigible Oh Seong-ryun, who knew his sins to be unforgivable, turned his thoughts back to the practice of war.

One evening, Oh Seong-ryun feigned illness and said he was unable to take a bath. Noting his pale face and sickly demeanor, the unsuspecting prison guard took the three other prisoners without asking any further questions.

This is truly a God-given opportunity! thought Oh Seong-ryun as he watched the guards march the other prisoners down the stairs. Filled with determination, he sat up and began using the tip of the small knife to loosen the screws on his leg restraints, turning them bit by bit. A considerable amount of time passed before he found that he had loosened the screws enough that they could now be removed entirely. Beside himself with joy, he attempted the same procedure with his handcuffs and successfully dismantled those as well. Worried that the other prisoners might soon return, he quickly put his restraints back on. But when they didn't come back immediately, he became anxious that he wouldn't be able to free himself again, so he took the screws out once more to make sure he could do so with ease. His experiment complete, he was just putting his restraints back on again when he heard the sound of feet on the stairs. The bathers were returning.

He pretended to be quietly sleeping.

Now that he had the small knife and could open his shackles, his heart was much less troubled than before. He had the means with which to kill anyone who got in the way of his escape, and he was not about to let some Japanese crook send him to heaven. And if escape proved impossible, he had a firm, unshakable conviction that he would kill himself.

Still contemplating such thoughts, he saw that the pitch-black snake of night had already escaped, trailed closely by the shimmering red glow of dawn. He was reminded of his homeland and the quiet, beautiful gardens of his youth. Joy and melancholy clashed in his heart. He felt almost crazy with excitement, knowing that even this new day, which would soon rule over all the land in the fullness and glory of her power, could not hold out forever, and would eventually have to yield to the dusk. The darkness of night would come once more.

Soon enough it was time for everyone to go to their daily bath.

The moment had come for Oh to put the plan he'd been hatching over the course of a day and a night into action. He thought: *If I am to escape, the best time to do so will be in the dead of night, when everyone is likely to be resting. The prison guards will probably be tired and doze off, but the three Japanese prisoners sleep all day so they're liable to wake at the slightest noise. Dastardly Japanese crooks!* He began to think. If he could make something resembling a gun, he could threaten the Japanese prisoners and stop them from preventing his escape.

Having thought the problem through, he fashioned the handle of a gun out of a small comb that Katō had given him, used a chopstick as its barrel, and tied the whole thing together with a leather string from his pants. He even made use of foil from the inside of a cigarette box, wrapping the front of the chopstick with it. Once he was finished, he brandished the contraption under the soft moonlight; it was such a good likeness that from a distance it would be hard to tell it was a fake. He smiled.

Shortly thereafter, his fellow prisoners returned from their bath. The prison guards did a cursory check before succumbing to fatigue and going downstairs to sleep. Oh Seong-ryun saw that the gate to his small cell had not been locked. Taking advantage of this opportunity, he used his knife to undo the cuffs on his hands and feet and ran into the cell where the three Japanese prisoners were resting. With the knife in his left hand and the fake gun in his right, he began to threaten them.

"Hey!" The Japanese prisoners were scared speechless. They could see that Oh Seong-ryun was no longer in shackles. His weapons flashed in the moonlight.

Oh Seong-ryun spoke:

"You are all about to die! Our Righteous Group of Korea has sent several hundred people to surround this consulate. If they don't see me walking out, or if they hear a shot from my gun, they'll set fire to the building and use bombs to destroy it." These words were meant to scare the three Japanese prisoners into letting him go.

"Oh no!" The carpenter cried out, panicked. "I was only sentenced to three months. My time is almost up. W-w-what am I supposed to do now?"

Filled with despair, Katō's brother-in-law also cried out: "If this is true, we're all done for, aren't we? Only yesterday your sister was telling me that I'm also going to be released sometime soon since I only have a six-month sentence. What will happen to me now?"

Katō experienced a wave of fear at the sight of the weapons in Oh Seong-ryun's hands. Rememberinghow his sister had told him that he, too, only had a one-year sentence made him even more distraught. He urged Oh to hurry up and escape.

Oh Seong-ryun was of course overjoyed to hear him say this. He replied, "In order for me to escape," he replied, "I'll need to destroy the metal bars on this window. But how am I going to do that?"

The carpenter came up with a plan. He suggested using water to wet the wooden frame around the window's metal grid and then carving it out using the knife. This was something that could be done very quietly. "Once the wooden frame is taken out, you'll be able to escape," the carpenter said.

The group agreed to this plan and exhorted Oh to proceed. However, after an hour of trying to dig out the window, there was still no sign of progress. Getting a little anxious, Oh Seong-ryun said, "It might be easier if we just force the door open."

So the three Japanese prisoners gathered together and heaved their bodies at the cell door—and in the blink of an eye, it was wide open. Fresh air flooded in, completely transforming the atmosphere.

Everyone was overjoyed. The only problem was that now the three Japanese prisoners wanted to escape with Oh.

But Oh was worried that a larger party would hold back his progress, so he only allowed Katō to join him.

Oh Seong-ryun suddenly realized that the officials at the Japanese consulate were likely to increase the sentences of the other prisoners for not having reported any suspicious activities. So, taking the string he had previously used to procure the pears along with some metal wires he had managed to dig out of the mesh walls, he tied the two remaining prisoners to the door of the cell. Then he stuck bundles of rags, paper, and handkerchiefs into their mouths to make it clear that there was no way the prisoners could have reported the escape.

After making these arrangements, Oh and Katō made their way furtively down from the fourth floor to the ground floor exit and climbed over the side of the wall outside. The patrol guards didn't notice a thing.

8

After After their escape, Oh Seong-ryun and Katō went their separate ways. Oh hurriedly hired a pedicab and sped to the area of the French Concession where Korean people lived. When he arrived, he got off and knocked on the gate. After a long while, someone came out at last and asked fearfully, "Who is it?"

Oh Seong-ryun gave his name and asked to be let in quickly, but the doorkeeper was unwilling to open the gate. As far as he knew, the real Oh Seong-ryun was still being held at the Japanese consulate, from which escape was impossible.

The two went back and forth like this for some time. By now, everyone inside the compound had woken up and was listening fearfully from under their blankets. At last they decided that the voice they heard was truly that of Oh Seong-ryun, and finally opened the gate.

As he stepped inside, Oh firmly gripped each of his friends' hands in turn, then began telling them about his capture in the wake of the failed assassination attempt on Tanaka, and about his vision for the future now that he'd managed to escape—a future that would be grand and glorious! His friends brought him tea and treats and raised their cups in celebration!

But just then, bad news came knocking.

It seemed Katō had gone directly to his sister's home after splitting ways with Oh. Realizing that her husband had not escaped with him, his sister had gone immediately to the Japanese consulate to report the jailbreak. Troops had quickly been sent, and a house-to-house search for the escaped prisoner was already underway in the Korean area of the French Concession.

Oh Seong-ryun was in the midst of a deep conversation when he heard that Japanese soldiers had surrounded their housing compound. He ran to an underground bunker to hide, and didn't emerge again until after the soldiers had moved on.

Getting his bearings again, Oh realized that he would never be safe as long as he stayed in Shanghai. So, shaving off all of his hair, he disguised himself as a civilian and hopped onto a Western ship bound for Germany. When it departed at first light, Oh became a refugee.

The following morning, Oh Seong-ryun's photograph was prominently featured in all the various newspapers of Shanghai, along with offers of a handsome reward for anyone who either captured him or had information about his whereabouts. Also included in the exposé about his escape was an account of the strange weapon he had left behind in his jail cell, the description of which was befuddling for the average reader. No one could make heads or tails of it.

Around this same time, it was reported that Oh's comrade Kim Iksang was deported to Tokyo, where he was given a life sentence.

As for Oh, he stayed in Germany for only a short while. Eager to strike down and wreak vengeance on those occupying his homeland, he decided that remaining in Germany would not be conducive to his goals. He moved on quickly instead to the center of world revolution, going to Moscow to learn tactics and theory.

By 1926, the Chinese revolutionary movement was expanding with unusual vigor. As an exiled youth hell-bent on changing the world, Oh began to chafe at playing it safe and wanted to join the fight. Both the Chinese and the Korean liberation movements sought to take aim at imperialism as part of a worldwide revolution. As long as that was what he was working towards, it didn't matter what country he was in. After all, national boundaries were merely constructs of feudal organizations and thus to be obliterated at any costs. The only difference that really mattered in the coming conflict would be the one between the oppressors and the oppressed.

When Oh had first set out to join the revolutionary movement, he had been absolutely dead set against Japanese imperialism and had categorized all Japanese people, including members of its lower classes, as mortal enemies. Now, however, he was ashamed of having had such a childish and crude understanding of things. His mission had become to awaken the oppressed peoples and classes of the world so that, united in solidarity, they could begin to attack the imperialists and the oppressor classes. Only then could all imperialists be vanquished and all oppressor classes obliterated! Only then would it be possible for the oppressed peoples and classes of the world to raise their bowed heads and rise to construct a new society of freedom and equality! Thinking thus, he felt a great swell of passion rise in his breast. This ultimately propelled him to China, where he became active in the revolutionary movement. He even eventually returned to Shanghai, where he continued to carry out the work of the revolution while hiding out in the small building where he had once lived.

But word of his presence somehow slipped out, and soon after his return to Shanghai, Japanese soldiers surrounded his residence. Luckily, he was out at the time, but when he heard about the incident, he left Shanghai once more and returned to his homeland where he continues to foment revolution.[4]

— March 8, 1930
To the East of Jingshan [Park]
in the Abandoned Capital City [Beijing]

TRANSLATED BY EVELYN SHIH

---

[4] *continues to foment revolution*: Oh Seong-ryun actually went to Manchuria in 1929, where he organized Korean communists and encouraged them to join the CCP. –DH

MOURNING COMRADE HAN HAE

KIM SAN

This English translation is based on a Korean translation by Professor Cui Longshui (Choe Yongsu), who provided his Korean translation of Kim San's original poem in Chinese to the *Yanbian Daily* (Yanbian ribao) on May 6, 2005, along with a photograph of Kim's handwritten poem. Professor Cui had offered his partial translation of it to the South Korean *Sisa Journal* magazine (joint issue of 205-206) in 1993, and this first translation was quite different from his later one in the *Yanbian Daily*. Since Kim's handwritten poem is unreadable on the picture, I have been unable to verify which of his translations is close to the original. For more on Han Hae, see note on p. 238 or Biographical Notes. –DH

1.
Oh! Fallen one, fallen one!
You who have become a stiffened corpse.
He gave up this dark world.
In suffering that pierced body and soul,
Ending his last war in bloodshed.
In a cold prison penetrated by resentment,
The long days spent in utter sleeplessness.
The world where bloody beasts roam
Mercilessly trampled one delicate life.

2.
Oh! Fallen one, fallen one!
You who have closed your eyes forever.
Truthless reality has
Forced you to take to the road of rebellion,
And reasonless reality has
Forced you to hold the flag of resistance.
Because you could not simply watch society's vampires
You raised revolution's red flag high.
Oh fallen one, society's rebel!
So this is how you fall to your bitter end!

3.
Oh! Fallen one, fallen one!
You of the stolen life!

Profound grief fills
Your sallow, bloodless face
And within your body of emaciated joints
Your violated soul lies.
See!
The loose, serpentine rope at the gallows –
That was this dark society's punishment.
The rope that once wound around his frail body
Is still wrapped around his cold corpse.

   4.
Oh! Fallen one, fallen one!
A traitor, they say, "a sinner even in death."
Up to the last drop, my blood boils.
I cannot even shed tears
Of pain in remembrance of him,
Since tears are the weak man's excuse.
Although you were delivered from your endless suffering,
Your countless brothers and companions still
Roam within the depths of oppression.

   5.
Oh! Fallen one, fallen one!
My heart that sees you aches.
Piercing rage blazes like a flame.
Death is not fearful to the oppressed.
However, fallen one!
Seven months you spent in Pyongyang Prison under false charges —
Your unyielding image is vivid before my eyes.
Oh! Your stiffened corpse on the second page of the *Joseon Ilbo* —
Who would have known one photo would sadden me so.

   6.
Oh! Fallen one, fallen one!
I respect you.
I adore you.
Death by strangulation, how could it be you were murdered so…

Is this the true fate of a revolutionary?
Since olden times, just how many revolutionaries
Lost their lives in this endless struggle?
The five thousand wretchedly fallen French warriors of the Paris Commune!
The countless sacrificed Russian warriors of the October Revolution!
The Chinese warriors who fearlessly fought in the Guangzhou Uprising!

7.
Oh! This is my last farewell, fallen one!
You disappeared like the morning dew.
I sadly look about my surroundings.
The enemy's venomous eyes are glinting.
Oh! Fallen one,
Perhaps today or tomorrow morning,
I will, as you did, disappear into dust.
I will forever hold your hand.
Even if we were both to be buried in the wilderness,
Many brothers and friends will follow us.

8.
Oh! Fallen one, fallen one!
This is the eternal farewell, the eternal farewell.
In the single photograph the deliveryman sent me,
I feel your disappearance.
Take care, our Han Hae.
Rest in peace, our Han Hae.
What we wish for is tomorrow.
Listen quietly to my pulse.
I will see you off with the resounding Internationale.
I will see you off with the resounding Internationale.

TRANSLATED BY HAYUN CHO

APPENDIX III

Foreword to the Second Edition (Ramparts Press)
by Nym Wales

First National Congress of the Workers and Peasants Red Army for Political Works in 1934

FOREWORD TO THE SECOND EDITION

NYM WALES

Helen Foster Snow (Nym Wales) prior to going to China.

In 1934 my husband Edgar Snow and I moved from Beijing to the village of Haidian about five miles away near the American-supported Yenching University. We had been studying Chinese and this was an enclave where the best court Mandarin of the Manchu monarchy was still spoken (though why we wanted to learn court Mandarin rather escapes me now). As part of learning Chinese and about China, Ed was editing translations of Chinese stories for his collection *Living China* (New York: The John Day Company, 1936), and I was doing an essay for it on "The Modern Chinese Literary Movement."

Ed was asked to teach in the Department of Journalism and I took courses there in almost all classes held in English. I even took one Chinese class in Hegel (my text was in English, of course) with the famous Zhang Dongsun, who may still be with the Beijing [Communist] government. I studied Buddhism, Daoism, and Confucianism with Xu Dishan, one of the chief scholars of China. I rode my bicycle in zero-degree weather to Tsinghua University for a class in the history of Chinese philosophy under Feng Youlan. I had a special class in Chinese aesthetics, and also studied Chinese economics and the history of Western philosophy. There were about eight Westerners studying at Yenching University then; one of my fellow students, Derk Bodde, later became known as the chief American scholar on China and taught at the University of Pennsylvania.

While we were living at Haidian, Pearl Buck and Richard Walsh came to spend the day with us (they were married a short time later) and we became friends. Pearl Buck had beautiful green eyes and a straight mouth cut like a gash in her expressive face. She also had a lovely speaking voice and an attractive personality.

From this time, I wrote articles regularly for *Asia* magazine, of which Walsh was editor. (Once I took up nearly one whole issue.) I used the pen name "Nym Wales" (invented by Edgar Snow—"Nym" means "name" in Greek and "Wales" because I am part Welsh). This was necessary to protect my sources. The Yenching students put my poem "Old Beijing"[5] on the bulletin board, not knowing at first that I was the author. It expressed exactly what we all felt—the living death, the suffocation, the dead calm before the storm, the December 9th mystique.[6]

We decided to move back to Beijing and rented half of a haunted house at No. 13 Kuijiachang, where in 1936-37 Edgar Snow wrote *Red Star Over China* in his separate office near the gatekeeper's house.

The students followed on visits, desolate, despairing, lost. The house at No. 13 became the nursery of the December 9th student movement, which broke the "white terror."

The end of 1935 was the peak of fascism in China. The communist apparatus in the "white" areas had been destroyed; nearly everyone in Beijing had been imprisoned or executed, or had joined the fascists for self-preservation. Demonstrations were illegal and students could expect to be executed just for starting one (though fortunately this did not occur); Japan was poised to take over North China, including Beijing, and anti-Japanese activity was illegal. But because the missionaries controlled Yenching University, and because Tsinghua University was also somewhat Westernized (it was a Boxer Indemnity school[7] originally, with American funds), the students there could count on some foreign protection.

And so the December 9th student movement was born. It started the mass of Chinese intellectuals on the path to the left; even the fascists began moving left. It spread like wildfire all over China and marked the first resistance to Japan by demanding an end to the civil war and a united front against Japan. It was a

---

[5] *my poem "Old Beijing"*: Originally published December 1935 in *Asia* magazine; later in Alan F. Pater, *Anthology of Magazine Verse and Year Book of American Poetry* (New York: Poetry Digest Association, 1936). —NW

[6] *December 9th*: On December 9, 1935, a mass protest took place in Beijing led by students who demanded that the National Government under Chiang Kai-shek halt it's appeasement of Japanese military aggression and initiate a united nationwide resistance against the aggressor. This is known as the December 9th Movement. —DH

[7] *Boxer Indemnity School*: After the suppression of the Boxer Uprising (1899-1901), the Qing Dynasty agreed to pay indemnity to eight foreign countries with whom it had been allied, including the U.S. The U.S. government used their indemnity to promote education in China, leading to, among other things, the establishment of Tsinghua University. —DH

landmark in modern Chinese history.

The December 9th movement was begun by three students from Yenching University: Zhang Zhaolin, president of the student government (now dead, I have been told); Huang Hua (Wang Rumei), an economics major, who went to the Northwest with Edgar Snow as an interpreter in 1936 (and in 1972 became the first ambassador from the People's Republic of China to the United Nations); and Chen Hanbo, a journalism student and later one of the chief journalists in China as editor of the *Commercial Press*. Zhou Enlai's spokesperson, from 1938 to her death in 1970, was a December 9th heroine—Gong Peng, wife of Qiao Guanhua, chief of the Beijing delegation to the United Nations. Her sister, Gong Pusheng, former national student secretary of the YWCA, is still in the Ministry of Foreign Affairs—she was one of the three women leaders of December 9th; the others were Li Min (she is now in Beijing, Huang Hua told me), and Zhang Shuyi, national industrial secretary of the YWCA in China for many years, who married Y.Y. Xu in New York.[1]

Thus it is the Yenching-Tsinghua students whom we knew in the 1930s as dear friends who are now trying to create a rapprochement between China and the United States, as part of the Zhou Enlai influence. These anti-fascist students risked their lives in 1935 to break the "white terror," and this was only possible because of foreign protection. It was part of this same December 9th mystique that got Edgar Snow the consent of Mao Zedong for President Nixon's visit.[2]

This brings me to the thought of Kim San. Though of course I didn't know it then, he was not only in and near Beijing but even hiding in Haidian about the time we were there. He had taken Chinese citizenship and was secretary of the Chinese Communist Party in Beijing during the worst of the "white terror," and though he survived physically,

---

[1] Just as I write this, the post brings my article on Li Min (her brief autobiography) entitled "Beriittelsen om Li Min," in *Rapport Fran Sida*, Jan.–Feb. 1972, Stockholm, p. 18. –NW

[2] I have just been watching the television reports of President Nixon's visit to Beijing, where his interpreter is Nancy Tang, who had been with her father Tang Mingzhao on the delegation to the United Nations. Nancy's mother, Constance Chang, was the star attraction at the December 9th demonstrations for foreign newsmen. When I introduced Constance to them as the daughter of a California lettuce grower (her family still lives in Los Angeles), their delight knew no bounds. In fact, J. B. Powell, editor of *The China Weekly Review*, allowed me as much space as I needed as their Beijing correspondent partly because Constance was a Californian. –NW

the party apparatus was completely destroyed. By the end of 1935, it is possible that no communist in Beijing existed with connections with the party, though a very few individuals may have been out of prison. The left-wing artists we knew went into hiding or escaped to Europe.

It was a dark time. Hitler and Mussolini were rising in power. Chiang Kai-shek had Nazi advisers in his fight against the communists. Japan was about to take over North China. It was a time when human nature showed its heights and its lowest depths.

One of those who showed the triumph of human nature at its best was the communist Huang Jing (his real name was Yu Qiwei), whom Huang Hua brought to call at No. 13 soon after the December 9th demonstration. He became the mentor and brains of the students after he arrived, though he was only about twenty-three. In Shandong he had been saved from execution in prison only by the intervention of his uncle, Yu Dawei, a close friend of Chiang Kai-shek and high in Chiang's army (Huang Jing belonged to the famous family of Marquis Zeng Guofan). His enduring role in history was as the mentor of the young actress Jiang Qing, whom he converted to the communist movement in Shandong. He escorted her to Yan'an in 1938, where she married Mao Zedong. In 1966 she became the most powerful woman in modem Chinese history. Huang Jing himself went on to become chief of the Ministry of Heavy Industry in Beijing until his death in the 1950s from the stress of his youth as an underground revolutionary.

It was early in 1937. Our friend Huang Jing, whom we called David, came with some news. A [Chinese] Communist Party congress was to be held in Yan'an on May 1st at which army and political people would be present, which had never before happened in any one gathering.

At this time I was at the peak of my literary career and had no wish to give it up. Earlier that year, J. S. Kennard, a missionary, had come to call. He had $1,000 for "a journal of applied Christian ethics," and he offered it to us if we would start such a journal to influence the students. I agreed to do the work. Ed agreed to serialize his book in each issue and to use some of his photographs. We named the magazine *Democracy*: it was to be a free press, a forum. We formed an editorial board, chiefly of Yenching professors, including Zhang Dongsun. Also, our agent, Henriette Herz (a real partner in our work), said she wanted to get a book of my verse published. I was asked by The Nation to be their China correspondent. I had collected material for histories of the student movement, of modern art and literature in China, etc. Life was important to me and I had not the least wish to risk it or my health in any way.

But David's news was vital. Such an opportunity might never come again. I had intended to go to Baoan when Ed sent for me to join him in the Northwest in 1936, but I could not get through the lines and was forced to turn back from Xi'an. Now the news of the party congress made the trip urgent.

When Ed had returned from the Northwest in 1936, two armies and their regional governments had not arrived there on the Long March as yet. These were the Second Front and Fourth Front armies of Zhu De, He Long, Xiao Ke, Xu Xiangqian, etc. My trip to Yan'an was necessary to collect historical information on the people my husband had missed, though he had written down half a dozen autobiographies, including that of Mao Zedong. When he was in Baoan, only the First Front Army under Mao had arrived on the Long March. The others ended their Long Marches a year later, meeting in the Northwest in October 1936, just after Ed left the Red areas; Yan'an was captured in December. So I felt I had to go to Yan'an; and because I did—because I managed to be in the right place at the right time—I got my scoops: thirty-four life stories.[3]

It is hard to explain why I felt such a categorical imperative to make the dangerous trip to Yan'an at any cost; it was a sense of history and of necessity. I had the same imperative about getting the December 9th student movement initiated in 1935, and later, in 1938, about starting the "Gung Ho ["Gonghe" in pinyin Romanization of Mandarin] Chinese Industrial Cooperatives—I knew it was right. These ideas had a life of their own, apart from my own volition and against my sense of self-preservation (which was rapidly disappearing in China). It was like being drawn into a powerful vacuum. I was a pilgrim in search of facts and in search of truth—the truth of history.

This trip was a turning point in my life. Never after that was I able to do "my own work," to be literary and do the GAN (Great American Novel), which had been my original aim. I became a writer of other men's

---

[3] Unfortunately, we both missed He Long, who is now in exile in Moscow. –NW [Nym Wales was obviously misinformed when she wrote this in 1972 for the Ramparts Press edition of this book. He Long actually died in 1969. –DH]

deeds, a doer of other men's good, a general factotum do-gooder.

David helped arrange my trip and went on the train with me to Xi'an, though we pretended not to know each other. He was the communist delegate from North China to the congress. In Xi'an, Chen Hanbo called on me (he and Zhang Zhaolin, our old friends from December 9th days, had gone to Xi'an in 1936 to stir up the Xi'an Incident in which Chiang Kai-shek was captured).

I was hiding in the rain among sacks of millet in a storehouse when Chen Hanbo came early in the morning, planning to help me escape to Yan'an. A few minutes later the chief of police arrived (having searched for me all night) and put me under the surveillance of seven spies and bodyguards, in relays. Chen had to escape to Yan'an secretly. I had nowhere to turn to get help to make the trip to Yan'an. A recent military order had been issued by Chiang Kai-shek's government in Nanjing forbidding any journalists to go to the Red areas. I was under extraterritoriality (that is, American law, not Chinese), but even so a military order was supposed to be obeyed.

The worst problem was that the name Snow was anathema in Xi'an. Ed had made his trip secretly to the Red areas in 1936 and published interviews which infuriated the Chiang Kai-shek government. I also had to pay retribution for my own trip to Xi'an the year before (1936), when I managed to get the biggest newspaper scoop of my career: Zhang Zhaolin, who had been escorting me around Xi'an, took me to interview Young Marshal Zhang Xueliang, who declared publicly that he was for stopping the civil war and cooperating with the Red armies against Japan. As he was the No. 2 Nationalist commander under Chiang Kai-shek, my story, published in the *London Daily Herald* (I was handling Ed's correspondence with them in his absence), rocked the chancelleries around the world—and in China almost caused a premature "Xi'an Incident" (the incident itself occurred only two months later). Because I was well known in Xi'an as a journalist my own right, as well as being married to Edgar Snow, I was doubly persona non grata.

On my second trip, in 1937, the friendly armies of the Young Marshal (who was now imprisoned) had been transferred out of Xi'an, and the fascist authority of Chiang Kai-shek was coming back, revengeful for loss of face—the result of our stories the previous year. I was told that Ed's life would be in danger if he should show up in Xi'an again. All this left me frightened, but even more resolute.

I would never have escaped from Xi'an at all had it not been for the help of two young men; they disapproved of my project but believed in making use of extraterritoriality. One was Effie Hill, son of a Swedish missionary, and a mechanic. He got a general's car so I could pass through military lines. The other was Kempton Fitch, whose father, George, was head of the national YMCA (Kempton is still in Asia, working for the U.S. government); I kept his name secret for many years as he was not proud of the incident. He escorted me to Sanyuan and made sure I was safely on my way. Except for them, I could not even have attempted the trip. My own contribution was to climb out of the back window of the Xi'an Guest House during martial law and evade my guards. The confiscation of my films and notebooks was likely on my return.

I spent four months in Yan'an. Mao Zedong and General Zhu De paid a formal call of welcome on me[4] as soon as I arrived (one of the few Mao ever made).

I sent a long list of questions to Mao Zedong and he was interested in answering them. I talked with him several times. He agreed to give me enough material for a booklet on the nature and history of revolution in China. We had the first interview for this booklet on July 7; unfortunately, that was the day of the incident at the Marco Polo Bridge and

Nym Wales with Red Army officers

---

[4] *paid a formal call of welcome on me*: So did nearly all of the top communist leaders, sometimes introduced by General Zhu. In fact, during the few days they were in Yan'an three of the legendary generals made a point of stopping by almost every day just to call on me—Gen. Xu Haidong (still with the Beijing government, as far as I know), and Gen. Luo Binghui and Gen. Xiao Ke, both of whom are dead. This was far beyond the call of diplomatic duty and it was a real people-to-people thing, because these generals were folk heroes who had scarcely even talked with foreigners before. –NW

the beginning of war with Japan, so he was unable to continue. He turned me over to Luo Fu [Zhang Wentian] and Wu Liangping.

I was received as "the wife of the American correspondent" and welcomed as one of a team. General Zhu De and his wife, Kang Keqing, especially went out of their way to make me feel at home. Both of them commended me by saying, "You are very brave," though this was never any news item in Yan'an usually; it was taken for granted.

Why was I made so welcome, and why was I told so many life stories? Mao Zedong was the key to everything. He not only admired Edgar Snow for breaking the nine-year news blockade but took a personal liking to him. Mao set the precedent. Once he opened up to Edgar Snow, the others followed. But for him, none of them would have told their autobiographies; it was not etiquette then and it is not now. But Mao Zedong received me well immediately because of his approval of Edgar Snow.

In September, Edgar Snow and Jim Bertram[5] arrived in Xi'an in search of me—four hours after I had left the city on my way home from Yan'an. Japan had attacked July 7, and I had been marooned in the interior. At the sinister military post of Dongguan, I was pulled off the train by gendarmes without explanation (my most terrifying moment of all, as I feared being tortured for information or disappearing without a trace). A telephone call to Xi'an revealed the Snow-Bertram search party, and I backtracked. The troop train I had been on with a special pass was bombed, destroying the engine and some coaches.

Jim went on the communist front to collect material for his book *Unconquered* (New York: The John Day Company, 1939). Ed escorted me as far as Qingdao, where we spent a few days together on the beach. Then he went to Shanghai to cover the war with Japan, while I returned to Beijing to close down the house.

---

[5] *Jim Bertram:* James Bertram was an Oxford Rhodes scholar from New Zealand who arrived in Beijing at the end of 1935 (after the December 9th demonstration). He became our best friend immediately. We all did the same things. He helped the students, made a dangerous trip to Xi'an alone just after the Incident occurred, wrote a book about the Red areas. He helped Madame Sun Yat-sen with her China Defense League in Hong Kong, where he was captured by the Japanese while defending the city. His book about his experiences as a Japanese prisoner of war, *Beneath the Shadow* (New York: The John Day Company, 1947), is another *Bridge Over the River Kwai*. He has published half a dozen books and is now professor of English literature in New Zealand. –NW

I had been gone six months. As soon as I returned to Beijing, I had to go to the German Hospital for its special treatment for dysentery (which included a large photograph of Hitler on the wall)—I had collected five kinds, including amoebic, and had lost over twenty pounds. Just the same I was smiling like the canary that swallowed the cat—the same expression Ed had on his face when he returned from the Northwest in 1936.

During my four months in Yan'an, I collected material for three books, all now being reprinted—*Inside Red China* (New York: Doubleday-Doran, 1939); *Song of Ariran* (New York: The John Day Company, 1941); and *Red Dust* (Stanford: Stanford University Press, 1952), of which an enlarged edition was published in 1972 under the title *The Chinese Communists: Sketches and Autobiographies of the Old Guard* (Westport, CT: Greenwood Press). I also collected material for a mimeographed volume, *My Yenan [Yan'an] Notebooks*, as well as parts of *The Chinese Labor Movement and Women in Modern China*. (I still have other unpublished material on my experiences in Yan'an and the people I talked with.)

I never expected to live long enough to become a museum piece. But in 1958–61 I compiled the Nym Wales Collection for the Hoover Institution at Stanford University. Then in 1972 the Costume Institute at the Metropolitan Museum in New York took for permanent use (available for copying) my "Yan'an sandals" and the blue cotton student gown I had tailored in Beijing and which I wore in Xi'an. The string (macramé) sandals, worn only in North Shaanxi, were made for me in Yan'an by a native Red soldier. I also gave the Metropolitan two bamboo workman's vests worn under the long-sleeved jackets for "air-conditioning."

Few things were brought on the Long March. I have two of the principal treasures—a thin black mirror from Germany and a dagger captured with the highest Guomindang officer ever taken in the South. The dagger was given to the German Comintern adivser, Li De (Otto Braun), as an honor. He gave it with his mirror to me in farewell—and to make up for not having been friendly all summer. (In the 1960s he was still attacking Mao Zedong from East Germany.) I also have a ring made of a Lama bead with a white band around it. General Luo Binghui, whom I knew in Yan'an, gave me the ring as one of his treasures, saying it was good luck: you would never fall off a horse while wearing it. He told me it had been given to him by a Lama during the Long March. (When I told this to Mao, he laughed and said, "I hope it was given to him" meaning it might have been confiscated.) Another memento from Yan'an is my pair of the original "Mao pants," the first ever made for a foreigner. Mao Zedong had a new uniform made in May when I was in Yan'an and I thought it would be fun to have a pair made by the same tailor out of the same piece of slate-grey cloth. I also still have my old indigo-dyed "Gung Ho" workman's jacket (all hand-sewn and worn as a beach coat for many years).

On February 15, 1972—the day of Edgar Snow's death at his home in Eysins, Switzerland—some of my three hundred Yan'an photographs were shown at the Metropolitan Museum as part of an exhibition of photographs of China from 1870 to the present. (The exhibition proved so successful it was held over for six months.)

Nym Wales photographed with CCP officer Peng Dehuai

These photographs and *My Yenan Notebooks* had a life of their own. My problem was how to avoid having them confiscated, either by the Chinese or Japanese during my trip back. In Yan'an I made a kind of lifebelt out of a man's undershirt, with compartments sewn in for the notebooks and rolls of film. This I wore around my waist under my coat at almost all strategic times. Wearing this I got into and out of Xi'an, into and out of Qingdao, into and out of Japanese occupied Tianjin and Beijing twice. Finally I went by coastal steamer to Shanghai, where I was met on the pier by Edgar Snow and J. B. Powell. The city was still burning from the Japanese attack, and I saw the victory parade.

Yes, black plague was endemic in Yan'an; my room had rats and fleas; typhus was not uncommon, and typhoid common. My bodyguard had active tuberculosis all summer (though I did not know it at the time). Every line of my Yan'an notebooks was written in my life's blood, every negative bathed in sweat and tears. But I was in league with history and I knew it—and I knew what had to be done to winnow out the grain from the chaff.

The death of Edgar Snow on February 15, 1972, is a landmark in the American experience in China. To the Chinese communists, he represented a kind of diplomatic liaison with the people of the United States. All during his career, Edgar Snow kept the watch on the Pacific, keeping Americans informed of what was happening, at any cost. We had a gung-ho marriage while it lasted, from 1932 to 1949 (and it was time for a change when we were divorced). The big things we did together (gung ho) were to spark the December 9th Student Movement and (with Rewi Alley) the Gung Ho Chinese Industrial Cooperatives[6] (which had spread all over China by 1958, when they were merged into communes). We separately, in 1936 and 1937, explored the then Soviet Republic of China and the Chinese communist mind, but it was a joint project, neither repeating what the other did.

My feeling now about Mao Zedong and Yan'an is one of nostalgic affection. I would not have made the dangerous trip had I not realized how important it was—and in retrospect it seems much more important than it did then. This was the Valley Forge of China and I was told the story of a revolution in the midst of it by the makers of the revolution.

But of all my experiences in China, none was more productive of knowledge and understanding than my talks with Kim San in Yan'an during those rainy days in 1937. Few persons were still alive even in 1937 who had gone through such an ordeal and survived the "white terror." Such a life story will never be told again.

—MADISON, CONNECTICUT
FEBRUARY 1972

---

[6] *Gung Ho Chinese Industrial Cooperatives*: As of 1972, these cooperative industries were still functioning in the communes to some extent in handicrafts. –NW

BIBLIOGRAPHY

BIBLIOGRAPHICAL ABBREVIATIONS USED IN NOTES

BDCC: Biographic Dictionary of Chinese Communism, 1921-1965, 2 vols.
BDRC: Biographical Dictionary of Republican China, 4 vols.
CIS: Chinil inmyeong sajeon (Biographical Dictionary of Pro-Japanese Koreans), 2 vols.
GCMR: Gendai chūka minkoku manshu teikoku jinmeikan (Contemporary Biographical Dictionary of the Republic of China and the Manchu Empire)
HHH: Hyeongmyeong gadeul ui hang-il hoesang: Kim Seongsuk, Jang Geonsang, Jeong Hwaam, Yi Ganghun ui dongnip tujaeng (Revolutionaries' Recollections of Anti-Japanese Struggles: Struggles for the Independence by Kim Seongsuk, Jang Geonsang, Jeong Hwaam, and Yi Ganghun)
HID: Han-guk inmul daesajeon (A Grand Biographical Dictionary of Korea), 2 vols.
HJS: Huangpu junxiao shiliao (Materials on the Huangpu Military Academy)
HSIS: Han-guk sahoejuui inmyeong sajeon (Biographical Dictionary of Korean Socialism)
ZGBZZ: Zhongguo gongchandang Beijingshi zuzhishi ziliao, 1921-1987 (Materials on the Organizational History of the Chinese Communist Party in the City of Beijing, 1921-1987)

Bibliography

Baek, Seon-gi (1993). *Miwan ui haebang norae – biun ui hyeongmyeongga Kim San ui saeng-ae wa Arirang* (The Song of Incomplete Liberation: The Life of Ill-Fated Revolutionary Kim San and Arirang). Seoul: Jeong-u sa.

_____ and Hong, Jeong-seon (1998). "Hanjang ui sajin gwa Kim San ui saeng-ae (One Photo and Kim San's Life), *Munhak gwa Sahoe* (Literature and Society) vol. 11, no. 4, 1515-1529.

Bak, Tae-won (1947). *Yaksan gwa Uiyeol-dan* (Kim Won-bong and the Uiyeol-dan). Seoul: Baekyangdang.

Boorman, Howard L. (1967). *Biographical Dictionary of Republican China* 4 vols. New York: Columbia University Press.

"Buhwal haneun han-guk ui Che Guevara 'Kim San'," ('Kim San,' a Resurrecting Korea's Che Guevara), *Ohmynews*.http://www.ohmynews.com/NWS_Web/view/at_pg.aspx?CNTN_CD=A0000270861. Accessed March 14, 2016.

Chang, Sei-yoon (2005). "Jungguk gongsandang gwangju bonggi wa hanin cheongnyeondeului hwaldong" (The Guangzhou Upring of the Chinese Communist Party and the Activities of Korean Youth). *Sarim* (The Historical Journal) no. 24, 215-245.

Chinil inmyeong sajeon pyeonchan wiwonhoe ed. (2009). *Chinil inmyeong sajeon* (Biographical Dictionary of Pro-Japanese Koreans) 3 vols. Seoul: Minjok munje yeon-guso.

Cui, Fengchun (1994). "Zhongshan daehak gwa 1920nyeondae joseonin ui hyeongmyeong undong" (Zhongshan University and the Revolutionary Movement of Koreans in the 1920s). *Sahak yeon-gu* (The Review of Korean History) no. 48, 113-126.

_____ (2015). "Yuanhun Zhang Zhiluo (Zhnag Zhiluo's Spirit). *Chaoxian hanguo lishi yanjiu* (Studies on the History of North Korea and South Korea) no.16 (August 2015), 350-368.

Cui, Longshui (2005). "Kim San (Jang Ji-rak) yeonbo" (Chronology of Kim San). *Hwanghae munhwa* (Yellow Sea Culture) winter issue, 338-351.

_____ and Jin, Dequan (1992). "Jiechude chaoxianzu gemingjia Zhang Zhile" (Zhang Zhile [Kim San]: An Outstanding Korean Revolutionary). *Fenghuo* (Beacon-fire). *Zhongguo chaoxian lishi zuji congshu* no.3, edited by Zhongguo chaoxian lishi zuji congshu bianwei, 202-

211. Beijing: Minzu chubanshe.

Cumings, Bruce (1997). *Korea's Place in the Sun: A Modern History*. New York: W. W. Norton.

Dirlik, Arif (1997). "Narrativizing Revolution: The Guangdong Uprising (11-13 December 1927) in Workers' Perspective". *Modern China* vol. 23, no. 4, 363-397.

_____, "Anarchism in East Asia." *Encyclopaedia Britannica*. http://www.britannica.com/topic/anarchism#toc224793. Accessed August 21, 2015.

Dong, Jianzhong, Zhang, Shouxian and Jin, Hengzhi (1986). "Li Tiefu" (Yi Cheolbu [Han Wi-geon]). In *Zhonggong dangshi renwuzhuan* (Biographies of the Persons in the History of the Chinese Communist Party), edited by Zhonggong dangshi renwu yanjiuhui, 168-195. Xi'an: Shaanxi renmin chubanshe.

Du, Junhui (1985). "Jin Kuiguang tongzhi canjia Guangzhou qiyi de wojian" (What I Saw about Comrade Kim Gyu-gwang's Participation in the Guangzhou Uprising). *Guangzhou qiyi ziliao* (Materials on the Guangzhou Uprising) vol. 2, edited by Guangdong geming lishi bowuguan,104-106. n.p.: Renmin chubanshe (Internal Publication).

Gaimushō jōhōbu ed. (1937). *Gendai chūka minkoku manshu teikoku jinmeikan* (Contemporary Biographical Dictionary of the Republic of China and the Manchu Empire). Tokyo: Tōa dōbun kai.

Gao, Kelin (1987). *Gao Kelin huiyilu* (Memoirs of Gao Kelin). Hohhot: Neimenggu renmin chubanshe.

Gordon, Andrew (2003). *A Modern History of Japan: From Tokugawa Times to the Present*. New York: Oxford University Press.

Graham, Robert ed. (2005). *Anarchism: A Documentary History of Libertarian Ideas* vol.1 (From Anarchy to Anarchism, 300 CE to 1939). Montreal: Black Rose Books.

Guangdong geming lishi bowuguan ed. (1982). *Huangpu junxiao shiliao* (Materials on the Huangpu Military Academy). Guangzhou: Guangdong renmin chubanshe.

Gwon, Rip (1986). "Kim San (1905-1938)." *Chaoxianzu geming lieshi zhuan* (Biographies of the Revolutionary Martyrs of Korean Ethnicity) vol. 2 (in Korean), edited by Bak Chang-uk, 24-66. Shenyang: Liaoning minzu chubanshe.

Han-guk jeongsin munhwa yeon-guwon ed. (1999). *Han-guk inmul daesajeon* (A Grand Biographical Dictionary of Korea) 2 vols. Seoul:

Jung-ang M&B.

He, Cheng (1985). "Dang a, Wo tingzhe ni huhuan – Guangzhou qiyi huiyi (jielu)" (The Party! I Heard Your Call - Memoirs of the Guangzhou Uprising (Excerpt). *Guangzhou qiyi ziliao* vol.2, edited by Guangdong geming lishi bowuguan, 116-120. Beijing: renmin chubanshe (Internal publication).

Hwang, Dongyoun (2016). *Anarchism in Korea: Independence, Transnationalism, and the Question of National Development, 1919-1984*. Albany, N.Y.: State University of New York Press.

Jeon, Myeong-hyeok. "Han Hae." *Encyclopedia of Korean Culture*. The Academy of Korean Studies. http://encykorea.aks.ac.kr/Contents/Index?contents_id=E0062056. Accessed August 10, 2016.

Jin, Mu (1990). "Yi dui 'Zuolian' kangli mengyuan de zhuangli yisheng" (A Splendid Life of a Married Member of the "Leftist League"). *"Zuolian" jinianji, 1930-1990* (A Volume to Commemorate the "Leftist League"), edited by Zhongguo zuoyi zuojian lianmeng chengli dahui huidi jinianguan and Shanghai Lu Xun jinianguan, 133-140. Shanghai: Baijia chubanshe.

Jo, Cheol-haeng (2002). "Kim San, Jasin ege seungri han hyeongmyeongga" (Kim San: A Revolutionary who Won Over Himself), *Naeil eul yeoneun yeoksa* (A History to Open Tomorrow) no. 10, 204-215

Jo, Gyu-tae (2008). "1920 nyeondae bukgyeong jiyeok hanin yuhaksaeng ui minjok undong" (The Nationalist Movement by the Korean Study-Abroad Students in Beijing in the 1920s). *Han-guk dongnip undongsa yeon-gu* (Journal of Korean Independence Movements Studies) no. 30, 201-255.

Kang, Man-gil and Seong, Dae-gyeong ed. (1996). *Han-guk sahoe juui inmyeong sajeon* (A Biographical Dictionary of the Korean Socialist Movement). Seoul: Changjak gwa bipyeong sa.

Kim, Chan-jeong (1990). (trans. by Yun Hae Dong). "Arirang yi deullyeo onda: hyeongmyeongga Kim San, geu uimun ui jugeum eul chajaseo" ('Arirang' is Being Heard: Revolutionary Kim San, A Quest for His Mysterious Death). *Yeoksa bipyeong* (Critical Review of History) no. 10, 140-166. [This is a Korean translation of Kim Chang-jeong's interviews in Beijing with scholars and Kim San's son, carried in *Mintō* (People Wave) Spring 1989.]

Kim, Changjeong (1989). "Ariran no uta to sono ato" (Song of Arirang and Afterwards). *Asahi shimbun* (Asahi Newspaper). Night edition (arch 14), second edition, 9.

Kim, Chang-sun and Kim, Jun-yeop (1986). *Han-guk gongsan juui undong-sa* (A History of the Korean Communist Movement) 5 vols. Seoul: Cheonggye yeon-guso, new edition.

Kim, Gwang-ji (1950). "Ariran no uta – Chōsen no ichi gakumeika no shōgai" (Song of Ariran – The Life of a Korean Revolutionary), *Tenbō* (An Outlook) no. 57, 64-71.

Kim, Hak-jun ed. (1988). *Hyeongmyeong gadeul ui hang-il hoesang: Kim Seongsuk, Jang Geonsang, Jeong Hwaam, Yi Ganghun ui dongnip tujaeng* (Revolutionaries' Recollections of Anti-Japanese Struggles: Struggles for the Independence by Kim Seong-suk, Jang Geon-sang, Jeong Hwa-am, and Yi Gang-hun). Interviewed by Lee Chong-sik. Seoul: Mineumsa.

Kim, San (1990). (trans. by Seo Eun-hye). "『*Arirang*』 ui juingong yi jikjeop sseun gimyohan mugi (A Stange Weapon written by the author of *Song of Ariran*)." *Wolgan Dari* (Monthly Bridge) January issue, 336-357

Kim, Yeong-beom (1997). *Han-guk geundae minjok undong gwa Uiyeol-dan* (Korea's Modern National Movement and the Uiyeol-dan). Seoul: Changjak gwa bipyeongsa.

Klein, Donald K. and Anne B. Clark (1971). *Biographic Dictionary of Chinese Communism, 1921-1965*, 2 vols. Cambridge, M.A.: The East Asia Research Center at Harvard University.

Lee, Chong-Sik (1978). *Korean Workers' Party: A Short History*. Stanford: Hoover Institution Press, Stanford University.

Lee, Ki-baik (1984). (trans. by Edward W. Wagner with Edward J. Schultz). *A New History of Korea*. Cambridge, M.A.: Harvard University Press for the Harvard-Yenching Institute.

Lee, Young Hee. (2005). "Arirang gwa na" (Arirang and I). *Arirang: Joseonin hyeongmyeongga Kim San ui bulkkot gateun sam* (Arirang: The Flame-like Life of a Korean Revolutionary Kim San), 6-14. Nym Wales and Kim San (trans. by Song Yeoung-in). Seoul: DongNyok, third edition.

Li, Zhengwen (1990). "Beiping zuolian" shiqide lilun douzheng" (Theoretical Struggles during the Period of "the Beijing Leftist Alliance"). "*Zuolian*" *jinianji, 1930-1990* (A Volume to Commemorate the "Leftist League"), edited by Zhongguo zuoyi zuojia lianmeng chengli dahui huidi jinianguan and Shanghai Lu Xun jinianguan, 160-166. Shanghai: Baijia chubanshe.

Luo, Qing (1987). "Yi wode sange chaoxain pengyou" (Remembering My Three Korean Friends). *Guannei diqu chaoxianren fanri duli yundong ziliao huipian* (Collection of the Materials on Anti-Japanese Independence Movement by Koreans in China Proper Area), edited by Yang Zhaoquan et al., 1352-1354. Shenyang: Liaoning renmin chubanshe.

Mizuno, Naoki (1995). "Yomigaeru 『Ariran no uta』 no shujinkō" (The Resurrecting Protagonist of *Song of Arirang*). *Tosho* (Books) no. 554, 34-37.

_____ (1992). "Tōhō hiappaku minzoku regōkai (1925–1927) ni tsuite" (On the United Society of the Eastern Oppressed Peoples, 1925–1927). *Chūkoku kokumin kakumei no kenkyū* (A Study of the National Revolution in China), edited by Hazama Naoki, 309–350. Kyōto: Kyōto daigakko jinbun kagaku kenkyūjo.

_____ (1990). "Kim San ui jakpum gwa saeng-ae: Joseon ui haebang eul hyang-han jeong-yeol" (Kim San's Novel and Life: Passion for Korea's Liberation). *Wolgan Dari* (Monthly Bridge) January issue, 358-365

Murata, Yōich ed. (1981). *Kominterun shiryōshū* (Collection of Materials on the Comintern) vol.4. Tokyo: Ōtsuki shoten.

Nie, Rongzhen (1983). *Nie Rongzhen huiyilu* (Memoirs of Nie Rongzhen) vol. 1. Beijing: Zhanshi chubanshe.

Sin, Jae-don (1946). "Yeokja ui mal" (Translator's Words). *Sin cheonji* (A New World) vol. 1, no. 9 (October), 268.

Sisa Journal [Current Issue Journal] (1993). "Minjok tonghap ui norae, Kim San ui 'Arirang'" (A Song that Integrates the Nation, Kim San's 'Arirang'). *Sisa Journal* (Current Issue Journal) joint issue 205-206 (September), 20-35.

"Sowi bukpyeong salin sageon eun mugeunhan jungsangjeok heoseol" (The so-called Beiping Murder Incident is a Groundless Defamatory Story). *Joseon ilbo* (Joseon Daily). November 6, 1929, 2.

Suh, Dae-suk (1967). *The Korean Communist Movement 1918-48*. Princeton: Princeton University Press.

Totten III, George O. (1966). *The Social Democratic Movement in Prewar Japan*. New Haven: Yale University Press.

Union Research Institute (1969). *Who's Who in Communist China*. Hong Kong: Union Research Institute, new edition.

Wales, Nym (1986). (trans. by Editorial office). *Arirang 2: Kim San ui saeng-ae mit han-guk e gwanhan bochung* (Arirang 2: A Supplementary to Kim San's Life and Korea). Seoul: Hakminsa. [This is a Korean translation of Nym Wales, "Notes on Korea and the Life of Kim San"]

_____ and Kim, San (2005). (trans. by Song Yeong-in). *Arirang: Joseonin hyeongmyeongga Kim San ui bulkkot gateun sam* (Arirang: The Flame-like Life of a Korean Revolutionary Kim San). Seoul: Dong-Nyok Publishing, third edition. [This is the Korean edition of Song of Ariran: A Korean Communist in the Chinese Revolution. San Francisco: Ramparts Press, 1972.]

Wēruzu, Nimu [Nym Wales] (1965). (trans. by Andō Jirō). *Ariran no uta – Chōsenjin gakumeika no shōgai* (Song of Ariran: The Life of a Korean Revolutionary). Tokyo: Misuzu shobō. [This is a Japanese translation of *Song of Ariran* by Andō Jirō.]

Wēruzu, Nimu [Nym Wales] and Kimu San [Kim San] (1987). (trans. by Matsudaira Ioko). *Ariran no uta – Aru chōsenjin gakumeika no shōgai* (Song of Ariran: the Life of a Korean Revolutionary). Tokyo: Iwanami shoten. [This is a Japanese translation of *Song of Ariran* by Matsudaira Ioko.]

Xie, Qiansheng (1988). "Hailufeng geming genjudi zhuyao lingdaoren jieshao" (Introduction to the Important Leaders of the Hailufeng Revolutionary Base). *Hailufeng geming genjudi yanjiu* (Studies on the Hailufeng Revolutionary Base), edited by Guangdongsheng sehuikexue xuehui lianhehui et al eds, 264-277. n.p.: Renmin chubanshe.

Ye, Zuoneng (1988). "Hailufeng geming genjudishi jige wenti de kaozheng" (Textual Research on Some Problems about the History of the Hailufeng Revolutionary Base). *Hailufeng geming genjudi yanjiu* (Studies on the Hailufeng Revolutionary Base), edited by Guangdongsheng sehuikexue xuehui lianhehui et al eds., 250-263. n.p.: Renmin chubanshe.

Yi, Won-gyu (2006). *Kim San pyeongjeon* (A Commentary Biography of Kim San). Seoul: Silchoen munhaksa.

Yi, Hoeseong and Mizuno Naoki (1991). 『*Ariran no uta*』 *oboe gaki: Kimu San to Nimu Wēruzu* (Notes on Song of Ariran: Kim San and Nym Wales). Tokyo: Iwanami shoten.

Yi, Hoeseong and Mizuno, Naoki ed. (1993). (trans. by Yun Hae Dong). *Arirang geu hu – Kim San gwa Nym Wales* (After Song of Ariran: Kim San and Nym Wales). Seoul: DongNyeok. [This is a Korean translation of Yi and Mizuno 1991.]

Yi, Myeong-yeong (1973). "Dongman ui pung-una Oh Seong-ryun" (Oh

Seong-ryun: A Man of Wind and Cloud). Wolgan Jung-ang (Monthly Jung-ang) no. 64 (July), 256-280.

Yim, Yeong-tae (1986). "'Arirang' ui deungjang inmul" (Characters in "Arirang"). *Yoeksa munje yeon-guso hoebo* (Newsletter of the Institute for the Research of Historical Problems) Inaugural issue, 10-12.

Young Korean Academy. https://www.yka.or.kr/html/eng/about.asp. Accessed August 12, 2016.

Yu, Ja-myeong (1999). *Yu Ja-myeong sugi: han hyeongmyeong ja ui hoeeok rok* (Yu Ja-myeong's Memoirs: A Revolutionary's Memoirs). Cheon-an: Dongnip gi-nyeom gwan han-guk dongnip undongsa yeon-guso.

Yun, Mu-han (2007). "Yeoksa sok euro saenghwan doen 'Arirang' ui Kim San, geu bulkkot ui sam" (Kim San in *Arirang*, Who Has Resurrected to History, His Sparkling Life). *Naeil eul yeoneun yeoksa* (A History to Open Tomorrow) no. 29 (September), 174-183

Zhang, Wenyuan (1988). "Tudi geming chuqi de dongjiang dangxiao" (The Dongjiang Party School in the Early Period of the Land Revolution). *Hailufeng geming gendiju yanjiu* (Studies on the Hailufeng Revolutionary Base), edited by Guangdongsheng shehui kexue xuehui lianhehui et al eds., 218-221. n.p.: Renmin chubanshe.

Zhonggong Beijing shiwei zuzhibu, Zhonggong beijingshiwei dangshi ziliao zhengji weiyuanhui, and Beijingshi dang'anju (1992).*Zhongguo gongchandang beijingshi zuzhishi ziliao, 1921-1987* (Materials on the Organizational History of the Chinese Communist Party in the City of Beijing). Beijing: Renmin chubanshe.

Index

──────── A

Ahn Byeong-chan, 99, 373
Ahn Chang-ho, 35, 94n, 100-104, 118, 119, 121, 125, 356n41, 358n60, 359nn64-65, 373, 401
Ahn Cheong, 179-181, 365n123
Ahn Dong-hui. *See* Ahn Dong-sik
Ahn Dong-sik (Ahn Dong-hui), 82, 85-87, 121, 357n48, 401
Ahn Ji-suk. *See* Ahn Mi-sam
Ahn Jung-geun, 46, 373
Ahn Mi-sam (Ahn Ji-suk, daughter of Ahn Dong-hui), 82, 85-87, 121, 357n48, 401
Ahn, Philip, 8
Anarchism, 77, 92, 100, 106, 127, 132, 376, 378, 390
Anarchist Federation, 109, 360n74
Anarchists, 28, 71, 73, 100, 106-110, 113, 115, 126, 128, 131-132, 150, 286, 304, 328, 329, 356n38, 360nn72-75, 362-363n101, 371n179, 376, 378, 390, 391, 401, 408. *See also* Black Youth League; Uiyeol-dan
Andong. *See* Dandong
Arirang (Hill of Arirang), 31-33

──────── B

Bai Xin, 209
Bak Eun-sik, 355n32
Bak Geun, 67, 69
Bak Geon-ung, 371n182, 408
Bak Geun-man, 144-146, 159, 161, 179, 217, 218, 223, 328, 373, 391, 402
Bak Geun-su, 144-146, 159, 161, 179, 217, 218, 223, 328, 373, 391, 402
Bak Jin (Bak Yeong), 144-146, 159, 161, 178-179, 217, 223, 373, 391, 402
Bak Yeol, 360n73
Bak Yeong. *See* Bak Jin
Bak Yong-man, 393, 405
Balzac, Honoré, 285
Baoan, 330-331, 408, 453
Baodingfu, 293, 406
Beijing, 10n, 11n, 64, 101, 107, 109, 119, 120, 123, 124, 126, 127, 130-131, 142, 187n, 196n, 219, 229, 251, 259n, 260, 262-263, 266, 270, 272, 278, 295, 296, 297n, 302n, 306n, 313, 352n8, 355n26, 356n34, 360nn35, 366n133, 368n146, 369n155, 370n170, 375, 376, 391, 394, 401, 402, 405, 406, 411, 449-452, 456-458

Beijing Union Medical College, 120, 131, 171, 219, 259n, 278, 279, 365n119
Berlin, 8, 116, 378
Black Flag League, 360n73
Black Friends Society, 360n73
Black Labor Society, 360n72
Black Wave Society, 360n73
Black Youth League, 109, 360n73
Blue Shirts Society, 297n, 302-306, 309-311, 370n168
Bodde, Derk, 449
Bolsheviks, 98n, 221, 337, 358n54, 373, 380, 381.
Borodin, Mikhail, 141, 143, 149-150, 362n97, 373, 402
Braun, Otto (Li De), 2n, 457
Browder, Earl, 149, 403
Buck, Pearl, 449
Byeong-in Volunteer Unit, 147, 363n108

──────── C

Cai Tingkai, 191, 194, 218
Chang-il dang (Creating-one Party), 362n94, 375, 402. *See also* Korean Communist Party, Irkutsk faction.
Chasan-ri, 39
Chen Gongbo, 161, 374
Chen Hanbo, 451, 454
Chen Jiongming, 190, 374
Cheng Qian, 150, 374
Cheondogyo, 56-58, 355n28, 378, 418.
Chiang Kai-shek, 10n, 29n, 103n, 149n, 151-152, 300, 311n, 331, 344, 353n15, 354n20, 363n106, 364n113, 368n156, 369n164, 369nn164-165, 370n168, 374, 375, 377, 381, 403, 450n6, 452, 454
China League of Left-Wing Writers, 314, 368n148, 370n170, 370n173
Chinese Communist Party (CCP), 10n, 18n, 29, 30, 96, 97, 131, 139n, 141-142, 152n, 156, 159, 170, 173, 177, 192, 200, 220, 229, 236, 238-239, 243n, 271-278, 284, 293-300, 302n, 305, 321, 328-330, 332n, 343n, 344n, 352nn4-6, 353n12, 354n20, 358n58, 362nn95-96, 362n98, 363n102, 364n115, 365n121, 365n128, 366n129, 366n133, 366n136, 367n140, 368n148, 368nn154-155, 368n155-156, 369n157, 369nn165-166, 370nn170-171, 371n173, 371n181, 373-380 passim, 385-387, 391-394, 402-410 passim, 451-453

Chinese Nationalist Party. *See* Guomindang (GMD)
Choe Nam-seon, 57-58, 374
Christianity, 34, 37, 44, 50-60, 64, 71, 85, 95, 120, 129, 187n, 346, 355n29
Comintern, 18, 99, 149n, 162n, 167, 358n54, 359n69, 361n85, 362n98, 364n117, 371n180, 375, 381, 391, 393, 457
Communist International. *See* Comintern
Communist Youth League, 128, 131, 131n, 141, 153, 159, 166, 169-170, 189, 192, 239-240, 241, 302n, 361n89, 381
Cui Longshui, 238n, 385n2, 443
Cultural Revolution, 385n1, 386

───────── D

Daegu, 59
Dalian, 263, 306n, 316, 406
Dandong, 4, 112, 113, 114, 244, 373, 378
December 9th Student Movement, 450-454, 456n5, 459
Diamond Mountains. *See* Geumgang-san
Dong-a Ilbo. *See* East Asia Daily
Dong Liang, 190, 374
Donghak. *See* Cheondogyo
Dongjiang Party School, 365n124
Dongjiaochang, 155, 364n114, 403
Doriot, Jacques, 149n, 403
Dostoevsky, Fyodor, 285
Du Junhui, 148, 363n109

───────── E

East Asia Daily (Dong-a Ilbo, Oriental Daily News), 43n, 61-62, 104, 356n33, 374
East Manchuria Young Men's League of Communist Youth, 241

───────── F

Feng Youlan, 449
Fengtian. *See* Mukden
Feuerbach, Ludwig, 57, 369n163, 407
French Concession, Shanghai, 35, 93, 94n, 103, 109, 115, 214-215, 357n50, 440
Friends of Korean Independence, 108, 359n70

───────── G

Gang Se-u, 88
Gao Gang, 385n1
Gao Kelin, 368n155
Gao Yongguang, 332n, 374, 384, 386, 387n3, 389, 410, 411

Gaoyang Xian, 294-296, 369n159, 369n161, 407
Geumgang-san (Diamond Mountain), 3, 56-57, 128, 129, 130
Go Yeong-gwang. *See* Gao Yongguang
Gong Peng, 451
Gong Pusheng, 451
Gongping, 191-193
Gorky, Maxim, 285
Great Kantō Earthquake (1923), 34, 72-75, 353n17
Great Revolution, 10n, 36, 139-157, 257, 294
Guangzhou, 18n, 29, 35, 112, 120, 139-142, 144, 146-150, 152, 155, 156-157, 160, 162n, 172n, 177, 188, 189, 207, 215, 361n86, 363n101, 363n110, 364n114, 364n116, 366n136, 370n171, 373, 375, 377, 389, 391, 402-404
Guangzhou Commune, 18n, 35, 57n, 132, 146, 152, 155, 156, 158-182, 189, 190, 201, 215, 217, 240, 251, 281, 351n2, 364n117, 365n119, 365nn121-122, 365n125, 376, 377, 379, 380, 387, 391, 403-404
Guangzhou Uprising. *See* Guangzhou Commune
Guo Sunhe, 2n
Guomindang (GMD), 10n, 18n, 29n, 30n, 76, 139, 142, 149n, 151, 152-155, 169, 170n, 178, 179, 182n, 185, 209, 253, 258, 275, 276, 297, 300, 303n, 306, 308-309, 312, 329, 343, 344n, 352n8, 353n12, 353n15, 362nn95-97, 363n106, 364n112, 366n129, 368n156, 369n157, 369n162, 370n168, 370n171, 373, 374, 375, 376, 377, 378, 379, 380, 391, 403, 407, 457
Gwak Jae-gi, 88

───────── H

Haifeng. *See* Hailufeng
Haifeng, battle of, 197-200
Hailufeng, 18, 29, 36, 101, 117, 146, 170n, 174-176, 182-194, 197-200, 207-209, 215, 217, 275, 281, 332n, 352n5, 365n124, 374, 377, 380, 381, 404
Hailufeng Soviet. *See* Hailufeng
Han. *See* Han Wi-geon
Han Fuju, 270, 374
Han Hae (Kim Jang-chun), 238n, 376, 443-445. *See also* Jang Il-jin.
Han Wi-geon, 221, 271-274, 279-280, 282, 286, 338, 366n132, 374-375, 405, 406
Hanihe, 83-84, 356n43, 401

Harbin, 46, 77, 86
Hatem, George, 2n
Hayakawa Sessue, 8, 375
He Cheng. See Zhong ying
He Long, 190, 200, 364n115, 366m29, 375, 453
He Zhongmin, 170n
Hegel, Georg W. F., 57, 124, 129, 130, 132, 449
Henan, 160, 161, 165, 171, 374
Heng Mu-kuan, 241
Heungsa-dan (Young Korean Academy), 101, 401
Hirohito, 360n82
Hitler, Adolf, 19, 69n, 300, 452, 457
Hong Kong, 18, 139n, 166, 172, 177, 205, 209-213, 216, 364n116, 365nn120-121, 378, 404, 410, 456n5
Hong Nam-pyo, 94n
Hongkou Park, 94n, 103n, 110, 359n67, 380
Hu Die. See Wu, Butterfly
Hu Yaobang, 386
Huang Hua (Wang Rumei), 451, 452
Huang Jing "David." See Yu Qiwei
Huang Pingchaun, 196
Huang Qixiang, 161, 375
Huangpu (Whampoa) Military Academy, 140, 143, 147, 172n, 365n121, 365n128, 370n168, 371n182, 374, 379, 380, 402
Huangpu River, 215, 421, 422-425, 431
Hunchun, 87, 357n46

———— I
Im Sa, 304
Inseong School, 92, 358n52, 401
Irkutsk faction. See Korean Communist Party
Ironsides, 150, 156, 364n115
Itō Hirobumi, 46, 373

———— J
Jaisohn, Philip. See Seo Jae-pil
Jang Geon-sang, 362n94, 402
Jang Il-jin, 238, 240. See also Han Hae
Jang Ji-rak (Kim San), 259n, 343n, 351n2, 398-399, 411
Japan, 5-12, 19, 32-37, 50, 52, 54, 67-76, 85, 95, 103, 114-115, 116, 150, 256, 261, 263-265, 346, 353n14, 354nn17-18, 356n37, 360n82, 367n141, 372n190, 390, 393, 422, 430, 450, 452, 456, 458
Japanese Communist Party, 71-72, 243n, 369n163

Japanese Occupation of China, 65, 94n, 172n, 174, 215, 355n26, 356n34, 357nn46-47, 371n179, 392, 456, 458
Japanese Occupation of Korea, 4, 8, 10, 15, 22n, 27, 29, 32, 35, 37, 39-42, 44, 52, 54-64, 66, 74, 85, 87, 93, 97, 107, 110-114, 127, 221, 237, 312, 344, 346-347, 353n9, 353n13, 354n19, 355n30, 355n32, 356n41, 373, 374, 379, 417-420
Japanese Occupation of Manchuria, 30, 93n, 238, 240-243, 328n, 339, 346-347, 352n7, 353n15, 377, 392, 415-416. See also Mukden Incident
Jeokki-dan. See Red Flag Society
Jeong I-so, 88
Jeong Yul-seong, 408
Jeong-uibu, 366n137
Jiang Qing, 452
Jiang Xiaoxian, 297n, 310n, 370n170
Jiangxi Soviet, 352n5, 364n115, 369nn164-165
Jiaodaotuan. See Special Training Regiment
Jilin, 34n, 36, 64, 236, 238-242, 298, 352n7, 356n41, 366m135, 367n138, 401
Jin Gong-mok (Kim Sang-seon), 196, 240, 365n128
Jin Yan. See Kim Yeom
Jo Bong-am, 94n
Jo Un-san, 87
Joseon Daily (Joseon Ilbo, Joseon Daily News), 62n, 259n, 405
Joseon Dynasty (Yi Dynasty), 31, 353n16, 354n22, 355n28
Joseon Ilbo. See Joseon Daily

———— K
Kang Keqing, 456
Kang Ruihua, 408
Kang Sheng, 385, 385m1, 409
Keijō. See Seoul
Kim Chung-chang (Kim Seong-suk), 19, 101, 123-125, 128-132, 142-143, 147-150, 173, 174, 177, 196, 214-217, 222-224, 321-322, 324, 345, 361n90, 362n91, 362n94, 363n109, 371n182, 371n184, 375, 391, 402, 404, 408
Kim Deok-rin. See Kim Yeom
Kim Dong-sam, 366n137
Kim Gi-chang, 406
Kim Gi-deuk, 88
Kim Gu (Kim Koo), 344, 346, 372n190
Kim Gyu-gwang. See Kim Chung-chang

Kim Hyeong-pyeong, 172n
Kim Ik-sang, 88, 114–116, 360n76, 360n78, 361n83, 375, 422, 426-432, 441
Kim Il Sung, 371n187, 378, 386, 389, 411
Kim Jang-chun. *See* Han Hae
Kim Jwa-jin, 241, 376
Kim Koo. *See* Ki Gu
Kim Mu-jeong (Mujeong), 331, 377
Kim Rip, 99–100, 359nn60–61, 359n63, 376
Kim Sang-seon. *See* Jin Gong-mok
Kim Seong-suk. *See* Kim Chung-chang
Kim Won-bong (Kim Yak-san), 34n, 88, 111–112, 142, 223, 343, 345, 346, 360n71, 360n76, 371n184, 376, 391, 402
Kim Yak-san. *See* Kim won-bong
Kim Yeom, 118, 376
KK (Koreanische Kommunisten), 143, 145, 146–148, 362n100, 402
Korean Anarchist Federation in China. *See* Anarchist Federation
Korean Anarchist League, 360n74
Korean Army of Independence, 34, 45, 64, 83–85, 87, 98, 141, 356n41.
Korean Communist Party, 96-99, 104, 131, 221-222, 236, 238-241, 243n, 328, 354n19, 358n54, 362n94, 365n128, 366n131, 366nn135–136, 367n139, 371n181, 374–375, 393, 419; and Chinese Communist Party, 142, 220, 236, 238–241, 244, 405; Irkutsk (Siberia) faction, 131, 143, 358n54, 362n94, 373, 375, 402; Marxist-Leninist faction (Third Korean Communist Party), 354n19, 358n54, 366n131, 366n136, 375; Shanghai faction, 97, 143, 358n54, 358n57, 359n69, 376, 380
Korean Communist Youth, 141, 239–240
Korean Daily News (Daehan Maeil Sinbo), 61, 358n32
Korean Declaration of Independence, 34n, 50–66, 374, 378, 380. *See also* March First Independence Movement
Korean Independence News, 92, 101, 358n51, 401
Korean Independence Party, 41, 252, 344, 354n21
Korean League for National Liberation, 329–330, 371n182, 371n184, 408
Korean National Front. *See* Union for the Korean National Front
Korean National Independence Party. *See* Uiyeol-dan
Korean National Revolutionary Party, 343, 344, 362n101. *See also* Uiyeol-dan
Korean nationalist movement, 29, 56–57, 62, 64, 75, 86, 98, 103, 390. *See also* March First Independence Movement
Korean Nationalist Party, 143, 344
Korean Peasants Alliance, 405
Korean People's Associations, 92, 98, 102, 357n50
Korean Provisional Government, 34n, 35, 66, 86, 93–96, 98–101, 103, 108, 114, 344, 357n50, 358n51, 358n53, 358n60, 367n139, 372n190, 374, 375, 376, 378
Korean Restoration Army (Gwangbok gun), 357n43.
Korean Revolutionary Army, 367n140, 419
Korean Revolutionary Young Men's League, 117, 142–143, 147–148, 150, 173, 236, 239, 260, 267, 361n86, 402, 403
Korean Social Science Research Society, 127
Korean Socialist Party. *See* Korean Communist Party, Shanghai faction
Korean Soviet Committee, 144
Korean Student Association, 126
Korean Student Union, 127, 401
Korean Union for Independence, 259n
Korean Volunteer Corps, 343, 344n, 345, 372n188
Korean Young Men's Independence Party, 70, 356n36
Korean-Chinese Peasants' Union, 239
Kropotkin, Peter, 77, 356n38, 376

───── L

League of Nations, 66
League of the Friends of Korea. *See* Friends of Korean Independence
Lenin, Vladimir Ilyich Ulyanov, 1, 98–99, 126, 336, 337, 381
Leninism, 100, 132, 339, 404
Li Dazhao, 131n, 230, 293, 302n, 339, 376, 402
Li De. *See* Braun, Otto
Li Fulin, 160, 161, 165, 174, 178, 190, 377
Li Jishen, 149n, 156, 160n, 163, 165, 190, 363n106, 377
Li Lisan, 274–276, 297
Li Min, 451, 451n1
Lingnan University, 146, 161, 178–179, 217
Liu Ling (Qi Shurong), 233–235, 245–250, 270, 366n134, 368n151, 377, 405–406
London, Jack, 284–285

Long March, 2n, 300, 369n164, 369n165, 377, 453, 457
Lu Xun, 370n173
Lufeng. *See* Hailufeng
Luo Binghui, 455n4, 457
Luo Fu (Zhang Wentian), 456
Luo Liumei, 153-155, 403

——————— M

Ma Cheon-mo (Ma Cheon-mok), 240, 366n136
Ma Cheon-mok. *See* Ma Cheon-mo
Malraux, André, 18
Manchu monarchy. *See* Qing Dynasty
Manchukuo, 92, 352n7, 377
Manchuria, 2, 3, 4-5, 10, 11, 19, 28, 30, 33, 34, 36, 37, 45-46, 62-64, 77, 80-86, 93, 95, 97-99, 107, 113, 130, 141, 151, 152, 224, 229, 236-244, 266, 298, 328, 331, 343, 345, 346-347, 351n2, 352n7, 356n41, 356n43, 357nn45-47, 359n69, 363n105, 365n128, 366n136, 366n137, 367nn139-142, 371n181, 373, 374, 376, 377, 379, 380, 385, 405, 415-416.
Manchurian Communist Party, 328-329
Manchurian Incident of 1931. *See* Mukden Incident
Mann, Thomas, 149n, 403
Mao Dun, 370n173
Mao Zedong, 10n, 162n, 207, 301n, 352n4, 369n165, 375, 378, 451-453, 455-459
March First Independence Movement, 24, 34, 51, 54-58, 62, 85, 93, 129-130, 346, 353n13, 354n25, 355n27, 358n53, 361n90, 366n132, 373, 374, 375, 378, 400. *See also* Korean Declaration of Independence
Marco Polo Bridge Incident, 11, 455.
Marxism, 70, 104, 110, 126, 129, 130, 258, 339, 391
Marxist-Leninist Party (Third Korean Communist Party). *See* Korean Communist Party
May 30th Incident, 139, 364n116
May Fourth Movement, 65, 355n26, 356n34
Minami Jirō, 346, 415
Mujeong. *See* Kim Mu-jeong
Mukden (Fengtian; Shenyang), 236, 240, 241
Mukden Incident, 328n, 359n66, 366n137, 367n140
Mun Seon-jae, 172n

Mussolini, Benito, 300, 452

——————— N

Nanchang Uprising, 156, 182n, 364n115, 366n129, 374, 375, 379, 380
Nanjing Regime. *See* Guomindang (GMD)
Nanjing, 150, 352n8, 369n162, 374
National Revolutionary Army (NRA), 10n, 150n, 152n, 362n96, 364n115, 375, 377, 381
Neumann, Heinz, 162, 165, 171, 174, 403
New Development School. *See* Sinheung Military School
Nixon, Richard M., 451
Northern Expedition, 10n, 140, 149n, 150-152, 362n96, 363n102, 364n113, 373, 374, 377, 381, 391

——————— O

October Revolution. *See* Russian Revolution
Oh Seong-ryun, 19, 111-117, 128, 147-149, 158-161, 170-176, 183, 195-206, 215-217, 223-224, 360n79, 361n83, 365n124, 377, 391, 402, 404, 421-442
Oriental Daily News. *See* East Asia Daily
Oriental League of Oppressed Peoples, 150, 364n111

——————— P

Park Chung Hee, 375, 386, 388
Peng Dehuai, 331, 377, 458
Peng Gui, 192
Peng Pai, 101, 156, 182-184, 189, 192, 205-209, 339, 378, 390
Political Training Regiment, 190, 365n125
Proletarian Federation, 130, 362n92
Provisional Government. *See* Korean Provisional Government
Puning. *See* Hailufeng
Pyongyang, 39, 102, 354n23, 400

——————— Q

Qi Shurong. *See* Liu Ling
Qiao Guanhua, 451
Qing Dynasty, 91n, 355n29, 357n45, 363n110, 377, 379, 449, 450n7
Qu Qiubai, 131n, 370n173, 402

——————— R

Red Army, 156, 159, 182n, 185-186, 187n, 189-190, 193-194, 197, 274n, 275, 279, 300, 314, 329-331, 352n6, 364n115, 365n125,

369nn164-165, 375, 377, 379, 404, 408
Red Flag Society (Jeokki-dan), 107, 359n69
Red Guards, 190, 192-194
Red Self-Protection Forces (Chiweidui). See Self-Protection Troops (Ziweijun)
Rhee, Syngman, 35n, 93, 94, 95, 372n190, 375, 378, 386
Rice Riots, 34, 73, 354n18
Rousseau, Jean-Jacques, 122, 125
Russia, 28, 33, 37n, 40, 99, 126, 132, 367n141. See also Soviet Union
Russian Revolution, 37, 97, 99, 126, 141, 195, 352n5, 353n14, 380. See also Soviet Union
Russo-Japanese War, 33, 37n, 39, 62, 97, 367n141

――――― S

Saitō Makoto, 61-62, 93, 104, 111, 360n76, 361n83, 375, 378
Sano Manabu, 369n163, 405, 407
Sanyuanpu, 80-82, 85, 87, 356n41, 357n43
Sao. See Shaw, George, L.
Second Normal School, 293, 406
Second United Front, 10n, 352n6, 354n20
Self-Protection Troops (Ziweijun), 168, 364n118
Seo Hwi (Yi), 371n187, 378, 409
Seo Jae-pil (Philip Jaisohn), 359n70
Seoul, 3, 31, 32, 34n, 35, 39n, 62, 93, 97, 104, 111, 136, 354n19, 355n31, 358n54, 359n64, 360n72, 362n92, 415
Shameen. See Shamian
Shamian, 16On, 172n, 174, 379
Shandong, 54, 65, 237, 355n26, 356n34, 375, 452
Shanghai, 29n, 31, 34, 35, 37, 62n, 66, 86, 91-94, 96, 98-101, 103, 106-116, 139n, 147, 151n, 208, 209, 215, 220, 223, 327, 339, 358nn51-52, 359n60, 359n67, 360n81, 363n108, 370n173, 374, 376, 378, 379, 380, 389-391, 421-442
Shanghai faction. See Korean Communist Party
Shanghai Massacre, 151n, 152, 363n106, 364n113, 403
Shanghai War, 103, 359n66
Shantou, 182n, 190, 206, 209, 404
Shaw, George L. (Sao), 113-114, 360n80, 378
Shi Cuntong, 131n, 402
Shigemitsu Mamoru, 103n
Shin Chae-ho, 109, 355n32, 360n73

Shirakawa Yoshinori, 103n
Si Lingke, 302n, 303
Siberia, 28, 33, 37, 46, 77, 85, 87, 95, 97-98, 107, 131, 141, 144-145, 347, 353n14, 357n44, 357n47, 358n54, 380, 401
Siberia faction. See Korean Communist Party
Sinclair, Upton, 285
Sinheung Military School (New Development School), 83-84, 356n43, 401
Sinheung, 356n41
Sinminhoe (New People Society), 356n41, 373, 380
Sino-Japanese War, 10n 11n, 352n4, 374, 377, 379
Sinuiju, 4n, 45, 244, 266, 406
Smedley, Agnes, 2n
Snow, Edgar, 162n, 331, 343, 344n, 449-451, 454, 456, 458-459
Socialist Youth League of China. See Communist Youth League
Son Byeong-hui, 57, 378
Son Gi-jeong, 7-8, 353n9, 379
Song Kuangwo, 371n177
Song of Arirang (folk song), 22, 23, 31-33, 196, 263, 267
Song Zheyuan, 296, 379
Soviet Union, 10n, 12, 18n, 29n, 66, 71, 97, 139, 243, 353n14, 362n95, 373, 395. See also Russian Revolution
Soviets, Chinese. See Hailufeng; Peng Pai
Special Training Regiment (Jiaodaotuan), 146, 156-160, 170, 174-179, 183, 189-194, 197-198, 201, 217, 363n107, 365n125, 366n136, 373
Stalin, Josef, 276n
Su Zhaozheng, 166, 379
Sun Yat-sen, 10n, 104, 139-140, 362n95, 363n102, 373, 374, 377, 379
Suwon, 59, 355n31

――――― T

Taiping Rebellion, 56, 355n29
Taiwan, 150, 345, 347, 354n20, 360n74, 364n111, 379, 380, 422
Tanaka Giichi, 114-115, 360nn81-82, 361n83, 380, 421, 426-433, 440
Tao Xijin, 408
Terrorism, 28, 58, 61, 66, 73, 95, 98, 100, 103n, 106-108, 110-111, 127-128, 354n17
Tianjin, 11n, 107, 114, 118-119, 263, 294, 306n, 313, 368n149, 368n155, 398, 458

475

INDEX

Tokyo, 67-74, 77, 104, 353n17, 356n36, 360n73, 380, 389, 390
Tolstoy, Leo, 111, 123, 125, 131-134, 187
Trotsky, Leon, 276n
Trotskyism, 276, 297, 332n, 369n161, 369n163, 385, 387, 387n3
Tsinghua University, 449-451

──────── U

Ugaki Kazushige, 415
Uiyeol-dan, 34, 88, 107-117, 128, 141-143, 147, 360n71, 360nn75-76, 360n79, 360n81, 361n83, 361n86, 362n101, 375, 376, 377, 378, 380, 391, 401.
Union for Korean Independence, 224
Union for the Korean National Front, 329, 343, 345, 371n184, 374, 375, 376, 408, 417-420
United Front (First), 10n, 29n, 140n, 152n, 353n12, 362n95, 363n102, 364n115, 373, 376-377, 380
United Front (Second), 10n, 329, 352n6, 354n20, 369n157, 369n166

──────── V

Versailles Peace Conference, 51-55, 62, 72, 97, 355nn25-27
Vladivostok, 97n, 108, 144, 145, 357n44, 359n69, 380
Volunteer Unit. *See* Byeong-in Volunteer Unit

──────── W

Walsh, Richard, 449
Wang Jingwei, 374, 381
Wang Ming, 300n, 370n171, 375
Wang Rumei. *See* Huang Hua
Wang Shuliang, 408
Wang Yizhen, 371n177
Washington Naval Conference, 75, 356n37
Whampoa Military Academy. *See* Huang-pu Military Academy
White Army, 177-178, 182n, 190, 193, 197-200, 296, 373
White Guards, 144
White Terror, 170n, 177-178, 222, 224, 299, 450-451
Wilson, Woodrow, 51-53, 56, 62, 64, 65, 95, 355n25
Wu Liangping, 456
Wu, Butterfly (Hu Die), 119, 361n87
Wuhan Military and Political Academy, 156

Wuhan, 150n, 152, 156, 365n128, 381

──────── X

Xi'an, 453-458
Xi'an Incident, 36, 311n, 331, 354n20, 381
Xiangshan, 119, 401, 406
Xiao Ke, 453, 455n4
Xiong Xiling, 119, 379
Xu Dishan, 449
Xu Guangying, 159, 174, 379
Xu Haidong, 455n4
Xu Xiangqian, 453

──────── Y

Yalu River, 4, 28, 33, 39n, 113, 356n41
Yan'an, 1, 2n, 11, 162n, 170n, 321n, 331, 352n5, 371n187, 378, 385, 386, 389, 392, 393, 409, 452-459
Yang Dal-bu, 158, 159, 161-165, 170-174, 379, 403
Yang Gi-tak, 355n32
Ye Jianying, 387
Ye Ting, 150n, 159-160, 162-164, 171, 172, 173, 177, 190, 200, 364n115, 366n129, 379, 403
Ye Yong, 159, 174-175, 190, 197, 379, 404
Yenching University (Yanjing University), 275, 449-452
Yi Bin, 172, 379
Yi Cheong-cheon, 241n, 344-345, 357n43, 366n137
Yi Dong-hwi, 45, 63, 93-100, 102, 358nn54-56, 359n62, 359n69, 376, 380, 400, 401
Yi Dynasty. *See* Joseon Dynasty
Yi Gwang-su, 32, 62n, 93, 100-102, 104-105, 121, 380, 401
Yi Hoe-seong, 387, 410
Yi Hoe-yeong, 360n74
Yi Jong-am, 114-115, 361n83, 380, 422, 426-428
Yi Seong-u, 88
Yi Tak, 366n137
Yi Won-hun, 94n
Yi Yong, 159, 172n, 380
Yu Dawei, 452
Yu Hanmou, 190, 191, 380
Yu Ja-myeong, 362n101, 371n184
Yu Qiwei (Huang Jing), 452
Yun Bong-gil, 103n, 110, 111, 380
Yun Daiying, 159, 174, 380

──────── Z

Zhang Dongsun, 449, 452

Zhang Fakui, 146, 150, 156-157, 160n, 161-163, 165, 172n, 381, 403
Zhang Gaoli, 332n
Zhang Shuyi, 451
Zhang Tailei, 159, 169, 171, 173, 174, 177, 365n122, 381
Zhang Wentian. *See* Luo Fu
Zhang Wenxiong (Zhang Wenxun), 302, 305-306, 309, 311
Zhang Wenxun. *See* Zhang Wenxiong
Zhang Xueliang, 36, 242, 295, 331, 354n20, 367n142, 381, 454
Zhang Zhaolin, 451, 454
Zhang Zuolin, 230, 377, 381
Zhao Eping. *See* Zhao Yaping
Zhao Yaping (Zhao Eping), 284, 303-304, 317-321, 323-324, 325, 326, 332n, 370n174, 381, 384, 386, 406, 407, 408, 409
Zheng Zhiyun, 183, 191-192, 205, 381
Zhong Ying (He Cheng), 171, 364n119
Zhongshan University, 143, 148, 155, 157, 173, 180, 363n102, 363n104, 375
Zhou Enlai, 366n129, 451
Zhu De, 182n, 378, 453, 455, 456
Zhu Lian, 408
Zhu Peide, 150, 381
Zinoviev, Grigori, 98

ABOUT THE AUTHORS

Born in 1905, KIM SAN (Jang Ji-rak) left his family in Korea as a teenager and crossed the border into China, where he joined Mao's Red Army. A participant in or witness to some of the most critical events of the Chinese Revolution, he became a leader in the fight against Japanese colonial rule, and was executed in China in 1937. He was awarded a posthumous "Patriot" award by the South Korean government in 2005.

HELEN FOSTER SNOW was born in Cedar City, Utah. She moved to China in 1931 and reported extensively on the Chinese Revolution, the Korean independence movement, and the Sino-Japanese War. Writing under the pseudonym of NYM WALES, she wrote and published over 40 books, including *Inside Red China*, *My China Years: A Memoir*, as well as *Song of Ariran*. Her clear-eyed, detailed accounts of life in revolutionary China have come to be considered some of the most valuable historical records of the era. In 1993, she was awarded the first China Writer's Association award, and in 1996, she became the first American ever to be honored as a Friendship Ambassador by the Chinese government.

ABOUT THE EDITORS

GEORGE O. TOTTEN III (1922-2009) obtained a Ph.D. from Yale University and was Distinguished Professor Emeritus of Political Science and Director of the Korea Project at the University of Southern California (USC). He was also founding director of the USC - UCLA Joint East Asian Language and Area Studies Center and served once as Director of East Asian Studies Center and Chair of Political Science Department at USC. A specialist in Japanese politics, he also authored, edited, or translated a wide range of numerous books and articles on Chinese and Korean politics. He was the editor of the Ramparts edition of *Song of Ariran* published in 1972.

DONGYOUN HWANG received a Ph.D. in history from Duke University and is Professor of Asian Studies at Soka University of America. He is the author of *Anarchism in Korea: Independence, Transnatioanlism, and the Question of National Development*. His research interests include nationalism, radicalism, and wartime collaboration in China during the Pacific War. Currently, he is working on a manuscript on anarchist education in China and Korea.

PUBLISHER'S ACKNOWLEDGMENTS

The Kaya edition of *Song of Arirang* has been made possible by the dedication and efforts of numerous people over the years. Without the dedication and expertise of Professor Dongyoun Hwang, who tirelessly pursued Kim San's story through multiple languages and sources, we would never have been able to make the scope of this project as ambitious and as comprehensive as it eventually became. In addition, Professor Sunyoung Park, a tireless cheerleader for this project, provided much-appreciated guidance, insight, and encouragement; Vicken Totten and Linnea Totten generously made available the notes and writings of their father, George O. Totten III, whose championing of the story of Kim San made it possible for future generations to appreciate him and his story; and Brigham Young University (Russ Taylor, Gordon Daines, and others) believed in Kaya's ability to steward this project to publication. We're grateful also to the translators—Evelyn Shih and Hayun Cho—who enabled us to present Kim San's own writings in English for the first time ever. And without the outstanding design vision of Chris Ro, this book would not be the beautiful object that it is today. Yvonne Cha, Shinhye Choi, and Dave Harris provided much needed assistance at important moments. Thanks also to USC East Asian Library, especially Joy Kim and Kenneth Klein, as well as to Sangyeoung Moon for their assistance.

Listing all the Kaya staff and volunteers who have helped bring this project to fruition would be impossible. But big thanks are due in particular to Managing Editor Neelanjana Banerjee and Dillon Sung, along with Maggie Deagon, Abigail Hora, Minyoung Huh, Anna Lee, Seokyoung Yang, Shuwen Zhang, and Evelyn Mingjie Zhong among others.

Special gratitude is also due to Whakyung Lee and Duncan Williams, for their constant, unstinting, and invaluable support of this project.

Finally, my own efforts on behalf of the Kaya edition of *Song of Arirang* are dedicated to Professor Hong Yung Lee, on whose shelf I originally found this book, and whose insistence on the importance of Korea in comparative East Asian Studies has been and remains an inspiration, and to Sonya Choi Lee, whose example of always questioning norms and received wisdom remains with me to this day.

—SUNYOUNG LEE, PUBLISHER